CCNP Guide to Advanced Routing

Michael Grice

**COURSE
TECHNOLOGY**
TM

THOMSON LEARNING

Australia • Canada • Mexico • Singapore • Spain • United Kingdom • United States

CCNP Guide to Advanced Routing

by Michael Grice

Managing Editor:
Stephen Soloman

Senior Vice President, Publisher:
Kristen Duerr

Product Manager:
Charles Blum

Developmental Editor:
Jim Markham

Production Editor:
Anne Valsangiacomo

Editorial Assistant:
Janet Eras

Associate Product Manager:
Tim Gleeson

Marketing Manager:
Toby Shelton

Text Designer:
GEX Publishing Services

Cover Designer:
Abby Scholz

BRIEF
Contents

TABLE OF
Contents

Preface

Welcome to the *CCNP Guide to Advanced Routing!* This book provides in depth coverage of the knowledge and skills required to pass Cisco's CCNP certification exam, *640-503: Routing*. It also maps to semester five of the Cisco Networking Academy curriculum. The material covered in this book will help prepare network administrators to build and maintain scalable networks. As networks grow larger, the effective use of routing protocols to manage their growth becomes more and more important. Cisco routers have played a huge roll in large and small networks, as well as connecting those networks to the Internet.

The Intended Audience

This book is intended for both students enrolled in the third year of Cisco's Networking Academy, as well as those students studying for Cisco's CCNP certification. It is designed to give a thorough grounding in the use of routing protocols.

Chapter 1, "Making Networks Scalable," gives an overview of the qualities that make a network scalable and general strategies you can use to make your networks scalable.

Chapter 2, "Managing IP Addresses and Broadcasts," describes techniques for allocating IP addresses, which can be essential for networks attached and unattached to the Internet. Additionally, this chapter describes how to use helper addresses to manage broadcasts.

Chapter 3, "OSPF," describes the use and operation of the Open Shortest Path First routing protocol. By the end of this chapter, you will be able to configure OSPF in a single area, and using several different topologies.

Chapter 4, "OSPF in Multiple Areas," you will learn how to partition your network into areas to make it even more scalable. Strategies to help make your network more stable are also discussed.

Chapter 5, "EIGRP", provides you with a thorough description of Cisco's Enhanced Interior Gateway Routing Protocol. By the end of the chapter you will be able to configure and troubleshoot the protocol, and use its features to make your network more scalable.

Chapter 6, "Route Filtering and Policy Routing", shows you how to finely control routing updates. In addition to learning several methods to filter routes and a review of access lists, you will learn how to use policy routing to finely tune the flow of traffic on your network.

Chapter 7, "Redistribution," describes how use multiple routing protocols on the same network. You will learn techniques to avoid common problems when redistributing routing protocols. Several common redistribution scenarios are discussed in detail.

Chapter 8, "BGP", describes Border Gateway Protocol, the routing protocol which connects the Internet backbone together. By the end of the chapter, you will have a thorough understanding of how the protocol operates.

Chapter 9, "Configuring and Troubleshooting BGP," you will learn how to configure and troubleshoot BGP.

Chapter 10, "Advanced BGP," shows you some of the features you can use to make BGP even more scalable. This chapter also discusses multihoming, or connecting your network to multiple Internet service providers.

Appendix A, "CCNP Guide to Advanced Routing Exam Requirements Matrix" tracks Cisco's exam objectives to the appropriate chapter in the book.

Features

To ensure a successful learning experience, this book includes the following pedagogical features:

- **Chapter Objectives:** Each chapter in this book begins with a detailed list of the concepts to be mastered within that chapter. This list provides you with a quick reference to the contents of that chapter, as well as a useful study aid.

- **Illustrations and Tables:** Numerous illustrations of server screens and components aid you in the visualization of common setup steps, theories, and concepts. In addition, many tables provide details and comparisons of both practical and theoretical information and can be used for a quick review of topics.

- **End of Chapter Material:** The end of each chapter includes the following features to reinforce the material covered in the chapter:

  - **Summary:** A bulleted list is provided which gives a brief but complete summary of the chapter

  - **Key Terms List:** A list of all new terms and their definitions

  - **Review Questions:** A list of review questions tests your knowledge of the most important concepts covered in the chapter

  - **Case Study Projects:** Case study projects take you through real world scenarios

- **On the CD-ROM:** On the CD-ROM you will find CoursePrep® exam preparation software, which provides 50 sample CCNP exam questions mirroring the look and feel of the MCSE exams.

Text and Graphic Conventions

Wherever appropriate, additional information and exercises have been added to this book to help you better understand what is being discussed in the chapter. Icons throughout the text alert you to additional materials. The icons used in this textbook are as follows:

 Tips are included from the author's experience and provide extra information on installation.

 The Note icon is used to present additional helpful material related to the subject being described.

 Case project icons mark the case project. These are more involved, scenario-based assignments. In this extensive case example, you are asked to implement independently what you have learned.

Instructor's Materials

The following supplemental materials are available when this book is used in a classroom setting. All of the supplements available with this book are provided to the instructor on a single CD-ROM.

Electronic Instructor's Manual. The Instructor's Manual that accompanies this textbook includes:

- Additional instructional material to assist in class preparation, including suggestions for classroom activities, discussion topics, and additional projects.
- Solutions to all end-of-chapter materials, including the Review Questions, Hands-on Projects and Case Projects.

ExamView® This textbook is accompanied by ExamView, a powerful testing software package that allows instructors to create and administer printed, computer (LAN-based), and Internet exams. ExamView includes hundreds of questions that correspond to the topics covered in this text, enabling students to generate detailed study guides that include page references for further review. The computer-based and Internet testing components allow students to take exams at their computers, and also save the instructor time by grading each exam automatically.

PowerPoint presentations. This book comes with Microsoft PowerPoint slides for each chapter. These are included as a teaching aid for classroom presentation, to make available to students on the network for chapter review, or to be printed for classroom distribution. Instructors, please feel at liberty to add your own slides for additional topics you introduce to the class.

ACKNOWLEDGMENTS

I'd like to thank Stephen Solomon and David George for starting me on this project, and Charlie Blum for helping me finish it. My thanks also go to my technical editor for catching the mistakes I made; if any are left in this book, they are my fault. I'd also like to thank Anne Valsangiacomo, the Production Editor, for making the book look great.

Finally, I'd like to thank my wife Nancy for her encouragement and inspiration, and for bearing with me while I wrote this book. There would be no book and much less joy in my life without you.

DEDICATION

The book is dedicated to my mother, Julia Grice Fitz. I just wish you were here to see it.

Read This Before You Begin

TO THE USER

Whether you are earning your Cisco Certified Network Professional certification or just learning about routing, this book will help you. Ideally you will have access to a classroom lab containing at least three Cisco routers and the cabling necessary to connect them. Additionally, you should have enable privileges in order to configure the routers.

VISIT OUR WORLD WIDE WEB SITE

Additional materials designed especially for you might be available for your course on the World Wide Web. Go to **http://www.course.com**. Search for this book title periodically on the Course Technology Web site for more details.

TO THE INSTRUCTOR

A classroom lab should have at a minimum three routers and the cabling necessary to connect them together. Students will need to have enable privileges to follow along with the examples in the book.

1

MAKING NETWORKS SCALABLE

After reading this chapter and completing the exercises you will be able to:

♦ Describe the features of a scalable network

♦ Describe some of the typical problems of an expanding network and the solutions

♦ Explain the benefits of redundancy and hierarchical design to a scalable network

♦ Compare and contrast the benefits of link-state routing protocols over distance-vector routing protocols in a scalable network

---

A network that grows continually, yet smoothly and stably, is a **scalable network**. Keeping networks scalable is becoming increasingly important for two primary reasons. The first is that networks everywhere are becoming larger. In addition to people and organizations connecting to the Internet, many organizations are expanding, or have plans to expand, their networks. The second reason is that networks are becoming more important. In addition to Internet commerce, many organizations rely on their networks to communicate to their employees, share documents, process orders, track inventory, control factory production, and many other functions.

A scalable network should be reliable, available, responsive, efficient, and secure. Growing networks tend to have several problems, which can make these objectives difficult or impossible to achieve, including congestion, haphazard growth, and the inability to easily manage the network. Redundancy and designing the network for easy manageability are strategies you can use to avoid these problems.

Finally, your choice of **routing protocol** can make a huge difference in the scalability of your network. A **router** uses a routing protocol to learn which route to each destination in the network is best. Some routing protocols, such as the Routing Information Protocol (RIP), work well in small networks, but become less efficient and slower to adapt to changes as the network grows. In this chapter, you will learn about some of the features that make a routing protocol scalable even in very large networks.

QUALITIES OF SCALABLE NETWORKS

The most important qualities of a scalable network are the ones your users will notice. If a network is not reliable, available, and responsive, you will have to deal with a lot of unhappy users. The efficiency of your network tends to be less obvious to your users, but it can affect the scalability of your network. Finally, your network should remain secure while it grows.

Reliability and Availability

Reliability and availability of a network are always major concerns for a network administrator. Downtime to an e-commerce Web site can cause headaches to many a business through lost sales, but network outages can cause even worse trouble. For years, businesses have tried to take greater advantage of their networks in order to reduce costs, share information, and control remote equipment.

For example, many factories nowadays rely on their networks to control and monitor production. A company may also use its network to access an inventory system, which can provide information about parts and supplies needed in a factory to produce goods, where goods need to be sent, or whether a slowdown or increase in production is required in response to demand. An outage in such a factory may mean that the factory management will not notice production defects, or it may stop production of millions of dollars of goods.

In an office, organizations use networks to share documents and other information. They can also use their networks to electronically track important packages, collect and process insurance claims, buy and sell goods, collect and analyze laboratory data, build and monitor shipping schedules, or do a thousand other things. If users cannot use the network, more and more often they will not be able to do their jobs. An unreliable or unavailable network can significantly affect the ability of an organization to function.

Responsiveness

Even if your network is consistently reliable and available, your users will quickly become frustrated if they cannot get their work done because the network does not respond quickly. Lack of responsiveness is one of the most common complaints network administrators receive. The effect of responsiveness will vary depending on the application. Time-dependent applications, such as terminal sessions, streaming video and IP telephony, are more affected by problems with responsiveness than less time-sensitive applications like File Transfer Protocol (FTP) clients. A terminal session, however, might be unusable if the words you type onto the screen do not appear until a minute after you type them.

Efficiency

On an efficient network, traffic devoted to maintaining the network uses as little of the network bandwidth as possible so that the vast majority of network bandwidth goes to the users. Every network needs maintenance traffic in order to function properly. This includes:

- Routing updates
- Servers advertising services
- Broadcast and multicast traffic

Without some of this traffic, the network is unusable. However, on an efficient network, this traffic will be minimized as much as possible, while still allowing the network to function properly.

Security

While network security is an immensely complicated subject well beyond the scope of this book, a scalable network should be designed with security in mind. In very broad terms, a scalable network should allow traffic to be controlled, where necessary, so that unwanted traffic can be prevented from reaching inappropriate areas of the network. For example, a user's miscellaneous Web browsing traffic on its way to the Internet should not cross networks dedicated to customer databases. This unnecessary traffic would make it difficult to tell which traffic belongs to legitimate users, and which traffic might belong to an intruder. In a scalable network, traffic of different types should be segmented as much as is practical, and each segment should have a clearly defined purpose.

PROBLEMS OF GROWING NETWORKS

The problems you encounter on a network will change as the network grows. Because a larger network involves a more sophisticated system with many more peripherals, more things can go wrong. However, some problems that exist on smaller networks become much more noticeable on a large network. The problems caused by an inefficient network, for example, may not be noticeable on a network with two routers and a couple dozen users. As the network grows, however, its inefficiency will have a greater effect on its users. Common problems on large networks include congestion, lack of manageability, and haphazard growth.

Congestion

Congestion occurs when traffic on the network uses most or all of the available bandwidth. As a network grows, more users are added, generating more traffic. If the network continues to grow, you will eventually need to add more bandwidth. For example, you may need to switch from 10 Mbps hubs to 100 Mbps switches, or from a 56 Kbps leased line to a 1.544 Mbps T-1.

On an Ethernet LAN, more traffic increases the risk of collisions. Because each frame in a collision must be retransmitted, traffic increases even more, and the problem becomes worse. In contrast, congestion on a WAN link may create a potential bottleneck and cost more money if the service provider charges for bandwidth.

Many congestion problems can be attributed to broadcast traffic. For example, on smaller networks where typically only a few devices broadcast, the percentage of bandwidth used by broadcasts is negligible. Routers running **Routing Information Protocol (RIP)** broadcast their entire routing tables every 30 seconds. If your network contains a total of five routers, the broadcast traffic will be manageable and not likely noticed by end users, much in the same way that five people talking normally in a cafeteria can carry on a conversation without any difficulty.

If your network expands to 500 routers, however, not only are 100 times as many routers broadcasting their entire routing tables every 30 seconds, but each routing table is also significantly larger. You added dozens, if not hundreds, of servers along the way, and each will probably broadcast service advertisements for the benefit of desktop clients. You also probably added thousands of those desktop clients, which also broadcast to request services. As a result, broadcast traffic may drown out other traffic, the same way that a thousand people talking in a cafeteria make it difficult to hear the person next to you. Even worse, each router, PC, and server on a LAN must look at every broadcast packet they receive to determine if they should respond. They will reject the vast majority of them, but the CPU time required will slow them down, and may cause performance degradation.

Manageability

Another common problem of larger networks is poor **manageability**. On a manageable network, the network administrator should be able to make many changes with only a minimal effect on other parts of the network. Unfortunately, on many networks, this is not true. On a network where all the subnets are allocated, adding a router might require re-addressing the other routers, which could in turn require re-addressing servers, and re-configuring the **Dynamic Host Control Protocol (DHCP) server** supplying IP addresses to clients attached to those routers. Generally, this type of problem is avoided with proper planning.

Additionally, many network designs and practices no longer work as the network grows. For example, network administrators often begin by manually assigning static IP addresses to their users. This manual assignment is acceptable for a small number of users, but as the user base grows, manual assignment becomes more problematic. In the same way, static routes can be used easily on small networks. While they are appropriate in certain places and situations on larger networks, maintaining several of them can be quite problematic. Changing 50 static routes on 50 different routers increases the odds of making a mistake on one or more of them. In general, any change you make manually on many routers is likely to result in mistakes.

Haphazard Growth

Haphazard growth can lead to congestion and manageability problems. Haphazard growth is the growth of a network without a plan in an arbitrary manner. When network administrators make decisions about a network's growth based on immediate acceptability rather than long-term effects, haphazard growth generally occurs. In other cases, a merger between two companies may require them to connect networks, which may be designed very differently. Similarly, cities grow in the same manner; buildings, roads, and parks are laid out without any regard as to how the rest of the city is designed. Traveling through a typical city is more difficult than traveling through a city laid out with a grid plan because the streets curve around, street names change at odd places, and generally, there are no direct routes across the city. A traffic accident on a city's main road might clog up traffic all across the city due to a lack of alternate routes. The same problems can occur on a poorly designed network.

Figure 1-1 contains an example of a network that grew haphazardly. As the imaginary Travigante Corporation expanded, its network administrators added new devices wherever they found it most convenient at the time. For example, the company connected offices on State Street and East Washington with ISDN lines to the headquarters on Doty Street, and remote offices in Manhattan and Lexington, KY with 56 Kbps leased lines. They also daisy-chained together a string of hubs, switches, and routers in their Doty Street headquarters to connect the entire building to the network.

One of the first things you will notice about the network diagram in Figure 1-1 is that much of the functionality of the network depends on only one network device. All the remote offices and both of the Internet connections from the headquarters are connected to the core_hq router. If that router goes down, headquarters will be disconnected from both the Internet and all remote offices. Inside the headquarters itself, most of the network is daisy-chained together in a bus topology. If the doty_street router goes down, the whole building follows. If the floor_1 router goes down, then all but the users attached to a few hubs go down. Single points of failure are often common with haphazard growth.

Traffic Drawbacks

Haphazard growth also makes it difficult to control traffic. In the corporate headquarters, the network is arranged with no regard to the purpose of each segment, or the type of traffic each segment should see. For example, nearly every segment has a file server of some type and some users, meaning that nearly every segment has both user traffic and server traffic. Both the workstations and the servers are in the same broadcast domain. Due to the grouping of users and servers, few logical places to control traffic exist (except at the doty_street or core routers). Restricting all traffic except TCP port 80 to WebServer1 cannot be done at the floor_3 router because the traffic to the users on that segment would also be restricted.

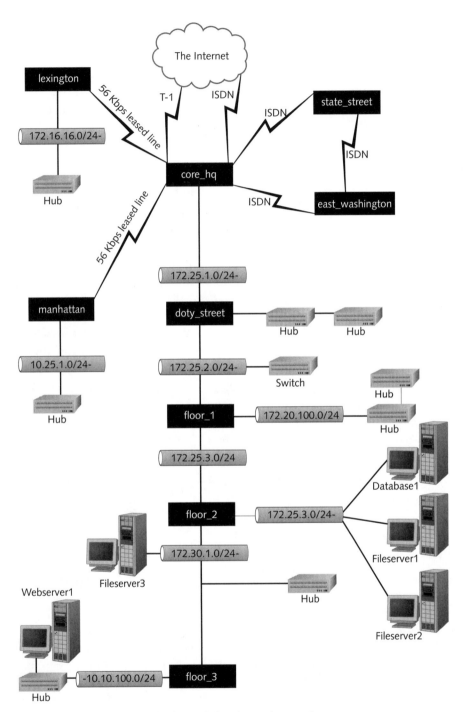

Figure 1-1   Network built through haphazard growth

Network Addressing Drawbacks

Haphazard growth can also cause problems with network addressing. In Figure 1-1, most of the network is on the 172.16.0.0/16 network with 24-bit subnet masks, except for the Manhattan office and WebServer1, which are on the 10.25.1.0/24 and 10.10.100.0/24 networks, respectively. Because these two networks have the same major network number, yet are discontiguous, some routing protocols will be unable to properly pass traffic between them. This can be a particularly serious problem in large organizations with IT departments in multiple locations if the departments do not communicate well with each other.

Documentation and Troubleshooting Drawbacks

Haphazard growth also tends to result in networks that are harder to document and troubleshoot. They are harder to document because they are not organized logically. Each piece of equipment is added to the network in a different way for different reasons each time, and few segments have a clear purpose. They are harder to troubleshoot because it is difficult to see how each part depends on the other, and changes may have unintended consequences. Often this is because a previous change that seemed to work did not.

For example, the Manhattan office might have a bad subnet mask, but packets arrive there anyway because the company uses a static route on the core router. If the network administrator replaces the static route with a dynamic routing protocol, such as RIP or Interior Gateway Routing Protocol (IGRP), the Manhattan office might lose connectivity with the rest of the office, even though the core router is advertising the route because of the bad net mask. Also, every location except State Street has its own connection to the Internet. Depending on how the network administrator configured the network, Internet traffic from the branch offices may travel over the line to the core router and use the T-1 to go out to the Internet, instead of using the local Internet connection. Depending on the amount of Internet traffic at each site, this might saturate the WAN connections and make accessing the file servers at each site much more difficult. While both these situations seem unlikely, they can occur on networks that grow haphazardly.

STRATEGIES FOR GROWING NETWORKS

You can employ several strategies to combat the problems found in expanding networks. In general, these strategies require advance planning. With good network design, you can avoid relying too heavily on any one piece of network equipment, and you can ensure that your network remains manageable. Finally, selection of an efficient routing protocol will help keep your network scalable.

Redundancy

Making a network redundant is a matter of removing all the single points where the network could fail. Unfortunately, since this generally requires additional equipment or links between sites, removing single points of failure from a network costs money. It also requires you to look at every aspect of the network in detail, including the network infrastructure. Routers with multiple power supplies do not help, for example, if both power supplies are connected to the same Uninterruptible Power Supply (UPS). In addition, multiple UPSs may not help if the two UPSs are connected to the same electrical circuit. Multiple circuits may not help if the building does not have a generator in case of an extended outage (and even a generator can fail). Building redundant infrastructure can be quite expensive. If you have multiple lines to remote offices or the Internet, you must ensure that each one goes through a different provider.

Functions Performed By Single Devices

Identifying functions performed by single devices is also helpful in making a network redundant. In the network shown in Figure 1-2, for example, each router and the connection to the Internet goes through the CoreRouter. In this situation, it may make sense to turn one of the remote routers into a second core router and add a second Internet connection. Then you could move some of the links to remote routers to the second core router. See Figure 1-3 for an example of how this might look. If either CoreA or CoreB fails, there will be a significant impact on the network, but remote routers attached to the remaining core router will still be able to connect to the Internet. This would require an additional connection to the Internet, which would result in additional expense.

Multiple Paths

Multiple paths through the network can also help. Creating a full or partial mesh can protect against downtime, since if any one router goes down, another router can do its job. In Figure 1-4, the two core routers each have a link to both the Internet and each remote router. The failure of either CoreA or CoreB will not prevent any of the remote routers from reaching the other core router and the Internet.

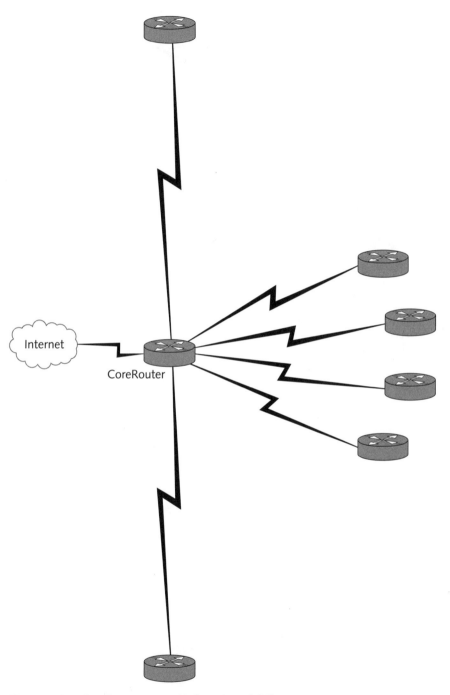

Figure 1-2 CoreRouter as a single point of failure

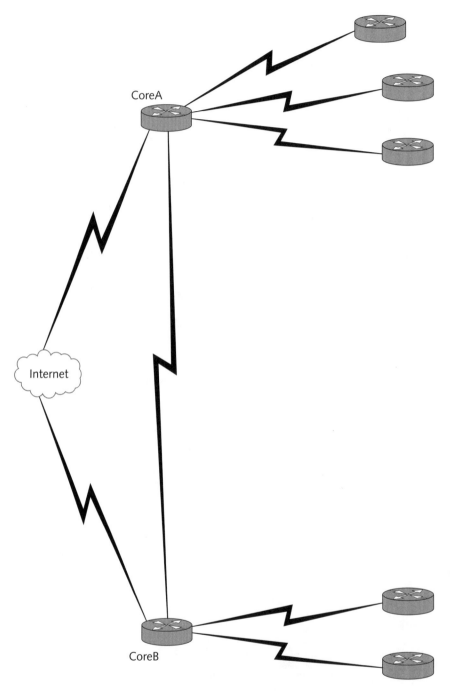

Figure 1-3 Two core routers reduce the consequences of any one failure

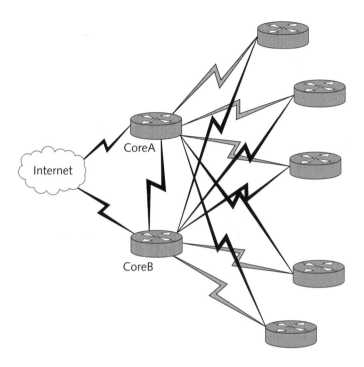

Figure 1-4   Two core routers and multiple paths through the network prevent outages after any one failure

Unfortunately, full or partial mesh designs will also significantly drive up the price of a network, especially with WAN links. The more nodes on a network, the more links needed to mesh them. With four routers in a mesh, it takes six links to make a full mesh; with 10 routers, it takes 45 links. You can calculate the number of links required to create a full mesh with **n (n −1) / 2**, where **n** is the number of links. Isolating one part of the network to control traffic also becomes much more difficult in a mesh topology, and troubleshooting a mesh network can be more difficult for the same reasons as described in the section on haphazard growth.

Hierarchical Design

A hierarchical design has several advantages for scalable networks. In a hierarchical design, the network is divided into layered parts, each with a clearly defined function. The most common models of hierarchical design consist of three parts: the core, distribution, and access layers. The purpose of the core layer is to switch packets as quickly as possible between other parts of the network. The **core layer** consists of the central parts of the network, and may connect different buildings on a campus network, or different offices on a large corporate network. The core layer may also be connected to the Internet, and tends to consist of the most powerful routers and switches on the network. The purpose of the **distribution layer** is to aggregate traffic and funnel it into the core layer. The distribution layer connects the core layer to the access layer. For instance, it might connect all the wiring closets and data centers on a campus network or corporate office to the core. The purpose of the **access layer** is to connect end users to the distribution network. For instance, users may connect to the access layer using hubs or switches in an office, or dial in with ISDN or modem connections.

Design Advantages

There are several advantages to this model. Primarily, it is easier to isolate problems on one part of the network. That is, if an access router goes down, then only the users on that part of the access network are affected. Problems in the distribution or core layers can be isolated there, and with multiple paths and an appropriate redundant design, these problems can be routed around. This also means that you can work on the distribution or access layers in one building without affecting the corresponding parts in any other building.

The second advantage of hierarchical design is that separating the functions of the three types of networks makes it easier to add to the network. For example, adding to the access network only affects the parts of the distribution network to which the new access network will be connected, and if the network design is sufficiently redundant, it may not affect the distribution network at all.

Regardless of redundancy, adding on to the access layer will affect the distribution layer to which you attach it.

The third advantage is traffic control. In a flat network, restricting certain types of traffic to certain parts of the network is difficult or impossible. Hierarchical design, on the other hand, enables you to easily restrict certain routing protocols and routing updates to the core, or the distribution networks. This allows you to use multiple routing protocols on a network. You can therefore minimize the effect on traffic by restricting each type to a certain area.

A fourth advantage is that it simplifies troubleshooting network problems. The network itself is simpler to visualize, and each component has well-defined functions.

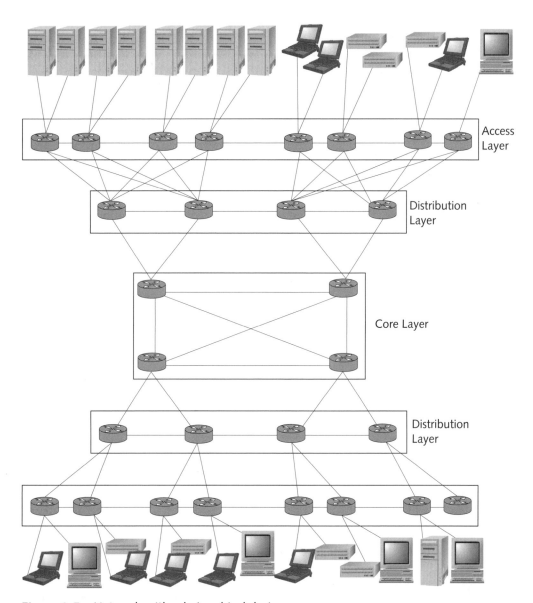

Figure 1-5   Network with a heirarchical design

Figure 1-5 contains an example of a network with a hierarchical design and clearly defined core, distribution, and access layers.

Redundancy and hierarchical design often conflict. For example, a fully meshed network design is highly redundant, but it does not work well as a hierarchical network design. Conversely, a purely hierarchical design will usually have single points of failure. When you design networks, you must weigh the benefits of redundancy against the benefits of hierarchical design.

Design Flavors

There are many possible variations on a hierarchical design. Smaller networks may do without the core network. If a company has a network with this design and adds another office later, you can simply add a core network to connect the two offices. You may use different routing protocols in each section since it is not uncommon to use one routing protocol on the core network, such as OSPF, and another routing protocol on the distribution and access networks, such as EIGRP. You can select the routing protocol that makes the most sense for the purpose and requirements of each section of your network.

Security

Network design plays a major role in network security. By allowing the network administrator to effectively segment a network, hierarchical design makes your network more secure. In a flat network, anyone who plugs into a network jack may be able to access important servers or routers. On the other hand, a hierarchically-designed network restricts users to the access portion of the network, and allows access only to needed services on other parts of the network.

Routing Protocols

Growing, scalable networks require several features of routing protocols that the early routing protocols did not have. Routing protocols should converge quickly and exchange routing information efficiently, without wasting bandwidth. **Convergence** occurs when routers rebuild their routing tables to reflect a change on the network, such as a router going down. Routing protocols should also allow flexible subnetting so that the size of networks is not restricted, and IP addresses may be used efficiently.

ROUTING PROTOCOLS ON GROWING NETWORKS

Routing protocols determine to a large extent the scalability of an expanding network. In order to see why, you will learn about the purposes of a router, and how different types of routing protocols fulfill these purposes.

Purposes of a Router

In essence, a router has two jobs. The first is to send packets to their destinations. Unless a packet is bound for a network directly attached to the router, the router will generally send the packet to the next router along the path towards its ultimate destination, based on Layer 3 network addresses. The router decides where to send the packet based on its routing tables.

A router's second job is to build and maintain its routing table. Routing tables give the router the information it needs to find the logical destinations (or networks) for the packet. The routing table also allows the router to identify its own interface to send the packet to the logical destination. Figure 1-6 shows a flow chart summarizing the process a router uses to decide where to forward a packet.

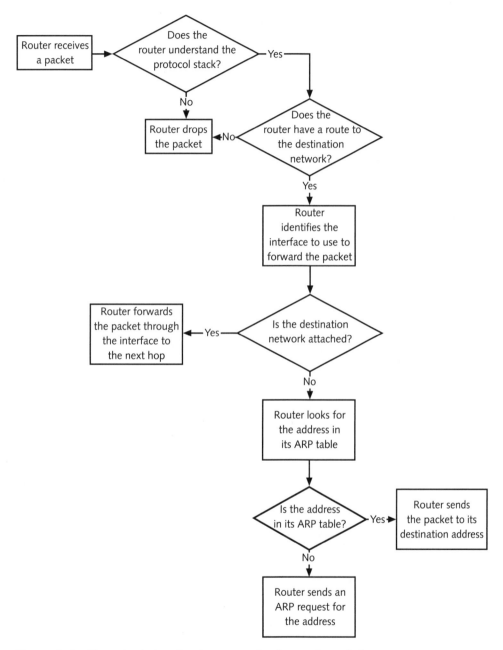

Figure 1-6   Flow chart showing how a router forwards packets

Obviously, the router also must understand the **routed protocol** with which the packet was sent. In order to forward an IP packet, a router must understand IP addresses and IP networks. If a router does not understand an incoming packet, it will usually drop it. For instance, a router without the IP protocol enabled, or without an IOS image capable of enabling IP, will not understand IP network addresses or numbers. Unless the router is configured as a bridge, it drops the packet, much like it does with broadcasts.

If the router does understand the protocol, it will attempt to find the ultimate destination of the packet by looking in its routing table. Figure 1-7 shows a simplified version of a routing table. It shows all the networks the router knows, as well as the next hop to get there. The routing table also tells the router which interface to use to send the packet to the next hop.

To the router, an IP address (or the address of any other routed protocol) consists of two parts: the network portion and the host portion. If you assume that a class C address such as 198.33.219.25, the IP address of www.cisco.com at the time of this writing, has a 24-bit netmask, then the router will see the first 24 bits of the address as the network address (198.33.219) and the last eight bits of the address as the host address (.25). A router would look for the 198.33.219.0 network in its routing table to decide where to send the packet. If the network is directly attached to one of its interfaces, the router would look in its **Address Resolution Protocol (ARP)** table to find that address. A router uses ARP to associate IP addresses with Layer 2 addresses, and it keeps a table containing each IP address it has learned, and the corresponding Layer 2 address. If it cannot find the Layer 2 address associated with an IP address, the router broadcasts an ARP request to find it. Then it sends the packet directly to the host. If the network is not directly attached, it uses the routing table to identify the next hop and the interface it should use to send the packet; then it forwards the packet out of that interface.

```
Send packets for 172.16.0.0 255.255.0.0 out of interface Ethernet 0 to 172.16.1.2.
Send packets for 10.0.0.0 255.0.0.0 out of interface serial 0 to 10.20.44.1.
Send packets for 192.168.1.0 255.255.255.0 out of interface serial 1 to 10.20.44.1.
Send everything else out of interface serial 0.
```

Figure 1-7   Simplified routing table

Distance Vector Routing Protocols

RIP and **Internetwork Gateway Routing Protocol (IGRP)** are both **distance vector routing protocols**. A distance vector routing protocol periodically broadcasts its entire routing table to all directly connected routers. Each routing update contains a list or vector of the networks known to the router sending the update, and a **metric** used to determine the best path to a particular network. RIP, formally defined in RFC 1058, uses the distance to the destination network (i.e., the **hop count**) as the metric. By default, Cisco's proprietary IGRP uses bandwidth and delay to calculate its metric, although it can be configured to also use load, reliability, and the **Maximum Transmission Unit (MTU)** in its metric calculations. Otherwise, each protocol uses the same techniques to avoid **routing loops**, and converge more quickly. In a routing loop, two routers pass the same packet back and forth without it ever reaching its destination; each router has the other router listed as the next hop in their routing tables.

Split Horizon

When a router receives a routing update from a neighbor on a connected interface, it puts all the routes it receives into its routing table. On its next update, it also broadcasts any routes received from its neighbors out of every interface, except the one from which it learned those routes. This is known as **split horizon**. Split horizon helps routers running distance vector routing protocols to avoid routing loops.

Split horizon prevents routing loops by preventing a router from learning about a route it initially advertised. For example, in Figure 1-8, RouterB advertises the router to the 172.25.0.0 network out of its Ethernet 0 interface connected to RouterA; RouterB can reach that network through RouterC. If RouterC goes down, RouterB will be unable to reach the 172.25.0.0 network. Without split horizon, however, RouterA will continue to advertise the route to 172.25.0.0 through its Ethernet 0 interface, even though RouterB cannot reach it; RouterB will put the route back into its routing table, indicating that it can instead reach that route through RouterA. As a result, when RouterB receives a packet intended for a destination on the 172.25.0.0 network, it will forward the packet back to RouterA. RouterA will in turn forward the packet back to RouterB, and so on. If RouterA cannot advertise the 172.25.0.0 route back through the Ethernet 0 interface from which it initially learned the route, RouterA and RouterB will avoid this routing loop.

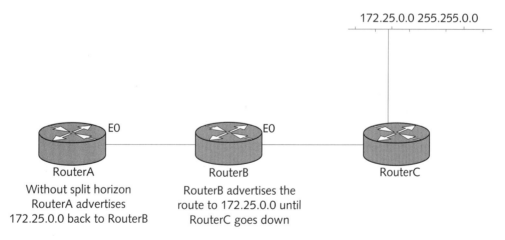

Figure 1-8   Routing loop prevented by split horizon

Hop Counts, Poison Reverse Updates, and Holddown Time

Two related techniques distance vector routing protocols use to avoid routing loops are hop counts and **poison reverse updates**. Distance vector routing protocols use the hop count to find routing loops. If a particular route is a loop, then the hop count for that route will keep increasing towards infinity. After the metric for a route reaches a hop count of 15 on an RIP network and 255 on an IGRP network, a router will declare it unreachable.

A router uses an unreachable hop count in a poison reverse update in order to prevent routing loops. On networks running distance vector routing protocols, routers on different parts of the network will learn about topology changes at different times. If a destination network becomes unreachable, routers that have not heard about the change will continue to advertise the route. As a result, other routers may add the now-invalid route to their routing tables. To prevent this, a router discovering an unreachable network will send out a poison reverse update with an unreachable metric out of all of its interfaces (including those which it normally does not use because of split horizon). On RIP, this is a route with a metric of 16.

 On IGRP, when a router sends out a reverse poison update, it uses a metric of 4,294,967,295, the maximum possible metric on IGRP.

The poison reverse update prevents routers from continuing to propagate the invalid route. In order to prevent a router from receiving a still-invalid route from one of its neighbors with a better metric, and installing it in its routing table, distance vector routing protocols also will not install a new route until it **flushes**, or completely removes, the route from its routing table. The amount of time a router waits between receiving a poison reverse update and accepting a route to that destination is called the **holddown time**. During the holddown time, the router will continue to advertise the invalid route with an unreachable metric; it will not accept a new route to that destination until the holddown time ends. However, a router will accept a route to the destination if its metric is better than the original metric since the metric of looped routes should be increasing.

Typically, the holddown time is slightly longer than three times the interval specified by the **update timer**, which controls how frequently the router sends routing updates. This is to allow a routing update enough time to propagate throughout the network so that all routers have up-to-date information. Finally, distance vector routing protocols use a flush timer, which determines how long a router will wait between the time it learns that a route is no longer valid, and the time it completely flushes the route from its routing table.

Flash Updates

If a neighboring router misses three consecutive routing updates, then a router running a distance vector routing protocol will declare that neighbor to be down. The interval a router will wait before declaring a neighbor unreachable is controlled by the **invalid timer**. Alternately, a router may detect that a neighbor is unreachable because an interface failed. In either case, it will also immediately send a poison reverse update to quickly notify its neighbors about a topology change. An update sent immediately after an outage detected is called a **flash update**. Flash updates speed up convergence by beginning it as quickly as possible after a topology change.

Disadvantages of Distance Vector Routing Protocols

Distance vector routing protocols have several disadvantages on larger networks. First, they have a tendency to converge slowly. A router on an RIP network knows of its neighboring routers because they send their complete routing tables to each other. Depending on the type of link, when a neighboring router goes down, a RIP router will wait 90 seconds for the invalid timer to expire before marking it down. It will then send a flash update (with a poison reverse update for the failed route) out of all of its interfaces indicating that the neighboring router is down. The other routers will put the poisoned route into holddown so they will not accept new information about the failed router until the holddown timer expires, and every router on the network has had enough time to learn about it. The net result of this is that, at a minimum, it takes several minutes for a distance vector network to converge. In practice, it can often take much longer, especially as the network grows. Table 1-1 summarizes timers affecting convergence for RIP and IGRP.

Table 1-1   Timers affecting convergence for RIP and IGRP

Routing Protocol	Update Timer (seconds)	Invalid Timer	Holddown Time	Flush Timer
RIP	30	180	180	240
IGRP	90	270	280	630

Another disadvantage of distance vector protocols on larger networks is the vast amount of bandwidth used to maintain their routing tables. Both RIP and IGRP require routers to send their entire routing tables during updates. According to Table 1-1, RIP routers do so every 30 seconds, and IGRP routers do so every 90 seconds. On a small network, this is generally not a problem. Only a few routers are broadcasting routing updates, and the routing tables contained in these updates consist of only a few routes. However, as a network increases in size, the effect of routing updates on bandwidth becomes noticeable. Not only are more routers broadcasting their updates, but also each update is significantly larger because there are more routes. Table 1-2 compares the estimated size of a routing update on networks of various sizes. On both a small network with only ten routes, and on a medium-size network with 100 routes, the routing update traffic is negligible. However, on a network with 1000 routes, the size of the routing update traffic is noticeable, especially on slower links (such as 56 Kbps leased lines or 128 Kbps ISDN lines).

Table 1-2   Estimated routing update sizes for RIP networks of different sizes

Number of Routes	Estimated Number of Packets in a Routing Update	Estimated Total Size of Routing Update (bytes)
10	1	168
100	4	1632
1000	40	16,320

Because RIP networks cannot contain routes with hop counts greater than 15, building a network with 1000 routes, as indicated in Table 1-2, would be very difficult, if not impossible.

Another disadvantage of distance vector routing protocols is their size restrictions. On RIP networks, for example, a router 16 hops away is unreachable, which clearly limits the potential size of a RIP network. IGRP also has a maximum hop count of 100, by default, which can be set as high as 255. IGRP does not use the hop count in its metric, but it does mark routes with hop counts greater than the maximum as invalid.

Finally, distance vector routing protocols typically do not understand **variable-length subnet masks (VLSMs)**, or subnet masks not on class boundaries. Neither RIP nor IGRP sends the subnet mask in their updates. A router running either of these protocols cannot determine the subnet mask of a route except by looking at the subnet masks on its own interfaces, or by looking at the class of the IP address. Consequently, a router running RIP or EIGRP may not be able to reach a network with a subnet mask that does not fall along a classful boundary, or that does not match the subnets of its connected interfaces. For instance, a router running RIP may not be able to reach a network with a subnet mask of 255.255.128.0. Additionally, neither RIP nor IGRP supports **discontiguous subnets**, or subnets separated by other networks. If the routers on the network shown in Figure 1-9 were running RIP or IGRP, hosts on the 172.16.10.0 network would be unable to reach hosts on the 172.16.20.0 network and vice versa. Unless a routing protocol supports VLSMs, all subnets of a network must be contiguous.

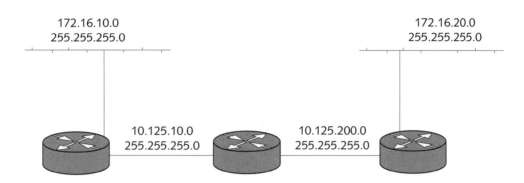

Figure 1-9 Discontiguous subnets

> A second version of RIP, RIP version 2, was designed to overcome some of these limitations. While RIP version 2 supports a larger hop count limit of 255 and VLSMs, it is otherwise quite similar to RIP version 1, and still suffers from the flaws of other distance vector routing protocols.

Link-State Routing Protocols

Link-state routing protocols were developed to remove some of these disadvantages. Link-state routing protocols require routers to advertise the state of each attached link to all other routers, allowing each router to build its routing table based upon complete knowledge of the network topology. **Open Shortest Path First (OSPF)** is a common example of a link-state routing protocol.

Link-state protocols tend to converge more quickly than distance vector protocols because when a link goes down somewhere on the network, that information is quickly flooded to all the routers on the network. Because each router on the network knows the status of every other router and all their links, a link-state protocol does not need to use a holddown time or send poison reverse updates to avoid routing loops.

Link-state routing protocols also tend to be more efficient than distance vector routing protocols. They generally send updated routing information only when a link changes status (with the exception of an update every 30 minutes in OSPF). As a result, on average, they use much less bandwidth to propagate routing updates.

Link-state protocols were also designed without hop count limitations. Distance vector routing protocols use the hop count to find routing loops. If the hop count for a route increases, the router can assume the route is in a loop. With link-state routing protocols, routers track the state of every link and every route on the network. Because they can see the whole network, they do not need to use the hop count to avoid routing loops.

Link-state protocols were also designed to handle variable-length subnet masks. This is a bigger advantage than it may seem since in addition to allowing you to arbitrarily subnet your networks, it enables address summarization, which allows you to summarize a whole range of IP addresses into one route. This can simplify routing on your network, and reduce the size of your routing tables.

You will find that there are tradeoffs in using link-state protocols over distance vector protocols. Both RIP and IGRP function quite well on small, stable networks. Link-state routing protocols require the router to use more CPU and memory since each router must keep track of the entire network, and use that information to calculate their routing tables. With a distance vector routing protocol, a router does not attend to anything but the networks attached to its own interfaces, and the updates it receives from its neighbors. However, distance vector routing protocols converge more slowly. The deciding factor in which type of routing protocol to use will generally depend on the size of your network. On small networks, you may safely use a distance vector routing protocol. In general, you should use link-state routing protocols over distance vector routing protocols on larger networks. Distance vector routing protocols are acceptable on smaller networks, but become less acceptable as they expand.

Other Types of Routing Protocols

Examples of other types of routing protocols include **Enhanced IGRP (EIGRP)** and **Border Gateway Protocol (BGP)**. Cisco designed EIGRP as a **hybrid routing protocol**, combining the best features of each type of protocol. Like a link-state routing protocol, EIGRP requires each router to know some of the network topology, but like a distance vector routing protocol, EIGRP requires routers to send updates only about attached networks.

BGP, on the other hand, is based on distance vector routing protocols. However, BGP uses information about each path, instead of the hop count, to ensure that each route it advertises is free of loops.

FINDING NETWORK TOPOLOGY WITH ROUTING TABLES

Mapping a network's topology can help you identify problems that can interfere with the scalability of a network. Routing tables supply a great deal of information about a network. The routing table in Figure 1-10 tells us:

- All the routes known by the router.
- How the router learned each route. Each route is marked with a code, explained at the top of the routing table. In this case, each route is marked with "R" for routes learned via RIP, and "C" for directly connected networks.

```
Router1#sh ip route
Codes: C - connected, S - static, I - IGRP, R - RIP, M - mobile, B - BGP
  D - EIGRP, EX - EIGRP external, O - OSPF, IA - OSPF inter area
  N1 - OSPF NSSA external type 1, N2 - OSPF NSSA external type 2
  E1 - OSPF external type 1, E2 - OSPF external type 2, E - EGP
  i - IS-IS, L1 - IS-IS level-1, L2 - IS-IS level-2, ia - IS-IS inter area
  * - candidate default, U - per-user static route, o - ODR
  P - periodic downloaded static route

Gateway of last resort is not set

     172.16.0.0/24 is subnetted, 8 subnets
R       172.16.8.0 [120/3] via 172.16.1.1, 00:00:09, Ethernet0/0
C       172.16.4.0 is directly connected, Ethernet1/0
R       172.16.5.0 [120/1] via 172.16.1.1, 00:00:09, Ethernet0/0
R       172.16.6.0 [120/1] via 172.16.1.1, 00:00:09, Ethernet0/0
R       172.16.7.0 [120/2] via 172.16.1.1, 00:00:09, Ethernet0/0
C       172.16.1.0 is directly connected, Ethernet0/0
R       172.16.2.0 [120/2] via 172.16.1.1, 00:00:09, Ethernet0/0
R       172.16.3.0 [120/1] via 172.16.1.1, 00:00:09, Ethernet0/0
```

Figure 1-10   Typical routing table

- The IP address of the next hop for each route.

- The interface through which the router will send packets for each route.

- The **administrative distance** of the route, which the router uses to choose between routes learned from different sources. If the router had both a static route and a route learned through RIP to the same destination, it would include the route with the lowest administrative distance in its routing table. In this case, all the routes learned through RIP have an administrative distance of 120.

- The metric of the route. This will vary depending on the routing protocol used. In this case, because each route is learned through RIP, the metric is the hop count for each route. For example, the metric to the 172.16.8.0/24 network is three hops.

- The default route, if any. In this case, the routing table tells us that the "**Gateway of last resort** is not set," which indicates that there is no default route. A router will forward a packet to the gateway of last resort when it has no other route for that packet. If the gateway of last resort isn't set, the router will discard the packet.

Mapping the Network Topology

You can use routing tables to map the topology of a network in greater detail. Looking at the routing table in Figure 1-10, you can see that it has two interfaces in use, Serial0/0 and Ethernet0/0, and eight networks in its routing table. Two of those routes are connected and six are remote. You also notice that the next hop of all the non-connected routes is 172.16.1.1, which is on the directly connected 172.16.1.0/24 network. There are no additional networks with a next hop on the other connected network, 172.16.4.0/24. It is possible that this network contains another neighboring router, which may not be advertising additional routes, or that it connects workstations or servers to the rest of the network.

Assuming you know the telnet password to the routers on the network, you can telnet to the next router at 172.16.1.1, and look through its routing tables for more neighbors. As you jump from router to router, you can gather a reasonably complete picture of the network. At this stage, it is a good idea to use the ping and traceroute commands to verify connectivity between all points on the network and that the network operates according to your network map.

Another good tool you can use to map a network is the **Cisco Discovery Protocol (CDP).** Typical output from the show cdp neighbor command is shown in Figure 1-11.

```
Router1#show cdp neigh
Capability Codes: R - Router, T - Trans Bridge, B - Source Route Bridge
               S - Switch, H - Host, I - IGMP, r - Repeater

Device ID        Local Intrfce     Holdtme    Capability  Platform  Port ID
Router2          Eth    0/0          155        R           2501      Eth 0
```

Figure 1-11   Output of the show cdp neighbors command

CDP is a proprietary protocol used to share information between Cisco routers about their hardware and interfaces. It supplements the information found in routing tables by providing information about any Cisco devices directly connected to the router, including switches (which normally do not appear in the routing table). On the other hand, CDP does not give any information when other vendors' devices are directly connected to a router, or if CDP was disabled on an interface.

CHAPTER SUMMARY

- ❑ A network administrator's goals are to ensure that a network remains available, responsive, efficient, manageable, and secure. However, as networks grow, problems may arise and jeopardize these characteristics. Such problems include congestion (which is often a result of or aggravated by network broadcasts), poor manageability, and haphazard growth.

❑ Redundancy, or eliminating all the points where the failure of one piece of equipment could bring down the network, can prevent some of these problems. Another strategy is hierarchical design. A hierarchical design segments the network into three main areas—the core layer, the distribution layer and the access layer—which all have clearly defined roles and purposes.

❑ Using efficient routing protocols is another strategy. Link-state routing protocols, which keep track of the state of every link on the network, have several advantages over distance vector routing protocols. These include faster convergence, support for VLSMs, no hop count limitations, and more efficient updates.

Key Terms

access layer — In a hierarchical network design, the access layer feeds traffic from end users into the distribution layer.

administrative distance — A value used by Cisco routers to decide between routes learned from different sources.

Address Resolution Protocol (ARP) — The protocol used in IP networks to associate an IP address with a Layer 2 address.

Border Gateway Protocol (BGP) — A path vector routing protocol.

broadcast domain — A group of devices receiving each other's broadcasts.

Cisco Discovery Protocol (CDP) — A protocol Cisco routers use to share information about their hardware and interfaces.

congestion — Traffic on the network using most or all of the available bandwidth, or when the amount of traffic exceeds the available bandwidth.

convergence — A process in which routers rebuild their routing tables to reflect a change on the network, such as a router going down.

core layer — In a hierarchical network design, the core layer switches packets between other sections of the network.

discontiguous subnets — Subnets of a major network number separated by other networks.

distance vector routing protocol — A dynamic routing protocol in which routers periodically broadcast their entire routing tables to neighboring routers.

distribution layer — In a hierarchical network design, the distribution layer funnels traffic from the access layer and aggregates it as it goes to the core network.

Dynamic Host Control Protocol (DHCP) — A protocol that allows a network administrator to dynamically assign IP addresses to host machines.

Enhanced IGRP (EIGRP) — A hybrid routing protocol containing features of both link-state and distance vector routing protocols.

flash update — When a router sends an update immediately after detecting an outage.

flushing a route — Completely removing a route from a routing table.

gateway of last resort — The default gateway through which a router will send all traffic without another route.

haphazard growth — Growth on a network without following any plan or design.

hierarchical design — A network design segmented into different parts with different functions.

holddown time — The period between the time a router receives a poison reverse update and the time it flushes that route from its routing table; the router will not place the route back into its routing table during this time.

hop count — The number of hops to a destination network, used as metric in some distance vector routing protocols.

hybrid routing protocol — A routing protocol combining the qualities of two or more types of routing protocols.

Interior Gateway Routing Protocol (IGRP) — A distance vector routing protocol designed by Cisco.

invalid timer — The timer that controls how long a router will wait before declaring one of its neighbors unreachable (typically three times the update timer).

link-state routing protocol — A routing protocol in which routers learn the state of every link on the network, and use that information to build their routing tables.

manageability — The degree to which network administrators can administer a network.

Maximum Transmission Unit (MTU) — The largest packet size usable on a particular network segment.

metric — A value used to distinguish between multiple routes to the same destination; for example, RIP uses the hop count to decide which route is the best route to a particular destination.

neighbor — A router sharing a common network segment.

Open Shortest Path First (OSPF) — A link-state routing protocol.

path vector routing protocol — A routing protocol similar to a distance vector routing protocol that uses information about the path to avoid routing loops, rather than the hop count.

poison reverse update — An update sent by a router running a distance vector routing protocol about an unreachable network with a metric larger than the largest acceptable hop count, in order to avoid routing loops.

routed protocol — A protocol that uses Layer 3 addresses and can be carried over multiple networks.

router — A device that forwards packets to their destinations, or to the next hop towards their destinations based on Layer 3 addresses; a router also keeps a routing table, which it uses to make decisions about where to forward packets.

Routing Information Protocol (RIP) — An Internet standard distance vector routing protocol defined in RFC 1058.

routing loop — When two routers pass a packet back and forth without it ever reaching its destination; the next hop for that packet in each router's routing table is the other router.

routing protocol — A protocol used by routers to dynamically exchange information about routes, including which routes are best to each destination.

routing table — A table built by a router containing a list of networks, and the next hop to reach those networks.

scalable network — A network that remains stable and smooth while continually growing.

segmentation — The process of breaking a network into smaller domains.

split horizon — A router running a distance vector routing protocol refuses to send routing information back out of the same interface through which it learned it in the first place.

update timer — The timer that controls the interval between routing updates.

variable-length subnet mask (VLSM) — A subnet mask not on a class boundary.

REVIEW QUESTIONS

1. Which of the following is not an advantage of hierarchical network design?

   a. It allows you to easily segment one area from another.

   b. It makes troubleshooting easier.

   c. It makes a full mesh for the network.

   d. It makes it easier to add devices to the network.

2. Which two of the following are likely to be causes of network congestion?

   a. routing update traffic

   b. redundant routes

   c. broadcast traffic

   d. larger networks segmented into smaller parts

3. It is possible for highly efficient networks to have congestion. True or false?

4. Which of the following is a potential problem caused by network congestion? (Choose all that apply.)

   a. Every device on the network must examine each packet crossing its network interface card to decide if it must respond.

   b. Ethernet collisions increase, resulting in more retransmitted packets.

   c. WAN connections use more bandwidth, increasing the charges for bandwidth used.

   d. Convergence times increase when a router goes down.

5. The type of routing protocol in which each router keeps track of each link on the network is called _____.

6. Which of the following information is not available from a routing table?

   a. the routing protocol through which a route was learned

   b. how long a route has been in the routing table

   c. the interface a router should use to forward a packet

   d. the responsiveness of a particular link

7. What are the disadvantages of greater redundancy on a network?

   a. higher availability and reliability

   b. greater complexity and expense

   c. more broadcast traffic

   d. increased routing update traffic

8. Which of the following is an advantage of link-state over distance vector routing protocols on large networks? (Choose all the apply.)

   a. Distance vector routing protocols require a router to use more memory and CPU.

   b. Link-state routing protocols are not restricted by network size.

   c. Link-state routing protocols tend to be less complex.

   d. Link-state routing protocols tend to use less bandwidth in routing updates.

9. Why do distance vector routing protocols converge more slowly than link-state routing protocols? (Choose all that apply.)

   a. Distance vector routing protocols cannot do flash updates.

   b. Distance vector routing protocols put routes into holddown after a route becomes invalid.

   c. Routers using distance vector routing protocols send out poison updates.

   d. They cannot alert other routers to topology changes.

10. Explain why some network applications are more sensitive to poor responsiveness than others.

11. What are the disadvantages of using a full or partial mesh in a network design? (Choose all that apply.)

   a. Mesh networks are unsupported by most routing protocols.

   b. Meshes are expensive to build because of the number of links required between routers.

   c. Isolating one segment of a mesh from another is difficult.

   d. Broadcast traffic is excessive.

12. On an efficient network, the amount of bandwidth devoted to routing table updates and service advertisements is irrelevant. True or false?

13. How does haphazard growth contribute to poor manageability? (Choose all that apply.)

    a. by making it difficult to segment the network

    b. by making the network more congested

    c. by requiring changes to be made manually

    d. by creating unnecessary dependencies between devices on the network

14. The number that a router assigns to a route and uses to choose between routes learned by different methods is called the _____.

15. What are the main functions of a router? (Choose all that apply.)

    a. to check the validity of incoming packets

    b. to build and maintain routing tables

    c. to filter unwanted packets

    d. to forward a packet closer to its destination

16. In a distance vector routing protocol, what happens when a route reaches the maximum hop count?

    a. Routers in the network will start counting at zero.

    b. Routers ignore further updates from any router at the other end of this route.

    c. Routers will consider it unreachable.

    d. Nothing because routers use the administrative distance to select a route.

17. Why do networks using link-state routing protocols converge more quickly? (Choose all that apply.)

    a. Link-state routing protocols require routers to have more memory and faster CPUs.

    b. Routers keep track of each link on the network and need not use a holddown time.

    c. Routers generally send routing updates when something changes.

    d. Link-state routing protocols understand VLSMs.

18. What is the purpose of split horizon?

    a. Split horizon prevents routers from learning about bad routes from networks attached to remote routers.

    b. Split horizon allows a router to immediately send an update after it detects a topology change.

    c. Split horizon prevents a router from sending invalid information about a route back to the router which originally advertised the route.

    d. Split horizon prevents any router from updating its routing table with false information.

19. How does the holddown time help prevent routing loops?

    a. by preventing routers from updating their routing tables before every router on the network has had an opportunity to learn about a topology change

    b. by preventing routers from learning about invalid routes

    c. by automatically flushing invalid routes from a router's routing table

    d. by immediately sending a poison reverse update after a topology change

20. Which of the following is a property of a link-state routing protocol? (Choose all that apply.)

    a. understands VLSMs

    b. sends the entire routing table during updates

    c. knows the topology of the entire network

    d. sends updates only after a topology change

21. Routing tables do not contain useful information about the topology of a network. True or false?

22. How can a routing table tell you whether or not a router has a default route?

    a. Cisco routers do not use default routes.

    b. The routing table will indicate whether or not a gateway of last resort was set.

    c. The routing table will give you the route with the highest administrative distance, which the router uses as its default route.

    d. Default routes are marked with a "D".

23. How does a Cisco router use administrative distance?

    a. to select the route with the best metric

    b. to determine which routes are administratively disabled

    c. to select which route to use when two routes have the same metric

    d. to select between two routes to the same destination learned from different sources

24. How might redundancy and hierarchical design conflict? (Choose all that apply.)

    a. Hierarchical design prohibits redundancy.

    b. Redundant networks with many paths can be difficult to segment.

    c. Hierarchical networks may have single points of failure.

    d. Redundancy requires a full mesh between all routers.

25. How can the Cisco Discovery Protocol (CDP) help you map a network?

    a. CDP provides information about directly connected routers and switches from all vendors.

    b. CDP provides information about directly connected Cisco routers and switches.

    c. CDP provides another source of routing information.

    d. The CDP table associates Layer 2 addresses with IP addresses.

CASE PROJECTS

Case 1

Cheryl is the network administrator for a large advertising firm in Los Angeles. Although it started quite small, the company's network now consists of about 5000 users, 60 servers, and about 120 routers. Cheryl has received complaints for some time about the responsiveness of the network. Users complain that they are unable to use network resources for minutes at a time. Additionally, they complain that even when it is available, the network responds so slowly that they can hardly watch streaming video clips of commercials in production, or run a terminal session to the billing system on the AS/400. Cheryl was successfully using IGRP since the network was quite small, so she is reluctant to change. What kind of suggestions would you make to Cheryl to improve the responsiveness and reliability of her network? What sorts of information do you need to gather to answer?

Case 2

You are brought in as a consultant at an insurance company. According to the network administrator, the insurance company recently acquired several smaller competitors. After each acquisition, the network administrator was given only a limited amount of time to integrate each network. As a result, he was unable to plan carefully before each integration. Now, users at several of the acquired firms complain that they cannot use network resources in some portions of the company. Additionally, the network administrator cannot restrict unnecessary traffic from the servers housing the company's billing system without cutting off network access for two departments. The insurance company runs IGRP on its network. What are possible explanations for the network problems described to you? How can you go about further diagnosing them? What kind of advice can you offer to help prevent future network changes from causing additional problems?

2

MANAGING IP ADDRESSES AND BROADCASTS

After reading this chapter and completing the exercises you will be able to:

♦ Learn strategies to efficiently use IP addresses

♦ Show how to use route summarization to decrease the size of your routing tables

♦ Understand the advantages and benefits of using variable-length subnet masks (VSLMs) and classless routing

♦ Allocate IP addresses using variable-length subnet masks

♦ Use IP helper addresses to control broadcasts

In the previous chapter, you learned about some of the techniques you can use to make a network scalable. Careful allocation of IP addresses will also help your networks become scalable. In recent years, inefficient IP addressing of hosts and networks on the Internet has been a major problem. How you address your network will obviously play an important role in how it interacts with the Internet. But that is not the only reason IP addressing and VLSMs are important. In this chapter, you will learn how you can use IP addressing and VLSMs to reduce the size of routing tables on your network, and efficiently allocate IP addresses with VLSMs. You'll also learn how to control broadcasts with IP helper addresses.

THE GROWTH OF THE INTERNET

The Internet was originally relatively small and limited to researchers. However, in the 1990s, governments, universities, corporations, not-for-profits, and the general public all began to use the Internet. The result was immense growth in both the number of people using the Internet, and the number of routers used to support them. At the same time, many of these organizations that are now connected to the Internet (and many others that are not) saw their private networks grow immensely. As a result, such organizations and the Internet are encountering problems related to the management of their IP addresses.

IP Address Exhaustion

Because each host connecting to the Internet needs a public IP address, there is now a great deal of concern about how IP addresses are allocated on the Internet. In theory, over four billion IP addresses are available in the 32-bit IP address space. In practice, however, many of the IP addresses allocated were wasted. For many years, addresses were allocated to whomever requested them, without much, if any, thought given to geographical location, or efficient planning. Additionally, IP addresses were originally allocated along class boundaries. This meant that some organizations were allocated entire Class A or Class B blocks of IP addresses despite not having enough hosts to make it worthwhile. A Class A, for example, contains 16,777,214 hosts, which is larger than the populations of some countries. As a result, many IP addresses in some Class A and Class B blocks are not used. The net result of this is the fear that the Internet may run out of usable IP addresses.

Routing Table Growth

Another IP addressing problem is the size of the Internet routing table. The Internet routing table increased from perhaps 5000 routes in 1990 to more than 100,000 in 2001. Large routing tables like these can increase the amount of CPU time and memory a router uses in order to maintain its routing tables, slow down routing table lookups and even make troubleshooting more difficult. While not all routers require the full Internet routing table, routers on any large network (even if it is not connected to the Internet) are vulnerable to the problem of large routing tables.

MANAGING IP ADDRESSES

To address these issues, network administrators used an evolving set of strategies over the years. These are all discussed in the following sections.

Hierarchical Addressing

One technique that helps manage both IP address exhaustion and routing table growth is **hierarchical addressing**. Hierarchical addressing operates in a layered, orderly fashion. One of the best examples of hierarchical addressing is the public telephone network.

To call a local number, you can usually dial a local exchange number, such as 267, and then the remainder of the phone number, 7740. The phone switch at the local central office recognizes the local exchange, realizes that the destination phone number is somewhere within its area, and routes the call to its specific destination. If you call this number from elsewhere in the country, you first dial a one to indicate a long distance call, and then the area code (for example, 608). The phone switch in your local central office looks up the central office associated with the 608 area code, and then transfers the call to the central office in Madison, Wisconsin. At this point, switching equipment in the Madison central office sends the call to its final destination as if it was a local call. Figure 2-1 shows how the public telephone system forwards calls to their destinations.

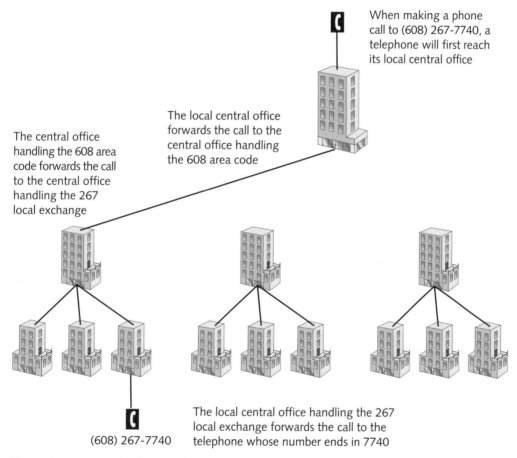

When making a phone call to (608) 267-7740, a telephone will first reach its local central office

The local central office forwards the call to the central office handling the 608 area code

The central office handling the 608 area code forwards the call to the central office handling the 267 local exchange

(608) 267-7740

The local central office handling the 267 local exchange forwards the call to the telephone whose number ends in 7740

Figure 2-1 Example showing how the public telephone system forwards calls to their destinations

The primary advantage of hierarchical addressing to the telephone company is that the central offices generally do not need to know anything about phone numbers in other areas. All they need to know about phone numbers outside their local areas is where to forward calls intended for other area codes. Otherwise, every central office would need to know the phone numbers of every other central office.

Hierarchical Routing

Hierarchical routing offers this benefit to IP addressing on large networks, including the Internet. For instance, suppose a router receives a packet with a destination address of 172.25.12.244. Under a hierarchical addressing scheme, a router might first forward the packet to a core layer router that handles all traffic bound for destination networks with a first octet of 172. This router would then forward the packet to a distribution layer router that handles all traffic bound for destination networks whose first two octets are 172.25, which would in turn forward the packet to an access layer router that handles all traffic bound for destination networks whose first three octets are 172.25.12. The access layer router would then forward the packet to its final destination. Any router but these three would simply need to know how to forward a packet to the appropriate core router.

Route Summarization

Route summarization, also known as **address aggregation**, is the combination of multiple routes that share the leftmost bits into one **summary route**. This is the rough equivalent of an area code on the public telephone network. For example, a large Internet Service Provider might have a customer with a large block of IP addresses, such as a Class A. In each of the customer's routing tables, there are 7000 routes. If you are a network administrator at the service provider, instead of adding all 7000 routes to your routing tables, you summarize all those routes into as few routes as possible. While you could theoretically summarize all your customer's routes into one, in practice, most networks of any size have multiple pathways for redundancy. While this makes it difficult to use just one summary route, you can often dramatically reduce the number of routes needed. This is particularly important if the service provider has many customers with large networks. Instead of advertising thousands of routes for each of hundreds of customers, you can advertise a small number of summary routes for each customer.

Figure 2-2 shows an example of route summarization. The Boston router is advertising a summary route to 10.25.0.0/16 to the Houston router and the rest of the network. Instead of individual routes to 10.25.1.0/24, 10.25.2.0/24, 10.25.3.0/24, 10.25.4.0/24, and 10.25.5.0/24, the Houston router will have one summary route to those networks in its routing table. A good place for route summarization is at routers between two different layers in a hierarchical design. For example, such a router might be a core router attached to the distribution network.

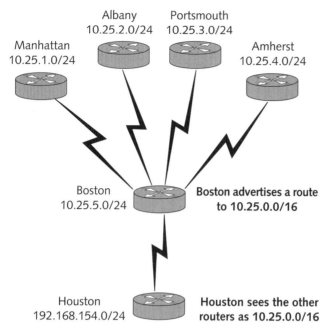

Albany   Portsmouth
10.25.2.0/24 10.25.3.0/24

Manhattan   Amherst
10.25.1.0/24   10.25.4.0/24

Boston   Boston advertises a route
10.25.5.0/24   **to 10.25.0.0/16**

Houston   **Houston sees the other**
192.168.154.0/24   **routers as 10.25.0.0/16**

Figure 2-2   Example of route summarization

What happens if a router has both a summary route and an ordinary route in its rout-ing table? The router selects the route with the **longest match**. This is possible because a router looks at the length of the **prefix**, or the number of bits in the subnet mask, when deciding which route to use. The prefix itself is the leftmost bits of the route, cor-responding to the network number. A Cisco router will always select the route with the longest prefix, or the most specific route. Figure 2-3 provides an example of the possi-ble routes a router might find in its routing table for a single destination. In a routing table, the length of the prefix appears directly after the network number. For the route to 172.30.0.0 in Figure 2-3, for example, the length of the prefix is 16 bits, while the prefix itself is the same as the network number, 172.30.0.0. For the route to 172.30.2.0, the prefix length is 24 and the prefix is 172.30.2.0. These routes will often be written as 172.30.0.0/16 and 172.30.2.0/24 as shorthand for the prefix and the prefix length, which are equivalent to the network number and the netmask, or subnet mask. The default route, for example, does not match any bits in the destination address so since all the other routes match at least 16 bits, the default route clearly is not the longest match for any 172.30.0.0 address. The routes to 172.30.0.0/16 and 172.30.2.0/24 match 16 and 24 bits, respectively, but there is a route to 172.16.2.104/30 that matches 30 bits in the destination address. Since this route is the longest match, the router will use it to forward packets to the destination address. Later in the chapter, you will learn how to perform route summarization.

```
Codes: C - connected, S - static, I - IGRP, R - RIP, M - mobile, B - BGP
       D - EIGRP, EX - EIGRP external, O - OSPF, IA - OSPF inter area
       N1 - OSPF NSSA external type 1, N2 - OSPF NSSA external type 2
       E1 - OSPF external type 1, E2 - OSPF external type 2, E - EGP
       i - IS-IS, L1 - IS-IS level-1, L2 - IS-IS level-2, ia - IS-IS inter
area
       * - candidate default, U - per-user static route, o - ODR
       P - periodic downloaded static route

Gateway of last resort is 172.30.254.2 to network 0.0.0.0
[Output omitted]
D       172.30.0.0/16 is a summary, 4w4d, Null0
D       172.30.2.0/24 [90/2174976] via 10.139.228.39, 7w0d,
FastEthernet0/0.1
S       172.30.2.104/30 [1/0] via 10.139.228.3
S*    0.0.0.0/0 [1/0] via 172.30.254.2
```

Figure 2-3   Routing table with several routes for the same destination

Variable-Length Subnet Masks

Unfortunately, route summarization does not make address allocation more efficient. Point-to-point links, for example, are particularly wasteful. Suppose you have a Class C address block and you need to connect two ends of a T-1 together. One end will be 192.168.154.1 and the other will be 192.168.154.2. If you use a netmask of 255.255.255.0 on this link, you will use only two IP addresses out of the 254 available—but you cannot use any of the others. **Variable-length subnet masks**, or VLSMs, defined in RFC 1812, allow you to subdivide that Class C, as necessary. A netmask of 255.255.255.252 will allow you to allocate only two IP addresses, one to each end of the point-to-point link. You can also carve up the rest of the Class C block however it makes the most sense for your network.

Each IP address consists of two portions. The first is the network portion and the second is the host portion. A router uses the network portion of an IP address to send a packet to the right network, and then a router, or switch on that network, uses the host portion to send it the rest of the way to its destination. In order to decide which portion of an IP address is the network portion and which portion is the host portion, a router uses the subnet mask.

To understand how the subnet mask works, you must look at an IP address and a subnet mask on a bit-by-bit level, the way a router does. For example, in Figure 2-4, you can see the bits for the IP address 192.168.12.57 and its subnet mask, 255.255.255.248.

IP Address	11000000	10101000	00001100	00111 001
Subnet Mask	11111111	11111111	11111111	11111 000
Network Number (binary)	11000000	10101000	00001100	00111 000
Network Number (dotted decimal)	192	168	12	56

Figure 2-4   Calculating the network number for 192.168.12.57

In mathematical terms, when the router sees this IP address and its subnet mask, it matches up all the bits and performs what is known as a logical AND operation on the two binary numbers. In a logical AND operation, you compare each bit of two binary numbers, one at a time. If both bits are ones, the result of the logical AND operation is a one. If either bit is a zero, the result is a zero. Table 2-1 shows all the possible combinations for the logical AND operation.

Table 2-1   Results of binary AND operation

IP Address	Subnet Mask	Result
0	0	0
0	1	0
1	0	0
1	1	1

If you match up the bits for the IP address and the subnet mask, you can perform the logical AND operation on each and get the network number. In Figure 2-4, the subnet number proves to be 192.168.12.56.

> The only time a binary AND operation results in a one is when the bits for both the IP address and the subnet mask are also ones. This means that if you match up the bits, the network number will be the bits where the subnet mask bits are ones, and the host portion of the address will be where the subnet mask bits are zeroes.

The number of subnets created by the subnet mask depends on the number of bits the default netmask was extended, or the number of subnet bits. In this case, the default subnet mask is 255.255.255.0 so the 255.255.255.248 subnet mask actually used extends the default subnet mask by five bits. The number of new subnets created is 2^5, or 32. In general, you can calculate the number of new subnets by 2^n, where n is the number of subnet bits.

If all the subnet bits are zeroes, this subnet is called subnet 0. In versions of Cisco IOS before 12.0, in order to use this subnet, you had to specifically enable subnet 0 with the IP subnet-zero command in global configuration mode. In IOS 12.0 and later, this command is on by default. The remaining bits, three in this case, are the host portion of the IP address. As you would expect, the host number must be unique on a given network. However, you cannot use all of the host numbers. If all the host bits for an IP address are zeroes, the address is reserved for the subnetwork number, and if all the host bits are ones, the address is reserved for the broadcast address. As a result, there are $2^n - 2$ host addresses in a subnet, where n is the number of host bits. This also means that the 255.255.255.254 netmask is effectively useless since this leaves only one host bit, $2^1 - 2 = 0$ host addresses. The 255.255.255.252 netmask leaves you with two host bits and $2^2 - 2 = 2$ host addresses. This is a perfect size for point-to-point links. With VLSMs, you can configure whatever subnet mask you need. You can even **supernet**, or use a smaller netmask than the traditional class boundaries. Addresses that follow the traditional class boundaries are called **classful routing**, while routing that does not is called **classless**. The network 212.156.0.0/20 is an example of a supernetted network, which you can use to summarize the classful networks 212.156.0.0/24, 212.156.1.0/24, and so on through the 212.156.15.0/24 network.

According to RFC 1812, all the bits in the subnet mask should be contiguous, or connected to each other. Cisco IOS will not allow you to configure a subnet mask with non-contiguous bits, as shown in Figure 2-5. The error messages show the subnet mask in hexadecimal instead of the usual dotted decimal format.

```
router(config-if)#ip address 172.16.1.1 255.255.253.0
Bad mask 0xFFFFFD00 for address 172.16.1.1
router(config-if)#ip address 172.16.1.1 255.224.255.0
Bad mask 0xFFE0FF00 for address 172.16.1.1
```

Figure 2-5   Configuring a subnet with discontiguous bits

Be careful trying to do calculations with IP address and subnet masks in your head. Unless you use a calculator, or draw out the bits on a piece of paper, it is very easy to make mistakes.

It is important to keep in mind that if you use VLSMs, you must also use a routing protocol that supports them. While neither RIP version 1 nor IGRP supports them, RIPv2 (which is not discussed in this text), OSPF, and EIGRP (which you will learn about in Chapters 3, 4, and 5) do.

Summarizing Routes Using VLSMs

In addition to more efficient allocation of IP addresses, VLSMs allow you to more flexibly summarize routes. Suppose you have a series of routes you want to summarize (as shown in Figure 2-6). Without VLSMs, you would have to summarize the routes along a boundary, such as 192.168.0.0/16, which may not be efficient or may not work because it might include other routes on other parts of the network. However, with VLSMs, you can summarize routes based entirely on the higher-order bits they share on the left (even if the routes are not contiguous).

192.168.98.0/24	11000000	10101000	0110 0010	00000000
192.168.99.0/24	11000000	10101000	0110 0011	00000000
192.168.101.0/24	11000000	10101000	0110 0101	00000000
192.168.102.0/24	11000000	10101000	0110 0110	00000000
192.168.105.0/24	11000000	10101000	0110 1001	00000000

Figure 2-6   Routes for summarization with a VLSM

Looking at the network numbers for the routes in Figure 2-6, you can see that each route shares each bit up to and including the 20th bit. The 21st bit, however, is not the same for all five routes. Therefore, the prefix for the summary route will be 20 bits long, and you can use that to calculate the network number of the summary route. As shown in Figure 2-7, the summarized route is 192.168.96.0/20.

| 11000000 | 10101000 | 01100000 | 00000000 |
| 192 | 168 | 96 | 0/20 |

Figure 2-7   Calculating the network number for a summary route

Classful and Classless Routing

While VLSMs help network administrators efficiently allocate IP addresses, they are not a complete answer because of the way IP addresses were originally allocated. When IP first came into use, IP addresses were thought of in terms of class. The class of an IP address is determined by the first octet of the IP address, or the first eight bits. Table 2-2 contains a list of IP classes. Each class is determined by the leftmost bits. Class A addresses begin with a zero as the leftmost bit, Class B addresses begin with a 10 as the first two bits, and Class C addresses begin with a 110 as the first three bits. Class D addresses are used for multicast, and Class E addresses are used for research. The octet beginning with 127, although by definition should be a Class A address, is reserved for internal loopback addresses. In classful routing, by default, the number of network and host bits depends on the class of the network. Class A networks have eight network bits and 24 host bits, while Class B networks have 16 network bits and 16 host bits, and Class C networks have 24 network bits and eight host bits. You may subnet classful networks, but only along octet boundaries. Additionally, classful routing protocols do not include the subnet mask in their routing updates. As a result, the only way a router using a classful routing protocol can learn the subnet mask of a route is by looking at the class of the route, or by looking at the subnet mask of its own directly connected networks.

In fact, in order to get a classful routing protocol, such as RIP, to properly route the summary route in Figure 2-7, you might have to use the ip classless global configuration command in Cisco IOS versions prior to 12.0. If a classful routing protocol is directly connected to one subnet of a network, it assumes that it knows all routes to all of the subnets for that network. If a packet arrives for a subnet of an unrecognized subnet of a directly connected network, the router discards the packet. With the ip classless command, classful routing protocols are not able to perform classless routing. Instead, they are able to use default or summary routes for unrecognized subnets of connected networks. For instance, without the **ip classless** command, a router running RIP with the 172.16.2.0/24 network directly connected drops packets intended for the unattached 172.16.200.0/24 network, even if a default route exists. With the ip classless command, the router forwards these packets to the next hop indicated by the default route. The ip classless command also enables the router to forward the packets to a summary route. In 12.0 and later versions, ip classless is turned on by default.

Table 2-2   Classful address distinctions

Class	First Octet (decimal)	Beginning Value of Leftmost Bits	Purpose	Number of Addresses
A	1 – 126	0	Routed	16, 777, 214
B	128 – 191	10	Routed	65, 532
C	192 – 223	110	Routed	254
D	224 – 239	1110	Multicast	Not Applicable
E	240 – 247	11110	Experimental	Not Applicable

Unfortunately, the allocation of address blocks under classful routing isn't as flexible as needed. For example, if you need 25,000 addresses, and you expect that need to double in the near future, a Class B block of IP addresses would be helpful. But what if you need 100,000 addresses? A Class B is too small, and if you use a Class A you'll waste over 16,600,000 addresses. Alternately, if you need only 1000 addresses, a Class C is too small, but a Class B wastes over 64,000 addresses.

In order to escape the inflexibility of classful routing, classless routing is commonly used throughout the Internet. As you might expect from the name, classless routing ignores the traditional class boundaries. Classless routing allows you to summarize routes in whatever manner best fits your network topology. Routing protocols, such as RIPv1 and IGRP, are classful, while OSPF and EIGRP are examples of classless routing protocols.

Classless routing also allows you to allocate and receive IP addresses, as necessary. As a result, the three **Regional Internet Registries (RIRs)** that allocate IP addresses throughout the world ignore class boundaries when they allocate IP addresses. The three RIRs are the **American Registry for Internet Numbers (ARIN)**, the **Réseaux IP Européens Network Coordination Centre (RIPE NCC)**, and the **Asia Pacific Network Information Center (APNIC)**. Table 2-3 shows the regions of the world for which each RIR allocates IP addresses.

You might also get a block of IP addresses from your service provider; however, ultimately, a RIR probably allocated a larger block of IP addresses to your provider, which it in turn divided into smaller Classless Inter-Domain Routing (CIDR) blocks that were allocated to you.

Table 2-3   RIRs and associated regions

RIR	Regions
ARIN	North America South America Caribbean Sub-Saharan Africa
RIPE NCC	Europe The Middle East Parts of Africa
APNIC	Asia Pacific

Instead of assigning you a classful block of IP addresses, such as a Class B, the RIRs will assign you addresses based on **Classless Inter-Domain Routing (CIDR)**, which is a strategy to allocate and aggregate (or summarize) IP addresses. CIDR and the allocation of IP addresses are discussed in RFCs 1518, 1519, and 2050. Each **CIDR block** is described by a prefix and prefix length, or an IP address and a subnet mask, similar to the way a VLSM describes a network number. In practice, a CIDR block often consists of a group of Class Cs, since this is the smallest block of addresses likely to be allocated by a RIR. However, CIDR blocks may also be assigned from within a Class A or Class B network, if they are available for the RIR to allocate. CIDR may be used to allocate a block of any size of IP addresses.

The CIDR block you receive from a RIR is a block like 10.33.96.0/21. This particular CIDR block allows you a maximum of 2,046 addresses, or the equivalent of eight Class Cs. You may allocate this block of addresses on your own network, or to your own customers, as necessary.

To better understand how this works, you can look at the address and the subnet mask in binary again in Figure 2-8. The prefix is 21 bits so the first 21 bits of the CIDR block address describe the network. The remaining bits are host addresses and can be used any way you need. In this case, you have 11 host bits remaining.

00001010	00100001	01100 000	00000000
11111111	11111111	11111 000	00000000

Figure 2-8   IP address and subnet mask in binary for the 10.33.96.0/21 CIDR block

> A prefix is calculated by counting bits from the left, and the number of host bits is found by counting bits from the right.

In classful terms, this CIDR block translates to eight Class C address blocks, or eight subnets with a prefix of 24. You have three bits between the start of your CIDR block at a prefix of 21 bits, and the traditional Class C boundary at 24 bits. You can allocate one smaller CIDR block for each possible bit pattern in those three bits. Figure 2-9 shows you how this works.

00001010	00100001	01100 000	00000000	10.33.96.0/24
00001010	00100001	01100 001	00000000	10.33.97.0/24
00001010	00100001	01100 010	00000000	10.33.98.0/24
00001010	00100001	01100 011	00000000	10.33.99.0/24
00001010	00100001	01100 100	00000000	10.33.100.0/24
00001010	00100001	01100 101	00000000	10.33.101.0/24
00001010	00100001	01100 110	00000000	10.33.102.0/24
00001010	00100001	01100 111	00000000	10.33.103.0/24

Figure 2-9   Allocating 10.33.96.0/21 into eight blocks with prefixes of 24

Keep in mind that you are not limited to allocating your CIDR block along traditional Class C boundaries. For example, it is possible to allocate this CIDR block in units with prefixes of 25, which gives you 16 blocks with 126 usable addresses, or in units with prefixes of 27, which gives you 64 blocks with 30 usable addresses. You can also allocate the 10.33.96.0/21 CIDR block into blocks with many different prefixes, which most network administrators will do in order to use their new address spaces as efficiently as possible. Table 2-4 summarizes how many usable addresses are possible for a given prefix, along with the number of host bits available, and the subnet mask.

Table 2-4   Number of IP addresses available, host bits, and subnet mask for a given prefix

Prefix	Host bits	Subnet Mask	Number of usable addresses possible
8	24	255.0.0.0	16, 777, 214
9	23	255.128.0.0	8, 388, 606
10	22	255.192.0.0	4, 194, 302
11	21	255.224.0.0	2, 097, 152
12	20	255.240.0	1, 048, 576
13	19	255.248.0.0	524, 286
14	18	255.252.0.0	262, 142
15	17	255.254.0.0	131, 070
16	16	255.255.0.0	65, 534
17	15	255.255.128.0	32, 766

Table 2-4   Number of IP addresses available, host bits, and subnet mask for a given prefix (continued)

Prefix	Host bits	Subnet Mask	Number of usable addresses possible
18	14	255.255.192.0	16, 382
19	13	255.255.224.0	8190
20	12	255.255.240.0	4094
21	11	255.255.248.0	2046
22	10	255.255.252.0	1022
23	9	255.255.254.0	510
24	8	255.255.255.0	254
25	7	255.255.255.128	126
26	6	255.255.255.192	62
27	5	255.255.255.224	30
28	4	255.255.255.240	14
29	3	255.255.255.248	6
30	2	255.255.255.252	2
31	1	255.255.255.254	0

2

ALLOCATING IP ADDRESSES

How you allocate IP addresses can have a significant effect on how well your network performs. This section discusses how to avoid some of the pitfalls with route summarization, and then gives you an example of how you might allocate your own CIDR block.

Pitfalls of Route Summarization

Despite its benefits on large networks, route summarization does have several potential disadvantages. One disadvantage, as you will see later in the chapter, is simply that it requires more planning, especially since route summarization works best with hierarchical addressing. Route summarization is most useful with a classless routing protocol, such as RIPv2, EIGRP, or OSPF. Classful routing protocols, such as RIP version 1 or IGRP, automatically summarize routes on classful boundaries, and therefore do not support summarization on any arbitrary boundary as do classless routing protocols.

Route summarization can also lead to poor path selection. Route summarization hides the details of large groups of networks; a router may choose a summary route through a low-bandwidth link, for example, when you would prefer it to choose a different path through a higher-bandwidth link.

Another potential problem involves discontiguous subnets. With classful routing protocols, such as IGRP or RIP version 1, all subnets on a particular network must be connected, or you will have trouble reaching all subnets. This is because of the automatic route summarization classful routing protocols do on the classful network boundaries.

This is also true when you use route summarization. Without route summarization, discontiguous subnets are not a problem for routing protocols that can handle VLSMs. However, route summarization hides the details of the network from routers. Figure 2-10 shows a diagram where the 172.16.2.0/24 subnet linking RouterD and RouterE is separated from the 172.16.1.0/24 and 172.16.5.0/24 subnets by the 192.168.154.0/24 subnet. When using OSPF or EIGRP without route summarization, you should have no trouble reaching any part of the network. However, if each network in the diagram has a summary route for 172.16.0.0/16, it will not know anything about the individual subnets on the 172.16.0.0/16 network. RouterD only knows to forward packets destined for any host in 172.16.0.0/16 to RouterE. RouterC only knows to forward packets destined for hosts in 172.16.0.0/26 to RouterB. Packets from neither RouterA, RouterB, nor RouterC are able to reach the 172.16.2.0/24 subnet, nor are packets from RouterD or RouterE able to reach the 172.16.1.0/24 and 172.16.5.0/24 subnets.

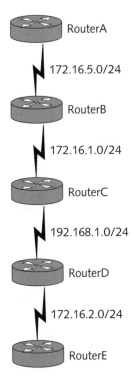

Figure 2-10   Discontiguous subnets

Depending on the topology of the network, discontiguous subnets may be created by an outage. This means that even though there are redundant paths through a network, some routers may not be able to reach others because the outage created discontiguous subnets while using route summarization. In Figure 2-11, all of the subnets for 172.20.0.0/16 are contiguous as long as the link between Router2 and Router3 remains connected. If that link goes down, and you are using a routing protocol that understands

VLSMs without route summarization, you should still be able to reach all parts of the network because of the link between Router4 and Router5. However, if you use route summarization, you will not be able to reach Router1 from Router3, Router5, or Router6. Because of the summarized route, Router5 only knows to forward packets destined for destinations on the 172.20.0.0/16 network to the attached subnets of that network. Router5 is therefore only able to forward packets to Router4 or Router6, neither of which can reach Router1.

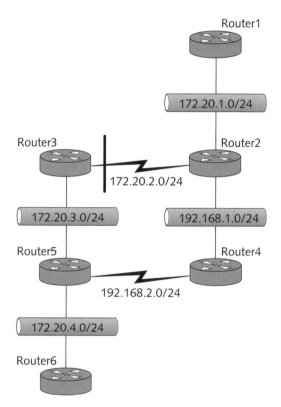

Figure 2-11   Discontiguous subnets created by an outage

Allocating IP Addresses Using VLSMs

Efficient allocation of IP addresses requires you to:

- Allocate enough IP addresses to each subnet for future growth.
- Assign no more IP addresses to each subnet than you predict necessary.
- Plan for route summarization.

How much weight you give each of these things will vary, of course, depending on your needs. If you allocate IP addresses on a first-come, first-serve basis (as many network administrators do), you may find that IP addresses are haphazardly allocated throughout your network, making route summarization difficult. Ideally, you allocate addresses based on the topology of your network, so that it is easy to summarize routes; however, that is not always practical for political or logistical reasons, and it certainly is not always easy to predict how you will use those IP addresses in the future.

Let's suppose you are given the CIDR block discussed earlier in the chapter, 10.33.96.0/21, and that you must allocate those IP addresses. You carefully examined your current network needs and you made every effort to predict future needs. As a result, you must divide your new CIDR block into one subnet for about 350 nodes at corporate headquarters, one subnet for about 300 nodes at the largest branch office, two subnets for 150–200 nodes at two more branch offices, six subnets for 40–50 nodes at six factories, and nine subnets for point-to-point links that connect the branch offices and factories to corporate headquarters. Figure 2-12 shows each building and how many nodes you need to allocate addresses for each of them.

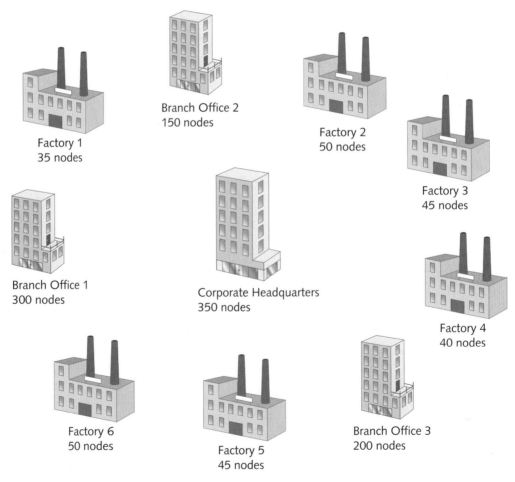

Figure 2-12   Physical layout of buildings for IP address allocation

Begin by dividing the network into subnets large enough to fit the largest block you need (sometimes known as the baseline subnet). As shown in Table 2-4, you can see that a prefix length of 23 (equivalent to a subnet mask of 255.255.254.0) supplies 510 addresses, which is the best fit for your largest two subnets, 300 and 350 nodes. You should carve up the rest of the CIDR block into four subnets with 23-bit prefixes.

You can calculate the number of subnets that can fit on a network with a particular prefix length by looking at the number of bits available for subnetting. In this case, you subdivided a subnet with a 21-bit prefix into subnets with 23-bit prefixes so there are two bits available. The number of subnets you can use is calculated with 2^n, where n is the number of bits available for subnetting. In this case, there are 2^2, or four, subnets available. Put your largest two networks, for corporate headquarters and the largest branch office, into the two lowest subnets, 10.33.96.0/23 and 10.33.98.0/23. In the past, the recommendation was to start allocating addresses from the subnets with the highest or leftmost bits. However, Cisco recommends that you allocate addresses from the lowest, moving up to the highest, because that makes it easier to summarize the routes for these subnets. Table 2-5 lists the first four address blocks allocated.

Table 2-5   Assignment of the largest IP address blocks in 10.33.96.0/21

Subnet	Assignment
10.33.96.0/23	Corporate Headquarters
10.33.97.0/23	Branch Office 1
10.33.98.0/24	Unassigned
10.33.99.0/24	Unassigned

Next, further subnet the first empty subnet so that it fits the next biggest block of IP addresses. According to Table 2-4, the best fit is a 24-bit prefix (or a subnet mask of 255.255.255.0), which provides 254 usable addresses, more than enough for the 150-200 addresses you need. Take the next unallocated subnet, 10.33.100.0/23, and divide it up, as necessary, to get the appropriate subnets. In this case, you can divide it in half to create two 24-bit subnets, 10.33.100.0/24 and 10.33.101.0/24. Since you still need one more 24-bit subnet, divide the next 23-bit subnet into two 24-bit subnets, 10.33.100.0/24 and 10.33.101.0/24. Table 2-6 shows the current list of assignments.

Table 2-6   Assignment of the next IP address blocks in 10.33.96.0/21

Subnet	Assignment
10.33.96.0/23	Corporate Headquarters
10.33.98.0/23	Branch Office 1
10.33.100.0/23	Subnetted further 10.33.100.0/24 Branch Office 2 10.33.101.0/24 Branch Office 3
10.33.102.0/23	Unassigned

One of the most important rules in subnetting a network is to not overlap subnets since overlapping subnets cause routing problems. It is extremely important to maintain records of how to subnet your network, such as a spreadsheet or a Web page containing a list of all the subnets you create, and their subnet masks or prefix lengths.

At this point, you must allocate IP address blocks for the factories, which each need 40–50 nodes. According to Table 2-4, the best fitting prefix has 26 bits, which provides 62 usable addresses. This will divide the remaining 23-bit subnet into eight 26-bit subnets. The first six of these will go to the six factories. However, you still need to assign addresses to the point-to-point links. Here, you can reserve one 26-bit subnet for future use, and subnet the remaining one even further. For the point-to-point links, you need only one IP address for each end of the link, so according to Table 2-4 you can use a 30-bit prefix. Between the 26-bit and the 30-bit prefix, you have four bits to use for subnetting, so you can divide that into 2^4 or 16 subnets, more than enough for the nine point-to-point links. See Table 2-7 for a final list of how you allocated your CIDR block.

Having allocated all the IP addresses in your CIDR block, it is important to keep in mind that there are several different ways that you can do this, depending on your needs and network topology. You can decide to subnet some of the larger blocks. For example, you might want to subnet the block assigned to corporate headquarters into blocks for each floor, or for different groups within the company. You may adjust your address allocation to account for route summarization.

Table 2-7   Final assignment of IP addresses in 10.33.96.0/21

Subnet	Assignment
10.33.96.0/23	Corporate Headquarters
10.33.98.0/23	Branch Office 1
10.33.100.0/23	Subnetted further: 10.33.100.0/24 Branch Office 2 10.33.101.0/24 Branch Office 3
10.33.102.0/23	Subnetted further: 10.33.102.0/26 Factory 1 10.33.102.64/26 Factory 2 10.33.102.128/26 Factory 3 10.33.102.192/26 Factory 4 10.33.103.0/26 Factory 5 10.33.103.64/26 Factory 6 10.33.103.128/30 Link 1 10.33.103.132/30 Link 2 10.33.103.136/30 Link 3 10.33.103.140/30 Link 4 10.33.103.144/30 Link 5 10.33.103.148/30 Link 6 10.33.103.152/30 Link 7 10.33.103.156/30 Link 8 10.33.103.160/30 Link 9 10.33.103.164/30 Free 10.33.103.168/30 Free 10.33.103.172/30 Free 10.33.103.176/30 Free 10.33.103.180/30 Free 10.33.103.184/30 Free 10.33.103.188/30 Free 10.33.103.192/26 Free

OTHER ADDRESSING STRATEGIES

There are several other IP addressing strategies currently in use to help you avoid one or more of the current sets of IP addressing problems.

Unnumbered Interfaces

Using **unnumbered interfaces** allows you to configure IP on an interface without explicitly using an IP address. This allows you to save IP addresses on serial links. In the following example, you can see how to configure an IP unnumbered interface. The ip unnumbered command must refer to an existing interface; the router uses this interface as the source address for any packets produced by the unnumbered interface. The router also looks to the existing interface, referenced in the ip unnumbered command, to decide whether or not to send routing updates out to the unnumbered interface.

```
toronto(config)#interface eth 0
toronto(config-if)#ip address 10.27.25.1 255.255.255.0
toronto(config-if)#int s0
toronto(config-if)#ip unnumbered ethernet 0
```

Unnumbered interfaces often get their IP addresses from a loopback address. Since a loopback interface is a logical interface implemented in software, it will not go down as long as the router remains up. Using loopback interfaces as the reference interface adds to the stability of unnumbered interfaces. Otherwise, unrelated problems with the reference interface can bring down the unnumbered interface.

While unnumbered interfaces do conserve IP addresses, they do have drawbacks. Since the interface does not actually have an IP address, you cannot get its status by pinging it. If you try to PING the interface referenced by the unnumbered interface, you will get a response as long as that interface is up and there is a path to it, regardless of the status of the serial interface, which makes both troubleshooting and network monitoring more difficult. However, it is possible to get the status of the interface through SNMP. Unnumbered interfaces are not supported by some serial protocols, such as X.25 and SMDS. Unnumbered interfaces also present problems if the two ends of the serial link are assigned to networks with different major network numbers. For example, if the unnumbered interface at one end of a serial link uses 192.168.100.1 as its address, and the unnumbered interface at the other end uses 192.168.101.1 as its address, Cisco recommends that any routing protocol used not advertise subnet information. In this case, you want to use a summary route.

Private Address Space

Because of the expansion of the Internet, and because not all organizations need public IP addresses, RCF 1918 set aside 10.0.0.0/8, 192.168.0.0/16, and 172.16.0.0 to 172.31.255.255 for use on private networks where connection to the Internet is either unnecessary, or limited to using network address translation (NAT). Addresses in these blocks should not be routed through the Internet. As a result, if you did not request a block of IP addresses from ARIN or the appropriate RIR, then you should number your networks using one of these blocks.

Network Address Translation

In **network address translation (NAT)**, a device, such as a router or firewall, translates a set of IP addresses on one side into another IP address or addresses on the other side. In this way, a private IP address of 172.16.97.38 might appear to the outside world as the public IP address 208.155.228.7. Because NAT allows translation between a large pool of private addresses and a small pool of public addresses (sometimes even just a single public address), NAT helps conserve IP addresses. NAT also allows a network to keep its original IP addressing scheme after a change in service provider, or after a merger with another organization's network. NAT has some disadvantages, including increased latency because the router must examine each packet in order to translate the appropriate address, and difficulties with any protocols or applications that put the IP address in the data portion of an IP packet.

IP Version 6

IP version 6 (IPv6) is the next version of the Internet Protocol, designed by the IETF to replace the current version (IP version 4, also known as IPv4). IPv6, specified in RFC 2460, potentially offers several advantages over IPv4, including a much bigger address space. IPv6 addresses are 128 bits long, which means that there are over 3×10^{38} possible IPv6 addresses. Other changes with IPv6 include more support for quality of service, and better security. Adoption of IPv6 appears to be moving slowly at the time of this writing, although the Cisco IOS and most of the major operating systems show at least experimental support for IPv6.

MANAGING BROADCASTS

By default, routers do not forward broadcasts. This prevents broadcasts from passing beyond the network where they originated and triggering other broadcasts. These broadcasts can in turn trigger other broadcasts, starting broadcast storms that can drown out other traffic on a network. However, in some situations, a device must broadcast in order to operate properly.

On many networks, for example, when a PC boots up, it does not know its own IP address. In order to find an IP address, it must contact a DHCP or BOOTP server, which responds with the IP address (and possibly other information). If a DHCP or BOOTP server is on the same segment, this is not a problem. Unfortunately, it is not always practical to have a DHCP or BOOTP server on every network segment where a PC might need to boot. In these cases, by not forwarding the broadcast, the router prevents the PC from getting an IP address after it boots.

One alternative, of course, is to hard code all the IP addresses for all machines not on the same network segment as the DHCP or BOOTP server. On a network with hundreds or thousands of PCs, however, this would be an administrative nightmare. A better solution is to allow broadcasts only in specific situations. Cisco routers do this with a helper address. A **helper address** on a router tells it to forward a broadcast or a directed broadcast to the helper address instead of the entire network segment. In this way, a PC can get its IP address upon booting, and routers can block the majority of broadcasts.

Additionally, you can configure more than one helper address. This allows you to send broadcasts to more than one server. You can also send a directed broadcast to a subnet containing multiple servers; you might have multiple servers on a segment running the same service for redundancy. However, in Cisco IOS 12.0 and later, you must use the ip directed-broadcast interface configuration command in order for this to work since directed broadcasts are not allowed, by default. You must configure the helper address on the router nearest the clients sending the broadcasts you want to forward. However, the ip helper-address command works by changing the destination address of the packet, so you will not need to add helper addresses on any routers between the nearest router and the destination servers. Here you can see how to configure an IP helper address.

```
toledo(config)#int e0/0
toledo(config-if)#ip address 10.1.1.1 255.255.255.0
toledo(config-if)#ip helper-address 10.1.100.15
toledo(config-if)#ip directed-broadcast
toledo(config-if)#ip helper-address 10.1.92.255
```

By default, the ip helper-address command turns on eight UDP ports, which are shown in Table 2-8. Every broadcast to one of these ports will be forwarded to the IP helper address, regardless of whether or not the service is actually running on the server. Each time a broadcast is forwarded to a server not running a particular service, an ICMP port unreachable message may be generated, which generates additional useless traffic. You can, however, turn off forwarding for these ports with the no ip forward-protocol udp [port] command, just as you can forward additional ports with the ip forward-protocol udp [port] command. Keep in mind also that if you configure multiple helper addresses on an interface, all broadcasts will be forwarded to both helper addresses; the router has no way to identify the service running on a helper address.

Table 2-8 Default UDP ports forwarded by the ip helper-address command

Port	Name
37	Time
49	Terminal Access Controller Access Control System (TACACS)
53	Domain Name Service (DNS)
67	BOOTP server
68	BOOTP client, DHCP
69	Trivial File Transfer Protocol (TFTP)
137	NetBIOS name server
138	NetBIOS datagram service

CHAPTER SUMMARY

❑ Because of the rapid growth of the Internet, it faces problems with both IP address exhaustion and growing routing tables. Many private networks also have problems with growing routing tables. In order to address these issues, network administrators turn to hierarchical addressing and route summarization, which help decrease the size of routing tables.

❏ VLSMs allow network administrators to more efficiently allocate IP addresses, and classless routing makes VLSMs even more efficient by removing classful network boundaries altogether. IP addresses now are allocated by the RIRs and service providers in CIDR blocks, described by a network number and a prefix. When subnetting your own CIDR block, you should try to allocate it in a way that allows for route summarization, but be careful to avoid discontiguous subnets.

❏ Other strategies for managing IP addresses include unnumbered interfaces, private address space, NAT, and IPv6. Finally, IP helper addresses can help you manage broadcasts by forwarding only certain broadcasts to the hosts that need to receive them.

KEY TERMS

address aggregation — *See* Route Summarization.

American Registry for Internet Numbers (ARIN) — The Regional Internet Registry for North and South America, the Caribbean, and Sub-Saharan Africa.

Asia Pacific Network Information Centre (APNIC) — The Regional Internet Registry for the Asia Pacific region.

Classless Inter-Domain Routing (CIDR) — A strategy to allocate and aggregate IP addresses based on classless routing; IP addresses are allocated in CIDR blocks.

CIDR block — A block of IP addresses allocated based on Classless Inter-Domain Routing; each block of addresses is described by a network number and a prefix.

classful routing — Routing that follows the traditional classful boundaries.

classless routing — Routing that ignores the traditional classful boundaries and uses VLSMs.

helper address — A specific IP address where Cisco routers will forward broadcasts without broadcasting them to the entire network segment.

hierarchical addressing — Addressing done in a layered, orderly fashion.

IP version 6 (IPv6) — The next version of the Internet Protocol, which has a 128-bit address space.

longest match — When deciding between multiple routes to the same destination, routers choose the route with the longest prefix.

netmask — Subnet mask.

network address translation (NAT) — Translation of one or more of the private IP addresses defined in RFC 1918 into publicly routable IP addresses.

prefix — The leftmost bits in an IP address or network number, corresponding to the network bits (equivalent to a network number).

Regional Internet Registries (RIRs) — The organizations (including ARIN, RIPE NCC, and APNIC) that provide IP registration services for the Internet.

Réseaux IP Européens Network Coordination Centre (RIPE NCC) — The Regional Internet Registry for Europe, the Middle East, and parts of Africa.

route summarization — The combination of many routes that share their leftmost bits into one route, called a summary route.

summary route — A route formed through route summarization.

supernet — Using a subnet mask or prefix shorter than the traditional class boundaries.

unnumbered interface — An interface without a specifically assigned IP address; these interfaces must reference another interface with an IP address (often a loopback interface).

variable-length subnet mask (VLSM) — A subnet mask with a variable prefix so that the same network may have many different subnet masks with prefixes of different lengths.

REVIEW QUESTIONS

1. What are some of the problems involving IP addressing that face the Internet today? (Choose all that apply.)

   a. inefficient allocation and wasting of IP addresses

   b. decrease in the size of Internet routing tables

   c. increase in the size of Internet routing tables

   d. use of private addressing

2. One of the best examples of hierarchical addressing is _____.

3. Which of the following is a benefit of using VLSMs? (Choose all that apply.)

   a. more efficient use of IP addresses

   b. understood by all routing protocols

   c. prevent routing to discontiguous subnets

   d. allow for route summarization

4. In classful routing, subnets are not advertised and therefore cannot be used. True or false?

5. Which of the following is the network number for the IP address 212.195.77.14/20?

   a. 212.195.77.14

   b. 212.195.76.0

   c. 212.195.77.0

   d. 212.195.64.0

6. Why are two IP addresses out of each subnet unusable? (Choose all that apply.)

   a. The host portion of the IP address must be separate from the network portion.

   b. The host address that consists of all zero bits is the network number.

   c. The host address that consists of all one bits is the broadcast address.

   d. The host address that consists of all one bits is reserved.

2

7. Why does classless routing allow for more efficient allocation of IP addresses than classful routing? (Choose all that apply.)

   a. Classful routing does not allow subnetting.

   b. Classful routing does not allow discontiguous subnets.

   c. Classless routing allows IP addresses to be allocated as needed.

   d. Classless routing allows IP addresses to be allocated in blocks of arbitrary size.

8. Referring to the prefix of an IP address means the bits on the _____ side of the IP address.

9. How many subnets with 62 usable addresses are possible out of 198.162.96.0/18?

   a. 256

   b. 512

   c. 128

   d. 1024

10. Which of the following is a potential benefit to route summarization on networks with thousands of routes? (Choose all that apply.)

   a. more efficient IP address allocation

   b. smaller routing tables

   c. faster routing table lookups

   d. less CPU utilization and memory use devoted to calculating the routing table

11. Classful routing could be described as a special instance of route summarization. True or false?

12. According to the principle of the longest match, which of the following routes would a router choose for a packet with a destination address of 10.212.17.144?

   a. 10.0.0.0/8

   b. 10.212.17.0/24

   c. 10.212.16.0/20

   d. 10.212.17.144/32

13. Which of the following is a potential disadvantage of route summarization? (Choose all that apply.)

   a. Route summarization requires more CPU time and memory in the routers that use it.

   b. Route summarization may result in less than ideal paths for some packets.

   c. Route summarization may result in a loss of connectivity to discontiguous subnets.

   d. Route summarization may result in larger routing tables.

14. You have a network with the following routes:

    172.16.252.0/24

    172.16.248.0/24

    172.16.198.0/24

    172.16.212.0/24

    Which of the following is a valid summary route for these networks? (Choose all that apply.)

    a. 172.16.0.0/16

    b. 172.16.128.0/17

    c. 172.16.0.0/24

    d. 172.16.192.0/18

15. How many networks with a subnet mask of 255.255.255.128 can you divide a network with a subnet mask of 255.255.192 into?

    a. 256

    b. 128

    c. 64

    d. 32

16. Why is it more difficult to troubleshoot unnumbered interfaces?

    a. Unnumbered interfaces are invalid.

    b. interferes with route summarization

    c. Unnumbered interfaces cannot be pinged.

    d. Loopback interfaces are software only.

17. Network address translation conserves IP addresses by:

    a. translating an IP address into another protocol with a larger address space

    b. increasing the number of possible IP addresses

    c. translating one IP address into another

    d. translating groups of IP addresses into smaller groups of IP addresses

18. Why does classful routing not allow for efficient allocation of IP addresses? (Choose all that apply.)

    a. Classful routing protocols have a hop limit, which limits the size of the network.

    b. The amount of IP addresses you can allocate with the traditional class boundaries does not fit very many organizations.

    c. You cannot subnet a classful IP address block however you need.

    d. Some of the IP addresses in classful routing schemes are reserved for multicast and experimental use.

19. After a helper address is configured on a router, how does it forward broadcasts?

    a. It allows all broadcasts to go across that router to the machine at the helper address.

    b. It changes the destination address in the broadcast packet.

    c. It forwards only broadcasts on certain ports.

    d. The ip directed-broadcast command is required for the router to forward broadcasts.

20. Which of the following is likely to happen after you configure multiple helper addresses on an interface?

    a. Broadcasts are forwarded to both addresses regardless of whether or not either machine is running a particular service.

    b. Broadcasts are forwarded only to those addresses where a machine is running the appropriate service.

    c. Nothing happens unless you configure the router to allow directed broadcasts.

    d. Broadcasts are forwarded only to the second helper address configured.

CASE PROJECTS

Case 1

You are the new network administrator for Luminant Lamination, Inc. (LLI) in Des Moines, Iowa. LLI was just bought out by a large conglomerate, which asks you to read-dress LLI's network in order to connect it to its network. In order to do this, you are given a block of IP addresses, 172.30.16.0/20. Given that LLI currently has two sites with about 500 nodes, eight sites with about 100 nodes, and 23 sites with about 50 nodes, and LLI's president expects to add another 20 sites in the next year, how can you allocate the CIDR block?

Case 2

You are brought in to consult for Carefree Toys, Inc., which is expanding rapidly at its corporate headquarters in Cherry Hill, New Jersey. The new CTO, Terry Wilcox, wants to summarize the routes in their routing tables as much as possible in preparation for the connection of the corporate network to that of Plane Jane Dolls, Inc., with which they just merged. A diagram of the network is shown in Figure 2-13. What sort of issues do you expect to encounter summarizing the routes on this network? What recommendations would you make to Terry Wilcox?

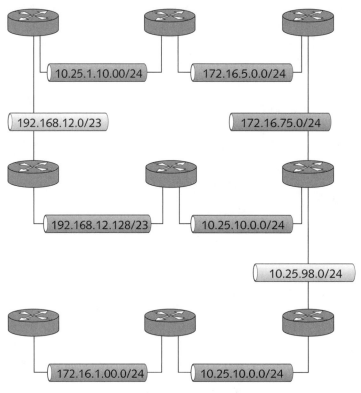

Figure 2-13   Network diagram for Carefree Toys, Inc.

3

OSPF

> **After reading this chapter and completing the exercises you will be able to:**
>
> ♦ Explain the advantages of using OSPF over RIP on a large network
> ♦ Explain how OSPF routers select their neighbors
> ♦ Explain how OSPF routers build and maintain their routing tables
> ♦ Configure OSPF on a network with a single area
> ♦ Configure OSPF in different network topologies

In this chapter, you'll learn about **Open Shortest Path First (OSPF)**. OSPF was designed to work on large networks, and it has several advantages over Routing Information Protocol (RIP). You'll learn about how OSPF builds its routing tables and updates them when the network changes. You'll also learn about how it operates differently in different types of network topologies. This will help you make decisions about configuring OSPF networks, which you'll learn how to do later in the chapter. Finally, you'll learn about how you can troubleshoot OSPF.

OVERVIEW OF OSPF

OSPF is a link-state routing protocol developed in 1988 by the **Internet Engineering Task Force (IETF)**, an organization devoted to the growth and operation of the Internet. RFC 2328 describes OSPF version 2, the latest version of OSPF, and the version supported by recent versions of Cisco IOS. The IETF designed OSPF to be an **Interior Gateway Protocol (IGP)**, a routing protocol used by routers in the same autonomous system. An **autonomous system** is a group of routers under the same administrative control, using the same routing policies. OSPF was designed to overcome some of the limitations of RIP, which is a distance vector routing protocol, on large IP networks.

In link-state routing protocols, such as OSPF, routers keep track of the status of each link in their sections of the autonomous system. Because each router knows the status of each link, and hence the topology of the entire network, routers using OSPF can avoid routing loops. Routers using distance vector routing protocols, such as RIP, only know the status of attached links. These routers use the hop count, split horizon, poison reverse updates, and the holddown time to avoid routing loops.

Advantages of OSPF over RIP

On large networks, OSPF has several advantages over RIP, such as:

- Support for variable-length subnet masks (VLSMs). RIPv1 does not support VLSMs.

- Faster convergence. Because RIP and other distance vector routing protocols are prone to routing loops, RIP networks must go through holddown before the network will converge. On an OSPF network, on the other hand, changes are flooded to all routers, and all routers simultaneously recompute their routing tables.

- More efficient use of bandwidth. Routers running RIP broadcast their entire routing tables every 30 seconds, which can use a lot of bandwidth as routing tables grow in size. Routers on an OSPF network send only updates every 30 minutes, or after a change on the network, resulting in a significant reduction of bandwidth used.

- No built-in size limitations. On a RIP network, routers must be within 15 hops of each other or they are unreachable. OSPF, on the other hand, has no hop count limit.

- Path selection based on cost. RIP metrics are based solely on the hop count, while OSPF uses the cost of a link as the metric. In Cisco routers, cost is, by default, based on the bandwidth of a link. This means that packets on a RIP network might be sent over a 56 Kbps leased line instead of a 1.544 Mbps T-1 because the path through the leased line has a lower hop count.

RIPv2 was designed to address some of the problems with RIP, but despite support for VLSMs and a hop count limit of 255, it is still at a disadvantage to OSPF on large networks.

3

OSPF Disadvantages

The disadvantage of using OSPF over RIP, however, is complexity. OSPF is significantly more complicated than RIP; RFC 2328, for example, is 243 pages long. As a result, OSPF is often more difficult to configure and often takes more planning to implement successfully. OSPF networks can also be segmented into multiple areas, which can add even more complexity. An **area** is a group of OSPF routers sharing the same knowledge of the topology of the network. Additionally, OSPF can use significantly more CPU time and memory than RIP.

OSPF OPERATION

In this section, you will learn how OSPF operates in a single area. You will learn about how OSPF works with multiple areas in the next chapter.

In order to operate successfully, neighboring OSPF routers must identify each other. Then they must share routing information with each other so that each router has the same information about the network topology. After identifying neighboring OSPF routers and exchanging routing information, then they can build their routing tables. After a link fails, or after another change in the network topology, routers must learn about the change and use the new information to rebuild their routing tables.

While basic OSPF operation is the same in all topologies, it does operate somewhat differently in other topologies. One primary factor in how it handles each type of topology is how a router identifies its neighbors. In this portion of the chapter, you will learn about how OSPF operates in **broadcast multiaccess topologies** like Ethernet. In this type of topology, the medium supports broadcasts and multicasts, and many routers may exist on a given network segment. Most of what you learn about OSPF will also apply to the other topologies it supports, which you will learn about later in the chapter.

Discovering Neighbors

In OSPF, neighboring routers discover each other with the **Hello protocol**, which is responsible for establishing and maintaining neighbor relationships. Packets sent using the Hello protocol are generally multicast instead of broadcast in order to minimize use of bandwidth. The Hello protocol and neighbor relationships work somewhat differently depending on the type of network.

In multiaccess network topologies, such as Ethernet, neighboring routers select a designated router (DR) and a backup designated router (BDR). The DR and the BDR form **adjacencies**, meaning that they exchange routing information with all the other routers on the segment.

When two routers form adjacencies with each other, they exchange their complete topology databases. Also known as a **link-state database**, a **topology database** contains the status of all the links on the network that each router knows about. In case of a network outage, the DR and the BDR on multiaccess networks, or the router discovering the outage on networks without DR and BDR, begin **flooding** all OSPF routers in the area with **link–state update (LSU)** packets describing the change. Afterwards, each router in the area recalculates its routing table using the **Djikstra** or **Shortest Path First (SPF) algorithm**. Nearly all packets are sent using **reliable transmission**. This means that if the sending router does not receive an acknowledgement packet, it will retransmit the packet to ensure that it arrives.

Until a router receives **hello packets** from its neighbors, it is considered to be in the Down state. This simply means that the router hasn't learned about any of its neighbors; later on, obviously, a router in the Down state will actually be down. To discover its neighbors and maintain its relationships with them, an OSPF router uses the Hello protocol. It will periodically send out hello packets using the IP multicast address 224.0.0.5, also called the **AllSPFRouter** address. This interval is known as the **hello interval** and will vary depending on the type of topology. On Ethernet segments, by default, the hello interval is 10 seconds. OSPF routers use the Hello protocol to determine the status of the networks attached to their interfaces. If a router hasn't seen a hello packet from a neighboring router for an interval usually equal to four times the hello interval, or 40 seconds on an Ethernet segment, it marks the neighboring router as down. This interval is known as the **dead interval**.

Forming Adjacencies

When a router receives a hello packet from one of its neighbors, it enters the **Init state**. At this point, it will look through the packet and several parameters to see if it can establish an adjacency with its neighbor. When two neighboring routers establish an adjacency with each other, they can share routing update information. Not all neighboring routers will form adjacencies, although they will still use the hello packets to determine the status of the link. Figure 3-1 shows the format of an OSPF packet header, which is common to all types of OSPF packets, while Figure 3-2 shows the format of a hello packet. The fields in the hello packet that must match are:

- Netmask. This should always match for two interfaces on the same segment.

- Hello interval

- Dead interval

- Area ID. You'll learn about OSPF areas in more detail in Chapter 4.

- Authentication type and password. OSPF supports authentication to prevent routers from accepting routing updates from unauthorized sources.

Other fields in a hello packet include:

- **Router ID**. Other routers in the autonomous system know routers by their router IDs. The router ID is usually either the highest IP address of an active interface on the router, or the highest IP address of a loopback interface.

However, if another interface is added with a higher IP address after the IP address is selected, it won't become the router ID until the interface that is currently supplying the router ID goes down.

- Designated router (DR) and backup designated router (BDR), identified by their router IDs. On networks where these are present, the DR and BDR handle the bulk of routing information.

- Each neighbor that the router received hello packets from, identified by their router IDs.

 Since mismatched parameters, such as timers, can often cause subtle routing problems that are hard to troubleshoot, two OSPF routers can't form adjacencies until important parameters match, such as the netmask, the hello interval, and the dead interval. This is part of the design of OSPF, and it helps you quickly learn about problems.

Length	1 byte	1 byte	2 bytes	4 bytes	4 bytes	2 bytes	2 bytes	8 bytes
Description	Version Number	Type	Packet Length	Router ID	Area ID	Checksum	Authentication Type	Authentication

Figure 3-1   Format of an OSPF packet header

Length	24 bytes	4 bytes	2 bytes	1 byte	1 byte	4 bytes	4 bytes	4 bytes	4 bytes	4 bytes each
Description	OSPF packet header	Netmask	Hello interval	Option	Router Priority	Dead interval	Designated router	Backup designated router	Neighbor	Additional Neighbor(s)

Figure 3-2   Format of an OSPF hello packet

A router also looks at the neighbors listed in hello packets it receives from its neighbors. Once it sees its own IP address inside a neighbor's hello packet, it knows that its neighbor also received its own hello packets. Now that the two neighboring routers are communicating in both directions, they enter what is called the **two-way state**. This is the final state before the two routers can begin to exchange their link-state databases.

Designated Router

In network topologies that elect a DR and BDR, not all neighboring routers will form adjacencies. While this adds to the complexity of OSPF, the DR and BDR do have benefits in multiaccess topologies.

Purpose of the Designated Router and Backup Designated Router   On a broadcast multiaccess network, many routers can share the same segment. If many routers simultaneously exchange routing information on the same network segment, this can

take up a lot of bandwidth. Each router updates its neighbors on the status of all its links to every other router on the segment. In many cases, these updates are sent back to the router on the other end of the link.

In order to reduce the amount of update traffic and the number of duplicate updates, in broadcast multiaccess networks, the routers on each network segment select a designated router (DR) and a backup designated router (BDR). Instead of each router on the network segment forming adjacencies with all the other routers, each router forms an adjacency with the DR and the BDR. The DR and the BDR also ensure that all the other routers on the network segment each maintain the most current routing information by handling the flooding of updates, which you will learn about later in the chapter. Because each segment has its own DR and BDR, one router can be a DR or BDR in multiple segments, or it can be a DR or BDR in one segment, and a regular router (in the state **DROTHER**) in other segments.

Electing the Designated Router   When a broadcast multiaccess network segment comes up for the first time, all the routers on that segment in the two-way state elect a DR and a BDR. They do this by examining the hello packets they receive from their neighboring routers, and comparing the **priorities** in their neighbors' hello packets with their own priorities.

In this first election, the router with the highest priority interface on that network segment is the DR, and the router with the next highest priority is the BDR. By default, the priority of any OSPF interface is one. You can configure this priority to make sure that routers with faster CPUs and more memory are more likely to become the DR or the BDR. You can also configure a router with a priority of zero to make sure that it doesn't become the DR or the BDR. However, OSPF won't function if none of the routers on a broadcast multiaccess segment are eligible to become DR and BDR.

If two routers have the same priority, the router with the highest router ID wins. The router ID is generally the highest IP address on an active interface, but you can override this by configuring a loopback interface with an IP address.

Designated Router Operation   Now that they've been elected, the role of the DR and the BDR is to handle the establishment of adjacencies on the segment. Both the DR and the BDR form adjacencies with all the other routers on the network segment. Additionally, the DR handles the flooding of updated routing information to the rest of the network segment after a change; the BDR sets a timer when it sees a change, and takes over for the DR if it doesn't begin to flood the network before the timer expires. When the DR does fail, the BDR allows the network to converge much more quickly than it would otherwise; the BDR already formed adjacencies with all the other routers on the network. As you'll see, forming adjacencies can take a fair amount of time and bandwidth depending on the size of each router's link-state database.

After the initial election of the DR and the BDR, they won't change until one of them goes down. This is even true if a router with a higher priority is added to the network. In fact, the new router can't become DR until two other routers fail. If the DR fails for any reason, the BDR and only the BDR becomes the new DR, and another BDR is elected. If the BDR goes down, another BDR is elected. The BDR uses a timer to decide if the DR is still up; if it sees that a network change took place, it starts the timer. If the DR doesn't begin to update the routers on the network about the changes before the timer expires, then the BDR assumes the DR is down and takes over.

In Figure 3-3, six routers are on the same Ethernet segment, 10.254.100.0/24. If each router had to form an adjacency with every other router, there would be a total of 15 adjacencies between routers, so there would be 15 different instances of routers exchanging routing information. If each router forms adjacencies with only the DR and the BDR, then a total of nine adjacencies form (two adjacencies for each of the four ordinary routers with the DR and BDR, plus one adjacency between the DR and the BDR). The difference in the number of adjacencies needed becomes more pronounced as the number of routers on a segment increases. Ten routers on a network segment, for example, require 45 adjacencies without a DR, and 17 with a DR.

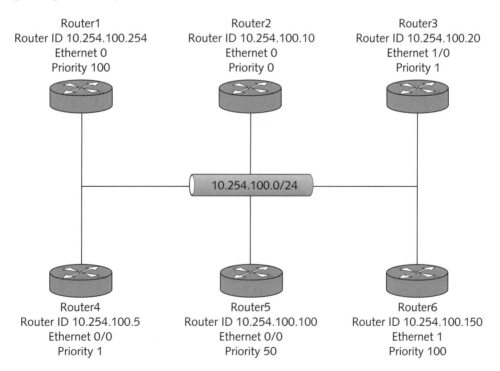

Figure 3-3 Designated router election

If all the routers in Figure 3-3 come up at the same time, the routers examine the priorities contained in the hello packets they receive in order to determine the DR and the BDR. Router2 isn't eligible to become DR or BDR because its priority is set to zero. Of the remaining routers, Router1 and Router6 both have priorities of 100, while Router5 has a priority of 50, and Router3 and Router4 have the default priority, one. Since Router1 has a higher router ID than Router6(10.254.100.254 to 10.254.100.150), Router1 is selected as the DR and Router6 is selected as the BDR.

What would happen if Router1 went down? The BDR, Router6, would become the new DR, and the router with the next highest priority would become the new BDR. In this case, Router5 has a priority of 50 and would be selected as the new BDR. In order for Router1 to become the DR again, Router1 would first have to become BDR (after the failure of the current DR or BDR). Then it would become DR after the current DR failed.

Exchanging Link-State Databases

After the election of the DR and the BDR, they will form adjacencies with all the other routers. Two routers about to form adjacencies with each other are in the **ExStart state**. The process of forming an adjacency is as follows:

1. Two routers in the ExStart state form a master-slave relationship with each other, where the master is the router with the highest router ID. The two routers also select an initial sequence number; they use the sequence number to detect stale or duplicate **link-state advertisements**, which provide the status of interfaces in the area, or other information about the topology of the network.

2. The master and slave enter the Exchange state and begin to exchange their link-state databases. The master router begins to send the slave its database in **database description (DD, DDP, or DBD) packets** with the sequence number agreed upon in the ExStart state. Table 3-1 contains a description of all the types of packets used by OSPF. Each DD packet contains the header for a link-state advertisement. The router must acknowledge the DD packet with another DD packet with the same serial number; the master will then send another DD packet after increasing the serial number by one. In either case, if the sequence number isn't correct, the receiving router will drop the packet since this means that there was some sort of error by either the sending router, or in the transmission of the packet.

3. When the two routers enter the Loading state, they can query any other router in the Exchange state or later for more recent information with **link-state request (LSR) packets**. Each router has a list of link-states that it needs from its neighbors. The routers will also receive link-state update (LSU) packets from routers responding to the LSR packets sent, which they will usually acknowledge with **link-state acknowledgement (LSAck) packets**, or with a LSU containing newer information.

4. When each router's list of needed link-states is empty, and each router's database is identical, the routers enter the Full state. At this point, the routers are ready to calculate their routing tables and begin routing packets.

Table 3-1   Types of OSPF packets

Packet Type	Type Code	Description
Hello packet	1	Used to establish and maintain neighbor relationships
Database Description packet (DD, DBD, or DDP)	2	Used to exchange databases; contains one or more LSA headers
Link-state request (LSR) packet	3	Used to request updated information about a LSA from other routers; contains summary information about one or more LSAs
Link-state update (LSU) packet	4	Used when flooding to give routers updated information about the network topology, and sometimes to acknowledge a LSU; contains one or more complete LSAs
Link-state acknowledgement (LSAck)	5	Used to acknowledge LSUs; contains one or more LSA headers

Table 3.2 shows each stage in the process of two routers forming an adjacency, including the exchange of each router's link-state database.

Table 3-2   Stages in the formation of an adjacency between two routers

State	Description
Down	No hello packets were received from either router.
Init	One router saw a hello packet from the other router.
two-way	One router saw its own router ID in a packet from the other router, so two-way communication was established.
ExStart	The two routers decide on a sequence number and establish which router is master and which is slave, based on the higher router ID.
Exchange	The two routers begin to use database description packets to exchange their complete link-state databases.
Loading	The two routers finalize their link-state databases, sending out link-state requests, as necessary.
Full	The two routers are completely adjacent and have identical link-state databases.

Calculating Routing Tables

A router running OSPF must recalculate its routing table after every network change, which, of course, includes the first time it joins the network. To do this, it uses the Djikstra algorithm, also known as the Shortest Path First (SPF) algorithm, to calculate the path with the lowest cost to each destination. Each router runs the Djikstra algorithm separately, but no routing loops are produced because each router in the area has complete and identical knowledge of the network. Each router produces a tree with itself at the root; the SPF algorithm calculates the cost of each path to every destination on the network, and the router places the paths with the lowest costs in its routing table. Where several paths have the same cost, OSPF load balances between equal cost paths. By default, Cisco IOS load balances between four paths with equal costs. However, Cisco routers can be configured with the **maximum-paths** command to use a maximum of six routes with equal costs.

Maintaining the Routing Table

Whenever a change takes place on the network, all the routers in the area must update their topology databases and recalculate their routing tables. On multiaccess networks, a typical example of the flooding process will go like this:

1. A router notices that the dead interval expired since it last received a hello packet from one of its neighbors. The router sends a LSU packet, indicating the neighbor is down, to the multicast address 224.0.0.6, also known as **AllDRouters**, to which all DRs and BDRs listen.

2. The DR sends an LSAck packet to the router that discovered the problem in order to acknowledge receipt of the LSU. Then the DR floods the LSU to all the other routers on that network segment. Each router receiving the LSU sends an LSAck packet to acknowledge it.

3. Every router receiving the LSU floods it to any other connected networks. If a router is connected to a multiaccess network, for example, it multicasts the LSU to the AllDRouters address, and the DR floods it to all the routers with which the DR of that network formed adjacencies. Those routers also flood the LSU to connected networks (other than the one from which they received the LSU), and so on, until all the routers on the network receive the LSU.

4. After receiving the LSU, each router updates its topology database, and then uses the SPF algorithm to recalculate its routing table.

A Cisco router can't forward packets to new routes until it finishes its SPF recalculation. However, it can forward packets to existing routes during SPF recalculation.

On OSPF networks, routers check the validity of LSAs in two ways. First, they run checksums of all LSAs every 10 minutes to verify that a LSA has not become corrupt. Second, to make sure a particular LSA doesn't become stale, a LSA has an aging timer that is monitored with the LS Age field in the LSA header. After the LS Age timer reaches 30 minutes, the router that originally advertised the LSA sends out a LSU to refresh the LSA. In order to prevent this from unnecessarily triggering SPF calculation, an OSPF router uses the sequence number in the LSA header like a timestamp to see if a LSA it received is older, newer, or the same age as a LSA already in its link-state database:

- If the LSU is for an identical entry in the router's link-state database, the router resets its aging timer for that LSA and discards the LSU. If the LSU is for an existing entry in the router's link-state database, but it contains older information, the router sends a LSU to the sending router with the more recent LSA.

- If the LSU is for an existing entry in the router's link-state database, but it contains newer information, the router sends a LSAck to the sending router, adds the LSA to its link-state database, floods the LSA to other routers, and runs through the SPC calculation in order to rebuild its routing table.

- If the LSU contains completely new information, the router adds the LSA to its link-state database, sends a LSAck to the router that sent it, floods the LSA to other routers, and runs through the SPF calculation in order to rebuild its routing table.

If a router doesn't receive a refresh packet for a LSA within an hour, it discards it.

In versions of Cisco IOS prior to 12.0, routers sent refresh packets for all LSAs at the same time because routers had a single timer for refreshing LSAs, while they had individual timers for checksumming and aging LSAs. Each router refreshed all of its LSAs at once, regardless of whether or not they needed refreshing, and although it only occurred every 30 minutes, it resulted in a brief period of high bandwidth. Beginning with Cisco IOS 12.0, Cisco routers have a refresh timer for each LSA. However, if only one LSA needs to be refreshed at a particular time, then a LSU is sent out containing only that one LSU.

If a router sends out many LSUs containing only single LSAs, this isn't efficient because of the overhead of the packet headers. Instead, Cisco routers use **group pacing**, which means that instead of sending refresh packets exactly as the aging timer hits 30 minutes, they wait for the **group pacing interval** to expire before sending many packets at once. By default, the group pacing interval is set to four minutes. On smaller networks, you may want to set this timer higher so that LSU packets contain more LSAs and are less likely to contain a single LSA. On larger networks, you may want to set this timer higher since the longer you wait between LSU packets, the more LSAs you're likely to have at one time. See Figure 3-4 for an example of configuring this timer (note that the interval is in units of seconds).

```
Orlando(config)#router ospf 1
Orlando(config-router)#timers ?
  lsa-group-pacing  OSPF LSA group pacing timer
  spf               OSPF SPF timers

Orlando(config-router)#timers lsa
Orlando(config-router)#timers lsa-group-pacing ?
  <10-1800>  Interval between group of LSA being refreshed or maxaged

Orlando(config-router)#timers lsa-group-pacing 120
Orlando(config-router)#timers spf ?
  <0-4294967295>  Delay between receiving a change to SPF calculation

Orlando(config-router)#timers spf 10 ?
  <0-4294967295>  Hold time between consecutive SPF calculations

Orlando(config-router)#timers spf 10 20
```

Figure 3-4   Setting OSPF timers

Because routers flood the network and recalculate their routing tables after any network change, any link that goes up and down repeatedly can generate many LSUs and use a lot of CPU time. Often this **route flapping** is caused by a serial interface since a router can often detect that its serial interface went down without waiting for the dead interval to expire. If the link generates LSUs often enough, it can put an OSPF network into a state where it is continually calculating and recalculating its routing table, and the network may never converge. In order to prevent this, Cisco uses two timers. The first is the **SPF delay timer**, which specifies how long after receiving a LSU a router will wait before recalculating its routing table. The default is five seconds.

This also allows a router to receive additional LSUs before running the SPF recalculation; these might either indicate that the original link is back up, or give information about a new outage on the network. The second timer is the **SPF holdtime timer**, which controls how long a router will wait between consecutive SPF calculations, and which has a default of 10 seconds. This timer prevents a router from continuously running through its SPF recalculation. See Figure 3-4 for an example of the configuration of both these timers.

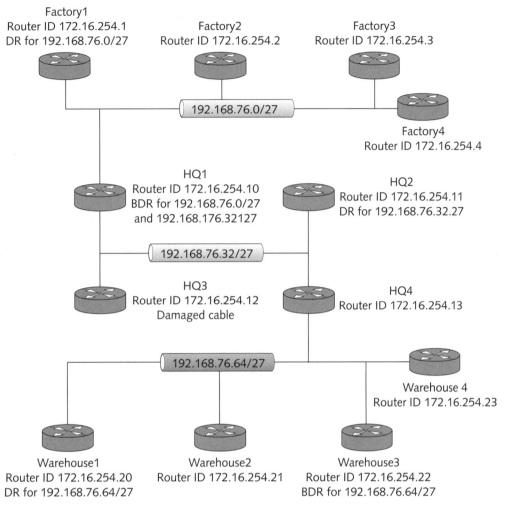

Figure 3-5 Flooding example

Figure 3–5 shows three Ethernet segments on an OSPF network. If the cable connecting router HQ3 to the 192.168.76.32/27 network is damaged, and the router becomes unable to connect to that Ethernet segment, for example, other routers on this network must run through the SPF calculation and rebuild their routing tables. It happens like this:

- HQ4 notices that HQ3 hasn't sent a hello packet in 40 seconds, or since the beginning of the last dead interval. This router multicasts a LSU packet to the AllDRouters address, 224.0.0.6, containing a LSA indicating that HQ3 is down. Since routers HQ2 and HQ1 are the DR and the BDR, respectively, they receive this broadcast. HQ2 or HQ1 might also notice the outage at the same time, in which case they also multicast a LSU packet to the AllDRouters address.

- HQ2 and HQ1 each send a LSAck packet acknowledging receipt of the LSU packet to each router that sends them a LSU.

- As the DR, HQ2 starts flooding the LSU to all other routers on this network using multicast address 224.0.0.5. In the meantime, HQ1, the BDR, watches to make sure that the DR begins flooding before its timer expires. In this case, HQ2 began flooding before the timer expired, so HQ1 does not need to take over for HQ2. Each router that receives a LSU packet from HQ2 also sends a LSAck to acknowledge receipt of the packet.

- After receiving the LSU from HQ2, HQ4 multicasts it to the AllDRouters address in order to forward the LSU to the DR and BDR on the 192.168.76.64/27 network. Router Warehouse3, the BDR on this network, sends a LSAck and starts its timer to see if router Warehouse1, the DR, will begin flooding this network. Router Warehouse1 sends a LSAck to HQ4 and floods the LSU out to the other routers on the 192.168.76.64/27 network before Warehouse3's timer expires.

- At the same time, since router HQ1 is also connected to the 192.168.76.0/27 network, it also multicasts the LSU to the AllDRouters address. Factory1 sends a LSAck and floods the rest of the routers on the 192.168.76.0/27 network with the new LSU, while HQ1 (also the BDR on this network) checks its timer to make sure Factory1 begins flooding in time.

Once each router on the OSPF network knows about the network change, they wait for the SPF delay timer to expire before running the SPF calculation and rebuilding their routing tables. Additionally, if another network change sparks another round of flooding immediately after this one, each router also waits for its SPF holdtime timer to expire before beginning the next round of SPF calculation.

OSPF Operation in Other Topologies

The three types of topologies commonly found on OSPF networks are:

- **Broadcast multiaccess.** This includes any network that can support more than two routers on the same segment, and which allows broadcasts to all the devices on a segment, such as Ethernet.

- **Point-to-point.** This includes any network that doesn't support more than two routers on a segment, such as a dedicated serial connection. OSPF routers discover their neighbors on point-to-point networks with a multicast.

- **Nonbroadcast multiaccess (NBMA).** This includes any network that can support more than two routers on the same segment, but which doesn't support broadcasts. Examples include frame relay, ATM, and X.25. Since it can't send multicasts on NBMA networks, an OSPF router may require additional configuration in order to discover its neighbors.

Point-to-Point Topologies

A point-to-point network consists of the two ends of a link; multiple routers on either end are not supported. A T-1 link and a 64 Kbps leased line are examples of point-to-point networks. In many ways, OSPF operates much the same in a point-to-point topology as it does on a broadcast multiaccess network. For example, a router discovers its neighbors using multicasts to the AllSPFRouters address. Since there can be only two routers on a point-to-point network segment, however, the DR and BDR don't offer any advantages and aren't used, and any two routers that can see each other's router IDs in a hello packet become adjacent. Unnumbered interfaces can also be used.

However, dial-up connections require more care. **Asynchronous** links, such as a modem connection, require the use of the **async default routing** command on the asynchronous interface; otherwise routing updates over the asynchronous interface aren't allowed. You should also use the **dialer map** command with both asynchronous links and BRI or PRI links with the **broadcast** keyword. The dialer map command associates a phone number with the IP address of the other end of the link, and the broadcast keyword enables broadcasts over the link.

NBMA Topologies

In NBMA topologies, you have several options for configuring a network. Which option you select depends on the specific topology you choose. A router may not be able to receive a broadcast or multicast from its neighbors unless the network is in a full mesh and all routers are directly connected to each other. On partially meshed networks, the path from one router to another may go through another router, which, by default, blocks the broadcast. Also, broadcasts must be enabled on the virtual circuits.

In NBMA topologies, Cisco increased the default hello interval to 30 seconds and the dead interval to 120 seconds. In general, NBMA topologies use serial interfaces, and a router can usually detect the failure of a serial interface. This is in contrast to Ethernet networks, where a router often can't detect the failure of an Ethernet interface, and must rely on the Hello protocol to determine whether or not any of the routers on the networks attached to the routers are still responding.

Figure 3-6 shows the following typical NBMA network topologies:

- **Star topology**. A central site connects all other sites. This form of topology is also known as a **hub-and-spoke topology**. Because it requires only one **permanent virtual circuit (PVC)**, or WAN connection, in many types of NBMA topologies, per remote site, this is the least expensive topology.

- **Partial mesh topology**. In this topology, many routers have connections to many other routers, but not all routers are connected to each other. The central site is not guaranteed to be connected to all remote sites; in some cases, there may not even be a clearly defined central site. Depending on the degree to which routers are connected to each other, this topology is usually more expensive than a star topology.

- **Full mesh topology**. All routers have virtual circuits to all other routers. As a result, all routers can be guaranteed to have connectivity with all other routers. This is the most expensive NBMA topology, and the expense increases with the number of virtual circuits. You can find the number of virtual circuits in a full mesh NBMA network with the formula $n(n-1)/2$, where n is the number of routers in the mesh.

The DR and the BDR must be connected to all other routers on the network, and the only topology that can guarantee this is full mesh.

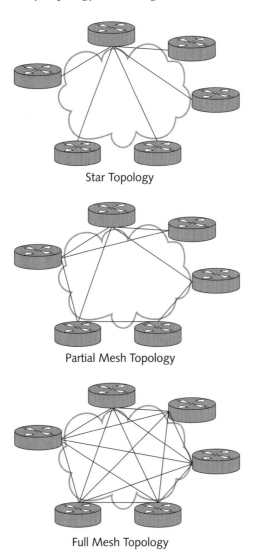

Star Topology

Partial Mesh Topology

Full Mesh Topology

Figure 3-6   Typical NBMA topologies

Subinterfaces

Since one interface in a NBMA topology can have multiple virtual circuits attached to it, Cisco recommends the use of **subinterfaces** when configuring routers in a NBMA topology. You use subinterfaces to divide a physical interface into multiple logical interfaces; each subinterface can be associated with a different virtual circuit. In Cisco routers, two types of subinterfaces can be configured:

- Point-to-point subinterfaces. Each point-to-point subinterface is on its own subnet.

- Multipoint subinterfaces. Multipoint subinterfaces will be on the same subnet.

Figure 3-7 provides an example of subinterfaces configured in both point-to-point and multipoint mode. Before you can configure a subinterface, you must remove the IP address from the physical interface with the no ip address command, or the subinterface will not work. Then you can configure the subinterface with the **interface serial** *number.subinterface number* **point-to-point** | multipoint command. The subinterface number can be anything from 0 to 4294967923, and the interface number is for the physical interface on which you're configuring the subinterface. You must also include either the point-to-point or multipoint keywords.

One disadvantage of using subinterfaces is the issue of keepalives. If you have multiple subinterfaces for one physical interface, as long as one subinterface receives keepalives, the physical interface will think that it is up — even if one or more subinterfaces are actually down. As a result, you'll have to rely on the expiration of the dead interval to tell you whether or not an interface is down, which may take longer, depending on the default dead interval (120 seconds in most OSPF modes for NBMA topologies).

RFC 2328 describes two ways NBMA topologies can be connected in NBMA mode:

- **NBMA mode.** This is very similar to the way OSPF operates on a broadcast multiaccess network; routers use the Hello protocol to identify their neighbors and select a DR and a BDR. Neighbors must be manually configured. Instead of sending broadcasts, the router simulates a broadcast by taking each broadcast packet and sending it individually to all destination routers. This mode is usually seen on fully meshed networks.

- **Point-to-multipoint mode.** Instead of emulating a broadcast multiaccess network, this mode emulates a series of point-to-point links. Routers can identify their neighbors, but as in a point-to-point topology, they don't select a DR and BDR. This mode is usually seen on partially meshed networks.

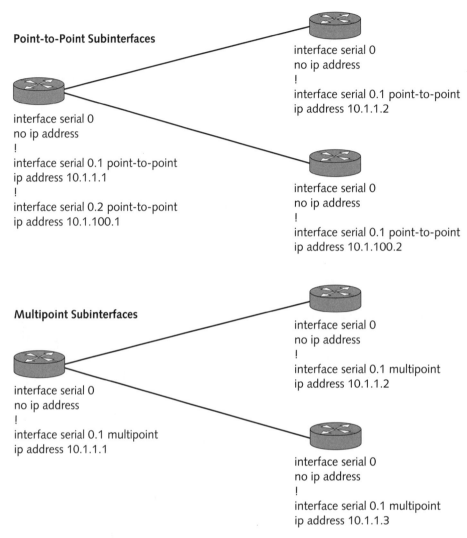

Point-to-Point Subinterfaces

interface serial 0
no ip address
!
interface serial 0.1 point-to-point
ip address 10.1.1.1
!
interface serial 0.2 point-to-point
ip address 10.1.100.1

interface serial 0
no ip address
!
interface serial 0.1 point-to-point
ip address 10.1.1.2

interface serial 0
no ip address
!
interface serial 0.1 point-to-point
ip address 10.1.100.2

Multipoint Subinterfaces

interface serial 0
no ip address
!
interface serial 0.1 multipoint
ip address 10.1.1.1

interface serial 0
no ip address
!
interface serial 0.1 multipoint
ip address 10.1.1.2

interface serial 0
no ip address
!
interface serial 0.1 multipoint
ip address 10.1.1.3

Figure 3-7   Configuring subinterfaces

NBMA Mode

OSPF in NBMA mode operates much like OSPF does on a broadcast multiaccess network. However, you must keep in mind the following:

- A DR and BDR must be connected to all routers because they must form adjacencies with all other routers on the network. If the network isn't fully meshed, you may need to force the selection of the DR and BDR. You can set the priority of any router that doesn't have physical connectivity to all other routers on the network to zero, which makes it ineligible to be the DR or BDR.

- Neighbors must be manually configured. Otherwise, without broadcasting or multicasting, the routers are unable to find each other.

- Neighbors are on the same subnet. This is just what you would find on a broadcast network, but this is not necessarily true in a NBMA topology; as you learned above, each point-to-point subinterface is on its own subnet.

- Routers replicate packets instead of broadcasting or multicasting. On an Ethernet network, for example, a router multicasts a LSU packet during flooding. However, since it can't multicast the packet, it instead copies the packet and sends it to each neighbor individually. This does increase CPU usage and the bandwidth used in flooding.

While NBMA mode tends to be efficient on networks with few neighbors, there are several potential issues to watch for when using it. The first is the requirement for either a full mesh, or physical connectivity between the DR, the BDR, and all other routers. This can make additions to a network in NBMA mode expensive. The second is the stability of the network itself. If one or more PVCs go down, this may affect the ability of OSPF to function properly since it may keep the DR and the BDR from forming adjacencies with all the other routers on the network, even though these routers still have physical connectivity to most of the other routers. Additionally, while OSPF is relatively efficient compared to RIP or IGRP, any changes on the NBMA network require flooding, which goes over the NBMA network and potentially costs you money in bandwidth charges. Additionally, since OSPF requires each router in the same area to have the same link-state database, any change on the rest of the network also causes routing traffic to be flooded through the NBMA network. In this situation, you can avoid this problem by putting the NBMA network into its own area, isolating it from changes on the rest of the network (and vice versa), as you will learn in Chapter 4.

Point-to-Multipoint Mode

If your NBMA network isn't a full mesh, and you can't have the DR and BDR connect to all other routers on the network, point-to-multipoint mode is usually a better choice for star or partial mesh topologies. Point-to-multipoint mode treats all connections as if they are point-to-point links. Some of the characteristics of point-to-multipoint mode include:

- Neither a DR nor a BDR is selected. This is similar to the way OSPF operates in point-to-point topologies.

- It works with partial mesh and star topologies. If two routers are connected only through PVCs to a third router, point-to-multipoint mode allows you to route between them since it treats all connections as point-to-point links.

- Neighbors can be dynamically discovered. Because each link is treated as a point-to-point link, routers can dynamically discover their neighbors. Neighbors can still be manually configured if desired (along with a cost for each neighbor).

- Each router is on the same subnet.

- Instead of broadcasting or multicasting, LSU and other packets are copied to each neighbor.

Keep in mind that the configuration of each router may vary a bit depending on how the router is connected to other routers. A router connecting multiple routers must be configured for point-to-multipoint mode, while a router connected only to one other router may be connected in point-to-point mode. However, if you add a second link to a router configured in point-to-point mode, you must change it to point-to-multipoint mode.

Cisco added several extensions to the OSPF specifications in RFC 2328. These include:

- **Point-to-multipoint nonbroadcast mode**. Cisco added this mode because the point-to-multipoint mode specified in RFC 2328 assumes that the virtual circuits carrying the connections support broadcasts and multicasts. However, this is not true for all point-to-multipoint networks, including classic IP over ATM and Frame Relay **switched virtual circuits (SVCs)**. If a router can't broadcast or multicast, then it can't discover its neighbors. To alleviate this problem, you must manually configure neighbors. Otherwise, this mode is the same as point-to-multipoint mode.

- **Point-to-point mode**. This mode is used to emulate a point-to-point network when there are only two nodes on a NBMA network, typically with point-to-point subinterfaces consisting of one subnet. As in a point-to-point topology, no DR or BDR is selected, and both ends of the link form adjacencies with each other. However, each point-to-point link requires its own subnet, and the more PVCs you add to a network, the more subinterfaces and subnets you must configure on your routers.

- **Broadcast mode**. Cisco added broadcast mode to avoid the manual configuration of OSPF neighbors. As in a multiaccess broadcast topology, the DR and the BDR are selected; if the network isn't a full mesh, the DR and BDR should be routers that can connect to all other routers on the network. As in NBMA mode, you can prevent routers that do not have connectivity to all other routers on the network from becoming DR or BDR by setting their priorities to zero.

Because another vendor's routers will unlikely be able to support these modes, you cannot use these modes on a multi-vendor network. Table 3-3 contains a summary of each NBMA mode a Cisco router can use, including its properties.

Table 3-3   Summary of NBMA modes used in Cisco routers

Mode	Topologies	Neighbor Configuration	DR/BDR	Comments
NBMA	Full mesh	Manual	Yes	Defined by RFC 2328
Point-to-multipoint	Partial mesh or star	Automatic	No	Defined by RFC 2328
Broadcast	Full mesh	Automatic	Yes	Defined by Cisco
Point-to-multipoint nonbroadcast	Partial mesh or star	Manual	No	Defined by Cisco
Point-to-point	Partial mesh or star	Automatic	No	Defined by Cisco; each subinterface uses a different subnet

Configuring OSPF

In this section, you'll learn how to configure OSPF on a Cisco router. You'll start with general OSPF configuration, followed by the specific configuration needed by different topologies.

Activating OSPF

Activating OSPF consists of two steps:

1. Enabling OSPF on the router with the **router ospf** *process-id* command. Unlike routing protocols, such as EIGRP (which you'll learn about in Chapter 5), the process ID need not be the same on each router on an OSPF network; its purpose is only to allow the router to tell if it's running multiple OSPF processes. Since a second OSPF process also creates a second set of databases, you do not normally need or want to run a second OSPF process on a router.

2. Telling OSPF which networks to use with the **network** *address wildcard-mask* **area** *area-id* command. All networks or interfaces on the router that match the network command are advertised by the router; the router also listens for OSPF packets on any matching interface. The area can either be a single number (such as zero or 10), or a dotted decimal (such as 10.200.25.1). Since you won't learn more about OSPF areas until the next chapter, put all networks into Area 0 for now.

To determine what networks a network mask will match, you must look at the bits in the mask. Any bits set to zero must exactly match the network number, and any bits set to one match anything; for this reason, ones in the wildcard mask are sometimes called **don't care bits**. For example, the mask 0.255.255.255 combined with the network 10.0.0.0 means that only the first octet must match so the networks 10.25.100.0, 10.254.254.0, and 10.0.0.0 all match this statement. The mask may also be more specific. The statement network 172.16.30.0 0.0.0.31 requires the first three octets to match and the first three bits of the fourth octet to match; the only don't care bits are the last five. So only 172.16.30.0 through 172.16.30.31 match. You may have multiple network statements. Each is read in order, and the first one that matches a network is used. Figure 3-8 shows two examples of routers configured to use OSPF; the Bowling Green router uses one network statement to match all interfaces on the router, while the Toledo router uses separate network statements for each interface. However, this isn't important until the next chapter, when you learn about putting interfaces into different areas.

```
Toledo(config)#int e0
Toldeo(config-if)#ip address 10.1.254.1 255.255.255.0
Toledo(config-if)#int s0
Toledo(config-if)#ip address 10.0.1.37 255.255.255.252
Toledo(config-if)#int s0
Toledo(config-if)#ip address 10.100.76.33 255.255.255.224
Toledo(config-if)#exit
Toledo(config)#router ospf 1
Toledo(config-router)#network 10.0.1.36 0.0.0.255 area 0
Toledo(config-router)#network 10.1.254.0 0.0.0.255 area 0
Toledo(config-router)#network 10.100.76.32 0.0.0.31 area 0

BowlingGreen(config)#int e0
BowlingGreen(config-if)#ip address 10.1.28.1 255.255.255.0
BowlingGreen(config-if)#int s0
BowlingGreen(config-if)#ip address 10.0.1.38 255.255.255.252
BowlingGreen(config-if)#exit
BowlingGreen(config)#router ospf 1
BowlingGreen(config-router)#network 10.0.0.0 0.255.255.255 area 0
```

Figure 3-8 Activating OSPF

Configuring a Router ID

Since the router ID identifies a router to its neighbors and other routers on the OSPF network, changes to a router's router ID can cause problems. If the router ID of a DR changes because an interface on another network goes down, for example, then the other routers on that network think that the DR went down, even though the DR is still up and forwarding packets. As a result, in addition to the SPF calculation, the BDR becomes the DR and a new router is elected the BDR. The new BDR then must form adjacencies with all the routers on the network and exchange link-state databases. Since this can consume a lot of bandwidth and cause stability problems, Cisco recommends that you use a loopback interface to set the router ID since a loopback address won't go down unless the whole router goes down.

Configure a loopback interface as follows:

```
Boston(config)#int loopback 0
Boston(config-if)#ip address 172.28.12.1 255.255.255.255
```

You'll notice that you can use a 32-bit netmask on a loopback interface to conserve IP addresses.

When configuring loopback interfaces for router IDs on your network, you have two options for their IP addresses:

- IP addresses from outside your address space, not advertised with a network statement. These should be within one of the private address ranges discussed in Chapter 2, such as 10.0.0.0/8. This saves public IP addresses and is especially useful if you have only a limited range of public IP addresses available. However, you also won't be able to telnet directly to the router ID, and you won't be able to ping it since the network containing the router IDs of your routers won't be advertised by any of your routers.

- IP addresses from within your address space, advertised with a network statement. Although this uses additional public IP addresses, it allows you to both ping and directly telnet to the router ID, which can significantly simplify troubleshooting.

If you're already using private IP addresses within your OSPF network, you'll usually want to use IP addresses within your address space for ease of troubleshooting. Otherwise, your choice will depend on how carefully you need to manage allocation of IP addresses.

Configuring Cost

In Cisco routers, cost is calculated, by default, using the bandwidth of a link. Since cost is the metric used by OSPF, a lower cost indicates a better path. To calculate the cost of an interface, divide 100,000,000 by the bandwidth of the link in bits per second (bps). For a T-1, for example, the bandwidth is 1.544 Mbps and the cost is 64, while for a 10 Mbps Ethernet link, the cost is 10. However, in many cases, you may have to specify the bandwidth of the link using the bandwidth command since OSPF won't be able to determine the bandwidth, and will assume the link has the default bandwidth of 1.544 Mbps. You can specify the bandwidth of an interface with the following:

```
Houston(config)#int s0
Houston(config-if)#bandwidth 64
```

The bandwidth is in units of Kbps so this sets the bandwidth of interface serial 0 to 64 Kbps, equivalent to a cost of 1562.

Manually Configuring Cost

In some situations, you may need to manually configure the cost. For example, you might wish to avoid routing packets unnecessarily over a particular WAN link because the service provider charges more for bandwidth on that link than other service providers do for your other WAN links. Load balancing may also result in packets arriving out-of-order. If you have a network application that has difficulty handling out of order packets, you may wish to set the cost on interfaces between the users of the application and the server or servers housing the application so that traffic will take only one path. Another reason to change the cost of a link is if your network includes non-Cisco routers. Another vendor may use another scheme to determine the default cost, and the cost should match on both sides of the link. You can manually configure the cost with the following:

```
Columbus(config)#int s1
Colombus(config-if)#ip ospf cost 500
```

Correcting Problems with the Reference Cost

Unfortunately, with this scheme, links of 100 Mbps or greater all have costs of one since the cost is rounded up to one. If you have 622 Mbps ATM or 1000 Mbps Gigabit Ethernet links on your network, by default, these have the same cost as a 100 Mbps Fast Ethernet link. As a result, OSPF might choose a suboptimal path through the Fast Ethernet link instead of through the two faster links.

In Cisco routers, there are two ways to correct this problem. The first is to manually configure the cost of each interface with the ip ospf cost command. The disadvantage of this is that it becomes more difficult to maintain and configure correctly as you add routers to your network, especially since each end of a link should have the same cost. But, in older versions of Cisco IOS, this is your only option.

In more recent versions of Cisco IOS, you can configure the value used to calculate the cost with the **auto-cost reference-bandwidth** command. You should select a value so that the cost of the interface with the highest bandwidth on your network is at least one, and the cost of the interface with the next highest bandwidth is at least two. This will allow OSPF to distinguish between them and route packets properly. However, if you do not make this change on all the routers in your autonomous system, then some routers will have incorrect costs. As a result, routers may forward packets along suboptimal paths. You can change the reference bandwidth with the following:

```
SanAntonio(config)#router ospf 1
  SanAntonio(config-router)#auto-cost reference-band—
  width 10000
```

Note that the reference bandwidth is in units of Mbps.

In Figure 3-9, you can see that each link attached to the Laboratory router has a cost of one, even though they vary in bandwidth from 1000 Mbps to 10 Mbps. Since the rest of the path from the Laboratory router to the Hospital router is the same, the Laboratory router performs load balancing on any packet it sends to the Hospital router, even though the bandwidth of each link is so different because each path has the same total cost. To fix this, you can set the reference bandwidth to 10,000 on each router on the network (the units of the reference bandwidth are Mbps). The precise value you choose isn't necessarily important, as long as your fastest links have a cost of at least one, and your next highest link has a cost of at least two. Additionally, you should use the same reference bandwidth throughout your network. In Figure 3-10, you can see that the cost of each interface on the Laboratory router is now different, so the Laboratory router does not attempt to do load balancing between these paths. You can also see that the reference bandwidth on the other routers changed too, along with that on the Laboratory router.

3

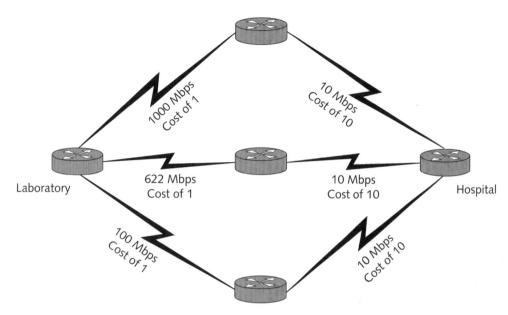

Figure 3-9   Links with different speeds but the same cost

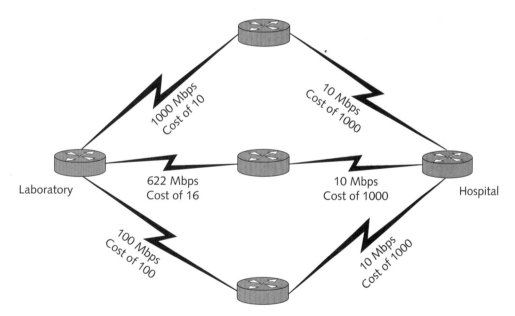

Figure 3-10   Path problems fixed by changing the reference bandwidth

Changing the bandwidth of a link, the reference bandwidth, or the cost of a link will cause routers to run through the SPF calculation and rebuild their routing tables.

Changing the Router Priority

Since each broadcast network elects its own DR and BDR, and since a single router may be a DR on one network and an ordinary router on another, setting the priority for DR and BDR elections is an interface command. The priority itself varies from zero to 255, with zero being ineligible. For instance, you might wish to ensure that a router with a fast processor and a lot of memory becomes DR by setting its priority to 255. Alternately, you might wish to ensure that a router with a slower processor and less memory is ineligible to become DR by setting its priority to zero. You can configure the priority on an interface with the following:

```
MexicoCity(config)#int eth 0/0
MexicoCity(config-if)#ip ospf priority 255
```

In this case, the priority of the Ethernet 0/0 interface on the MexicoCity router is set to 255, the maximum possible priority.

Configuring OSPF in NBMA Topologies

Because of the added complexity of OSPF in NBMA topologies, configuration of OSPF is also more complex in these topologies. Depending on the mode used, you may have to manually configure the neighbors and the network type. You can use the **ip ospf network** command to configure the network type depending on the topology and characteristics of a NBMA network. Table 3-4 shows the options for this command. Keep in mind that while use of this command is probably most important in NBMA topologies, it may also be used in other topologies.

Table 3-4   Options for the **ip ospf network** command

Command	Mode	Comments
ip ospf network nonbroadcast	NBMA	Default for NBMA interfaces and point-to-multipoint subinterfaces
ip ospf network point-to-multipoint	Point-to-multipoint	Similar to point-to-multipoint mode, but requires manual configuration of neighbors
ip ospf network point-to-point	Point-to-point	Default for point-to-point interfaces and subinterfaces;
ip ospf network point-to-multipoint nonbroadcast	Point-to-multipoint nonbroadcast	Added in Cisco IOS 11.3a
ip ospf network broadcast networks such as Ethernet	Broadcast	Default for broadcast multiaccess

NBMA Mode

In NBMA mode, the two issues are the selection of the DR and the BDR, and the fact that the DR and BDR need manual configuration of neighbors because they can't dynamically discover them without broadcasts. See Figure 3-11 for an example of how to configure both the neighbors and their priorities for this sort of a network topology. In this instance, four neighbors are configured; the Seattle router set its own interface priority to 200 and the priority of the neighbor at 192.168.24.30 to 200, so (depending on the router ID of the Seattle router) these two routers will be selected the DR and the BDR. The neighbor at 192.168.24.40, however, has a priority of zero and is ineligible to be selected DR. Keep in mind that some of the options for the neighbor command depend on which mode you're configuring. Also, note that the network type can be configured with the ip ospf network nonbroadcast command; however, this is the default for NBMA networks so it isn't necessary in this instance.

```
Seattle(config)#int s0
Seattle(config-if)#ip address 192.168.24.1 255.255.255.0
Seattle(config-if)#encapsulation frame-relay
Seattle(config-if)#ip ospf priority 200
Seattle(config-if)#router ospf 25
Seattle(config-router)#network 192.168.24.0 0.0.0.255 area 0
Seattle(config-router)#neighbor 192.168.24.10
Seattle(config-router)#neighbor 192.168.24.20
Seattle(config-router)#neighbor 192.168.24.30 ?
  cost              OSPF cost for point-to-multipoint neighbor
  database-filter   Filter OSPF LSA during synchronization and flooding
                    for point-to-multipoint neighbor
  poll-interval     OSPF dead-router polling interval
  priority          OSPF priority of non-broadcast neighbor
  <cr>

Seattle(config-router)#neighbor 192.168.24.30 priority 200
Seattle(config-router)#neighbor 192.168.24.40 priority 0
```

Figure 3-11   OSPF configuration in NBMA mode

Broadcast Mode

Although this can work in other network topologies, broadcast mode works best in a fully meshed NBMA topology. The advantage of using broadcast mode is that you don't need to manually configure the neighbors since broadcasts are enabled, and on a fully meshed network, all routers can reach each other. You can configure broadcast mode on a NBMA network simply by changing the OSPF network type in interface configuration mode:

```
SanFran(config)#int s1
SanFran(config-if)#ip ospf network broadcast
```

Point-to-Point Mode

Point-to-point mode doesn't require any special configuration other than the configuration of the subinterfaces themselves since point-to-point mode is the default for point-to-point interfaces and subinterfaces. See Figure 3-12 for an example of an OSPF configuration in point-to-point mode with subinterfaces.

```
interface Serial0/0
 no ip address
 encapsulation frame-relay
 frame-relay lmi-type ansi
!
interface Serial0/0.1 point-to-point
 ip address 10.0.1.1 255.255.255.252
 frame-relay interface-dlci 101
!
interface Serial0/0.2 point-to-point
 ip address 10.0.1.5 255.255.255.252
 frame-relay interface-dlci 102
!
interface Serial0/0.3 point-to-point
 ip address 10.0.1.10 255.255.255.252
 frame-relay interface-dlci 103
!
[Output omitted]
!
router ospf 1
 network 10.0.0.0 0.255.255.255 area 0
!
```

Figure 3-12   OSPF configuration in point-to-point mode with subinterfaces

Point-to-Multipoint Mode

If broadcasts are supported on the network, configuration of point-to-multipoint mode can be as simple as defining the OSPF network type in interface configuration mode:

```
Dublin(config)#int serial 0/0
Dublin(config-if)#ip ospf network point-to-multipoint
```

In this case, neighbors do not need to be manually defined. However, if you do manually configure neighbors, you should configure them with a cost:

```
Dublin(config)#router ospf 77
Dublin(config-router)#neighbor 192.168.154.1 cost 200
```

If broadcasts are not supported on the network, then you must use point-to-multipoint with the nonbroadcast keyword.

```
Dublin(config)#int serial 0/0
Dublin(config-if)#ip ospf network point-to-multipoint
nonbroadcast
```

Additionally, neighbors must be manually configured. You should also configure these with a cost.

MONITORING AND TROUBLESHOOTING OSPF

You can use a variety of show and debug commands to verify that OSPF is operating properly, or to troubleshoot it, when necessary.

Since running debug commands can be a CPU-intensive process (which can sometimes crash a busy router), you'll want to start by using show commands and move on to the debug commands after you narrow down the potential source of the problem.

Confirming that OSPF is Running

Especially on a strange network, it's often useful to quickly find out whether or not a router is running a particular routing protocol. One quick way to find out is to run the **show ip protocols** command. This will quickly show you whether or not OSPF is enabled on a router, what networks OSPF is advertising, and the hosts from which a router is receiving routing information. You may use this command to quickly determine if any other routing protocols are active on a router, or if there are any additional OSPF routing processes active. Figure 3-13 shows a typical example of the **show ip protocols** command.

```
Hilo#show ip prot
Routing Protocol is "ospf 1"
  Sending updates every 0 seconds
  Invalid after 0 seconds, hold down 0, flushed after 0
  Outgoing update filter list for all interfaces is
  Incoming update filter list for all interfaces is
  Redistributing: ospf 1
  Routing for Networks:
    10.0.0.0
  Routing Information Sources:
    Gateway         Distance      Last Update
    10.1.28.1            110       00:02:06
    10.1.16.1            110       00:02:06
    10.0.1.37            110       00:02:06
    192.168.1.1          110       03:45:29
  Distance: (default is 110)
```

Figure 3-13   Output of the **show ip protocols** command

Confirming Interface Parameters

The **show ip ospf interface** command can help you determine whether or not an interface is configured properly, among other things. See Figure 3-14 for typical output from this command, showing interfaces Ethernet 0/0 and serial 1.1 on the Lahaina router. In this case, it's obvious that OSPF was activated on both interfaces; however, without the name of an interface, this command won't show you the results for any interfaces where OSPF was not activated. Suppose you expected to see interface serial 0 in addition to the other interfaces. Running the command with the name of the serial 0 interface produces no output, which tells you that OSPF was not activated on that interface.

```
Lahaina#show ip ospf interface
Ethernet0 is up, line protocol is up
  Internet Address 10.1.22.1/24, Area 0
  Process ID 1, Router ID 10.1.22.1, Network Type BROADCAST, Cost: 10
  Transmit Delay is 1 sec, State DR, Priority 1
  Designated Router (ID) 10.1.22.1, Interface address 10.1.22.1
  No backup designated router on this network
  Timer intervals configured, Hello 10, Dead 40, Wait 40, Retransmit 5
    Hello due in 00:00:05
  Index 1/1, flood queue length 0
  Next 0x0(0)/0x0(0)
  Last flood scan length is 0, maximum is 0
  Last flood scan time is 0 msec, maximum is 0 msec
  Neighbor Count is 0, Adjacent neighbor count is 0
  Suppress hello for 0 neighbor(s)
Serial1.1 is up, line protocol is up
  Internet Address 10.0.1.30/30, Area 0
  Process ID 1, Router ID 10.1.22.1, Network Type BROADCAST, Cost: 64
  Transmit Delay is 1 sec, State DR, Priority 1
  Designated Router (ID) 10.1.22.1, Interface address 10.0.1.30
  Backup Designated router (ID) 10.0.1.37, Interface address 10.0.1.29
  Timer intervals configured, Hello 10, Dead 40, Wait 40, Retransmit 5
    Hello due in 00:00:01
  Index 2/2, flood queue length 0
  Next 0x0(0)/0x0(0)
  Last flood scan length is 1, maximum is 1
  Last flood scan time is 0 msec, maximum is 0 msec
  Neighbor Count is 1, Adjacent neighbor count is 1
    Adjacent with neighbor 10.0.1.37  (Backup Designated Router)
  Suppress hello for 0 neighbor(s)
Lahaina#show ip ospf interface serial 0

Lahaina#
```

Figure 3-14 Output of the **show ip ospf interface** command

You can use this command to find other valuable information. For example, this command will tell you the network type and, if applicable, the router ID of the DR and the BDR. In Figure 3-14, both interfaces are on broadcast networks; you can see that the Lahaina router is the DR for the network attached to Ethernet 0, but that there is no BDR. Whether or not this is a problem depends on what you expect to see. For example, the Lahaina router did not discover any other routers on this network, which probably means that there aren't any other routers connected. In a NBMA environment, on the other hand, a lack of neighbors could mean that the router can't discover its neighbors, and you may need to manually configure them. The output for serial interface 1.1, for example, indicates that the Lahaina router is also the DR for the network attached to this interface, and its only neighbor is the BDR. You can also find out how the hello and dead intervals are set, and the cost of the link.

Verify that OSPF is Learning Routes

You can use the **show ip route** command to verify that the OSPF process on a router is learning routes. In Figure 3-15, you can see the results of the **show ip route** command on the Lima router. Especially if a router is running more than one routing protocol (which you'll learn about in Chapter 7), you may have to sort through quite a bit of output before you can identify the routes learned from OSPF. In fact, none of the output at the top of the command shows any OSPF routes. You can see only the OSPF routes with the **show ip route ospf** command, as shown in the bottom of Figure 3-16.

```
Lima#sh ip route
Codes: C - connected, S - static, I - IGRP, R - RIP, M - mobile, B - BGP
       D - EIGRP, EX - EIGRP external, O - OSPF, IA - OSPF inter area
       N1 - OSPF NSSA external type 1, N2 - OSPF NSSA external type 2
       E1 - OSPF external type 1, E2 - OSPF external type 2, E - EGP
       i - IS-IS, L1 - IS-IS level-1, L2 - IS-IS level-2, * - candidate
default
       U - per-user static route, o - ODR, P - periodic downloaded static
route
       T - traffic engineered route

Gateway of last resort is 10.1.254.1 to network 0.0.0.0

     10.97.87.0/24 is variably subnetted, 7 subnets, 2 masks
R       10.97.87.128/27 [120/9] via 10.1.254.3, Ethernet0/0
R       10.97.87.129/32 [120/9] via 10.1.254.3, Ethernet0/0
R       10.97.87.96/27 [120/9] via 10.1.254.3, Ethernet0/0
R       10.97.87.97/32 [120/9] via 10.1.254.3, Ethernet0/0
R       10.97.87.64/27 [120/2] via 10.1.254.3, Ethernet0/0
R       10.97.87.32/27 [120/1] via 10.1.254.3, Ethernet0/0
R       10.97.87.33/32 [120/1] via 10.1.254.3, Ethernet0/0
S    192.168.40.0/24 [1/0] via 10.1.254.5
     10.97.81.0/24 is variably subnetted, 6 subnets, 2 masks
R       10.97.81.192/27 [120/8] via 10.1.254.3, Ethernet0/0
R       10.97.81.193/32 [120/8] via 10.1.254.3, Ethernet0/0
R       10.97.81.64/27 [120/3] via 10.1.254.3, Ethernet0/0
R       10.97.81.65/32 [120/8] via 10.1.254.3, Ethernet0/0
R       10.97.81.32/27 [120/1] via 10.1.254.3, Ethernet0/0
R       10.97.81.33/32 [120/1] via 10.1.254.3, Ethernet0/0
     172.16.0.0/21 is subnetted, 1 subnets
S       172.16.8.0 [1/0] via 10.1.254.5
     10.97.80.0/24 is variably subnetted, 8 subnets, 2 masks
R       10.97.80.225/32 [120/7] via 10.1.254.3, Ethernet0/0
 --More-

Lima#show ip route ospf
     10.0.0.0/8 is variably subnetted, 13 subnets, 2 masks
O       10.0.1.12/30 [110/1626] via 10.0.1.29, 00:40:53, Serial1.1
O       10.0.1.0/30 [110/1626] via 10.0.1.29, 00:40:53, Serial1.1
O       10.0.1.4/30 [110/1626] via 10.0.1.29, 00:40:53, Serial1.1
O       10.0.1.24/30 [110/1626] via 10.0.1.29, 00:40:53, Serial1.1
O       10.1.28.0/24 [110/1636] via 10.0.1.29, 00:40:53, Serial1.1
O       10.1.16.0/24 [110/1636] via 10.0.1.29, 00:40:54, Serial1.1
O       10.0.1.16/30 [110/1626] via 10.0.1.29, 00:40:54, Serial1.1
O       10.0.1.20/30 [110/1626] via 10.0.1.29, 00:40:54, Serial1.1
O       10.0.1.32/30 [110/1626] via 10.0.1.29, 00:40:54, Serial1.1
O       10.0.1.36/30 [110/1626] via 10.0.1.29, 00:40:54, Serial1.1
O       10.1.254.0/24 [110/74] via 10.0.1.29, 00:40:54, Serial1.1
```

Figure 3-15   Output of the **show ip route** command

The **clear ip route *** command will clear the routing table if you have any doubts about the routes it contains. While this does force the router to rebuild its routing table, it neither affects the router's link-state database, nor forces it to run through the SPF calculation.

Show Information About the OSPF Process

The **show ip ospf** command shows information about the OSPF process (see Figure 3-16). For example, you can see the number of times the SPF algorithm was calculated (47), which gives you a sense of the stability of an OSPF area. You can also get a good idea of the size of the area (11 interfaces), and whether or not the area is configured for authentication (no), among other things.

```
Kihei#show ip ospf
 Routing Process "ospf 1" with ID 10.0.1.37
 Supports only single TOS(TOS0) routes
 SPF schedule delay 5 secs, Hold time between two SPFs 10 secs
 Minimum LSA interval 5 secs. Minimum LSA arrival 1 secs
 Number of external LSA 0. Checksum Sum 0x0
 Number of DCbitless external LSA 0
 Number of DoNotAge external LSA 0
 Number of areas in this router is 1. 1 normal 0 stub 0 nssa
 External flood list length 0
    Area BACKBONE(0)
        Number of interfaces in this area is 11
        Area has no authentication
        SPF algorithm executed 47 times
        Area ranges are
        Number of LSA 9. Checksum Sum 0x27935
        Number of DCbitless LSA 0
        Number of indication LSA 0
        Number of DoNotAge LSA 0
        Flood list length 0
```

Figure 3-16   Output of the **show ip ospf** command

Show Information about Neighboring Routers

To see information about neighbors, you can use the **show ip ospf neighbors** command. This command gives the router ID of each neighbor, its state, and whether the neighbor is the DR, the BDR, or in the DROTHER state (this field is left empty on networks without a DR or BDR). It also provides the interface on the router through which the neighbor was discovered, and the address of the neighbor's adjacent interface. You can also use this command to examine neighbors by interface, or in greater detail with the detail keyword. Typical output of the **show ip ospf neighbors** command follows:

```
Montevideo#show ip ospf neighbor
Neighbor ID   Pri   State          Dead Time   Address       Interface
10.96.0.254   1     FULL/DROTHER   00:00:37    10.96.0.27    FastEthernet0/0
10.89.95.249  90    FULL/DROTHER   00:00:32    10.96.0.30    FastEthernet0/0
10.96.0.250   1     FULL/DROTHER   00:00:38    10.96.0.26    FastEthernet0/0
10.89.95.243  1     FULL/BDR       00:00:39    10.96.0.2     FastEthernet0/0
10.96.0.225   1     FULL/DROTHER   00:00:33    10.96.0.1     FastEthernet0/0
10.96.0.252   1     FULL/DROTHER   00:00:38    10.96.0.28    FastEthernet0/0
10.89.95.245  95    FULL/DROTHER   00:00:37    10.96.0.34    FastEthernet1/0
10.96.0.254   1     FULL/DROTHER   00:00:37    10.96.0.59    FastEthernet1/0
10.89.95.249  1     FULL/DROTHER   00:00:33    10.96.0.62    FastEthernet1/0
10.96.0.250   1     FULL/DROTHER   00:00:38    10.96.0.58    FastEthernet1/0
10.89.95.244  100   FULL/BDR       00:00:33    10.96.0.33    FastEthernet1/0
```

3

```
Montevideo#show ip ospf neighbor ?
  FastEthernet  FastEthernet IEEE 802.3
  Loopback      Loopback interface
  Null            Null interface
  Serial          Serial
  detail          detail of all neighbors

Montevideo#show ip ospf neighbor FastEthernet1/0

Neighbor ID    Pri  State        Dead Time  Address      Interface
10.89.95.245   95   FULL/DROTHER 00:00:39   10.96.0.34   FastEthernet1/0
10.96.0.254    1    FULL/DROTHER 00:00:36   10.96.0.59   FastEthernet1/0
10.89.95.249   1    FULL/DROTHER 00:00:36   10.96.0.62   FastEthernet1/0
10.96.0.250    1    FULL/DROTHER 00:00:37   10.96.0.58   FastEthernet1/0
10.89.95.244   100  FULL/BDR     00:00:39   10.96.0.33   FastEthernet1/0
10.96.0.252    1    FULL/DROTHER 00:00:37   10.96.0.60   FastEthernet1/0
Montevideo#show ip ospf neighbor FastEthernet1/0 detail
 Neighbor 10.89.95.245, interface address 10.96.0.34
  In the area 0 via interface FastEthernet1/0
  Neighbor priority is 95, State is FULL, 6 state changes
  DR is 10.96.0.61 BDR is 10.96.0.33
  Options is 0x42
  Dead timer due in 00:00:35
  Index 8/8, retransmission queue length 0, number of retransmission 71
  First 0x0(0)/0x0(0) Next 0x0(0)/0x0(0)
  Last retransmission scan length is 1, maximum is 2
  Last retransmission scan time is 0 msec, maximum is 0 msec
 Neighbor 10.96.0.254, interface address 10.96.0.59
  In the area 0 via interface FastEthernet1/0
  Neighbor priority is 1, State is FULL, 6 state changes
  DR is 10.96.0.61 BDR is 10.96.0.33
  Options is 0x42
  Dead timer due in 00:00:35
  Index 10/10, retransmission queue length 0, number of retransmission 123
  First 0x0(0)/0x0(0) Next 0x0(0)/0x0(0)
  Last retransmission scan length is 0, maximum is 2
  Last retransmission scan time is 0 msec, maximum is 0 msec
[Output omitted]
```

Show the OSPF Topology Database

The following example shows a link-state database produced with the **show ip ospf database** command. As OSPF routers require knowledge of the entire area in order to route packets properly, any discrepancies in the link-state database should be investigated. In this sample, you can see the router advertising each link, as well as the number of links the advertising router has in the area (although interfaces such as serial interfaces in a point-to-point link do generate two links in the OSPF database). As you might imagine, as your OSPF area grows larger and more complicated, so does the link-state database. You will learn more about this in the next chapter.

```
Nashville#show ip ospf database

    OSPF Router with ID (10.0.1.37) (Process ID 1)

       Router Link States (Area 0)

Link ID        ADV Router     Age    Seq#       Checksum Link count
10.0.1.37      10.0.1.37      432    0x8000001E  0x4432       10
10.1.16.1      10.1.16.1      815    0x8000000E  0x4D29        2
10.1.22.1      10.1.22.1      911    0x8000001B  0x788F        2
10.1.28.1      10.1.28.1      494    0x8000002A  0x2DA9        2

       Net Link States (Area 0)

Link ID        ADV Router     Age    Seq#        Checksum
10.0.1.22      10.1.16.1      815    0x8000000B   0xA207
10.0.1.29      10.0.1.37      13816  0x80000001   0x78B
10.0.1.30      10.1.22.1      911    0x8000000A   0x6036
10.0.1.37      10.0.1.37      13884  0x80000001   0x57F
10.0.1.38      10.1.28.1      494    0x80000009   0x1E65
```

Debugging

A variety of debugging commands is available. See Table 3-5 for details of some common debugging commands.

Table 3-5 Debug commands for OSPF

Command	Description
debug ip ospf adj	Adjacency events, such as the Hello protocol and the election of the DR and BDR
debug ip ospf events	General OSPF events (overlaps with most other categories)
debug ip ospf flood	Details of LSA flooding
debug ip ospf lsa-generation	Details of LSA generation
debug ip ospf packet	Details of individual OSPF packets; can be extremely CPU-intensive during flooding
debug ip ospf retransmission	Retransmission events
debug ip ospf spf	Details of SPF calculation
debug ip ospf tree	Details of the operation of the OSPF database tree

The following example is some sample output of two debugging commands. At the top, the **debug ip ospf adj** command was run; the output indicates that while most hello packets appear to be processed properly, one of the neighbors has some mismatching parameters. Specifically, the hello interval was set to five seconds and the dead interval to 20. Debugging was turned off and the **debug ip ospf events** command was run right before the mismatched timers were fixed on the remote router. You can see the neighbor go back into the two-way state, the DR and the BDR election, and the exchange of database information. Most of all of this information is also available with adjacency debugging.

```
SanAntonio#deb ip ospf adj

[Output omitted]

4w5d: OSPF: Mismatched hello parameters from 10.0.1.22
4w5d: Dead R 20 C 40, Hello R 5 C 10  Mask R 255.255.255.2
52 C 255.255.255.252
4w5d: OSPF: Rcv hello from 10.1.28.1 area 0 from Serial0/0
.10 10.0.1.38
4w5d: OSPF: End of hello processing
4w5d: OSPF: Rcv hello from 10.1.16.1 area 0 from Serial0/0
.6 10.0.1.22
4w5d: OSPF: Mismatched hello parameters from 10.0.1.22
4w5d: Dead R 20 C 40, Hello R 5 C 10  Mask R 255.255.255.2
52 C 255.255.255.252
4w5d: OSPF: Rcv hello from 10.1.22.1 area 0 from Serial0/0
.8 10.0.1.30
4w5d: OSPF: End of hello processing

[Output omitted]

SanAntonio#deb ip ospf events

4w5d: OSPF: Mismatched hello parameters from 10.0.1.22
4w5d: Dead R 20 C 40, Hello R 5 C 10  Mask R 255.255.255.2
52 C 255.255.255.252
4w5d: OSPF: Rcv hello from 10.1.22.1 area 0 from Serial0/0
.8 10.0.1.30
4w5d: OSPF: End of hello processing
4w5d: OSPF: Rcv hello from 10.1.28.1 area 0 from Serial0/0
.10 10.0.1.38
4w5d: OSPF: End of hello processing
4w5d: OSPF: Rcv hello from 10.1.22.1 area 0 from Serial0/0
.8 10.0.1.30
4w5d: OSPF: End of hello processing
4w5d: OSPF: Rcv hello from 10.1.16.1 area 0 from Serial0/0
.6 10.0.1.22
4w5d: OSPF: 2 Way Communication to 10.1.16.1 on Serial0/0.
6, state 2WAY
4w5d: OSPF: Neighbor change Event on interface Serial0/0.6
4w5d: OSPF: DR/BDR election on Serial0/0.6
4w5d: OSPF: Elect BDR 0.0.0.0
```

```
4w5d: OSPF: Elect DR 10.1.16.1
4w5d: OSPF: Elect BDR 10.0.1.37
4w5d: OSPF: Elect DR 10.1.16.1
4w5d:           DR: 10.1.16.1 (Id)    BDR: 10.0.1.37 (Id)
4w5d: OSPF: Send DBD to 10.1.16.1 on Serial0/0.6 seq 0x25B
9 opt 0x2 flag 0x7 len 32
4w5d: OSPF: Set Serial0/0.6 flush timer
4w5d: OSPF: Remember old DR 10.0.1.37 (id)
4w5d: OSPF: End of hello processing
4w5d: OSPF: Rcv DBD from 10.1.16.1 on Serial0/0.6 seq 0x26
2E opt 0x2 flag 0x7 len 32   mtu 1500 state EXSTART
4w5d: OSPF: NBR Negotiation Done. We are the SLAVE
4w5d: OSPF: Send DBD to 10.1.16.1 on Serial0/0.6 seq 0x262
E opt 0x2 flag 0x2 len 172
4w5d: OSPF: Rcv DBD from 10.1.16.1 on Serial0/0.6 seq 0x26
2F opt 0x2 flag 0x3 len 52   mtu 1500 state EXCHANGE
4w5d: OSPF: Send DBD to 10.1.16.1 on Serial0/0.6 seq 0x262
F opt 0x2 flag 0x0 len 32
4w5d: OSPF: Rcv DBD from 10.1.16.1 on Serial0/0.6 seq 0x26
30 opt 0x2 flag 0x1 len 32   mtu 1500 state EXCHANGE
4w5d: OSPF: Exchange Done with 10.1.16.1 on Serial0/0.6
4w5d: OSPF: Synchronized with 10.1.16.1 on Serial0/0.6, st
ate FULL
4w5d: OSPF: Send DBD to 10.1.16.1 on Serial0/0.6 seq 0x263
0 opt 0x2 flag 0x0 len 32
4w5d: OSPF: Rcv hello from 10.1.28.1 area 0 from Serial0/0
.10 10.0.1.38
4w5d: OSPF: End of hello processing
4w5d: OSPF: Rcv hello from 10.1.22.1 area 0 from Serial0/0
.8 10.0.1.30
4w5d: OSPF: End of hello processing
4w5d: OSPF: Rcv hello from 10.1.16.1 area 0 from Serial0/0
.6 10.0.1.22
4w5d: OSPF: Neighbor change Event on interface Serial0/0.6
4w5d: OSPF: DR/BDR election on Serial0/0.6
4w5d: OSPF: Elect BDR 10.0.1.37
4w5d: OSPF: Elect DR 10.1.16.1
4w5d:           DR: 10.1.16.1 (Id)    BDR: 10.0.1.37 (Id)
4w5d: OSPF: End of hello processing
4w5d: OSPF: Rcv hello from 10.1.28.1 area 0 from Serial0/0
.10 10.0.1.38
4w5d: OSPF: End of hello processing
```

CHAPTER SUMMARY

❑ Because OSPF was designed for large IP networks, it has several advantages over RIP and other distance vector routing protocols. These include support for VLSMs, faster convergence, no hop limit, more efficient use of bandwidth, and path selection based on cost rather than hop count.

❑ OSPF routers establish and maintain routers with the Hello protocol. Parameters such as the hello interval and dead interval must match in order for two routers to become neighbors. Not all neighboring routers form adjacencies, a relationship in which two routers exchange routing information. On broadcast multiaccess networks, routers elect a designated router (DR) and a backup designated router (BDR) based on their priorities. The DR and the BDR both form adjacencies with all the routers on the network; the DR takes the responsibility of flooding each router on the network with any network changes.

❑ When two routers form adjacencies, the router with the highest router ID becomes the master and starts sending database description (DD) packets. The other router, the slave, sends DD packets in response until each exchanges its full link-state database. At this point, each router runs through the Shortest Path First (SPF) calculation and rebuilds its routing table. Each time a router receives a link-state update (LSU) packet containing a link-state advertisement (LSA) about a network change, it makes sure that the LSA really does contain new information. If it does, it begins the flooding process, and then it does the SPF calculation and rebuilds its routing table, along with the other routers on the OSPF network.

❑ In nonbroadcast multiaccess (NBMA) network topologies, OSPF must behave somewhat differently because NBMA network topologies don't support broadcasts, and in many cases, not all routers are physically connected. Cisco routers support several different modes in NBMA topologies. Which mode you choose depends in large part on whether the NBMA network is a star topology, a partial mesh, or a full mesh.

❑ After activating the OSPF process on each interface, you must activate OSPF on each interface with a **network** statement, a wildcard mask, and an area. You can set a router's router ID by assigning it a loopback interface. On NBMA networks, you can choose the type of mode used with the **ip ospf network** command in interface configuration mode.

❑ By default, Cisco routers calculate the cost of a link by dividing the bandwidth by 100,000,000. However, any link with a bandwidth of 100 Mbps or faster has the same cost. To correct this, you can use the **auto-cost reference-bandwidth** command, or you can manually configure the cost of each interface. You can also use the **ip ospf priority** command to influence the selection of the designated router and the backup designated router.

❏ You can use a variety of show and debug commands to monitor and troubleshoot OSPF operation. For instance, you may use the **show ip protocols** command to see which routing protocols a router is running, the **show ip ospf** command to see information about the OSPF process, the **show ip ospf neighbors** command to see information about neighboring routers, and the **show ip ospf database** command to look at the OSPF topology database. You can also use the **debug ip ospf events** command to monitor OSPF events as they happen.

KEY TERMS

adjacency — A relationship between two neighboring routes in an OSPF area where each router shares its link-state database with the other router; not all routers in an area form adjacencies.

AllDRouters — The multicast address 224.0.0.6, to which all designated and backup designated routers listen.

AllSPFRouters — The multicast address 224.0.0.5, to which all OSPF routers listen.

area — A unit into which an OSPF network can be divided.

asynchronous communication — Communication method using start and stop bits; for example, used by modems over the public telephone network.

Autonomous System — A group of routers under the same administrative control, using the same routing policies.

broadcast mode — A mode that can be used with OSPF on NBMA networks, in which OSPF emulates a broadcast multiaccess network and elects a designated router and backup designated router.

broadcast multiaccess topology — A network topology that can support more than two routers on a segment, and where routers can send broadcasts to all other devices on the segment.

cost — The metric OSPF uses to decide between routes; in Cisco routers, cost is based on the bandwidth of a link, by default.

database description packet (DD, DBD or DDP) — The packets used in OSPF by two routers forming an adjacency to exchange their link-state databases.

dead interval — The interval between the time an OSPF router last receives a hello packet and the time it declares it unreachable; typically, this is four times the hello interval.

Djikstra algorithm — The algorithm used by OSPF to calculate routing tables.

dialer map — Configuration statement that associates a destination IP address with a dialer string or phone number.

don't care bits — Bits in the wildcard mask on an OSPF network configuration statement set to one, which matches all possible bits.

DROTHER — A router that isn't a designated router or a backup designated router.

ExStart state — The state when two OSPF routers are about to form adjacencies with each other.

flooding — The process of sending updated link-state advertisements throughout an area in order to ensure that each router in the area has up-to-date knowledge of the network topology.

full mesh topology — Topology in which all routers are connected to all other routers.

Full state — When an OSPF router has exchanged its complete topology database with a neighbor and is ready to route packets.

group pacing — The practice of sending packets to refresh LSAs in small groups at intervals set by the group pacing interval, rather than all at once.

group pacing interval — The interval at which groups of refresh packets are sent in group pacing.

hello interval — The interval between hello packets sent by an OSPF router; in multiaccess and point-to-point topologies, this is typically 10 seconds, while in nonbroadcast multiaccess topologies, the hello interval is typically 30 seconds.

hello packets — Packets sent out by a router using the Hello protocol in order to discover new neighbors, and identify the status of existing neighbors.

Hello protocol — The protocol responsible for establishing and maintaining neighbor relationships with other OSPF routers.

Hub-and-spoke topology — *See* star topology.

Interior Gateway Protocol (IGP) — A routing protocol used by routers in the same autonomous system.

Internet Engineering Task Force (IETF) — An organization devoted to the growth and operation of the Internet.

link-state acknowledgement (LSAck) packet — OSPF packet that acknowledges the receipt of another packet.

link-state advertisement (LSA) — Describes the state of a network or neighboring router; sent in routing updates during flooding, and used by routers to build their link-state databases.

link-state Aging timer — The timer set by each router to determine when it should attempt to refresh a LSA by flooding it out (after 30 minutes), and when it should discard the LSA (after 60 minutes).

link-state database — Contains a LSA for every router and network in an OSPF area so that a router has complete knowledge of the area's topology.

link-state update (LSU) packet — Packet containing a LSA; sent to update other routers' link-state databases during flooding.

multipoint subinterfaces — Logical interfaces on the same subnet.

neighbors — Other routers with interfaces in the same area.

nonbroadcast multiaccess (NBMA) topology — A network topology that can support more than two routers on a segment, but which doesn't support broadcasts.

NBMA mode — A mode for the operation of OSPF on a nonbroadcast multiaccess network; the network is usually in a full mesh, uses the Hello protocol to discover neighbors, and selects a designated router and a backup designated router.

3

partial mesh topology – A topology in which many routers, but not all, are connected to each other, sometimes without a clearly defined central site.

permanent virtual circuit (PVC) — A logical connection in a nonbroadcast multiaccess network topology, such as frame relay or ATM; one port may have multiple such connections.

Point-to-multipoint mode — Operation of OSPF on nonbroadcast multiaccess networks, typically used on partially meshed networks; each link is treated as a point-to-point link.

point-to-multipoint nonbroadcast mode — Operation of OSPF on nonbroadcast multiaccess networks where circuits do not support dynamic discovery of neighbors; each link is treated like a point-to-point link.

point-to-point mode — An extension to RFC 2328, developed by Cisco, which treats point-to-point subinterfaces in NBMA topologies as if they are point-to-point links.

point-to-point subinterfaces — Logical interfaces in their own subnet.

point-to-point topology — A network topology that supports only two routers on a segment, such as a dedicated serial connection.

priority — Determines how likely a router is to be elected DR or BDR; higher priorities win the election, while priorities of zero indicate that a router isn't eligible to be DR or BDR.

reliable transmission — To ensure that a packet arrives, the receiver must send an acknowledgement packet to the sender, or the sender will retransmit the packet.

route flapping — When a route goes up and down repeatedly.

router ID — The 32-bit number representing a router on an OSPF network; usually this number is either the highest IP address of an active interface, or the highest IP address of a loopback interface.

shortest path first (SPF) algorithm — *See* Djikstra algorithm.

SPF delay timer — The timer that specifies how long a router will wait after receiving a LSU before undergoing the SPF calculation; the default is five seconds.

SPF holdtime timer —The amount of time between two consecutive SPF calculations; the default is 10 seconds.

star topology — All remote sites are connected to a central site.

subinterface — A logical interface used to divide a physical interface into multiple parts, each of which can be associated with a different virtual circuit.

switched virtual circuit (SVC) — A virtual circuit established dynamically and torn down when no longer needed; used in NBMA topologies, such as frame relay.

topology database — *See* link-state database.

two-way state — A router receives a hello packet from a neighbor containing its own address; at this point, the two routers may form an adjacency with each other, depending on the network topology.

REVIEW QUESTIONS

1. Which of the following is an advantage of OSPF over RIP on large networks? (Choose all that apply.)

    a. Each OSPF router sends its entire routing table in each update.

    b. OSPF routers send updates only after changes, or every 30 minutes.

    c. OSPF has no hop count limit.

    d. OSPF does not support VLSMs.

2. What is the purpose of the Hello protocol in OSPF? (Choose all that apply.)

    a. flood the network with updates after a network change

    b. multicast link-state advertisements to the designated router

    c. discover neighboring routers

    d. determine the status of neighboring routers

3. Hello and dead intervals do not need to match for two neighboring routers to form an adjacency. True or false?

4. How does a router determine whether or not a LSA in its topology database is older than, newer than, or the same as a LSA received in a LSU packet?

    a. It looks at the LS Aging field in the LSU packet and compares it to the LS Aging field in its topology database.

    b. It checks the timestamp applied by the router sending it.

    c. It checks the sequence number in the LSA and compares it to the sequence number in its topology database.

    d. It automatically uses the LSA just received since any LSA received in a LSU packet is assumed to contain newer information than the LSA in the router's topology database.

5. Which of the following is an advantage of having a designated router and a backup designated router? (Choose all that apply.)

    a. Routers need to form adjacencies only with the DR and the BDR, instead of all other routers on a network segment.

    b. The BDR can take over for any router in case of failure.

    c. The DR and the BDR have the fastest CPUs on the network.

    d. The DR makes sure all routers on the segment have identical link-state databases.

6. You just added a new router with the highest priority possible, 255, to an existing Ethernet segment. None of the other routers have priorities above 100. When will it become the designated router?

   a. immediately

   b. after the election caused by the failure of the current DR

   c. only after the current DR fails, followed by the failure of the next DR

   d. after the election caused by the failure of the current BDR

7. What is the advantage of the BDR in the fast convergence of a network?

   a. There isn't one.

   b. Without a BDR, when the DR fails its replacement must form adjacencies with all neighboring routers before flooding the network with updated LSUs.

   c. The BDR shares some of the load of flooding the network with the DR.

   d. Because of the BDR, the DR can send out hello packets twice as fast.

8. At what state in the adjacency process do two routers have complete knowledge of the OSPF area?

   a. Loading state

   b. Routing state

   c. Exchange state

   d. Full state

9. What is the SPF holdtime timer designed to prevent from happening?

   a. By delaying the time between when a router receives a LSU and when it begins flooding, this timer prevents unnecessary flooding.

   b. By delaying the time between SPF calculations, this timer prevents a router from recalculating its routing table with incomplete information.

   c. By delaying the time between when a router receives a LSU and when it begins flooding, this timer prevents a router from recalculating its routing table with incomplete information.

   d. By delaying the time between SPF calculations, this timer prevents a router from continuously recalculating its routing table because of route flapping.

10. What does a router do with a LSA when the LS Aging timer reaches 30 minutes?

   a. It runs through the SPF calculation and recalculates its routing table.

   b. It floods the network with a LSU containing the LSA in order to refresh it.

   c. It discards the LSA from its topology database.

   d. It performs checksumming to verify that the LSA is not corrupt.

11. Which of the following statements is true about the flooding process? (Choose all that apply.)

    a. The DR floods the entire OSPF area with LSUs after a network change.

    b. The DR floods its attached network with LSUs after a network change, and each router receiving a LSU sends it to the DR (if present) on any attached networks, or floods it itself if there is no DR.

    c. The DR and the BDR share the flooding of their attached network after a network change, and each router receiving a LSU sends it to the DR (if present) on any attached networks, or floods it itself if there is no DR.

    d. The BDR starts a timer when it receives a LSU and makes sure the DR begins flooding before the timer expires.

12. A router begins the SPF calculation and rebuilds its routing table immediately after receiving a LSU with a network change. True or false?

13. In which of the following network topologies is a DR and BDR elected? (Choose all that apply.)

    a. Point-to-point

    b. Broadcast multiaccess

    c. NBMA in broadcast mode

    d. NBMA in point-to-multipoint mode

14. Why must neighboring routers be manually configured in some NBMA modes?

    a. Only two routers are possible on any NBMA segment.

    b. OSPF requires all neighbors to be manually configured.

    c. NBMA media doesn't support broadcasts or multicasts.

    d. This was designed to prevent unwanted discovery of neighboring routers.

15. Which is the most expensive NBMA topology?

    a. star topology

    b. hub-and-spoke topology

    c. partial mesh topology

    d. full mesh topology

16. Why can't adjacencies to all routers by the DR and BDR be guaranteed on partial mesh NBMA networks?

    a. Each spoke router is connected only to the hub router.

    b. Broadcasts aren't supported on NBMA networks.

    c. Not all routers have physical connectivity to each other, and routers in OSPF must have physical connectivity with each other in order to form adjacencies.

    d. Each router must have neighbors manually configured.

17. What are some of the potential problems in a frame relay network in NBMA mode if a PVC goes down on a partial mesh network? (Choose all that apply.)

    a. One or more routers may become unreachable for some routers, but not for all.

    b. The BDR and the DR may not be able to form or maintain adjacencies with one or more routers.

    c. The DR and BDR must re-establish adjacencies with all routers.

    d. None since the BDR will take over for any router on the network.

18. Which of the following is true about point-to-point mode in a NBMA topology? (Choose all that apply.)

    a. Each point-to-point subinterface must be on its own subnet.

    b. Point-to-point mode is a Cisco extension to OSPF.

    c. Point-to-point mode is ideal for a fully meshed topology.

    d. The fuller the mesh between sites, the more configuration of subinterfaces and IP addresses is required.

19. When activating OSPF with the router **ospf process-id** command, the process ID must be the same throughout the entire OSPF network. True or false?

20. Assuming each of the following interface/IP address combinations is on the same router, which would be selected as the router ID?

    a. Ethernet 0: 192.168.254.1

    b. Serial 0: 192.168.100.1

    c. Loopback 0: 192.168.1.2

    d. Loopback 1: 192.168.2.1

21. Which of the following networks would be matched by the following configuration statements (and hence activated for OSPF)? (Choose all that apply.)

    Detroit(config)#router ospf 89
    Detroit(config-router)#network 192.168.0.0 0.0.127.255 area 0

    a. 192.168.1.16/28

    b. 192.168.254.0/24

    c. 192.168.125.0/24

    d. 192.170.1.0/24

22. You discovered that OSPF has actually been load balancing through some of your 100 Mbps Fast Ethernet links and 1000 Mbps Gigabit Ethernet links. What can you do to correct this? (Choose all that apply.)

    a. Change the reference bandwidth on the routers with the Gigabit Ethernet links.

    b. Manually change the cost on all ends of each of the Gigabit Ethernet links to one.

    c. Change the reference bandwidth on all routers.

    d. Manually change the cost on all ends of the Fast Ethernet links to two or higher.

23. While trying to troubleshoot a problem on an OSPF network, you discover that you cannot ping the router ID of any of the routers on the network—even after the network is working normally. Why might this be normal?

   a. Since the router ID isn't an IP address, you can't ping it.

   b. The routers are using the addresses of loopback interfaces as their router IDs, and these interfaces aren't being advertised by OSPF.

   c. The routers are using the addresses of interfaces that aren't up for their router IDs.

   d. The routers are using IP unnumbered interfaces to get their IP addresses.

24. Which commands will show you which neighbors are associated with an interface? (Choose all that apply.)

   a. show ip route

   b. show ip ospf interface

   c. show ip ospf

   d. show ip ospf neighbor

25. Two neighboring routers aren't becoming neighbors even though OSPF is running on both routers and activated on both interfaces. How can you go about trying to identify the cause of the problem? (Choose all that apply.)

   a. Attempt to ping across the link.

   b. Run the **show ip ospf interface** command on both routers and look for mismatched parameters.

   c. Run the **debug ip ospf adj** command and look for error messages.

   d. Run the **show ip route ospf** command to see if the route is properly advertised.

26. Running the **show processes cpu** command on all the routers on your network running OSPF shows that CPU use on each is extremely high almost all the time. Since the problem seems to be affecting all routers, you think it's related to OSPF. What might you do to troubleshoot the problem? (Choose all that apply.)

   a. Run the **debug ip ospf event** command to see what sort of OSPF events are happening.

   b. Run the **show ip ospf interface** command to look for excessive hello packets.

   c. Run the **show ip protocols** command to make sure OSPF is the only routing protocol running on each router.

   d. Run **show ip ospf** to see how often the SPF calculation is running, and what the SPF holdtime and delay timers are.

27. Which of the following will make a router run the SPF calculation and rebuild its routing table? (Choose all that apply.)

    a. receiving a LSU containing a LSA about a new network

    b. running the **clear ip route** * command

    c. running the **auto-cost reference-bandwidth** command

    d. a LSU containing a LSA older that the one already in the router's database

CASE PROJECTS

Case 1

You are brought in by Dalton Advertising to help with network problems. Dalton Advertising is a large firm with offices in New York and Los Angeles; the previous network administrator was also the chief software developer and didn't devote a lot time to maintaining the network before he left six months ago. The network is running RIP. Users are having all kinds of problems accessing file servers on either end of a T-1 line (1.544 Mbps) connecting the two offices; accessing files over the line is extremely slow. Additionally, in the New York office, the wiring is suspect and can cause two or three brief outages a day. After each outage, many users on the network are unable to access network resources for up to 20 minutes after the routers and servers come back up again. Why do you think the T-1 appears to be so slow? What sort of information do you need? Why can't users access network servers for so long after an outage? What sort of benefits might you expect after implementing OSPF for Dalton Advertising?

Case 2

You are hired as network administrator for Galleon Brokerage, Inc. at its New York headquarters. Galleon has remote offices all over the country and in Hong Kong, London, and Buenos Aires, each of which has at least one frame relay network in a partial mesh (shown in Figure 3-17); however, the frame relay network was running SNA traffic for an obsolete legacy application, and none of the IP networks were ever connected. Your supervisor, the CIO, is under pressure to connect each and every office as seamlessly as possible, and integrate them into the sizeable OSPF network at the New York office. However, she is also under pressure to do it as cheaply as possible. Your job is to evaluate the current network, come up with a plan, and choose the network topology. Which modes can you use to run OSPF on this network? The CIO is partial to NBMA mode. How many links must you add to create a full mesh? If you run this network in NBMA mode as a partial mesh, which routers can you choose as the DR and the BDR? How can you ensure that these routers are selected? Do you have to add frame relay circuits in order to get this working properly? What must you do to configure it in point-to-multipoint mode instead?

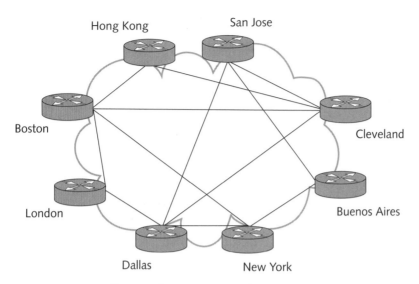

Figure 3-17   Galleon Brokerage's network

Case 3

You are brought in as a consultant for the Krumbly Cereal Company in Richmond, Virginia, which has a multi-vendor network consisting of approximately 500 routers. The network manager, Tom Brown, has run OSPF on the network for a couple of years now. Recently, however, he received numerous user complaints about the network response times. His management is particularly upset because Tom also added several Gigabit Ethernet links, which should have alleviated some of the problems the network had with congestion at key points. However, Tom discovered through use of the traceroute command that packets don't appear to be using the Gigabit Ethernet links as much as they should, while some of the Fast Ethernet links are saturated. Tom also has high bills for WAN links from Richmond to the Denver and Battle Creek, Michigan offices, as well as on the WAN link from Denver to Battle Creek. He thinks that some of the Richmond WAN traffic for Denver was routed through to Battle Creek first, instead of going through directly to Denver. Management wants Tom to switch back to RIP since they didn't have these sorts of problems when the network ran RIP. Tom wants you to solve his problem with path selection, and help him make the case to management to stick with OSPF. What sort of information do you need to gather to find out what's happening with path selection on the network? What sorts of steps might you take in order to fix the problems?

Case 4

You are brought in as a consultant to help a large department store design and build a network to connect each of its 1,250 stores to redundant data centers at its corporate headquarters in Church Falls, Virginia, and its office in Annapolis, Maryland. Each store needs access to inventory, accounting, personnel, and payroll systems in both data centers for load balancing and failover. The CIO of the department store already decided to use a frame relay network to connect each store to the two data centers, but his staff doesn't have the skills necessary to design the actual network. Your job is to present the CIO with options for building the network in partial and full mesh topologies (since each store will be connected to the two data centers, this network can't be in a star topology). For each topology, make sure to calculate the number of PVCs you need, which will in large part determine the monthly cost of the network. The CIO knows a full mesh network will be expensive, but the president of the company wants to connect all stores so they can work more closely together. Estimate the cost of each frame relay PVC at $100 each. Additionally, come up with a sample configuration for each router, and a rough plan for allocating IP addresses to the stores and to the Annapolis and Falls Church offices. Assume that each remote store will need no more than 10 IP addresses, each office will need no more than 2000 IP addresses, and use a private IP address block, such as 10.0.0.0/8.

Case 5

Let's suppose that you are brought in as the new network administrator to help rapidly expanding Adler Auto Parts convert its network to OSPF. In addition to its headquarters in Detroit, Adler has sales offices in Auburn Hills, Stuttgart, Tokyo, Osaka, and Seoul, which are connected by a frame relay in a full mesh topology. The **committed information rate (CIR)**, or the minimum guaranteed transfer rate, of the PVC from Detroit to Auburn Hills is 1.544 Mbps. The CIR of a link is roughly equivalent to its bandwidth (although the actual bandwidth can be just above that). Except for the PVC in Tokyo (128 Kbps), the other permanent virtual circuits on the frame relay network have CIRs of 64 Kbps. According to your supervisor, the CIO, Adler Auto Parts put together the frame relay network in order to take better advantage of the inventory system, which can run either from the main server at the Auburn Hills data center, or from servers at any of the remote offices. The inventory system is saving the company so much money, in fact, that it pays for the full mesh topology several times over. Figure 3-18 shows the Adler Auto Parts network.

3

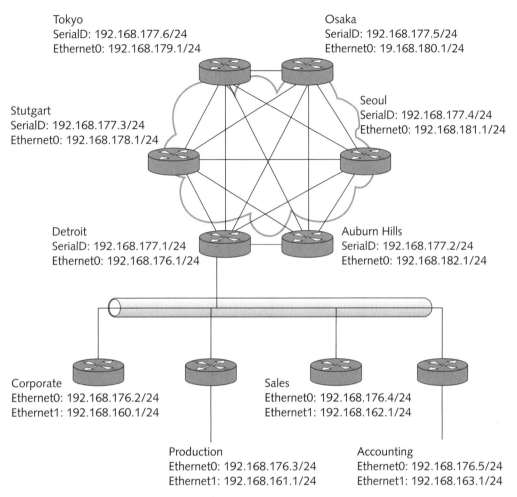

Tokyo
SerialD: 192.168.177.6/24
Ethernet0: 192.168.179.1/24

Osaka
SerialD: 192.168.177.5/24
Ethernet0: 19.168.180.1/24

Seoul
SerialD: 192.168.177.4/24
Ethernet0: 192.168.181.1/24

Stutgart
SerialD: 192.168.177.3/24
Ethernet0: 192.168.178.1/24

Detroit
SerialD: 192.168.177.1/24
Ethernet0: 192.168.176.1/24

Auburn Hills
SerialD: 192.168.177.2/24
Ethernet0: 192.168.182.1/24

Corporate
Ethernet0: 192.168.176.2/24
Ethernet1: 192.168.160.1/24

Sales
Ethernet0: 192.168.176.4/24
Ethernet1: 192.168.162.1/24

Production
Ethernet0: 192.168.176.3/24
Ethernet1: 192.168.161.1/24

Accounting
Ethernet0: 192.168.176.5/24
Ethernet1: 192.168.163.1/24

Figure 3-18   Alder Auto Parts' network

You must configure each router on the network. In order to successfully switch over to OSPF, you must:

❐ Configure the frame relay network in NBMA mode so that other vendors' equipment will be supported when Adler Auto Parts adds its factories to the frame relay network later in the year.

❐ Make sure that on the frame relay network the Detroit router is selected as the DR and the Auburn Hills router is selected as the BDR.

❐ Ensure that the bandwidth of each frame relay link is configured properly (treat the CIR of each link as the bandwidth).

❐ Ensure that the Detroit router cannot be selected as the DR or BDR on the Ethernet network it shares with the Corporate, Sales, Production, and Accounting routers.

4

OSPF IN MULTIPLE AREAS

After reading this chapter and completing the exercises you will be able to:

♦ Explain the benefits of using multiple areas on an OSPF network

♦ Design an OSPF network using multiple areas

♦ Configure an OSPF network with multiple areas

♦ Use and configure route summarization between OSPF areas

♦ Troubleshoot an OSPF network with multiple areas

In the last chapter, you learned how Open Shortest Path First (OSPF) operates, and how to configure OSPF in a single area. Because an OSPF network in a single area will eventually have scalability problems as the network grows, you may need to divide your network into several different areas. This chapter will show you how to use multiple OSPF areas to create a reliable, available, and scalable network.

USING MULTIPLE OSPF AREAS

Inside each individual area, OSPF works much the way you learned in Chapter 3. Each OSPF area is its own separate domain, with its own link-state database. Each router in an area has the same link-state database and routes to the same destinations in its routing table as all the other routers in the area. Allowing you to divide an Autonomous System into multiple areas is how OSPF supports hierarchical routing.

Even though OSPF allows you to create much more scalable networks than distance vector protocols like RIP, OSPF begins to have scalability problems as you increase the size of your network while using only one area. In order to avoid this, OSPF was designed to support the use of multiple areas within an Autonomous System.

Scalability Problems in Large OSPF Areas

Scalability problems in large OSPF areas include:

- Large routing tables. As the size of an OSPF area increases, the number of routes in each router's routing table can only increase. Since OSPF routers can load balance between several different paths with the same cost, the number of routes in an OSPF area will be larger than the number of networks in the area because there may be multiple paths to many destinations. Large routing tables present several problems. Routers must spend more time looking up routes and use more memory to store them.

- Large topology databases. Each router must store the complete topology of the area inside its topology database. As the size of an area grows, this requires more and more memory.

- Frequent recalculation of the Shortest Path First (SPF) algorithm. Because all the routers in an OSPF area must do the SPF calculation and rebuild their routing tables every time a network change occurs, every router in an area is affected by every network change. As the area grows, the odds that some section of the network will change also increase. Even one unstable link can cause the entire area to run through the SPF calculation.

- Slow synchronization. OSPF operates under the assumption that each router in an area has complete knowledge of the area's topology. However, routers in the far corners of an OSPF area may not receive link-state updates (LSUs) for network changes as quickly as other routers, especially if these routers are separated by a slow link. In this situation, the remote routers may recalculate their routing tables without having up-to-date information about the rest of the network. The problem should be corrected when the remote routers receive the new LSUs and recalculate their routing delays after the SPF holdtime timer expires, but in addition to an extra SPF calculation, they may experience reachability problems with at least some portion of the area in the meantime.

Advantages of Using Multiple Areas

Advantages of using multiple OSPF areas within an Autonomous System include:

- Smaller routing tables. While each router in an OSPF area must know the complete topology of its own area, it doesn't need to know everything about the topology of other areas (although routers in an area must at least have a default route or summarized routes to other areas). As a result, you can summarize routing information between areas and reduce the size of your routing tables.

- Less frequent SPF recalculations. Depending on network topology, network changes in one area may not need to be flooded to routers in other areas. As a result, routers in other areas may not need to recalculate their routing tables.

- Less routing update overhead. Since you can summarize routing information between areas, routers can advertise routers between areas with a handful of summary LSAs instead of LSAs for every network within each area. This reduces the amount of LSUs that must be sent during flooding.

- Faster synchronization. Routers in smaller areas are less likely than routers in large areas to have problems receiving LSUs on time. You can also design your areas to minimize or prevent this problem.

In order to use OSPF in multiple areas, you should know how to connect OSPF areas, and how to route between OSPF areas.

Connecting OSPF Areas

In order to connect two OSPF areas, you just need a router with at least one interface in both areas. With multiple OSPF areas, OSPF uses several different types of routers and areas.

Types of Routers

Types of OSPF routers include:

- **Internal routers.** These include any router that has all of its interfaces within the same area. Every internal router within the same area has identical link-state databases.

- **Backbone routers.** Backbone routers have at least one interface connected to the **backbone area**, Area 0. Whenever an area connects to another area, it must go through the backbone area. Backbone routers with all of their interfaces within Area 0 are also internal routers.

- **Area Border Routers (ABRs).** An ABR has interfaces connected to multiple areas. These routers are the only connection points between areas. In order for traffic to travel between areas, it must go through an ABR. In order to perform this role, an ABR must have complete link-state databases for each connected area. An ABR can summarize routing information for each of its connected areas and distribute it within the backbone area. Backbone ABRs will in turn pass the summarized routing information to all of their connected areas. Each area may have as many ABRs as necessary.

- **Autonomous System Border Routers (ASBRs)**. Every ASBR is connected to another Autonomous System, such as a vendor's Autonomous System or a service provider's Autonomous System. For example, an ASBR may have one or more interfaces connected to an OSPF area, and one interface connected to an Internet Service Provider's Autonomous System, which in turn connects the OSPF Autonomous System with the Internet. ASBRs can **redistribute** or import routing information from external Autonomous Systems.

A router may simultaneously be several different types of router. For example, the Cleveland router in Figure 4-1 has two interfaces in Area 0, one interface in Area 2, and one interface connected to an Internet Service Provider. As a result, it is a backbone router because of its connection to Area 0, an ABR because of its connections to Area 0 and Area 2, and an ASBR because it connects the OSPF Autonomous System with the Internet Service Provider's Autonomous System.

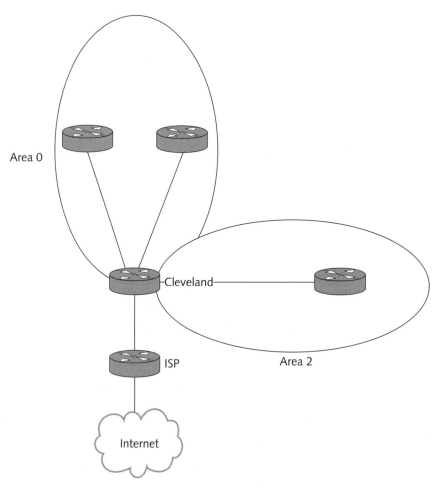

Figure 4-1   Example of a router with more than one type

As a router fulfills more roles in an OSPF Autonomous System, however, you must keep in mind the cost of performing each function. The Cleveland router in Figure 4-1, for example, must maintain complete topology databases for both Area 0 and Area 2. Depending on the type of networks attached to its interfaces, it must form adjacencies and exchange its topology databases with either the neighboring routers or the DR and BDR for those networks. It may also have to be the DR or BDR on some of those networks. Finally, it may be required to run another routing protocol to exchange routing information with the Internet Service Provider's router (although often this can be done with a static route).

4

An interface may be in only one area at a time.

The Backbone Area

The backbone area is the most important area in any OSPF Autonomous System. The backbone is almost always Area 0. It behaves just like a **standard area** does (discussed in Chapter 3). However, all other areas must connect to it in order to exchange routing information. Any packets sent between areas must also go through the backbone area. As a result, any OSPF network design should take special care to ensure that the backbone area remains stable and reachable.

If you have only one area in an Autonomous System, by definition, this area is the backbone area. You can configure it as something other than Area 0. However, this is not recommended since it may make adding other areas to the Autonomous System difficult.

Other Types of Areas

Besides the backbone, other types of areas are classified by how they interact with other areas. Other types of areas include:

- **Standard area**. A standard area, which you learned about in Chapter 3, can accept link updates and route summaries from within and from external areas, and it can accept external routes from an ASBR.

- **Stub area**. A stub area does not accept routing information from ASBRs about routes to destinations outside the Autonomous System. This does not mean that routers or other devices in stub areas can't reach external destinations. Stub areas instead use a **default route** to reach them. A default route is usually described as a route to 0.0.0.0 or 0.0.0.0/0, and is taken only when no other route matches a packet's destination address.

- **Totally stubby area**. In addition to not accepting external routes, a totally stubby area will refuse summary routes from other areas. If a router in a totally stubby area needs to send a packet to any destination outside the area, it uses a default route. This is a Cisco proprietary extension to the OSPF protocol.

- **Not-so-stubby area (NSSA).** This type of area is defined in RFC 1587 and supported beginning with Cisco IOS 11.2. A NSSA will accept limited information about external routes. Like other stub areas, NSSAs don't accept routing information from ASBRs. However, unlike other stub areas, they can connect to external Autonomous Systems. NSSAs can also send this information to ASBRs. While a NSSA will accept routing information from attached Autonomous Systems, it will not accept information about external routes from ASBRs outside the NSSA. NSSAs are useful when you need to connect a stub area to another Autonomous System. This may be necessary to connect a stub area to a small customer network, or a network with legacy equipment running a routing protocol, such as RIP. The NSSA option was designed with Internet Service Providers in mind. Figure 4-2 shows an example of an OSPF network with NSSAs (Areas 8 and 9 are NSSAs redistributing routes for two external customers).

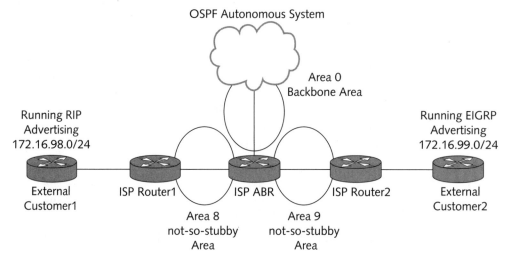

Figure 4-2   Example of a not-so-stubby Area

Routing Between Areas

While each internal router behaves much the same as you learned in Chapter 3, routing between multiple areas adds some additional complexity to OSPF. In order to see how this works, you must start by learning about the different types of LSAs used to describe the topology of a network.

Types of LSAs

Because all OSPF routers must know the complete topology of each connected area, OSPF uses several different types of LSAs to describe the topology of a network. Types of LSAs include:

- **Router link entry LSAs** (LSA type 1). Every router generates router LSAs, which describe the state of the router's links to an attached area. These LSAs are flooded only to the areas for which they were generated.

- **Network link entry LSAs** (LSA type 2). Designated routers generate these on multiaccess networks. They describe the routers attached to a network. These are flooded only to the area containing the network they describe.

- **Summary link entry LSAs** (LSA types 3 and 4). Summary LSAs describe routes to inter-area destinations, sent by ABRs. The key difference in type 3 and type 4 LSAs is the type of router to which they're flooded. ABRs send type 3 LSAs to other ABRs in the backbone area and type 4 LSAs to ASBRs. These LSAs may or may not contain summarized information. This is the case, for instance, if route summarization is not configured on an ABR.

- **Autonomous System external link entry LSAs** (type 5). An ASBR uses these to describe routes to destinations outside the OSPF Autonomous System. They're flooded throughout the Autonomous System, with a few exceptions, which you'll learn about a little later in the chapter.

- **NSSA Autonomous System external link entry LSAs** (type 7). These LSAs are flooded within a NSSA to describe the external routes learned by the NSSA. If any of these routes are advertised to other areas, they will be converted into type 5 LSAs at the ABR, and flooded to the backbone.

Table 4-1 summarizes the types of LSAs. Type 6 LSAs are not listed because they are not supported by Cisco routers.

Table 4-1   Types of LSAs

LSA Type	LSA Name	Originated By	Areas Flooded To	Description
1	Router LSA	All routers	Area where generated	Describes the states of a router's link to a particular area
2	Network LSA	Designated routers only	Area where generated	Describes the routers attached to a particular broadcast multiaccess network
3	Summary LSA	ABRs only	ABRs in the backbone area	Describes the links between an ABR and internal routers in another area

Table 4-1   Types of LSAs (continued)

LSA Type	LSA Name	Originated By	Areas Flooded To	Description
4	Summary LSA	ABRs only	Backbone area, but not totally stubby areas	Describes links to ASBRs
5	Autonomous System external LSA	ASBRs only	The entire OSPF Autonomous System, excluding stub, totally stubby and not-so-stubby areas	Describes routes to destinations outside the OSPF Autonomous System
7	Not-so-stubby area (NSSA) Autonomous System external LSA	ASBRs within a not-so-stubby area	The entire not-so-stubby area; some of these LSAs are converted into type 5 LSAs and flooded into the backbone	Describes routes to destinations outside the OSPF Autonomous System

Cost of Inter-Area and External Routes

For routes between areas or to external destinations, routers must calculate the cost of the route differently than they do for an intra-area route. For each inter-area route, Cisco routers add the cost of the inter-area route in the summary with the smallest cost and the cost of the ABR's link to the backbone area. If an ABR has an inter-area route with a cost of 64 in the summary updates it receives, and the cost of its link to the backbone is 10, the total cost of the summary route is 74. The routes in an ABR's routing table already include this calculation in the total cost.

The cost of an external route, however, depends on the configuration of the ASBR. An ASBR may be configured to generate one of two types of external routes, which is controlled with **bit E** in a type 5 LSA. Bit E is a field in the LSA consisting of a single bit. The two types of external routes include:

- Type 1 (or E1). If bit E in an AS external LSA isn't set (or is equal to zero), then the metric for the route described with this LSA is calculated by adding the cost necessary to leave the Autonomous System to the cost of crossing each individual link along the way.

- Type 2 (or E2). If bit E is set (equal to one), then the metric of the route advertised in this LSA will include only the external cost, no matter what path it takes to reach the external route. This is the default.

In general, Cisco routers will select type 2 routes over type 1 routes because of their lower cost, unless two routes with the same cost exist (in which case they will load balance over the paths). Type 2 routes are useful when you have only a single ASBR advertising routes to destinations outside your Autonomous System, while type 1 routes make more sense if you have multiple ASBRs advertising external routes.

Routes Between Multiple Areas

In general, the path a packet takes in an OSPF Autonomous System depends on whether or not the destination is within a single area. If a packet's destination is within the same area as its source, then the packet is passed from internal router to internal router until it reaches its destination.

If a packet's destination is outside the area in which it originates, it first goes to an ABR in its own area. The ABR sends the packet through the backbone area to an ABR in the same area as the destination network. This ABR then forwards the packet from internal router to internal router until it reaches its destination.

Since an OSPF Autonomous System may include a wide variety of types of routes (intra-area, inter-area, and external types 1 and 2, as shown in Table 4-2), RFC 2328 indicates that a router should prefer routes generated locally over routes generated externally or in other areas. When forwarding a packet, routers prefer to first use routes generated within the same area as the source network, followed by inter-area routers, followed by external type 1 routes, and then external type 2 routes.

Table 4-2   OSPF Autonomous System routes

Type of Route	Preference
Internal routes (destination network is in the same area as the source)	Most preferred
Inter-area routes	
External type 1 routes	
External type 2 routes	Least preferred

Calculating Routing Tables and Flooding in Multiple Areas

In order for ABRs to learn about routes and network changes in other areas, each ABR must generate LSAs for the areas attached to its interfaces, and flood them to other ABRs. On an ABR, flooding occurs as follows:

1. The router completes all intra-area processing for all attached areas, as described in Chapter 3. All routers in each area receive LSUs describing the change. Inside each area, each router has identical link-state databases. They also calculate their routing tables for each area.

2. The router generates new summary LSAs for any attached areas, and looks at summary LSAs from other areas. Unless you configure route summarization (which you'll learn about later in the chapter), an ABR sends summary LSAs for each network in the area. In a good area design, you can reduce the number of summary LSAs generated with route summarization.

3. Summary LSAs for an area are sent in one or more LSU packets out of all ABR interfaces attached to other areas. However, the ABR will not send summary LSAs to interfaces attached to totally stubby areas, nor will it send summary routes to interfaces attached to neighbors below the Exchange state. The ABR

will also not send summary LSAs to stub, totally stubby, or not-so-stubby areas if they contain type 5 LSAs with information about external routes.

4. Any summary LSAs received by an ABR or an ASBR are added to its link-state database and flooded to local areas. Internal routers in those areas will add them to their link-state databases.

Figure 4-3 shows an example of an Autonomous System divided into multiple OSPF areas. Suppose an interface attached to Router7 in Figure 4-3, an internal router in Area 2, failed. This event would generate the initial flooding within Area 2, as described in Step 1. The ABR would generate new summary LSAs for Area 2, as described in Step 2, and it would flood them out its interface attached to Area 0, as described in Step 3. After the ABR recalculates the routing table for Area 2 (as in Step 1), it generates new summary LSAs and floods them to the interface connected to Area 0, the backbone area, and the interface connected to Area 3, a standard area. It does not flood them through the interface connected to Area 1 since totally stubby areas do not accept any outside routing information.

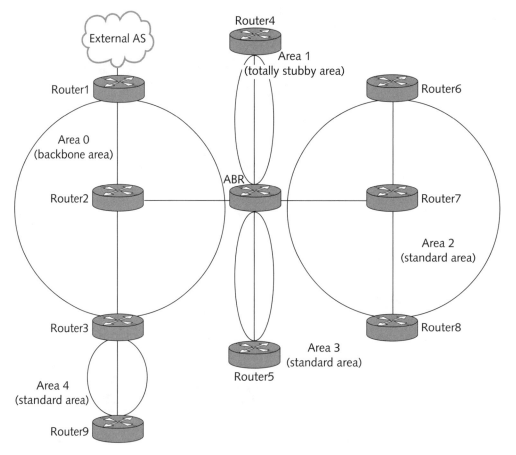

Figure 4-3   Flooding in multiple areas

When Router3 receives the new summary LSAs, since it's also an ABR, it will flood them out its interface attached to Area 4, as described in Step 4. Router1, an ASBR, will redistribute this information to the external AS (assuming that it is redistributing routing information for the external AS instead of using a default route).

After all routers eligible to receive the new summary LSAs receive them (all routers except those internal to the totally stubby area), they recalculate their routing tables as follows:

1. A router begins by calculating intra-area routes (advertised with type 1 and 2 LSAs), and adding the routes with the lowest costs into its routing table.

2. A router then uses type 3 and 4 LSAs to calculate intra-area routes. As you learned above, a router prefers any route within the area to any external route. Routers in totally stubby areas skip this step.

3. All routers calculate external routes advertised with type 5 LSAs. Routers in stub, totally stubby, or not-so-stubby areas skip this step.

Virtual Links

The fact that each area in an OSPF Autonomous System must be connected to the backbone area limits how you can add areas. Any area not connected to the backbone is unable to send or receive routing information from other areas, and none of the routers in the new area is able to communicate with routers in other areas.

To get around this obstacle, OSPF uses virtual links. A **virtual link** is a logical link used to connect an area to the backbone when it doesn't have an interface physically connected to the backbone. A virtual link must be between two ABRs connected via a common area (sometimes called the **transit area**), and one ABR must have an interface attached to the backbone.

Figure 4-4 shows an example of a virtual link used to connect an area to the backbone. The SanJose router doesn't have a physical connection to the backbone area, but the SanDiego router does. Without the virtual link connecting San Jose to San Diego, Area 2 would have no connection to the backbone, and routers and hosts in Area 2 would be unable to connect to other routers.

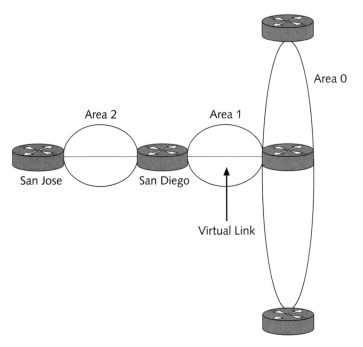

Figure 4-4   Adding an area with a virtual link

Virtual links have three basic purposes:

- Connecting areas to the backbone when they don't have an ABR with an interface in the backbone area

- Connecting the backbone itself in situations where it has been partitioned

- Adding a redundant connection to the backbone to prevent the failure of a single link, or the backbone area itself, from partitioning an area from the backbone

A backbone area can be partitioned by an outage. Or, it can be created by the merger of two existing networks. See Figure 4-5 for an example of a virtual link used to connect a discontiguous backbone. A better long-term solution is usually to redesign the backbone area so that a virtual link isn't necessary to connect all the routers in a backbone. However, a virtual link will work as a short-term solution. It is also unlikely to cause outages, as modifying the backbone area might, without sufficient planning.

Since a virtual link is really a logical link, OSPF must handle the link differently than it handles any other link. Since a virtual link can logically connect two routers across an area, a router must make sure to use the true next hop in calculating the cost of its routes, rather than the interface on the ABR attached to the virtual link. Additionally, since a virtual link crosses an area instead of a physical link, the IP addresses of the interfaces attached to each end of the virtual link won't be on the same subnet. So, OSPF treats a virtual link as if both ends of the link are unnumbered interfaces.

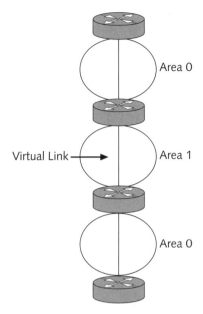

Virtual Link

Figure 4-5   Connecting a discontiguous backbone with a virtual link

DESIGNING AREAS

In designing an area, you must consider several factors. You should design areas on your network to minimize the size of the routing tables and frequency of SPF calculations in the area, as well as the CPU utilization on any one router. Each of your areas must also be contiguous. None of the routers in an area should be isolated from the rest of the area. As you learned earlier, if a network outage forces a router interface to be temporarily isolated from the rest of an area, you will need to use a virtual link to attach it to its area, or move it to another area.

Some of the factors involved in designing OSPF areas include:

- The size of an area, to keep link-state databases small
- The number of neighbors each router has, in order to reduce the stress on any one router
- Problem isolation, by the isolation of unstable links
- The restriction of routing information, to reduce routing information from outside an area
- Stable backbone design, in order to maximize stability in the entire Autonomous System
- Addressing areas, to maximize your ability to summarize routes

Size of an Area

The size of an area affects the number of routes in the routing table, as well as the frequency of SPF calculations inside the area. Historically, Cisco recommended no more than 50 routers inside any one area. However, Cisco somewhat relaxed this recommendation. Areas on your network may be larger or smaller, depending on the network topology and the memory and processors in your routers. On a stable network connected with high-speed links, for instance, you may have no problem expanding the size of your areas to 100 routers, and possibly more.

However, if your network contains several slow, unstable WAN links, you may need to partition your network into smaller areas. Since storing the link-state database and doing the SPF calculation can be CPU- and memory-intensive, the amount of memory and the speed of the CPUs in your routers may also play a factor in area design. If your network consists mostly of newer routers with faster CPUs and more memory, expanding the size of your areas may work well.

At the same time, Cisco also recommends that an ABR have interfaces in no more than three areas. For each area attached to an ABR's interfaces, the ABR must maintain link-state databases. However, the maximum number of areas in which a router has ABR interfaces will depend on the processor speed and the amount of memory in your ABRs, as well as the size of the areas attached to each interface. While you may be able to safely increase the number of areas attached to a particular ABR, keep in mind that an overloaded ABR may be a source of instability if it cannot perform the SPF calculation as quickly as other routers in an area. If you can't avoid ABRs with more than three attached areas, you should carefully monitor them.

Number of Neighbors Per Router

Another factor that will influence the performance of routers on an OSPF network is the number of neighbors. A router must exchange hello packets with its neighbors, and link-state databases with those neighbors with which it forms adjacencies. Cisco recommends that a router have no more than 60 neighbors, although this may vary depending on the stability of your network, and the CPU speed and memory of your routers. Since a DR or BDR forms adjacencies with all the routers on a network, limiting the number of networks where a router is DR or BDR may also be wise.

Isolating Potential Network Problems

One of the great advantages of the hierarchical design that OSPF allows you to use is that you can keep potential network problems from affecting other areas of the network. With OSPF, you can do this easily by placing potentially unstable routers and links in their own areas.

For example, route flapping on WAN links is a common cause of instability on OSPF networks. In extreme cases, a link may go down several times a minute, requiring a SPF calculation each time. In a large area, requiring every router to recalculate its routing table every time a WAN link flaps generally doesn't make a lot of sense.

In Figure 4-6, you can see an example of how you might use areas to isolate your WAN links. The WAN links are kept in Areas 1, 2, and 3, isolated from the backbone. A summary LSA flooded into the backbone can still cause it to recalculate its routing table. However, you can stop this by carefully summarizing the routes allowed into the backbone. Hiding the details of the routes inside the areas containing the WAN links can prevent an ABR from generating a different summary LSA for those areas when it recalculates its routing tables after a WAN link goes down. If the summary LSA stays the same, the backbone area routers don't need to recalculate their routing tables.

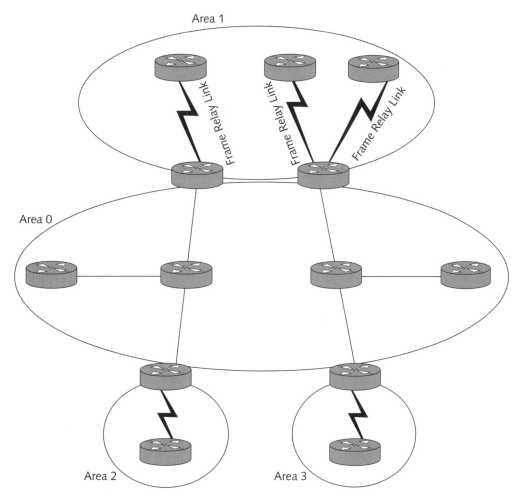

Figure 4-6   Isolating WAN segments with areas

Restricting Routing Information From an Area

Restricting the routing information coming into an area has several benefits. First, it reduces routing table size in an area, as well as the amount of flooding traffic after a topology change. Second, it aids stability by insulating the routers inside the area.

One way you can restrict routing information into an area is by configuring it as a stub area, a totally stubby area, or a not-so-stubby area. In either case, routing inside the area is handled as it normally is with OSPF, while routes coming from outside the area are restricted. All three types of stub areas reject type 5 LSAs, meaning that they won't receive any information about routes outside the Autonomous System (with the exception of not-so-stubby areas, which only receive limited information about connected external networks). Instead, routers inside stub areas use a default route to exit the area. With a default route, any packet whose destination network isn't in the routing table is matched. The packet is forwarded to a router that does have that network in its routing table.

Selecting a Stub Area

Stub areas work very well for branch offices, or in hub-and-spoke topologies, where the stub area is likely to have only one exit point. In a hub-and-spoke topology, the spokes generally don't need to know anything about the rest of the network, except how to get to the hub. Since an ABR is likely to be advertising a default route, a router still chooses the default route even though choosing a path through another ABR (if present) might result in a better path. In general, if suboptimal path selection is acceptable in an area, then it is a good candidate for a stub area.

Additionally, stub areas can't be either the backbone area or a transit area for a virtual link. Using a stub area as the backbone area completely defeats the purpose of a stub area since OSPF uses the backbone area as a place to accumulate routing information about the whole Autonomous System. A virtual link also requires the injection of additional routing information into an area. Additionally, ASBRs within a stub network make little sense since an ASBR injects external routes into an area. Stub areas do not accept external routes (with the exception of the limited external routing information generated by NSSAs).

Totally Stubby Areas

In addition to rejecting external routes, totally stubby areas also reject intra-area routes. Since totally stubby areas rely completely on default routes to reach any destination outside the totally stubby area, use of totally stubby areas eliminates every route outside the area but one, which can significantly reduce the size of routing tables. If an area consists entirely of Cisco routers, and the area has a single exit point, you should use totally stubby areas over stub areas because they will allow you to have smaller routing tables. However, since totally stubby areas are proprietary to Cisco, you must use a stub area if you have routers from multiple vendors.

Not-so-stubby Areas

While stub areas reject external routing information, in some situations this requirement is too restrictive, and you may find it helpful to use a not-so-stubby area. The first situation where a NSSA may be useful is for a service provider. As a service provider, your network may have many small customer networks attached. Since most of these have only one exit point, making the portion of your network that connects to the customer network a stub area makes sense. However, incorporating the customer network into your OSPF Autonomous System may not be desirable for several reasons, including that your customer may not want or need this, and the fact that you have little or no control over the stability of your customer's network. Using a NSSA allows you the benefits of using a stub area, without having to configure OSPF on the customer's routers and include them in your area.

In addition to service providers, network administrators who need to redistribute other routing protocols into their OSPF Autonomous Systems might find NSSAs useful. For example, a branch office containing a segment that still uses RIP might be a spot to use a NSSA. The RIP segment might contain old but important devices that don't support any protocol but RIP, as is sometimes the case with old UNIX servers. In this case, you can't include the RIP segment in your OSPF area, but without using a NSSA, you can't get the benefits of using a stub area. Figure 4-7 contains an example of both situations where you might find a NSSA useful.

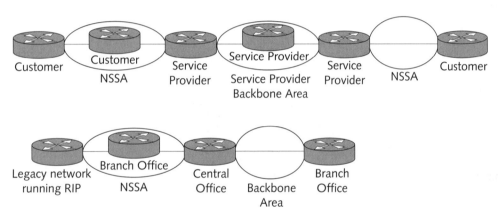

Figure 4-7 Examples of not-so-stubby areas

Designing the Backbone Area

Since areas exchange routing information through the backbone area, and since all intra-area packets must go through the backbone, a stable backbone area is essential. How you design your backbone area will affect the stability of the entire OSPF Autonomous System.

Keeping the Backbone Area Small One method to stabilize a backbone area is to keep it small. The fewer routers and interfaces in an area, the less likely the area is to have a router or interface fail at any one time. Since a backbone router must have all intra-area and external routes throughout a network, it also makes sense to keep its link-state database and inter-area routing tables small. You can reduce the size of the routes received from other areas with route summarization, but since a router must know the complete topology of its own area, you can't reduce the number of routes it knows from its own area.

Keeping the Backbone Area Contiguous   Additionally, your backbone area should remain contiguous. Partitioning your backbone area prevents each portion of your network from reaching the other half. Figure 4-8 shows a simple backbone area design, which has the disadvantage of relying upon a single link between each router for backbone connectivity. If any of these links fails, at least one area will be isolated from the rest of the network. In general, you should have redundant links between backbone routers, wherever possible.

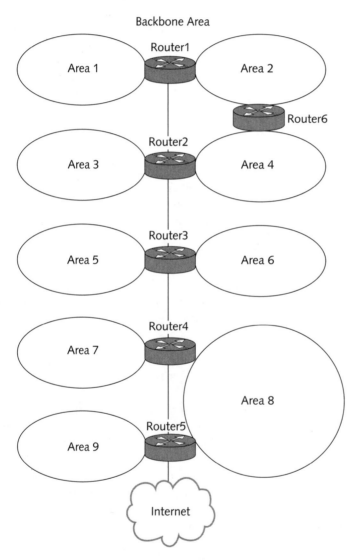

Figure 4-8   Non-redundant OSPF backbone design

Figure 4-9 shows an example of a backbone design where each backbone router is connected to each other backbone router by at least two links. The disadvantage of this design, of course, is complexity and cost, which you should balance against the cost of a partitioned network.

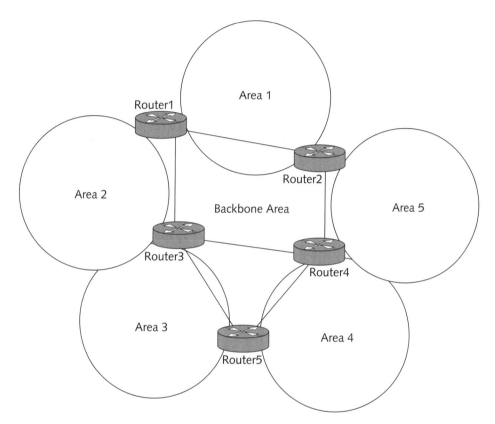

Figure 4-9   Redundant OSPF backbone design

Connecting Areas to the Backbone With Virtual Links   In some situations, you can use virtual links as backups in order to prevent the backbone area from being partitioned. In Figure 4-8, for example, you could configure a virtual link through Area 8, connecting Area 9 to the backbone since Area 8 connects to each of these routers. However, you would no longer be able to configure Area 8 as a stub area, making it more difficult to restrict the number of entries in routing tables in that area.

Since each area in an OSPF Autonomous System must be connected to the backbone, you should use redundant links between an area to the backbone, wherever possible. In the network design in Figure 4-8, each individual area, excluding Area 8, has only one connection to the backbone. As a result, each area, except Area 8, could be isolated from the rest of the network with the failure of a single link. In Figure 4-9, each area is connected to the backbone area at two different spots so that the outage of any one backbone router will not partition any area from the rest of the Autonomous System. Again, you can also use virtual links in cases where two non-backbone areas connect. For example, in Figure 4-8, you could use a virtual link from Router6 to Router1 through Area 2 to ensure that Area 4 remains connected to the backbone in case Router2 fails. However, this still has the disadvantage of preventing you from making Area 2 a stub area.

In general, however, you should avoid virtual links, whenever possible, for three reasons:

- Virtual links prevent you from using the transit area as a stub area.

- The stability of a virtual link depends on the stability of the transit area crossed by the virtual link, and the specific path crossed by the virtual link. If either is unstable, the area connected to the backbone by the virtual link will be affected.

- Because virtual links cross other areas, using virtual links adds an extra layer of complexity to your network design. As a result, troubleshooting problems in the area connected to the backbone area by the virtual link will be more difficult.

However, you may find it necessary to use virtual links from time to time to prevent the backbone from being partitioned, or for redundancy when an area is connected to the backbone with a single link.

Using WAN Links in the Backbone Area   In an OSPF Autonomous System containing WAN links, designing the backbone may require special care. In a star topology, you may wish to keep the WAN links out of the backbone since those are more likely to flap than any other kind of link. You can accomplish this by keeping WAN interfaces on backbone routers out of the backbone area. However, you must watch the number of areas each backbone router is in to avoid overwhelming the individual routers.

In extended star topologies, some of the spokes may also be hubs. On this sort of a network, you generally want to include the WAN links connecting each hub, as shown in Figure 4-10. The backbone routers in Figure 4-10, however, are linked with only a single link, which (especially with a WAN link) may partition the backbone with a single failure. You want to be careful to add redundant links, as you would in a full or partial mesh on a frame relay network, in order to maximize the odds that the backbone will be contiguous at all times. In Figure 4-11, each backbone router has two links to each other backbone router so that a single failure will not partition the backbone.

4

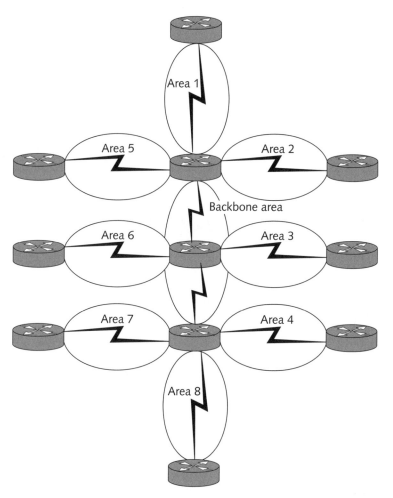

Figure 4-10   OSPF Autonomous System in extended star topology without redundant
backbone links

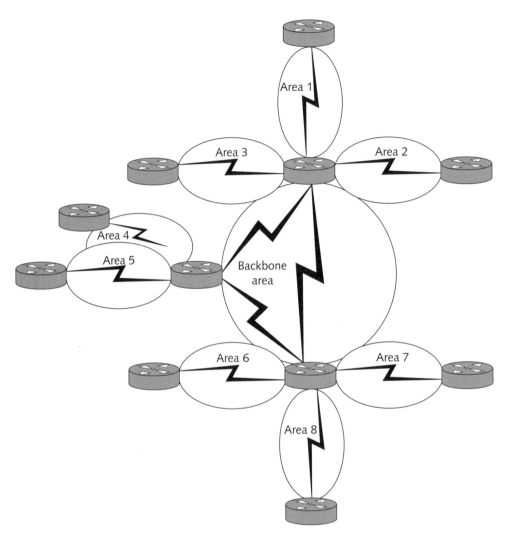

Figure 4-11 OSPF Autonomous System in extended star topology with redundant links between backbone links

Avoiding Other Devices in the Backbone Area Finally, you should avoid placing anything but routers in the backbone area. Servers and workstations will use bandwidth better devoted to routing traffic between other areas, and a traffic spike to a server inside your backbone area may cause performance problems with intra-area traffic throughout the rest of your network. Additionally, servers and workstations may cause other problems that can affect the stability of your network. A malfunctioning network interface card, or an IP address on a workstation duplicating one of your router interface's IP addresses, could cause serious problems within your network. The presence of other devices in your backbone area might also make troubleshooting more difficult. The obvious exception to this rule is when you have only one area.

Addressing with Multiple Areas

How you address your areas helps determine how well your OSPF Autonomous System scales as it grows. While you can restrict the number of routes in the routing tables of individual routers by using stub and totally stub areas wherever possible, routes to destinations inside every area must be advertised into the backbone, or routers in different areas are not able to exchange information. As the number of routes in the backbone area increases, so does the load on your backbone routers. However, you can minimize the number of routes injected into your backbone area by carefully using route summarization. Without route summarization, a network change in a non-backbone area will require routers in both that area and the backbone area to run through the SPF calculation and recalculate their routing tables. Routers in other areas in the Autonomous System might also have to recalculate their routing tables, depending on how the areas are configured.

Route Summarization in OSPF

In OSPF, each router in an area must have the same knowledge of the network in order to properly build its routing table. This has two consequences for route summarization in OSPF. The first is that routes cannot be summarized within an area, because that would mean that some routers in the area would have a different view of the topology than other routers. The second is that summarization of routes from an area must occur at ABRs since ABRs advertise those routes to other areas.

Summarizing External Routes   In OSPF, you can also summarize external routes. External routes are generally routes redistributed into OSPF from another Autonomous System, or from a router running another routing protocol. While this is generally done at an ASBR, it may also be done at an ABR.

Summarizing Contiguous Blocks of Routes   In each case, you should make certain to summarize only contiguous blocks of IP addresses. In Figure 4-12, for example, the ABR is summarizing two different ranges of IP addresses. The result is that nine routes advertised within Area 1 are summarized into two routes advertised by routers in the backbone area. This has the advantage of shielding the backbone from changes within Area 1. As long as a route exists to any one of the five networks summarized within 10.96.128.0/21, for example, the ABR still advertises a route to 10.96.128.0/21. This means that, unlike all the routers within Area 1, the backbone doesn't have to recalculate its routing table when individual networks, such as 10.96.129.0/24, are no longer reachable.

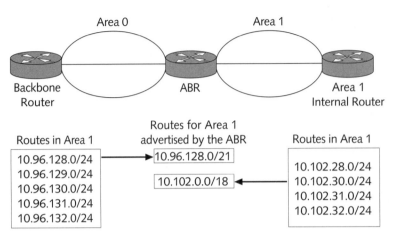

Figure 4-12   Summarizing routes injected into the backbone area

In general, you may wish to summarize routes on ABRs connecting non-backbone areas to the backbone. This means that while routers in the backbone are able to connect to every subnet on the network, they don't have to know every detail of the outlying areas, and can maintain reasonably small routing tables. Additionally, this minimizes the amount of information other areas have about each other since they learn about routes to other areas from ABRs connected to the backbone. Summarizing the routes in the backbone to other areas, however, may not be desirable since it may result in suboptimal routing through the backbone. If you keep the size of the backbone reasonably small, the number of routes injected into other areas about the backbone will remain small.

While route summarization is extremely useful on large networks, you must make sure that all summarized routes are in the same area. For example, in Figure 4-12, networks 10.96.133.0/24, 10.96.134.0/24, and 10.96.135.0/24 would also be summarized as part of 10.96.128.0/21. If these networks are added to another area while 10.96.128.0/21 is advertised to the backbone by the ABR, you will have problems connecting to these networks from outside their areas.

Limitations of Route Summarization   Route summarization can lead to poor path selection. If an ABR is advertising a summarized route, packets intended for any of the networks contained within that summary route are sent to it. This often means that packets are sent through the ABR on the way to their destinations even though better paths may exist. The advantages of route summarization, however, often outweigh the effects of poor path selection, especially on larger networks. Because of route summarization, other routers aren't able to see the details of the path selected, and can't find a better path.

For example, if you have multiple paths into your backbone area, you may not want to summarize routes in your backbone area since many packets will take a poor path into the backbone. Also, a packet must travel nearly to the destination before discovering that the destination network is down. For example, suppose that Area 5 contains the network 172.25.200.0/24, which is summarized at the ABR connecting Area 5 to the backbone area as 172.25.0.0/16. If the 172.25.200.0/24 network goes down, packets from Area 2 must go through the backbone area to learn that this network is down. Without route summarization, the closest router to the packet's source knows that the network is down. On large networks, the unnecessary traffic generated by this behavior is usually an acceptable tradeoff for smaller routing tables.

Finally, route summarization in OSPF does not allow you to summarize groups of areas. For example, on a network with thousands of areas, you might be able to configure each area as a totally stubby area so that each internal router outside the backbone has a manageable routing table, and uses a default route to get to any destination outside its area. Even if each area can be summarized into a single route, however, each backbone router must have a route for each area in its routing table, so its routing table would have thousands of entries. Unfortunately, OSPF does not allow you to add an extra level of summarization. You cannot use route summarization to summarize a hundred contiguous summary routes into one.

 Although type 3 and type 4 LSAs are called summary LSAs, the routes contained within these LSAs do not include summarized routes unless specifically configured to do so on the router sending them.

Addressing Areas

Even if you're not planning to use route summarization immediately, you should seriously consider numbering your OSPF areas in contiguous blocks. If you do need to use route summarization later, then you won't need to readdress your network. Ideally, your addressing scheme will be relatively simple, and will allow you to address areas based on the topology of the network, or some other scheme. Ideally, you will be able to easily add new routers to an area, and divide an area into smaller areas after it becomes too large.

Addressing based on the topology of the network means assigning each router a block of IP addresses, which you can easily summarize. You can also base addressing schemes on location. For example, you may find it very useful to be able to associate a certain block of IP addresses with each location on your network. Addressing based on other schemes, such as the department structure of an organization, can lead to problems. For instance, you might need to readdress if the organization restructures itself, or if some departments have people in multiple areas.

If possible, you may wish to assign address blocks at an octet boundary so that you can easily recognize when an IP address belongs to a particular area. For example, you might divide your networks into 16-bit blocks. This might mean assigning the 10.1.0.0/16 block to Area 0, the 10.2.0.0/16 block to Area 1, the 10.3.0.0/16 block to Area 2, and so on. This type of scheme is easy to remember and configure, and allows you to easily add new routers to an area. If you carefully add routers to an area, you can split into two areas with a minimum of trouble. If you assign blocks of addresses based on geographical location, you can also easily associate a particular block of addresses with both a location and an area. While this obviously works well using private IP address space, it may not be efficient if you need to use public IP addresses.

If you can't assign IP addresses based on an octet boundary, you must make especially certain to keep thorough and accurate documentation about your addressing scheme. Any overlapping subnets, or subnets assigned in discontiguous blocks, can potentially cause routing problems later. Subnetting your network to use IP addresses as efficiently as possible can often be confusing if you need to use lots of small subnets with large prefixes. You may find it useful to assign IP addresses in contiguous blocks based upon the router to which each subnet is attached in order to facilitate route summarization.

CONFIGURING OSPF IN MULTIPLE AREAS

In many ways, configuring OSPF in multiple areas is similar to configuring it in only one area, but with an added layer of complexity.

Activating Multiple Areas on an ABR

For internal routers in an area, you don't need to do anything special to use multiple areas in an Autonomous System. On ABRs, configuring OSPF to use multiple areas just requires a **router ospf** statement to activate OSPF, followed by **network** statements putting each interface on the ABR into the appropriate area. For example, Figure 4-13 shows how the BackboneRouter's four interfaces can be added to three different areas with four network statements.

Keep in mind when adding interfaces to multiple areas that both the order in which you add interfaces to areas and the network mask make a difference regarding where an interface lands. A Cisco router processes network statements in the order in which they were made. The first statement matching a particular interface activates OSPF on that interface and includes it in that area. As a result, you may need to be careful about how you add interfaces to an area. Too broad a mask may put interfaces in the wrong area. Since the area must match for two routers to become neighbors, the router will not be able to form adjacencies with its neighbors on those interfaces. For example, if the first network statement on the BackboneRouter in Figure 4-13 is **network 10.0.0.0 0.255.255.255 area 0**, this includes all interfaces in Area 0, regardless of the later statements. Some network administrators prefer to specifically add the address of each interface to avoid confusion (as the statement **network 10.1.1.5 0.0.0.0 area 1** does). However, this can lead to a lot of additional configuration on routers with many interfaces, which in turn makes it easy to make a mistake. You can also cover several networks with one carefully chosen network statement. In Figure 4-13, for example, instead of using two statements to add interfaces S0 and S1 to Area 1, you can use the statement **network 10.1.1.0 0.0.0.7 area 1** to add both interfaces to Area 1 at the same time.

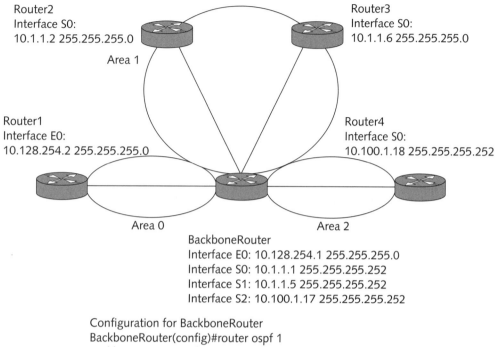

Configuration for BackboneRouter
BackboneRouter(config)#router ospf 1
BackboneRouter(config-router)#network 10.128.0.0 0.0.255.255 area 0
BackboneRouter(config-router)#network 10.1.1.1 0.0.0.0 area 1
BackboneRouter(config-router)#network 10.1.1.5 0.0.0.0 area 1
BackboneRouter(config-router)#network 10.100.1.16 0.0.0.3 area 2

Figure 4-13   Activating multiple areas on an ABR

If you have trouble activating OSPF on an ABR's interface, you may need to either reboot the router, or use the **no router ospf** command to momentarily deactivate OSPF on the router. Either option requires routers in attached areas to use the SPF algorithm and recalculate their routing tables. If you use the **no router ospf** command, you also must add all the OSPF configuration statements back in again. If so, you must have the original OSPF configuration readily available. Ideally, of course, you should avoid this with careful use of the network statement when you initially configure OSPF on an ABR.

Configuring Stub Areas

While stub areas have several advantages, configuring them requires some additional work. Each router in a stub area must be specifically configured as a stub router. This sets the Stub Flag in the hello packets sent out a router's interfaces, and if the Stub Flag on two neighboring routers doesn't match, then they can't become neighbors. To configure Area 6 as a stub area, you can use the following commands in each router in the area after activating OSPF on the router's interfaces:

```
Router(config)#router ospf 7
Router(config-router)#area 6 stub
```

Configuring Totally Stubby Areas

Totally stubby areas are configured much the same as regular stub areas. Since the difference between a stub area and a totally stubby area is that an ABR in a totally stubby area doesn't accept type 3 and type 4 summary LSAs, the ABR is a logical place to configure a totally stubby area. You can do that with:

```
Router(config-router)#area 6 stub no-summary
```

While the **no-summary** keyword must be used on each ABR in a totally stubby area, it is not necessary on any of the internal routers. However, you can configure it on internal routers. It just doesn't have any effect unless another area is configured on the router, and the internal router becomes an ABR.

Additionally, you would need to configure each router in the totally stubby area with the **area** *area-number* **stub** command, just as you would for a stub area.

Not-so-stubby Areas

As in other types of stub areas, each router in the NSSA must be specifically configured to be part of a NSSA. You can configure Area 7 to be a NSSA by configuring each router in the NSSA with:

```
Router(config-router)#area 7 nssa
```

Default Routes

Although you can use a default route in all types of areas, the configuration will vary from area to area. In normal areas, you can generate a default route with the **default-information originate** command in router configuration mode. If you have a router with a default route (such as a route out to the Internet), you can use this command to propagate the default route to the rest of the OSPF Autonomous System. This command will begin to advertise an external route (to network 0.0.0.0 with a netmask of 0.0.0.0) and convert the router into an ASBR. You can do this with:

```
Router(config)#ip route 0.0.0.0 0.0.0.0 172.16.1.1
Router(config)#router ospf 1
Router(config-router)#default-information originate
```

You can also configure a default route on a router even if it doesn't have a default route by adding the **always** keyword. By default, this route will be an external type 2 link. You can configure the type of external link to be advertised, calculate the cost of the default route, and identify a route map to be used on the default route. A **route map** is a mechanism to manually adjust routing decisions and updates; if a particular route matches a certain condition configured in the route map, then the router will alter the route as configured. Table 4-3 shows the default-information originate command and its arguments.

Table 4-3   The default-information originate command and its arguments

Command or Keyword	Description
default-information originate	Generates a default route
Always	The router will generate a default route even when it does not have a default route
metric *metric-value*	Cost of the route to be advertised
metric-type *type-value*	Type of external route generated (either type 1 or type 2)
route-map *map-name*	Tells the router to use a route map

In stub areas and totally stubby areas, however, ABRs automatically generate default routes by creating a summary LSA to the 0.0.0.0 network. Since the ABR is connected to the backbone and has all the same routes as all the other backbone routers, it can forward packets on to their final destinations. It doesn't actually need to have a default route itself, and you don't need to use the **default-information originate** command.

In a NSSA, an ABR must be forced to generate a default route when you configure it to be part of a NSSA with the **area** command using the **default-information originate** keyword. After you configure this, the ABR advertises a type 7 LSA for the network 0.0.0.0. Additionally, you can configure an ABR for a not-so-stubby area to control route redistribution with the **no-redistribution** keyword. This allows an ABR to distribute routes into the normal area attached to it without injecting them into the not-so-stubby area. The following command configures the ABR for Area 8 to generate a default route without redistribution into the NSSA:

```
Router(config-router)#area 8 nssa default-information-
originate no-redistribution
```

While each router in the area must configure as part of the NSSA, only an ABR must use this command.

Route Summarization

Configuring route summarization in OSPF depends on whether you are summarizing intra-area routers or external routes. To summarize intra-area routes, you use the **area range** command. For example, suppose Area 1 contains a contiguous block of networks that you can summarize with 172.20.0.0/16. On the ABR connecting Area 1 to the backbone, go into router configuration mode and use this command:

```
Router(config-router)#area 1 range 172.20.0.0 255.255.0.0
```

The address and the netmask are for the summary route. Afterwards, the ABR advertises an LSA with a summary route of 172.20.0.0/16 into the backbone (and hence to all areas), instead of the many individual routes Area 1 actually contains.

To summarize an external route, use the **summary-address** command. This command can be used not only by the ASBR, but by an ABR to summarize the external routes injected into an area. You might want the backbone area to know all the external routes so that your backbone routers select the best path, but you may want to advertise only the summary route to other areas. For example, an ASBR in the backbone area might have a series of external routes that can be summarized with 10.0.0.0/18. In order to summarize these, use the following command in router configuration mode on the ASBR:

```
Router(config-router)#summary-address
10.0.0.0 255.255.192.0
```

Additionally, you can use the **summary-address** command to avoid advertising a route with the **not-advertise** keyword. For example, you might prefer to have routers outside the backbone use a default route. At your ABRs, you can prevent this route from being advertised with:

```
Router(config-router)#summary-address
10.0.0.0 255.255.192.0 not-advertise
```

You can also attach a numeric tag value to the summary route with the **tag** keyword. This can be useful in redistribution, or with route maps, when you need to manipulate a group of routes.

Configuring Virtual Links

Figure 4-14 shows how to configure a virtual link with the **area virtual-link** command. The routers at each end of the virtual link must know both the transit area and the router ID of the router on the other end. In Figure 4-13, the router with router ID 10.50.165.1 is configured with the transit area Area 1, as well as the router ID of the router at the other end, 192.168.254.1.

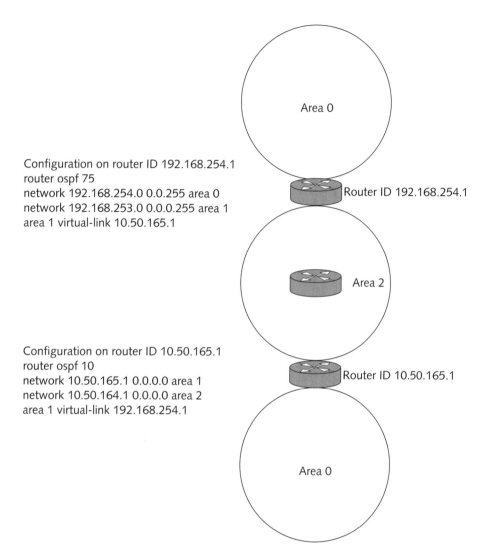

Configuration on router ID 192.168.254.1
router ospf 75
network 192.168.254.0 0.0.255 area 0
network 192.168.253.0 0.0.0.255 area 1
area 1 virtual-link 10.50.165.1

Router ID 192.168.254.1

Area 2

Configuration on router ID 10.50.165.1
router ospf 10
network 10.50.165.1 0.0.0.0 area 1
network 10.50.164.1 0.0.0.0 area 2
area 1 virtual-link 192.168.254.1

Router ID 10.50.165.1

Figure 4-14   Configuring a virtual link

MONITORING AND TROUBLESHOOTING OSPF IN MULTIPLE AREAS

In order to monitor and troubleshoot OSPF in multiple areas, you use largely the same set of commands you learned in Chapter 3. However, you now have another set of potential problems to look for.

To get an idea of what area a particular interface is in, or whether or not a router is properly configured as an ABR, you can use the **show ip ospf** command. This tells you which areas a router has interfaces in, as well as the type of router. Output from this command in an OSPF Autonomous System with multiple areas follows:

```
Dulles#show ip ospf
 Routing Process "ospf 1" with ID 10.1.254.2
 Supports only single TOS(TOS0) routes
 It is an area border router
 SPF schedule delay 5 secs, Hold time between two SPFs 10
secs
 Minimum LSA interval 5 secs. Minimum LSA arrival 1 secs
 Number of external LSA 0. Checksum Sum 0x0
 Number of DCbitless external LSA 0
 Number of DoNotAge external LSA 0
 Number of areas in this router is 3. 3 normal 0 stub 0
nssa
 External flood list length 0
    Area BACKBONE(0)
        Number of interfaces in this area is 2
        Area has no authentication
        SPF algorithm executed 3 times
        Area ranges are
        Number of LSA 7. Checksum Sum 0x2A371
        Number of DCbitless LSA 0
        Number of indication LSA 0
        Number of DoNotAge LSA 0
        Flood list length 2
    Area 1
        Number of interfaces in this area is 1
        Area has no authentication
        SPF algorithm executed 3 times
        Area ranges are
        Number of LSA 6. Checksum Sum 0x1AD5B
        Number of DCbitless LSA 0
        Number of indication LSA 0
        Number of DoNotAge LSA 0
        Flood list length 0
    Area 2
        Number of interfaces in this area is 1
        Area has no authentication
        SPF algorithm executed 2 times
        Area ranges are
        Number of LSA 6. Checksum Sum 0x16093
        Number of DCbitless LSA 0
        Number of indication LSA 0
        Number of DoNotAge LSA 0
        Flood list length 0
```

Since each interface can be in only one area at a time, the **show ip ospf interface** command is useful to identify whether or not an interface is in the proper area. It also shows whether or not an area is a stub area; as you learned earlier, each router in a stub area must be configured as such, and this can tell you whether or not this is true. Typical output from the **show ip ospf interface** command follows:

```
dallas#show ip ospf interface fastethernet 0/0
FastEthernet0/0 is up, line protocol is up
    Internet Address 10.173.0.29/27, Area 0
    Process ID 10, Router ID 10.197.195.241, Network Type
BROADCAST, Cost: 100
    Transmit Delay is 1 sec, State DR, Priority 89
    Designated Router (ID) 10.197.195.241, Interface
address 10.173.0.29
    Backup Designated router (ID) 10.197.195.243, Interface
address 10.173.0.2
    Timer intervals configured, Hello 10, Dead 40, Wait 40,
Retransmit 5
        Hello due in 00:00:09
    Index 1/1, flood queue length 0
    Next 0x0(0)/0x0(0)
    Last flood scan length is 1, maximum is 45
    Last flood scan time is 0 msec, maximum is 4 msec
    Neighbor Count is 6, Adjacent neighbor count is 6
        Adjacent with neighbor 10.173.0.254
        Adjacent with neighbor 10.197.195.249
        Adjacent with neighbor 10.173.0.250
        Adjacent with neighbor 10.197.195.243  (Backup
Designated Router)
        Adjacent with neighbor 10.173.0.225
        Adjacent with neighbor 10.173.0.252
    Suppress hello for 0 neighbor(s)
    Message digest authentication enabled
        Youngest key id is 100
```

Additionally, you can use the **show ip ospf database** command to take a look at the topology database as a router knows it. Typical output from the **show ip ospf database** command follows:

```
dallas#show ip ospf database

        OSPF Router with ID (10.197.195.241) (Process ID 10)


                Router Link States (Area 0)

    Link ID            ADV Router         Age      Seq#   Checksum
    10.173.0.225       10.173.0.225       273      0x80002C0F 0xAE0B
    10.173.0.250       10.173.0.250       459      0x8000110F 0xE478
    10.173.0.251       10.173.0.251       269      0x800015AC 0x31BD
    10.173.0.252       10.173.0.252       606      0x80002C11 0xCED1
    10.173.0.254       10.173.0.254       1450     0x800007FF 0x14BE
    10.197.195.241     10.197.195.241     385      0x80002C14 0xECB7
```

4

```
10.197.195.243   10.197.195.243   1533      0x80002C0B 0x7B9C
10.197.195.244   10.197.195.244   529       0x80002C11 0x784C
10.197.195.245   10.197.195.245   833       0x80002C0B 0xDFF3
10.197.195.249   10.197.195.249   1758      0x80002C0D 0xA6F4

                  Net Link States (Area 0)

Link ID          ADV Router       Age    Seq#         Checksum
10.173.0.29      10.197.195.241   385    0x800016E3   0x492
10.173.0.61      10.197.195.241   385    0x800016E7   0xBC9A
10.173.0.130     10.197.195.243   1533   0x8000009E   0x2081

              Summary Net Link States (Area 0)

Link ID          ADV Router       Age    Seq#         Checksum
10.173.0.64      10.173.0.225     273    0x80002C0F   0x855D
10.173.0.64      10.197.195.244   535    0x8000009D   0x7FB
10.173.0.193     10.173.0.225     279    0x8000233A   0xFF1F
10.173.0.193     10.197.195.244   535    0x8000009D   0xD0F4
10.173.0.194     10.173.0.225     531    0x8000009F   0x9447
10.173.0.194     10.197.195.244   536    0x8000009D   0xC6FD
10.173.0.200     10.173.0.225     280    0x80000CB0   0x12A6
10.173.0.200     10.197.195.244   536    0x8000009D   0x8A34
10.173.0.201     10.173.0.225     280    0x80000CDE   0xABDD
10.173.0.201     10.197.195.244   537    0x8000009D   0x803D
10.173.0.202     10.173.0.225     280    0x80002C0A   0xEA52
10.173.0.202     10.197.195.244   537    0x8000009D   0x62F5
—More—
(Output omitted)
```

You can also use this command to see the topology database for each area configured on the router. You can check and see where a router is receiving updates from and what sorts of LSAs it is receiving. You can get more specific information about different types of links with the keywords listed in Table 4-4.

Table 4-4 Keywords used by the **show ip ospf database** command

Keyword	Description
asbr-summary	Displays information about ASBR summary links
database-summary	Displays summary information about the link-state database, including the total number of each type of link
External	Displays information about the status of links to destinations outside the Autonomous System
Network	Displays link-state information about networks
nssa-external	Displays information about the status of external links advertised in not-so-stubby areas
Router	Displays router link-state information
Summary	Displays summary link-state information

To see internal OSPF routing table entries to ABRs and ASBRs, you can use the **show ip ospf border-routers** command. The following is an example of the output of this command. In this example, most of the border routers shown are ASBRs. This information can be useful when you need to identify the path that a packet takes when leaving an area in order to troubleshoot path selection problems.

```
dallas#show ip ospf border-routers

OSPF Process 10 internal Routing Table

Codes: i - Intra-area route, I - Inter-area route

I 10.173.0.194 [110] via 10.173.0.33, FastEthernet1/0, ASB
R, Area 0, SPF 118
I 10.173.0.194 [110] via 10.173.0.1, FastEthernet0/0, ASBR
, Area 0, SPF 118
I 10.173.0.193 [110] via 10.173.0.33, FastEthernet1/0, ASB
R, Area 0, SPF 118
I 10.173.0.193 [110] via 10.173.0.1, FastEthernet0/0, ASBR
, Area 0, SPF 118
I 10.173.0.198 [110] via 10.173.0.33, FastEthernet1/0, ASB
R, Area 0, SPF 118
I 10.173.0.198 [110] via 10.173.0.1, FastEthernet0/0, ASBR
, Area 0, SPF 118
I 10.173.0.200 [110] via 10.173.0.33, FastEthernet1/0, ASB
R, Area 0, SPF 118
I 10.173.0.200 [110] via 10.173.0.1, FastEthernet0/0, ASBR
, Area 0, SPF 118
I 10.173.0.201 [110] via 10.173.0.33, FastEthernet1/0, ASB
R, Area 0, SPF 118
I 10.173.0.201 [110] via 10.173.0.1, FastEthernet0/0, ASBR
, Area 0, SPF 118
I 10.173.0.202 [110] via 10.173.0.1, FastEthernet0/0, ASBR
, Area 0, SPF 118
i 10.173.0.225 [100] via 10.173.0.1, FastEthernet0/0, ABR/
ASBR, Area 0, SPF 118
i 10.173.0.251 [101] via 10.173.0.2, FastEthernet0/0, ASBR
, Area 0, SPF 118
i 10.173.0.250 [100] via 10.173.0.58, FastEthernet1/0, ASB
R, Area 0, SPF 118
i 10.173.0.250 [100] via 10.173.0.26, FastEthernet0/0, ASB
R, Area 0, SPF 118
i 10.173.0.254 [100] via 10.173.0.59, FastEthernet1/0, ASB
R, Area 0, SPF 118
i 10.173.0.254 [100] via 10.173.0.27, FastEthernet0/0, ASB
R, Area 0, SPF 118
i 10.173.0.252 [100] via 10.173.0.60, FastEthernet1/0, ASB
R, Area 0, SPF 118
```

4

```
i 10.173.0.252 [100] via 10.173.0.28, FastEthernet0/0, ASB
R, Area 0, SPF 118
—More—
(Output omitted)
```

The **show ip route** command can be very useful when troubleshooting route summarization problems, or problems with intra-area or external routes. For route summarization problems, this is a matter of identifying the routes a router should see, and looking in the routing table to determine if they're present. For problems with intra-area or external routes, Cisco routers use a code to tag the source of an OSPF route in their routing tables. Table 4-5 shows a list of the tags and what they mean.

Table 4-5   Codes for the source of an OSPF route in a routing table

Code	Description
O	OSPF inter-area route
O IA	OSPF intra-area route
E1	OSPF type 1 external route
E2	OSPF type 2 external route

Following is output from the **show ip route** command:

```
lasvegas#show ip route
Codes: C - connected, S - static, I - IGRP, R - RIP, M -
 mobile, B - BGP
       D - EIGRP, EX - EIGRP external, O - OSPF, IA -
 OSPF inter area
       N1 - OSPF NSSA external type 1, N2 -
 OSPF NSSA external type 2
       E1 - OSPF external type 1, E2 -
 OSPF external type 2, E - EGP
       i - IS-IS, L1 - IS-IS level-1, L2 - IS-IS level-
2, ia - IS-IS inter area
       * - candidate default, U - per-
user static route, o - ODR
       P - periodic downloaded static route

Gateway of last resort is 172.20.0.60 to network 0.0.0.0

       172.20.0.0/16 is variably subnetted, 73 subnets,
7 masks
O IA    172.20.0.64/27 [110/110] via 172.20.0.1, 5d12h,
FastEthernet0/0
O       172.20.35.96/28 [110/20] via 172.20.0.2, 5d12h,
FastEthernet0/0
                        [110/20] via 172.20.0.34, 5d12h,
FastEthernet4/0
```

```
O          172.20.66.0/28 [110/130] via 172.20.0.1, 5d12h,
FastEthernet0/0
                        [110/130] via 172.20.0.33, 5d12h,
FastEthernet4/0
O          172.20.34.96/27 [110/20] via 172.20.0.2, 5d08h,
FastEthernet0/0
                        [110/20] via 172.20.0.34, 5d08h,
FastEthernet4/0
O IA    172.20.69.0/26 [110/130] via 172.20.0.1, 5d12h,
FastEthernet0/0
                        [110/130] via 172.20.0.33, 5d12h,
FastEthernet4/0
O IA    172.20.72.12/30 [110/130] via 172.20.0.1, 5d12h,
FastEthernet0/0
                        [110/130] via 172.20.0.33, 5d12h,
FastEthernet4/0
O IA    172.20.68.0/27 [110/130] via 172.20.0.1, 5d12h,
FastEthernet0/0
                        [110/130] via 172.20.0.33, 5d12h,
FastEthernet4/0
O E1    172.20.64.4/30 [110/130] via 172.20.0.1, 5d12h,
FastEthernet0/0
                        [110/130] via 172.20.0.33, 5d12h,
FastEthernet4/0
O E2    172.20.36.96/27 [110/20] via 172.20.0.2, 5d12h,
FastEthernet0/0
                        [110/20] via 172.20.0.34, 5d12h,
FastEthernet4/0
O          172.20.6.64/26 [110/130] via 172.20.0.1, 5d12h,
FastEthernet0/0
O          172.20.89.0/28 [110/130] via 172.20.0.1, 5d12h,
FastEthernet0/0
                        [110/130] via 172.20.0.33, 5d12h,
FastEthernet4/0
O          172.20.88.1/32 [110/130] via 172.20.0.1, 5d12h,
FastEthernet0/0
                        [110/130] via 172.20.0.33, 5d12h,
FastEthernet4/0
O IA    172.20.72.16/30 [110/130] via 172.20.0.1, 5d03h,
FastEthernet0/0
B     206.70.138.0/24 [200/0] via 207.170.6.41, 2w2d
 —More—
(Output omitted)
```

Finally, the **show ip ospf virtual-links** command provides the status of a virtual link, its cost, and its transit area.

CHAPTER SUMMARY

❒ In this chapter, you learned about how to make an OSPF network even more scalable by dividing it into areas. While OSPF is much better suited to large networks than RIP or IGRP, in a single area, large routing tables, large topology databases, slow synchronization, and frequent SPF calculation can cause performance problems.

❒ In order to solve these problems, OSPF divides an Autonomous System into several different areas. A router with an interface in two or more areas is an Area Border Router, while a router that redistributes external routes is an Autonomous System Border Router. Routers flood different types of LSAs depending on the type of router they are.

❒ Each area must have an ABR connected to the backbone area, through which all intra-area traffic must travel. Stub, not-so-stubby, and totally stubby areas each restrict the amount of routing information routers inside those areas receive about external routes or other areas. You can use a virtual link to connect an area to the backbone when an area does not have a direct connection to the backbone.

❒ A rough guideline is that an area should contain no more than 50 to 100 routers, an ABR should be in no more than three areas, and a router should have no more than 60 neighbors. The backbone area is the most important area in an OSPF Autonomous System, and it should be both stable and small.

❒ Route summarization allows you to significantly reduce the number of routes an area advertises to the rest of the Autonomous System. It also allows you to hide the details of an area so that network changes will not affect the entire Autonomous System. However, you must be careful in order to avoid summarizing non-contiguous routes.

❒ In order to verify that the OSPF Autonomous System is functioning properly, you can use show and debug commands like **show ip ospf database** to look at the link state database, and **show ip route** to make sure that you see the expected routes.

KEY TERMS

Area Border Router (ABR) — A router with interfaces in multiple areas. An ABR must build link-state databases for each area it is connected to.

Autonomous System Border Router (ASBR) — A router with one or more interfaces connected to an OSPF area, and one or more interfaces connected to another Autonomous System. An ASBR can redistribute routing information between the OSPF Autonomous System and the external Autonomous System.

Autonomous System (AS) external link entry LSA — An LSA (of type 5) advertising an external route, sent by ASBRs and flooded throughout the entire Autonomous System with the exception of stub, totally stubby, and not-so-stubby areas.

backbone area — On OSPF networks, the backbone area (Area 0) connects all other areas; all intra-area traffic must pass through the backbone area.

backbone router — A router with at least one interface inside the backbone area.

bit E — A field in an Autonomous System external LSA consisting of a single bit, which is used to determine the type of external route the LSA is advertising.

default route — A route used to send traffic when no other destination is known; default routes are usually described as routes to 0.0.0.0 or 0.0.0.0/0.

internal router — A router with all of its interfaces within the same area; all internal routers within an area have identical link-state databases.

link-state advertisement (LSA) — Describes the state of a network or neighboring router; sent in routing updates during flooding, and used by routers to build their link-state databases.

Link-state update (LSU) — Packet containing a LSA; sent to update other routers' link-state databases during flooding.

network link entry LSA — A LSA (of type 2) advertising a network, generated by a Designated Router and flooded throughout the area, including the network.

not-so-stubby area (NSSA) — A stub area that accepts a limited number of external routes.

not-so-stubby area (NSSA) Autonomous System external link entry LSA — A LSA sent throughout a not-so-stubby area.

redistribute — The process of importing or exporting routing information between one Autonomous System and another, or between two different routing protocols.

router link entry LSA — A LSA (of type 1) generated by each router in an OSPF area, describing the state of its links and flooded throughout the area containing those links.

route map — A mechanism to manually adjust routing decisions and updates; if a route matches certain conditions configured in the route map, the route map will alter it, as necessary.

standard area — An area that can accept link updates and route summaries from both routers within the area, and from ABRs outside the area, as well as external routes from an ASBR.

stub area — An area that does not accept information about routes external to the Autonomous System; routers inside the stub area instead use a default route to reach these destinations.

summary link entry LSA — A LSA (of types 3 or 4) advertising inter-area routes, sent by ABRs, and usually flooded throughout the backbone area.

totally stubby area — An area that does not accept routing information about routes external to the Autonomous System, or about routers outside its own area; to reach any destination outside the totally stubby area, routers use a default route.

transit area — The area through which a virtual link passes.

virtual link — A logical link used to logically connect an area to the backbone area when it isn't physically connected; a virtual link must be between two ABRs over a common area.

REVIEW QUESTIONS

1. What are some of the scalability problems associated with OSPF in a single area? (Choose all that apply.)

   a. memory used to store large routing tables

   b. CPU time used by frequent SPF calculations

   c. routing problems caused by summarization of discontiguous routes

   d. memory used by large link-state databases

2. How does OSPF get around the scalability problems associated with OSPF in a single area?

   a. by summarizing all the routes within an area

   b. by dividing an Autonomous System into multiple, largely independent areas

   c. by using default routes whenever possible

   d. by keeping the maximum size of an autonomous area at 50-100 routers

3. Which type of router floods summary LSAs (types 3 and 4) with routing information about intra-area networks?

   a. ASBR

   b. internal router

   c. backbone router

   d. ABR

4. Why should you limit the number of areas for ABR interfaces? (Choose all that apply.)

   a. in order to limit the size of the routing tables

   b. because a router keeps a complete link-state database for each area

   c. because a router in too many areas has too many neighboring routers, which requires more CPU time

   d. because a router must go through the SPF calculation every time any one of its areas undergoes a network change

5. What are the advantages of using a totally stubby area over a stub area? (Choose all that apply.)

   a. A totally stubby area doesn't accept any information about external routes.

   b. A totally stubby area uses a default route.

   c. A totally stubby area doesn't accept any information about intra-area routes.

   d. A totally stubby area allows limited access to external networks.

6. Why is it important that the backbone area be stable and reliable? (Choose all that apply.)

    a. so that the backbone routers don't undergo excessive SPF calculations

    b. because all intra-area traffic must go through the backbone area

    c. because the backbone area propagates information about intra-area routes throughout the Autonomous System

    d. because you can't use route summarization in the backbone area to hide flapping links

7. A typical path for a packet going from a host in one area to a destination in another area is to an ABR in the originating area, through the backbone area, to an ABR in the destination area, and then through the destination area to the final destination. True or false?

8. How does route summarization help prevent route flapping from causing other areas to recalculate their routing tables?

    a. Route summarization prevents routing information about the flapping route from being propagated at all within any area.

    b. It automatically creates a default route to an area so that routing information about the flapping link doesn't need to be shared with other areas.

    c. Route summarization increases the dead interval on flapping interfaces.

    d. Route summarization hides the details of the individual networks in an area so that routers in other areas will only know if all of the summarized networks go down.

9. Which of the following is true about intra-area routes? (Choose all that apply.)

    a. Routers in the backbone area must know all intra-area routes.

    b. Routers in a stub area don't know any intra-area routes since they use a default route to get to other areas.

    c. Routers in a standard area don't know any intra-area routes since they use a default route to get to other areas.

    d. Routers in a totally stubby area don't know any intra-area routes since they use a default route to get to other areas.

10. Your OSPF Autonomous System contains an area that has only one ABR bordering the backbone, and a mixture of routers made by Cisco and other vendors. Which type of area can you make it?

    a. not-so-stubby area

    b. stub area

    c. backbone area

    d. totally stubby area

11. A router on your network has two interfaces in Area 0, one interface in Area 1, and one interface attached to an Internet Service Provider's network. Which of the following types of routers is it? (Choose all that apply.)

    a. an ABR

    b. an ASBR

    c. an internal router

    d. a backbone router

12. Why might type 3 or type 4 LSAs (a summary LSA) not advertise summary routes?

    a. because route summarization only occurs at ABRs

    b. because summary routes are advertised only with type 5 LSAs

    c. because type 3 and type 4 LSAs advertise a summary of routes inside an area, which may or may not be summarized

    d. because type 3 and type 4 LSAs contain all the LSAs within an area unless they're summarized

13. Which of the following commands would put an interface with the IP address 192.168.244.1 and a netmask of 255.255.255.128 into Area 2? (Choose all that apply.)

    a. network 192.168.0.0 0.0.255.255 area 2

    b. network 192.168.0.0 0.0.0.255 area 2

    c. network 192.168.244.1 0.0.0.0 area 2

    d. network 192.168.244.0 0.255.255.255 area 2

14. Why might summarizing routes in your backbone area result in poor path selection?

    a. Route summarization hides the details of the backbone area so that a router in another area might forward a packet over a poor path into the backbone because it can't see the details of the better path.

    b. Route summarization in the backbone area prevents other backbone routers from finding the best path out of the backbone.

    c. Route summarization hides the details of routes in your non-backbone areas so routers in non-backbone areas are unable to find the best path out of those areas.

    d. Route summarization in backbone areas is irrelevant to path selection.

15. Which of the following types of routers requires you to manually (instead of automatically) configure a default route? (Choose all that apply.)

    a. a router in a totally stubby area

    b. a router in a not-so-stubby area

    c. an ASBR

    d. a backbone router

16. Which of the following is a potential disadvantage of using virtual links? (Choose all that apply.)

    a. You must troubleshoot the transit area, as well as the two areas connected by the virtual link.

    b. You can't use a virtual link in an area where you also use route summarization.

    c. You can't use a default route in an area with a virtual link.

    d. You can't use a virtual link in a stub area.

4

17. Which of the following commands would summarize routes including 172.16.96.0/24 as part of Area 8? (Choose all that apply.)

    a. Area 8 range 172.16.0.0 255.255.255.0

    b. Area 8 range 172.16.0.0 255.255.224.0

    c. Area 8 range 172.16.0.0 255.255.192.0

    d. Area 8 range 172.0.0.0 255.224.0.0

18. After the following sequence of commands, which area would an interface with an IP address of 192.168.221.1 and a netmask of 255.255.255.240 be in?

    network 192.168.100.0 0.0.0.255 area 0
    network 192.168.0.0 0.0.128.255 area 1
    network 192.168.0.0 0.0.255.255 area 2
    network 192.168.221.1 0.0.0.0 area 3

    a. Area 0

    b. Area 1

    c. Area 2

    d. Area 3

19. An ABR is connected to two areas, Area 0 and Area 5. If there is a network change in Area 0, what sort of LSAs about Area 0 would the ABR be most likely to flood into Area 5?

    a. type 2

    b. type 1

    c. type 3

    d. type 5

20. Routers in Area 5 are having performance problems because of the large number of routes injected from the backbone area. How can you reduce the number of routing table entries injected by backbone routers into Area 5? (Choose all that apply.)

    a. summarize the routes injected from Area 5 into Area 0

    b. summarize external routes injected into Area 5 at the ABR

    c. summarize the routes injected from Area 0 into Area 5

    d. turn Area 5 into a stub or totally stubby area

21. After an ABR with interfaces in Area 0 and Area 1 processes a LSU received from Area 1 and recalculates its routing table, what happens if it discovers that the summary LSAs it advertises have changed?

    a. The ABR floods the summary LSAs back to Area 1 where the change originated.

    b. Nothing, since the change doesn't affect Area 0.

    c. The ABR floods LSUs containing the new summary LSAs.

    d. The ABR doesn't flood the LSUs containing the new summary LSAs because of route summarization.

22. Given multiple routes leading to the same destination, which type of route does OSPF prefer to use?

    a. an external type 1 route

    b. an external type 2 route

    c. an intra-area route

    d. an inter-area route

23. In which of the following situations could you **not** summarize a block of IP routes?

    a. The block of IP routes is not contiguous.

    b. The routes are to destinations outside the OSPF Autonomous System.

    c. The routes are inside a stub area.

    d. The routes are inside a totally stubby area.

24. Which of the following commands in router configuration mode would you use to summarize 172.16.1.0/24, 172.16.2.0/24, 172.16.3.0/24, and 172.16.4.0/24 to Area 5? All routes are to destinations outside the OSPF Autonomous System.

    a. Area 5 range 172.16.0.0 255.255.255.0

    b. summary-address 172.16.0.0 255.255.255.0

    c. Area 5 range 172.16.0.0 255.255.224.0

    d. summary-address 172.16.0.0 255.255.224.0

25. You just divided your network into multiple OSPF areas. Which of the following areas would it make sense to configure as a NSSA?

    a. an area with multiple exit areas and a single link to an external service provider

    b. an area with multiple exit areas connected to several different areas

    c. an area with a single connection to the backbone

    d. an area with a single connection to the backbone, and a handful of routes redistributed from a single link to an external Autonomous System

26. What happens if you place an interface on RouterA into Area 2 while the interface on the other end of the link is in Area 0? All of the other interfaces on RouterA are in Area 0.

    a. RouterA becomes an ABR.

    b. RouterA becomes an ASBR.

    c. RouterA is unable to form an adjacency with the link on the other side of that interface.

    d. Area 2 becomes a stub area.

4

CASE PROJECTS

Case 1

You are called in as a consultant to Happy Hotel, which is having trouble with its nationwide OSPF network of routers. Individual hotels in the Happy Hotel chain use the network to connect to the central reservation system. Each hotel router is attached through a single frame relay PVC to a single router at the central office, which in turn is attached to an extensive network at the corporate headquarters in Sacramento, California; all of this is in a single area. The Help Desk tells you that approximately five out of 1200 frame relay links to remote hotels flap. The CIO is furious because the CPU usage by each router on the network is nearly always very high, and some of the older routers with slower CPUs and less memory have been prone to crash.

Additionally, sometimes hotels are unable to check the reservation system for brief periods, which is increasing the time that customers must wait while checking in, thereby decreasing customer satisfaction. The hotels at the other end of the flapping frame relay links often can't get into the reservation system for hours at a time. The CIO is convinced that OSPF is at fault and wants to replace it with IGRP, which the company hasn't used since there were routers at only six hotels. What arguments do you use in trying to talk the CIO out of using IGRP? What can you do to improve the performance of OSPF? How do you suggest the company make sure that the hotels with flapping frame relay links can get into the reservation system?

Case 2

You worked as network administrator for East Bay Community College (EBCC) long enough to design and build a small OSPF network (see Figure 4-15). However, EBCC has put a greater emphasis on distance learning so the network has expanded greatly in both size and importance. When you initially designed the network, however, the school's administration put the emphasis on cost so you designed it as cheaply as possible. As a result, the network you designed has several single points of failure. All of the buildings on campus have wiring closets in basements, and unfortunately, most of these basements leak, which has caused several outages (due both to loss of power and loss of equipment). The administration now charges you with maintaining high availability for all parts of the network, and wants you to prepare a plan showing how you would go about doing that. Aside from the need to move the wiring closets out of the basements, how can you decrease the odds that any one-link failure will cause a network outage for a large portion of the network? Make two different plans, one using virtual links to back up each area's links to the backbone, and another using direct redundant links from a router in each area to the backbone.

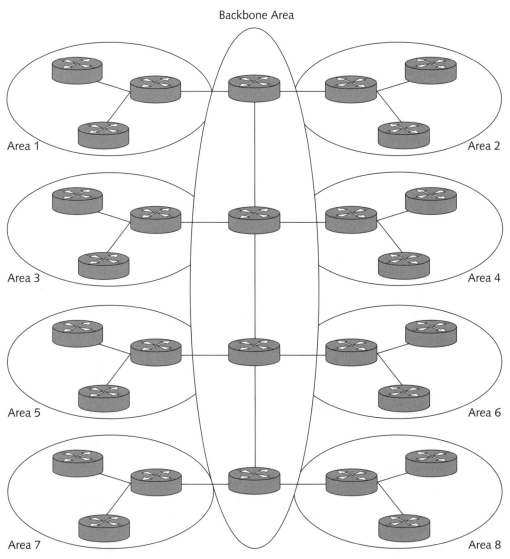

Figure 4-15   Diagram of the East Bay Community College network

Case 3

You are brought in as a consultant to help the new CTO at Benzworth Chemical Company solve some problems with the network. The previous CTO wasn't able to retain a network administrator for more than a few months for the last several years, and did much of the day-to-day administration himself when he could find the time. See Figure 4-16 for a diagram of Benzworth's network. With the help of her new network administrator, the new CTO identified some problems with flapping links in two of the non-backbone areas, and wants to summarize the routes in those areas to protect the rest of the network, as well as reduce the size of her router's routing tables. However, neither the CTO, nor the network administrator, yet feels comfortable summarizing routes on the new network without your help. What prevents you from summarizing each area's routes now? How can you group the network numbers in the current addressing scheme in order to summarize them as best as possible? If you can readdress the network by moving the existing networks around, how and where would you summarize routes? What other potential problems do you see in this network design?

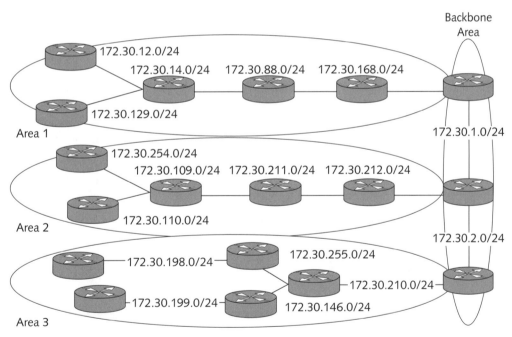

Figure 4-16   Diagram of the Benzworth Chemical Company network

Case 4

The Siesta Hammocks Company in Phoenix, Arizona just hired you as its new network administrator. The person handling network administration before you were hired is also the primary software developer, and is mystified by recent network problems. Siesta Hammocks has a nationwide frame relay network running OSPF to each of its 22 factories and stores, consisting mostly of links with CIRs of 64 or 128 Kbps in a star topology. The OSPF network is divided into areas; the Ethernet interface of each remote router is in its own area (sometimes along with a small or medium-sized network at the remote site), while the backbone area contains each frame relay link, as well as a large network at the corporate headquarters. However, recently, each frame relay link was saturated much of the time, including the middle of the night, when hardly anyone is using the network. After some research, you traced the source of the problem to routing update traffic. How can you rearrange the area design so that routers pass less update traffic across the frame relay links? What sort of areas might go well with this sort of design?

Case 5

You are hired as the network administrator for Kramer Kabinets. Currently, the network uses OSPF, but every router is in the same area, and the network isn't very stable. Additionally, Kramer Kabinets plans to significantly expand its network in the coming year in order to network production and inventory software at each factory, and integrate the network of a small chain of lumber mills into the existing network. After careful planning, you come up with the network design in Figure 4-17, which you think will both make the network more stable, and allow for expansion. Figure 4-17 also summarizes the networks that will be included in each network; you tried to assign addresses to each area based on geographic location, as much as possible.

You will develop configurations for the key routers in the Autonomous System. Most of the configurations will be done in the backbone area. Your design goals are as follows:

❑ Configure BackboneA with a default route to the Internet. The IP address on the end of its link to the Internet is 55.21.176.1 (with a 30-bit netmask). The default route should be advertised even when the link is down.

❑ Configure Area 2 on BackboneC as a totally stubby area. How can you configure the other routers in Area 2 to know that this is a totally stubby area?

❑ Summarize the routes in Area 2 to the backbone.

❑ Configure a summary route for the routes in Area 3 to the backbone.

❑ Configure a virtual link connecting Area 4 to the backbone. This will require configuration on router Area3ABR.

❑ Configure Area 4 as a totally stubby area.

❑ Summarize routes from Area 4 into the backbone.

4

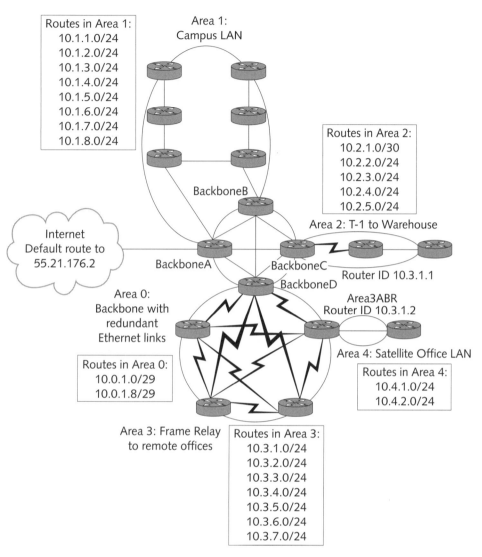

Routes in Area 1:
  10.1.1.0/24
  10.1.2.0/24
  10.1.3.0/24
  10.1.4.0/24
  10.1.5.0/24
  10.1.6.0/24
  10.1.7.0/24
  10.1.8.0/24

Area 1:
Campus LAN

Routes in Area 2:
  10.2.1.0/30
  10.2.2.0/24
  10.2.3.0/24
  10.2.4.0/24
  10.2.5.0/24

BackboneB

Area 2: T-1 to Warehouse

Internet
Default route to
55.21.176.2

BackboneA   BackboneC   Router ID 10.3.1.1

BackboneD

Area 0:
Backbone with
redundant
Ethernet links

Area3ABR
Router ID 10.3.1.2

Area 4: Satellite Office LAN

Routes in Area 0:
  10.0.1.0/29
  10.0.1.8/29

Routes in Area 4:
  10.4.1.0/24
  10.4.2.0/24

Area 3: Frame Relay
to remote offices

Routes in Area 3:
  10.3.1.0/24
  10.3.2.0/24
  10.3.3.0/24
  10.3.4.0/24
  10.3.5.0/24
  10.3.6.0/24
  10.3.7.0/24

Figure 4-17   Network for Kramer Kabinets

CHAPTER

5

EIGRP

After reading this chapter and completing the exercises you will be able to:

♦ Describe the features and benefits of using EIGRP

♦ Explain how EIGRP builds routing tables, and how the DUAL algorithm allows EIGRP networks to converge quickly

♦ Describe how to use EIGRP on very large networks

♦ Configure and troubleshoot EIGRP

In this chapter, you'll learn about **Enhanced Interior Gateway Routing Protocol (EIGRP or Enhanced IGRP)**, another routing protocol that works well on large networks. Cisco designed EIGRP to be more scalable than traditional distance vector routing protocols, but less complex than link-state routing protocols. As a result, EIGRP is both less complex and easier to configure than OSPF. However, EIGRP offers many of the benefits of OSPF, including quick convergence and scalability. While you may use EIGRP to build hierarchically designed networks, EIGRP does not require you to design networks in this way.

EIGRP Overview

EIGRP is a routing protocol designed by Cisco to combine some of the best features of link-state and distance vector routing protocols. As you might guess from the name, EIGRP is the successor to IGRP, and remains compatible with it. Cisco released two major versions of EIGRP, version 0 and version 1; versions of Cisco IOS software released after May 1996 use version 1.

Advantages of EIGRP

EIGRP offers several important advantages over traditional distance vector protocols on a large network:

- Rapid convergence. Because a router running EIGRP learns back-up routes to each destination, whenever possible, it can usually quickly update its routing table to reflect a topology change. If it doesn't have a back-up route, it queries its neighbors to find an alternate route; if its neighbors can't find a route, they query their neighbors, and so on, until a route is found.

- Low routing update traffic. EIGRP routers don't send periodic updates; they send incremental updates only about paths that changed, and only to routers that need the information.

- Support for multiple protocols. In addition to support for IP, EIGRP supports Apple's **AppleTalk** and Novell's **Internetwork Packet Exchange (IPX)** protocols, but an involved discussion of these is beyond the scope of this chapter. In order to support these protocols, EIGRP uses **protocol dependent modules (PDMs)** for each additional protocol. Using EIGRP with multiple protocols adds memory and processing overhead. In addition to a separate routing table for each protocol supported, EIGRP also maintains separate neighbor and topology tables.

- Support for VLSMs and classless routing. Since EIGRP includes the netmask in routing updates, you can use VLSMs, as needed, on EIGRP networks. You can also route to discontiguous subnets.

- Support for route summarization along arbitrary boundaries. While EIGRP automatically summarizes routes along classful boundaries, you can configure it to summarize routes, as needed, along any bit boundary.

Hybrid Routing Protocol Features

As a hybrid routing protocol, EIGRP offers features of both link-state and distance vector routing protocols. Similar to using a distance vector routing protocol, EIGRP routers generally learn about routes only from connected interfaces or their neighbors. Because EIGRP routers do not need to know the entire network topology, they do not require as much memory or CPU time to calculate their routing tables as routers running link-state routing protocols. EIGRP routers also send routing updates only to routers who need the information, saving bandwidth, compared to a link-state routing protocol like OSPF after a topology change. Traditional distance vector routing protocols, however, are prone to routing loops, while EIGRP is not.

In order to avoid routing loops, EIGRP uses some of the strategies used by link-state routing protocols. EIGRP routers use the **Diffusing Update Algorithm (DUAL)**, which allows routers to store back-up routes by storing part of the network topology in a **topology table**. Rather than containing the complete network topology, however, in EIGRP, the topology table contains only those routes advertised by neighboring routers. In OSPF, routers flood topology changes to the entire area, while in EIGRP, routers ask for information about the topology from neighbors only when necessary. If a router's topology table contains a back-up route to a destination affected by a topology change, it uses it. When a back-up route isn't available, a router queries its neighbors for a route to the destination; they look in their topology tables for a new route, and if not found, they query their neighbors.

Table 5-1 compares the features of EIGRP with those of OSPF, a pure link-state routing protocol, and with those of RIP, a pure distance vector routing protocol.

Table 5-1 Comparison of EIGRP to RIP and OSPF

Protocol	EIGRP	OSPF	RIP
Type of protocol	Hybrid	Link-state	Distance vector
Knowledge of network topology	Maintains limited topology table	Maintains table with complete knowledge of each area	None
Routing updates	Incremental updates sent to affected routers when necessary	Incremental updates sent to all routers in an area when necessary	Complete routing table sent to all neighbors every 30 seconds
Sends acknowledgements after receiving routing updates	Yes (ACK packet)	Yes (LSAck packet)	No
Convergence	Fast	Fast	Slow
Prone to routing loops	No	No	Yes
Supports VLSMs	Yes	Yes	No
Supports route summarization on arbitrary boundaries	Yes	Yes	No
Supports hierarchical routing	Yes	Yes	No
Proprietary to Cisco	Yes	No	No
Supports multiple protocols	Yes	No	No

Disadvantages of EIGRP

The chief disadvantage of EIGRP is that it is proprietary to Cisco. As a result, routers from other vendors aren't able to use or understand it. However, you can still use it in multi-vendor environments with careful use of redistribution, which you'll learn about in Chapter 7.

EIGRP Operation

Like other routing protocols, routers running EIGRP must identify neighbors, exchange routing information with them, and build and maintain their routing tables. Like OSPF, EIGRP uses hello packets to identify neighbors and determine their status. In order to ensure that each router receives routing updates, EIGRP uses reliable transport to exchange routing information. An EIGRP router stores information about its neighbors and their routes, and it uses this information to build its routing table.

Transmission of EIGRP Packets

While EIGRP does support multiple protocols, this chapter mostly covers EIGRP operation on IP networks. On IP networks, EIGRP is sent in IP packets, identified as protocol 88 in the IP header. Like OSPF, EIGRP packets are sent reliably to ensure that a router that needs updated routing information actually receives it.

Reliable Transport Protocol

In order to send routing updates reliably, EIGRP uses the **Reliable Transport Protocol (RTP)**. RTP uses a sequence number in each packet to ensure reliability, and requires an explicit acknowledgement for each packet sent reliably.

Additionally, RTP builds a **retransmission list** for each neighbor. This list contains a list of packets requiring acknowledgement sent to neighbors; a router removes each packet from the list after receiving an acknowledgement. A router retransmits each packet in the retransmission list a total of 16 times, or until the hold time expires, whichever is longer. The **hold time** is similar to the dead interval in OSPF; it is the length of time in seconds that a router will wait to receive packets from one of its neighbors before declaring the neighbor unreachable.

However, reliable transmission doesn't make sense in all situations. For example, like OSPF, EIGRP sends hello packets. On network media supporting multicast, sending a single multicast packet to all neighbors is far more efficient than sending multiple hello packets requiring acknowledgements. In these situations, RTP puts a flag in the packet indicating that the packet doesn't need acknowledgment. RTP uses this same flag in packets carrying routing updates to indicate that an acknowledgement is necessary.

If a router sends a multicast packet requiring an acknowledgement to multiple neighbors on a multiaccess network, ordinarily the router wouldn't be able to send the next multicast packet until it receives acknowledgements from all of its neighbors. However, if one or more neighbors respond slowly (or not at all), this can delay the next packet while the router waits for either an acknowledgement, or the hold timer to expire. To get around this, the router retransmits the packet to the slow router with a unicast so that it can continue to send multicast packets to the other routers.

Types of EIGRP Packets

Like OSPF, EIGRP uses a limited number of packets to maintain neighbor relationships and routing tables. The five types of EIGRP packets are:

- **Hello packets**. As in OSPF, hello packets are used to discover neighbors. They are sent using multicast with an acknowledgement number of zero.

- **Update packet**. Like a LSU packet in OSPF, update packets contain the routes used by an EIGRP router. When a new route is discovered, and after convergence is finished, a router sends multicast update packets. In order to synchronize topology tables when a router first comes onto the network or starts up, a router sends update packets as unicast packets. In either case, all update packets require acknowledgements.

- **ACK packet**. An ACK packet is sent to acknowledge receipt of a packet sent reliably, such as an update packet. ACKs are essentially hello packets sent with a non-zero acknowledgement number.

- **Query packets**. Query packets, or **queries**, contain a request for information about a route. These are sent when an EIGRP router doesn't have a **feasible successor (FS)**, or back-up route, in its topology table. Query packets are multicast packets and require acknowledgements.

- **Reply packets**. Reply packets, or **replies**, are the responses an EIGRP router sends to a query packet. Reply packets are unicast packets and also require acknowledgements.

Building and Maintaining Neighbor Relationships

As in OSPF, EIGRP routers use hello packets to discover and maintain relationships with neighboring routers.

Sending Hello Packets

Out of each interface where EIGRP is activated, an EIGRP router sends hello packets to the multicast address 224.0.0.10. The frequency of EIGRP's hello interval depends on the type of media for the interface. For LAN interfaces, such as Ethernet or token ring, and for point-to-point links, such as **Point-to-Point Protocol (PPP)** or **High-level Data Link Control (HDLC)** serial links, the default hello interval is set to five seconds. For multipoint links, such as ISDN Primary Rate Interface (PRI) or **Switched Multimegabit Data Service (SMDS)**, the default is also set to five seconds. But on slower links, such as ISDN Basic Rate Interface (BRI), hello packets are sent every 60 seconds.

In EIGRP, the default hold time is three times the hello interval. On LAN interfaces, and fast WAN interfaces, the hold time is 15 seconds, while on slow WAN interfaces, the hold time is 180 seconds.

The longer hold time on slower links is a trade-off between the bandwidth used by the Hello protocol, and the significantly longer time it may take a router to notice that it can no longer see one of its neighboring routers. However, depending on the link type, a router often notices that one of its interfaces is down well before the router realizes that the hold time expired without a hello packet from a particular neighbor.

In the earliest versions of EIGRP, a router used hello packets only to determine the status of a neighbor. However, an EIGRP router now uses any packet it receives from a neighbor to reset the hold timer. This includes all five types of EIGRP packets.

Adjusting EIGRP Timers

Unlike OSPF, both the hold time and the hello interval can be adjusted, if necessary, without preventing two neighbors from becoming neighbors. Each timer is configured independently of the other. If you change the hello interval, you must manually change the hold time, and vice versa.   Additionally, each hello packet contains the hold time. However, changing the hold time and the hello interval should be done carefully since this can lead to situations where one router marks another as down because the hold time on one router is set too low for the hello interval on another router.

Exchanging Neighbor Information In Hello Packets

In order to become neighbors, two routers must share a common subnet. Additionally, two parameters in hello packets sent between two neighboring routers must match if the two are to exchange routing information. These parameters are the Autonomous System number and the constants used to calculate EIGRP's metric, which you'll learn about later in the chapter.

Through the hello packets it receives from other routers, an EIGRP router learns not only of the presence of its neighbors, but also about the interfaces and addresses used by these neighbors. This information is kept in the neighbor table. The **neighbor table** contains much useful information about an EIGRP router's neighbors:

- **Neighbor address.** The address of the neighbor's adjacent interface.

- **Neighbor interface.** The interface on the local router through which the neighbor can be reached.

- **Hold time.** The time to wait before marking a router down (in seconds).

- **Uptime.** This is the amount of time the router has been receiving packets from the neighbor (in seconds).

- **Smooth round trip timer (SRTT).** The SRTT is the length of time (in milliseconds) between when a router sends a packet requiring an acknowledgement and the ACK packet arrives from the other router.

- **Retransmit timeout (RTO)**. This is the amount of time (in milliseconds) an EIGRP router waits before retransmitting a packet. The length of the RTO is determined by the SRTT.

- **Handle (H)**. This is the number EIGRP assigns to each router for tracking.

- **Queue count.** This is the number of packets waiting to be sent to a neighbor.

- **Sequence number**. This is the sequence number of the last EIGRP packet received from a neighbor.

Building the Topology Table with Update Packets

Once a router discovers a new neighbor, each router rebuilds its topology table by sending an update packet containing all of the routes each router is advertising. Any EIGRP router's topology table consists of all of the routes each of its neighbors is advertising. Unlike OSPF, EIGRP routers do not need to know the entire network's topology. An OSPF router also calculates all paths in its area, and then chooses the paths with the lowest cost. An EIGRP router, however, only needs to store information about its neighbors and their routes. In addition to its neighbors' routes, a router's topology table also contains the metrics advertised by its neighbors for these routes, as well as the metrics the router itself would use to forward packets to those destinations. In order to calculate the metrics to get to these destinations through its neighbors, a router adds the metric to get to the neighbor and the metric advertised by the neighbor.

Similar to OSPF, routers rebuild their topology tables whenever a directly connected interface or network changes, or when a neighbor reports a change. Unlike OSPF, however, a router is usually unaffected by a change to a route that neither it nor its neighbors advertise. A router running EIGRP is less likely to even learn about the failure of a particular network attached to a router five hops away than a router running OSPF because neither it nor its neighbors advertise the network. However, a router might receive query packets about a path to a network neither it nor its neighbors advertise.

Building and Maintaining Routing Tables

In order to learn about how an EIGRP router builds and maintains its routing tables, first we'll look at how a router initially builds its routing tables.

Building Routing Tables for the First Time

When a router first becomes part of an EIGRP network, the first thing it does is send hello packets out all of its interfaces. Establishing a neighbor relationship for the first time in EIGRP is much less complicated than in OSPF; any neighbor that receives a hello packet sends update packets containing all of the routes in its routing table to the initiating router. Because the two routers are establishing a neighbor relationship for the first time, the neighboring router will set the **Init bit** in its update packets to indicate that this is a new neighbor relationship.

Because update packets must be sent reliably, the new Router replies with an ACK packet to each update packet it receives. It then builds its topology table using the information in the update packets.

Having processed the update packets from its new neighbor, the router sends out update packets describing the routes it knows about to its neighbor. The update packets contain information about all the routes that the neighbor knows, and the metric of each route. However, EIGRP uses **split horizon**. To avoid routing loops, a router won't send out information it learned from a particular interface back out that interface. Without split horizon, when an interface on a router fails, its neighbors can send it updates indicating that they have routes to the network attached to the failed interface—which are through the router with the failed interface. They forward packets to the original router, which forwards the packets to one of its neighbors, which would, in turn, forward it back to the router with the failed interface, and so on.

Since at this point, the router knows only about networks directly attached to its interfaces and networks learned about from the interface attached to its neighbor, its update packets don't contain any routing information sent by its neighbor. After receiving each update packet, the neighbor sends an ACK packet to acknowledge receipt of the update packet.

The router goes through this process more or less simultaneously with each of its neighbors. Table 5-2 summarizes the process of building a routing table for the first time. Note that this is the only time that a router exchanges its full routing table with its neighbors; all other updates are incremental. On larger networks, this can result in significant savings in bandwidth over traditional distance vector routing protocols like RIP or IGRP.

Table 5-2   Building a routing table for the first time

Step	Description
1	The new router sends hello packets out all of its interfaces.
2	A neighbor replies with a series of update packets.
3	The new router sends an ACK packet for each update packet received.
4	The new router builds its topology table with the information contained in the update packets.
5	The new router sends update packets to all of its neighbors.
6	Each neighbor replies with an ACK packet for each update packet it receives.

Building Routing Tables

When selecting routes in a router running EIGRP, the DUAL algorithm selects both primary and back-up routes for each destination (up to a total of six routes per destination). It includes both sets of these in its topology table. EIGRP supports internal, external, and summary routes. As you'd expect, internal routes are routes from inside an Autonomous System, summary routes are simply summarized routes, and external routes are routes from outside an EIGRP Autonomous System, or redistributed from another routing protocol.

EIGRP routers add the best route into the routing tables as the **successor** route. Additionally, EIGRP routers keep back-up routes in the topology table as feasible successors.

EIGRP Metric

Since EIGRP is the successor to IGRP, its metric is nearly identical. However, the final EIGRP metric value is multiplied by 256, resulting in a 32-bit metric value instead of the 24-bit metric value used by IGRP, and the ability to control the metric more finely. Like IGRP, EIGRP uses the five following variables in calculating the metric:

- **Bandwidth**. Instead of using the bandwidth of a link, EIGRP uses the smallest bandwidth along a particular path to calculate the metric of that path.

- **Delay**. EIGRP adds the interface delay along the path to calculate this parameter.

- **Reliability**. This is the worst reliability along the path.

- **Load**. EIGRP uses the worst load along the path.

- **Maximum transmission unit (MTU)**. EIGRP uses the smallest MTU along a path. The MTU is the maximum packet size supported on a network segment.

By default, however, only bandwidth and delay are used to calculate the metric of a route. If the other parameters are used in the metric calculation, EIGRP routers tend to frequently recalculate their routing tables. Like IGRP, EIGRP uses a series of constants, sometimes called the **K-values**, to calculate the final metric. Table 5-3 shows a list of the K-values, their default values, and the variables associated with each constant. Note, however, that some variables are affected by more than one constant.

Table 5-3   Default K-values and their associated variables

Constant	Default Value	Associated Variable
K1	1	Bandwidth
K2	0	Load
K3	1	Delay
K4	0	Reliability
K5	0	MTU

The formula used to calculate the metric is:

```
EIGRP metric = (K1 x bandwidth) + ([K2 x band-
width] / [256 — load]) + (K3 x delay)]
```

If K5 is greater than zero, then the metric calculated with this result is:

```
EIGRP metric = EIGRP metric x (K5 / [reliability + K4])
```

This calculation is not performed when K5 is equal to zero, since the calculated metric is always zero. Since K2, K4, and K5 are set to zero by default, however, the metric is usually calculated by:

```
EIGRP metric = (K1 x bandwidth) + (K3 x delay)
```

Unlike OSPF, EIGRP routers put the K-values they use to calculate metrics into their hello packets. If a neighbor receives K-values in a hello packet from a neighbor that does not match its own K-values, it can reset that neighbor.

While you can manipulate the K-values to change the characteristics of the metric, poorly selected K-values can prevent a network from converging. As a result, you only want to change the K-values on your network after careful planning.

 Since bandwidth is one of the two primary variables used, by default, in calculating the EIGRP metric, you must make sure that EIGRP knows the proper bandwidth for each link. This is particularly important for serial interfaces. As you learned in Chapter 3, the default bandwidth for a serial interface is 1.544 Mbps; you often have to manually set the bandwidth of a serial interface with the **bandwidth interface configuration** command.

MAINTAINING ROUTING TABLES WITH THE DUAL ALGORITHM

In order to deal with topology changes, EIGRP uses the DUAL algorithm. DUAL is a **finite state machine**, or a computer program that starts at one state and uses input variables to go to the next state. Each state is a loop-free routing table, and the variables it uses to go from one state to the next are topology changes. In addition to changes on connected interfaces, DUAL watches for topology changes sent by neighboring routers.

Selecting the Best Path with the DUAL Algorithm

In order to select the best paths to each destination, DUAL calculates the best path to each destination by searching through its topology table and looking at the metric for each possible path. It calculates the route with the lowest cost (or metric) by adding the cost advertised by each neighboring router with a route to the same destination, and the cost between itself and the neighbor advertising the route. The cost advertised by the neighboring router (or the next hop router) is known as the **advertised distance (AD)**, while the total metric to the destination is known as the **feasible distance (FD)**. The FD is the sum of all the metrics along the way to the destination. If a neighboring router has a path with the lowest cost to a particular destination, and this path is guaranteed to be loop-free, then this route is known as a successor and added to the routing table. A router may put more than one successor in its routing table if it has the same FD. The primary route to any destination is also known as the **current successor**.

The terminology describing the EIGRP metric can be somewhat confusing. Cisco sometimes talks about both cost and distance in discussing the EIGRP metric, but both refer to the same thing.

Selecting Feasible Successors

For the back-up route, DUAL selects a feasible successor in much the same way that it selects a successor. The feasible successor is the next best route to a particular destination. While DUAL keeps the feasible successor and the back-up route in the topology table, it doesn't use the back-up route to forward packets. Again, an EIGRP router can keep more than one feasible successor in its topology table.

In order to be selected as a feasible successor, the next hop router must have an advertised distance to the destination less than the feasible distance of the route for the current successor. This helps routers running EIGRP prevent routing loops. It works somewhat like the hop count limit in traditional distance vector protocols like RIP and IGRP. In distance vector routing protocols, a routing loop results in a route with an increasing hop count. If the route to a destination is a loop on an EIGRP network, then the EIGRP metric also increases.

Failure of the Primary Route

When the primary route to a destination fails, the DUAL algorithm looks at each feasible successor in its topology database, chooses the one with the lowest metric, and uses it to replace the failed primary route in the routing table. If it doesn't have a feasible successor installed in its topology table, a router queries its neighbors to find a new route. At this point, the route goes from the **passive state** to the **active state**, meaning that the router must recalculate this route. An EIGRP router does not need to recalculate its routing table when a route fails if its topology database contains a feasible successor; however, if the DUAL algorithm can't find a feasible successor, then it recalculates its routing table. The combination of the topology table and queries for routes enables EIGRP to avoid the holddown and flush timers used by RIP and IGRP. As a result, convergence on an EIGRP network occurs more quickly than on a comparable network using RIP or IGRP.

When a route fails without a feasible successor, and goes into the active state, it follows the split horizon rule to send queries out all interfaces in order to reach all neighbors except for the one that advertised the failed route. Each neighbor that has another route to the destination replies with an update packet. However, if a neighbor doesn't have an alternate path, it queries all of its neighbors until a new route is found. When a router replies to a query with an update packet, it does not query its neighbors. Rather, other routers on other interfaces continue to query their neighbors until they have no more neighbors to query for the route, or the query reaches a neighbor that has no knowledge of the route. The path of a query throughout an EIGRP Autonomous System is known as the **query range**, while efforts to limit the query range are known as **query scoping**.

Since EIGRP routers transmit query packets reliably, they must receive an answering packet for each query packet sent. A router cannot take a route out of the active state without a reply to all of its query packets; if it receives responses to each query packet, but none contains a feasible successor, the router discards that particular route. If a router in the active state doesn't receive a response to a query packet within an interval equal to three minutes, by default, then the router enters the **stuck-in-active (SIA) state**. At this point, the router responds by **resetting** the neighbor, or putting all of its routes into the active state.

Topology Change on an EIGRP Network

In Figure 5-1, RouterA just came up on the network. It will build its routing table with the information it receives from its neighbors. Based on the link metrics shown in Figure 5-1, we can see all the possible topology and routing table entries RouterA might have (see Table 5-4).

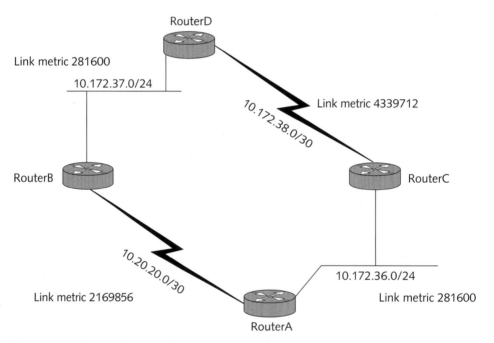

Figure 5-1   Example network

Table 5-4 Possible topology table entries for RouterA in Figure 5-1

Network	Via	Feasible distance	Advertised distance	Added to topology/routing tables?
10.20.20.0/30	Connected	2169856	0	yes/yes
10.172.37.0/24	RouterB	2451456	281600	yes/yes
10.172.37.0/24	RouterC	4902912	4621312	yes/no
10.172.38.0/30	RouterB	7241168	4621312	yes/no
10.172.38.0/30	RouterC	4621312	4339712	yes/yes
10.172.36.0/24	Connected	281600	0	yes/yes

Although there are two possible paths to three networks, RouterA does not necessarily put each of them into its routing table. Two paths to connected networks through other routers are left out. For unconnected destination networks, RouterA chooses the paths with the best feasible distances. So, it selects the path through RouterB to reach the 10.172.37.0/24 network, and it selects the path through RouterC to reach the 10.172.38.0 network, both of which have the lowest feasible distances of the two possible paths.

In selecting feasible successors, however, RouterA looks at the advertised distance. EIGRP's rule is to select only paths that can be guaranteed to be free of loops, which it does by selecting only paths with advertised distances less than the feasible distance of the existing path. If the advertised distance of an alternate path is greater than the existing path's feasible distance, the alternate path may not be a loop, but the router can't guarantee it. In this case, the alternate paths to each network advertised distances equal to or greater than the feasible distance of the best route. As a result, RouterA adds them to its topology table, but not as feasible successors.

If the serial link to RouterB goes down (as you can see in Figure 5-2), RouterA is no longer able to reach either the 10.20.20.0/30 network or the 10.172.37.0/24 network through its current paths. The router will try to do the following in order to find routes to the two networks:

1. RouterA will mark the metric of both routes as −1 (unreachable).

2. RouterA will look in its topology table for feasible successors. Since each feasible successor is the next hop of the back-up route, if it can find one, it will put that route into its routing table, and stop without the route ever leaving the passive state. However, in this case, RouterA has no feasible successors for either network; in both cases, the advertised distance for either route through RouterC is greater than the last known feasible distance for the failed routes.

3. In order to find a new route to the destination networks, RouterA will put the routes into the active state. It will send query packets for each route out of any active interfaces, except the interface used for the old routes; in this

case, RouterA sends query packets out of the Ethernet interface on the same network as RouterC. RouterA notes that it has a reply to its query pending from RouterC.

4. RouterC receives the query packets from RouterA. It also receives a query packet from RouterD about the route to 10.20.20.0/30. In its routing table, it has a route to 10.172.37.0/24 through RouterD, with a metric of 4621312. RouterC marks the route to 10.20.20.0/30 unreachable (since both possible next hops sent it query packets for that route), and sends reply packets to both routers indicating no change for that route. For the 10.172.37.0/24 route, RouterC replies to RouterA with information about its route to 10.172.37.0/24.

5. RouterA receives RouterC's replies and removes the flag indicating that it expects a reply from RouterC. It installs the new route to 10.172.37.0/24.

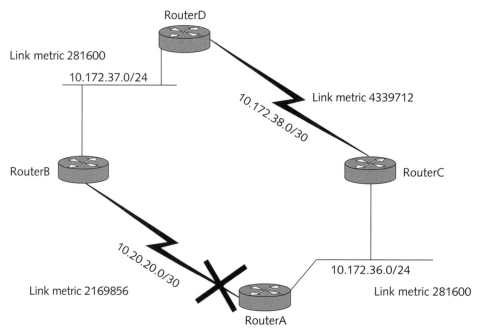

Figure 5-2   Example network after the serial interfaces go down

USING EIGRP ON VERY LARGE NETWORKS

As on every large network, EIGRP requires special care in order to minimize routing problems and convergence time. As you learned, EIGRP routers primarily share routing information with their neighbors. If an EIGRP router does not have a feasible successor to a destination after a topology change, it queries each of its neighbors, who query their neighbors until either an answer is found, or all query packets are answered negatively. Because of this, EIGRP scalability is primarily affected by these variables:

- The number of routers involved in each network change. As this number increases, so do the resources used by EIGRP.

- The amount of routing information exchanged by EIGRP neighbors. The number of routes an EIGRP router passes to its neighbors also affects the resources used by EIGRP, and network performance.

- The number of hops that information must travel in order to reach all affected routers. This will affect both queries and routing updates.

- The number of redundant paths on the network. While redundant paths are necessary to prevent outages, too many paths can complicate the topology and cause problems for EIGRP convergence.

Ideally, any EIGRP design for a large network restricts and eliminates queries as much as possible. When a router puts a route into the active state, it does not update routing information for that route until it enters the passive state again. If a router doesn't receive replies to its query packets, the router will:

- Send ICMP destination unreachable messages to any packets sent to that destination network.

- Put all routes known through that neighbor into the active state.

Since all routes for the neighboring router now go into active mode, any unanswered query packets sent to query these routes also put the router into the SIA state again (and the router also sends destination unreachable messages to any device that tried to reach hosts on these routes in the meantime). If reply packets are lost, or returned too slowly, serious convergence problems can result.

Typically, a wide query scope does not directly cause problems with routers in SIA mode. More common reasons include heavy CPU or memory usage on a router, and packet loss on WAN links. Depending on the percentage of packets lost over a point-to-point serial link, for example, the two routers on the ends of the link may be able to become neighbors, but may lose individual packets, including reply packets. Circuit problems can also result in one-way traffic, where one end of the link can send out query packets successfully to the other end of the link, but the other end of the link can't send any traffic in return.

However, in general, the larger the query scopes are in an Autonomous System, the more likely routers are to end up in SIA mode. Larger query scopes mean that more routers may be queried, and as a query propagates to more routers, the odds increase that one or more will have trouble answering. The size of the query scope depends on the number of neighbors and the number of paths a query might take through the network. Another reason to avoid large query scopes is to avoid the network traffic generated by queries, especially over WAN links.

Restricting Query Scope

One strategy sometimes used in an attempt to restrict query scope is segmenting a network into multiple Autonomous Systems. Unfortunately, this doesn't actually address the problem. In Figure 5-3, RouterC is redistributing routes between two EIGRP Autonomous Systems, AS 318 and 2897. If a network connected to one of RouterE's interfaces in AS 2897 goes down, for example, it will query its neighbor, RouterD. RouterD will, in turn, query RouterC and RouterF.

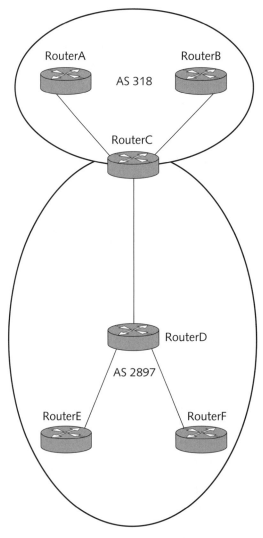

Figure 5-3   Attempting to restrict queries with multiple EIGRP Autonomous Systems

At this point, the design is intended to stop the query by preventing it from going into AS 318. Since this is the edge of AS 2897, RouterC no longer sends queries for the EIGRP process for AS 2897. Unfortunately, the EIGRP process for AS 318 on RouterC also has knowledge of the route since RouterC is redistributing routes from AS 2897. As a result, the EIGRP process for AS 318 must send queries to its neighbors in AS 318, RouterA, and RouterB, which, in turn, must send queries to any of their neighbors (not pictured). You shouldn't use multiple EIGRP Autonomous Systems on a network design unless you've thought carefully about all the issues involved. Key issues include the redistribution of routes between Autonomous Systems (which you will learn about in Chapter 7), and the design of each individual Autonomous System.

In general, the best way to restrict query scope is through route summarization. In Figure 5-3, for example, you can eliminate the queries sent through Autonomous System 318 by having RouterC redistribute summary routes instead of the individual subnets. Another example is shown in Figure 5-4. If the CorpLan router goes down, Core1 will be unable to reach the 10.198.172.0/24 network. Since it doesn't have another path to that network, Core1 can't have a feasible successor, and it must send query packets to all of its neighbors. This includes Core2, all of the WAN links, Remote1, Remote2, Remote3, and Remote4.

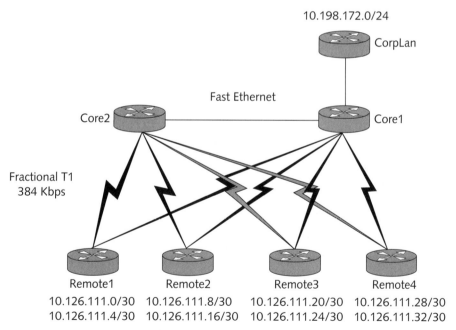

Figure 5-4   Multiple query packets sent on networks with multiple paths

Unfortunately, each neighbor also must send out query packets since each has a route to the 10.198.172.0/24 network, but none of them has an alternate path. While they won't send query packets out the interface through which they received the initial query packet, they will have to send query packets through all of their other interfaces. This means that after receiving the initial query from Core1, Core2 also sends query packets to all four of the remote routers. Additionally, each remote router also sends out query packets to Core2 after receiving the initial query packet from Core1. Core2 and the remote routers all receive and respond to multiple query packets. This complicates the convergence process and increases the odds that something will go wrong. For example, if the link from Core2 to Remote4 is dropping packets because of errors on the line, then Remote4 may not receive the reply packet to the query packet it sent to Core2, and it will enter the SIA state. In turn, it will put any routes it knows through Core2 into the active state.

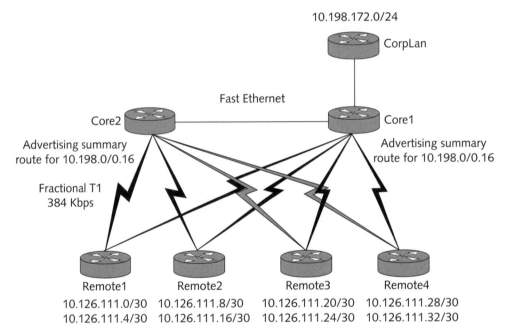

Figure 5-5   Query scope restricted by summary routes

In order to avoid this, you can use appropriately placed summary routes. For example, you can place a summary route to 10.198.0.0/16 on both Core1 and Core2. Routers Remote1, Remote2, Remote3, and Remote4 will then know about the summary route, but won't have any knowledge of the 10.198.172.0/24 subnet, so when they receive Core1's query packets, they will respond with empty query packets, and they will not attempt to propagate the query any further.

Scalable EIGRP Network Designs

The key to a scalable EIGRP network design is route summarization. Since each individual router on the network needs information only about part of the network, your job is to make sure that each router and each section of the network has the information they need, and only that information. Potential advantages include smaller routing tables and smaller query scopes. Careful allocation of IP addresses will make this easier.

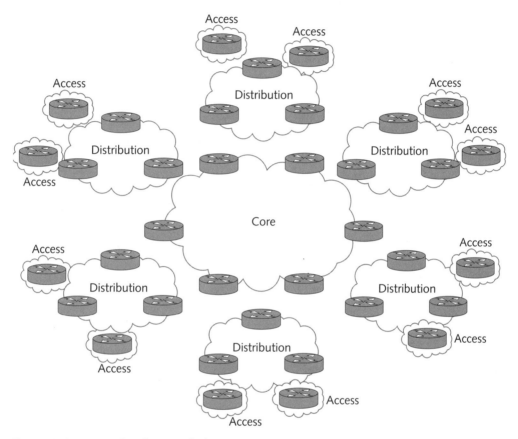

Figure 5-6   Hierarchical network design

In Figure 5-6, you can see an example of a hierarchical network design, segmented into core, distribution, and access layers. The distribution and access layers are further segmented into smaller sections. How you summarize routes on this network will depend on how you allocate IP addresses, as well as on what information each section of the Autonomous System needs to know about the rest. For the purposes of this chapter, you'll assume that you allocated IP addresses throughout the network in Figure 5-6 so that each section of the network has a contiguous block of IP addresses you can easily summarize.

In the core, each router needs to know which distribution router is the next hop for any packet sent to it, and how to forward packets to other core routers. An individual router may need to know details about the section of the distribution layer closest to it, especially if there are multiple paths, but it doesn't need to know anything about any section of the access layer. In general, you'll want to summarize routes sent from the distribution layer into the core so that the core routers have routes only for the next hop to the distribution layer. For example, a core router doesn't need to know that the distribution layer contains networks 10.221.16.0/28, 10.221.16.16/28, 10.221.16.32/28, and 10.221.16.48/28, and that the access layer contains networks 10.221.17.0/24 through 10.221.31.0/24; a core router needs to know that it can send any packets destined for anything in the summary route 10.221.16.0/20 to the next hop at 10.221.16.2. These summary routes can be configured on distribution routers.

In the distribution layer, routers need to know how to send packets to the core, and to any attached sections of the access layer. A distribution router doesn't need to know any of the details of the core or the attached sections of the access layer, except as much as it needs to know to send packets through redundant paths to either of these sections. It doesn't need to know anything at all about unattached sections of the access network, and it doesn't need to know anything at all about other sections of the distribution layer. Generally, you will want to summarize routes going from the attached sections of the access layer into the distribution layer; you also want to summarize routes for other sections of the distribution and access layers (or consider using default routes).

Finally, routers in each section of the access layer need to know only the details of their own sections, as well as how to connect to the distribution layer. In general, routers in the access layer should know as little about the rest of the network as possible; you should consider using default routes and summarizing as much as possible.

How well your IP addresses are allocated will affect how easy it is to summarize routes on your network. You will find it far easier to plan ahead and carefully allocate IP addresses than to readdress later. In addition to running the risk of outages while you readdress your routers, you will face numerous issues readdressing servers, and possibly even end hosts. Another potential source of problems is the number of paths through your system. More paths make route summarization and convergence more complicated and increase the query scope. In Chapter 6, you will learn about some ways you can control the number of paths EIGRP and other routing protocols choose by controlling the routes advertised.

CONFIGURING EIGRP

In this section, you'll learn how to configure EIGRP and adjust its parameters to summarize routes, do load balancing, and improve performance and stability over WAN links.

Activating EIGRP

Activating EIGRP on a router is just a matter of activating the routing protocol in an Autonomous System, and then indicating which networks you want EIGRP to advertise. To activate EIGRP on a router in Autonomous System 89, for example, you type:

```
Router(config)#router eigrp 89
```

To tell EIGRP to advertise the 192.168.200.0/24 network, you type:

```
Router(config-router)#network 192.168.200.0
```

The router summarizes each network along classful boundaries so that configuring EIGRP to advertise the network 10.105.15.0 also configures it to advertise all networks on the 10.0.0.0/8 Class A network. However, with EIGRP, you don't need to worry about putting an interface into a particular area, as you do with OSPF.

Since the bandwidth is, by default, one of the two variables used in EIGRP's metric calculations, you must make sure to configure each serial interface with the correct bandwidth since the router will otherwise assume that the link speed is 1.544 Mbps. You can configure the bandwidth on a serial interface to 128 Kbps in interface configuration mode with:

```
Router(config-if)#bandwidth 128
```

This command sets the bandwidth in units of Kbps. If EIGRP does not know the correct interface speed, sub-optimal routing will result. In cases where EIGRP thinks that the interface is significantly faster than it actually is, the router may have trouble receiving routing updates from its neighbors on networks attached to that interface, or it may have trouble converging.

 This is particularly important on frame relay and SMDS networks since the bandwidth can be set by the service provider.

On point-to-point links, Cisco recommends using the line speed for the bandwidth. This includes interfaces encapsulated with HDLC or PPP. For frame relay point-to-point interfaces or subinterfaces you should use the CIR, while with multipoint subinterfaces, you should use the sum of the CIRs of each connected link.

Changing EIGRP Timers

You can configure both the hello interval and the hold time on EIGRP routers. For example, you might wish to do this on a high-bandwidth frame relay subinterface. The default hello interval and hold time are 60 and 180 seconds, respectively, and the router may not notice until the end of the hold time if a frame relay subinterface goes down unless the entire physical interface also goes down. As usual, the EIGRP Autonomous System is required. You can set the hello interval to five seconds and the hold timer to 15 seconds in Autonomous System 9717 by entering the following in interface or subinterface configuration mode:

```
Router(config)#interfaces serial 0.1
Router(config-subif)#ip hello-interval eigrp 9717 5
Router(config-subif)#ip hold-time eigrp 9717 15
```

You should also make this change on any neighbors the router learned of through this subinterface. In general, you should avoid changing EIGRP's timers without both good reason and careful planning.

In some situations, you might wish to change the interval a router will wait for query packets before it enters the SIA state. On smaller networks, for example, you might wish to decrease this value since you can reasonably expect the query to be answered in less than three minutes. To set the active state timer to one minute in Autonomous System 214, you enter the following:

```
Router(config)#router eigrp 214
Router(config-router)#timers active-state 1
```

Additionally, you can disable the active state timer altogether by using the keyword **disable**, instead of an interval.

Configuring Route Summarization in EIGRP

Unlike OSPF, EIGRP automatically summarizes routes along classful boundaries, just like the classful distance vector routing protocols RIP and IGRP. Automatic summarization results in smaller routing tables with minimum configuration. Unlike RIP and IGRP, however, EIGRP includes the netmask with routing updates. As a result, you can turn off automatic summarization on any EIGRP router, and summarize routes along whatever boundaries you need.

In order to turn off automatic summarization on a route, you can use the following command in router configuration mode:

```
RouterA(config-router)#no auto-summary
```

Suppose RouterA has routes for 192.168.128.0/24, 192.168.129.0/24, 192.168.130.0/24, and 192.168.133.0/24, which are attached to Ethernet interfaces 0 through 3. On interface serial 0 and in Autonomous System 89, you can configure a summary route of 192.168.128.0/21 for these networks with the following command in interface configuration mode:

```
RouterA(config-if)#ip summary-address eigrp
89 192.168.128.0 255.255.248.0
```

As an interface command, the interface under which you configured the summary route advertises it; other interfaces won't advertise your manually configured summary route unless you specifically configure them to do so.

 A Cisco router won't advertise manually configured summary routes unless at least one of the subnets for the summary route is in its routing table.

When you configure route summarization on an interface, a Cisco Router l adds a summary route to the routing table. This summary route uses a **null interface** (numbered as interface Null0) as the next hop; a null interface is a software-only interface, like a loopback interface. Unlike a loopback interface, however, packets sent to a null interface are discarded. This kind of route is known as a **null route**. Routers receiving advertisements from the router with the summary route configured do not learn anything about the null interface; they only learn the summary route.

As a result, downstream routers forward packets to the router advertising the summary route. The router doing the summarizing looks in its routing table for the route with the longest match. If it finds a route with a longer match than the summary route, it sends the packet out the appropriate interface. If only the summary route matches, the router discards the packet.

For example, look at RouterA in the last configured example. Figure 5-7 shows all the individual routes included in the summary route for 192.168.128.0/21, which exists in RouterA's routing tables as a null route. Any routers receiving routing updates through RouterA's serial interface (and any routers further downstream) see this route only as 192.168.128.0/21, without ever learning about the null interface. They forward any packets for any subnet summarized by this summary route over to RouterA.

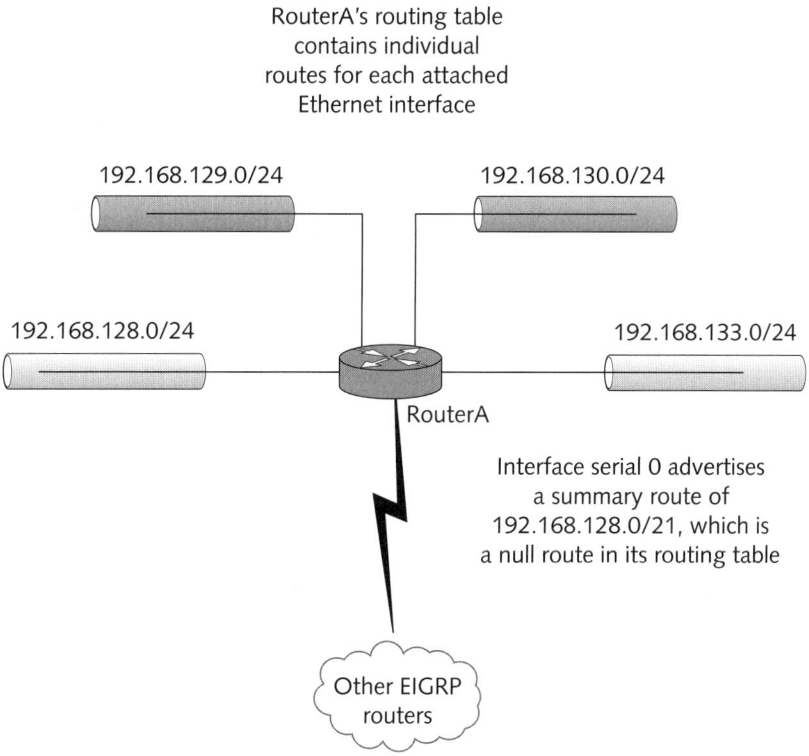

RouterA's routing table
contains individual
routes for each attached
Ethernet interface

Figure 5-7 Example of routes summarized

If a packet sent to a destination address on the 192.168.130.0/24 network reaches RouterA, RouterA looks in its routing table for the best match. Since its routing table contains a route for the 192.168.130.0/24 network, and since this route is a longer match than the null route to 192.168.128.0/21, RouterA forwards this packet out the appropriate Ethernet interface to its destination.

However, a packet for a destination address on the 192.168.134.0/24 network is also sent to RouterA. This network is not attached to any of RouterA's interfaces, but is included within the 192.168.128.0/21 summary route. As a result, RouterA is unable to find a better match for this packet, so only the null route matches. As a result, RouterA discards the packet. This is similar to the way a classful routing protocol discards packets on a network with discontiguous subnets. If your network contains discontiguous subnets, you must turn off automatic summarization with the **no auto-summary command** on the affected routers, or you will have connectivity problems between these subnets. This accidental summarization of routes is one of the reasons IP addressing requires such careful planning.

Additionally, keep in mind that EIGRP routers only do automatic summarization for attached networks. In Figure 5-8, for example, automatic summarization was turned off on the San Jose router. As a result, it does not summarize 172.16.100.0/24 and 172.16.120.0/24, and advertise a summary route to the Cupertino router; instead, it advertises both individual routes. Since these networks are not attached to Cupertino, it will not perform automatic route summarization on them and it will also advertise the individual routes. You can, however, manually configure an appropriate summary route.

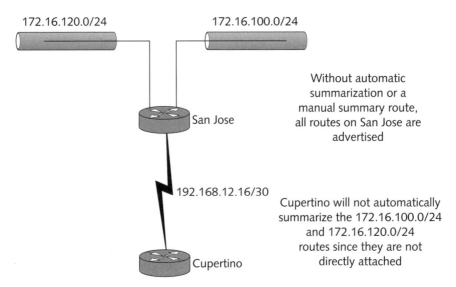

Figure 5-8   Without automatic summarization, all routes are advertised.

Finally, Cisco routers assign an administrative distance of five to summary routes they are advertising. Otherwise, internal and external EIGRP routes have administrative distances of 90 and 170, respectively.

Load Balancing in EIGRP

By default, Cisco routers load balance between a maximum of four paths with the same metric. You can configure this value from one path to six paths with the maximum paths command in router configuration mode:

```
Router(config-router)#maximum-paths 6
```

Packet Switching Methods

Typically, the manner in which a router sends packets depends on the method the router uses to switch packets. Cisco routers use several methods of switching packets to their destinations, depending on the type of hardware in use. The two methods found on all Cisco routers are **process switching** and **fast switching**. In process switching, when a packet is received on an interface, the system processor is interrupted as the router copies the packet from the interface buffer into system memory. The processor then looks at the Network layer address in order to find which interface to send it out, rewrites the packet header, and then copies the packet to the outgoing interface. The processor also places a copy of the header into the **fast-switching cache** for subsequent packets to that destination.

 Because the processor is interrupted, and must look at the Network layer of every process-switched packet, process switching is the slowest of Cisco's switching methods.

If a router uses process switching when it is load balancing between several different paths, the router sends each packet through a different route. Each time it rewrites the packet header, it also uses its load-balancing algorithm.

In fast switching, on the other hand, the router doesn't need to rewrite the packet headers or interrupt the system processor. It simply takes the packet header out of the fast-switching cache and sends it to its destination. This is significantly faster than process switching. However, the router must still put the header of the first packet in the fast-switching cache, which means that it must do process switching on that packet. At this time, the router uses its load-balancing algorithm. As a result, a router using fast switching load balances between destinations. Each packet to the same destination uses the same path, but packets sent to different destinations use different paths.

Using Variance to Configure Load Balancing

In EIGRP, you can also configure a router to load balance over paths with unequal metrics. EIGRP uses a parameter called the **variance** in selecting routes to be added to the routing table. By default, the variance is set to one, which results in load balancing over paths with equal metrics. EIGRP uses the variance as a multiplier, which you can configure to be any value from one to 128. When selecting routes to add to its routing table for a particular destination, an EIGRP router must verify that the feasible distance—the metric of the best path—is greater than the advertised distance, the best metric on the next hop router. It must also verify that the variance times the feasible distance of the best path to the destination is greater than the metric through the next hop router. If both these conditions are met for a path, then it is added to the router's routing table.

In Figure 5-9, HomeRouter has four paths to the destination network; the advertised distance and feasible distance of each path are summarized in Table 5-5. The metric values across each link were selected because they're easier to understand than typical EIGRP metrics, which can be rather large. The path with the best metric is through R1; the feasible distance is the sum of the cost of all links to reach the destination network, or 700 (200 for the link to R1, plus 500 for the link from R1 to the destination network). In this case, the advertised distance is just the metric for the link to the destination network, or 500. For this path, as well as the other three paths in Table 5-5, the feasible distance is larger than the advertised distance so they pass the first test.

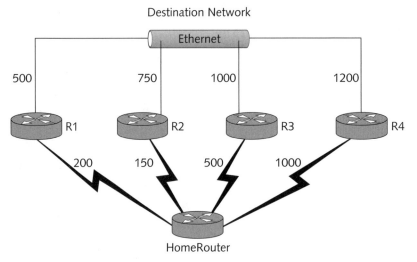

Figure 5-9   Variance example

Table 5-5 Feasible distances and advertised distances for the paths in Figure 5-9

Next Hop Router	Feasible Distance	Advertised Distance
R1	700	500
R2	900	750
R3	1500	1000
R4	2200	1200

However, whether or not HomeRouter will add any of the other routes besides the path through R1 depends on the variance. The path through R1 has the lowest feasible distance so it is automatically added; none of the other paths will be used to route packets if the variance is one since none of the other paths has a feasible distance less than 700 times one (or 700).

If you configure the variance on HomeRouter to be two, however, then any of the paths with a feasible distance less than 700 times two (or 1400) are included in the routing table. The path through R2 has a metric of 900, and is therefore added to the routing table. As you increase the variance, more routes are added to the routing table. With a variance of three, the path through R3 is added to the routing table (since its feasible distance of 1500 is less than 2100), and with a variance of four, each route in Figure 5-9 is included in HomeRouter's routing table (since the feasible distance of each route is less than 2800). So you can use the variance to have a router do load balancing down paths that it would not, by default, include in its routing table.

You can configure a variance of three by typing the following in router configuration mode:

```
Router(config-router)#variance 3
```

One final parameter controlling load balancing among routes with different metrics is traffic sharing. By default, EIGRP routers send traffic down each path inversely proportional to the ratio of the metric for each path. For example, if one path has a metric twice that of another path, then an EIGRP router sends half the traffic down the path with the higher metric. You can configure this with the **traffic-share** command. This command has two possible keywords, *balanced* and *min*. The balanced keyword (the default) shares traffic in inverse proportion to the metric, while the min keyword only sends traffic out the routes with the best metric. This means that routes with higher metrics remain in a router's routing table, but the router won't send any traffic through them. You can configure balanced traffic with this command in router configuration mode:

```
Router(config-router)#traffic-share balanced
```

EIGRP Over WAN Links

Because of the issues of bandwidth consumption and metric calculation, configuring EIGRP over WAN links requires additional caution.

Reserving Bandwidth for Routing Updates

After a network topology change, every EIGRP interface uses output rate queues to throttle the bandwidth used by routing protocol updates. By default, EIGRP will use a maximum of 50% of the bandwidth of an interface to send routing updates. However, you can configure this as needed. For example, you might need to increase the bandwidth percentage used by EIGRP if you manually configured the bandwidth on an interface to be lower than the actual bandwidth, in order to make sure that an expensive WAN link is used less often than other links. You can even configure the bandwidth percentage to be a value over 100%. To set the bandwidth percentage used by an interface in Autonomous System 89 to 150%, you can type the following command in interface configuration mode:

```
Router(config-if)#ip bandwidth-percent eigrp 89 150
```

You are likely to have routing problems if an interface is incapable of actually transmitting packets at 150% of the bandwidth configured on the interface.

Configuring Bandwidth for Multipoint Interfaces

EIGRP treats point-to-point frame relay interfaces and subinterfaces the same as other serial interfaces so configuring the bandwidth is just a matter of setting the bandwidth to be equal to the CIR. However, multipoint interfaces (such as a multipoint frame relay subinterface) are more complicated. Logically, EIGRP divides the bandwidth configured on a multipoint interface between each of the neighbors connected to that interface. If a multipoint interface has a bandwidth of 128 Kbps, and four neighbors, each with 128 Kbps bandwidth connected to that interface, then EIGRP assumes that each neighbor has 128 Kbps divided by four, or 32 Kbps of bandwidth. As a result, EIGRP assumes that each link is significantly slower than it actually is; the metrics for each link, as well as the bandwidth percentage used by routing updates, will be affected.

The situation becomes more complicated if some of the neighbors have circuits provisioned with different bandwidths or CIRs. If the value EIGRP uses for the bandwidth is too low, the metrics it advertises will be poorer than they should be for the links with the higher CIRs, and these links may be underused. On the other hand, if EIGRP uses too high a value for the bandwidth, the advertised metrics for the links with lower CIRs will be too low, and these links might become overloaded. If the CIRs of each link are more or less the same, you generally want to take the lowest CIR and multiply it by the number of neighbors to determine the appropriate bandwidth. So if you have a multipoint interface with three neighbors with 64 Kbps CIRs, and one neighbor with a 128 Kbps CIR, you should configure the bandwidth to be four times 64 Kbps, or 256 Kbps.

On the other hand, the more the CIRs of each link vary, the less effective this approach will be. For example, Router1 in Figure 5-10 has a frame relay multipoint interface. Two of its neighbors have CIRs of 1.544 Mbps, and a third has a CIR of 256 Kbps. If you configure the bandwidth at 768 Kbps (three times 256 Kbps), this will work well for only the slowest link. The other two links, on the other hand, will be significantly underused.

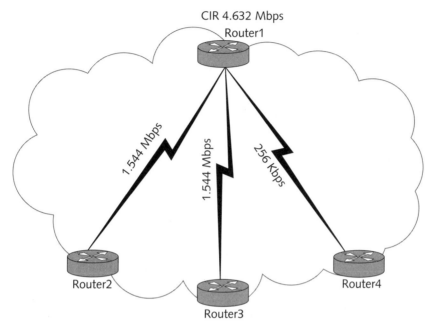

Figure 5-10   Multipoint frame relay interface with neighbors with different CIRs

In situations like the one shown in Figure 5-10, the best solution may be to configure the slowest link as a point-to-point link, and keep the two faster links as multipoint links. You can then configure the bandwidth of the multipoint interface at 3.088 Mbps so that EIGRP will use the correct value of 1.544 Mbps for each link. You can also configure the link to Router4 with its CIR of 256 Kbps as the bandwidth.

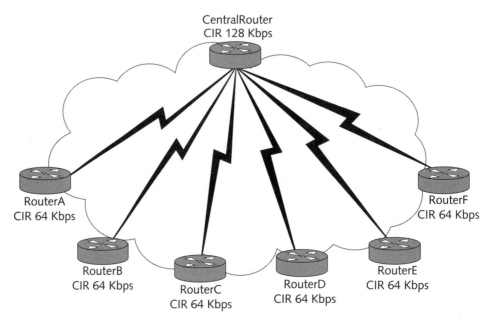

Figure 5-11   Oversubscribed frame relay network

Another situation that can cause problems is oversubscription. For example, in Figure 5-11, CentralRouter has a CIR of 128 Kbps, and its six neighboring routers each have CIRs of 64 Kbps. While with multipoint subinterfaces you would configure the CentralRouter with the sum of neighbors' bandwidths, in this case, the sum of bandwidths is 384 Kbps, three times its CIR. You might overload the CentralRouter. In this topology, it makes sense to configure each link as a point-to-point link, and set the bandwidth on each link on the CentralRouter and each hub router to one-sixth of the CentralRouter's CIR, 21 Kbps. On RouterA, for example, you do that by typing this in configuration mode:

```
RouterA(config)#interface ser 0
RouterA(config-if)#bandwidth 21
```

However, in case one of the spoke routers needs to send routing updates, EIGRP will use only 50% of the configured bandwidth, or approximately 10 Kbps. You may wish to set this value higher to increase the odds that EIGRP update packets get through properly. For example, in order to increase the bandwidth used by each router during EIGRP updates to 50% of the actual bandwidth, you must configure the percentage of bandwidth used to 152%. Assuming that the routers in Figure 5-11 are in Autonomous System 89, you do this on RouterA by entering the following in interface configuration mode:

```
RouterA(config-if)#ip bandwidth-percent eigrp 89 152
```

TROUBLESHOOTING AND MONITORING EIGRP NETWORKS

```
Router#debug ip eigrp
3d08h: IP-EIGRP: Processing incoming QUERY packet
3d08h: IP-EIGRP: Int 10.172.37.0/24 M 4294967295 - 1657856 4294967295 SM
4294967295 - 1657856 4294967295
3d08h: IP-EIGRP: 10.172.37.0/24 routing table not updated
3d08h: IP-EIGRP: 10.172.37.0/24 - do advertise out Serial1
3d08h: IP-EIGRP: Int 10.172.37.0/24 metric 2221056 - 1657856 563200
3d08h: IP-EIGRP: Processing incoming UPDATE packet
3d08h: IP-EIGRP: Int 10.172.37.0/24 M 2195456 - 1657856 537600 SM 281600 -
256000 25600
3d08h: IP-EIGRP: 10.172.37.0/24 - do advertise out Ethernet0
3d08h: IP-EIGRP: Int 10.172.37.0/24 metric 2195456 - 1657856 537600
3d08h: IP-EIGRP: Int 10.172.37.0/24 metric 2195456 - 1657856 537600
3d08h: IP-EIGRP: Processing incoming UPDATE packet
3d08h: IP-EIGRP: Int 10.243.15.0/24 M 2323456 - 1657856 665600 SM 409600 -
256000 153600
3d08h: IP-EIGRP: Int 10.172.38.0/30 M 2707456 - 1657856 1049600 SM 2195456 -
1657856 537600
3d08h: IP-EIGRP: 10.172.38.0/30 routing table not updated
3d08h: IP-EIGRP: Int 10.243.15.0/24 metric 2323456 - 1657856 665600
3d08h: IP-EIGRP: Int 10.243.15.0/24 metric 2323456 - 1657856 665600
```

Figure 5-12   Output of the debug ip eigrp command

In troubleshooting EIGRP, you can primarily look at four types of information: neighbors, network topology, routing tables, and protocol parameters.

One of the general tools you can use to debug EIGRP on a router is the **debug ip eigrp** command. This command displays summary information about EIGRP packets sent and received. Figure 5-12 shows an example of output from the **debug ip eigrp** command.

```
AMHERST#deb ip eigrp neighbor 1 10.9.5.38
First enable IP-EIGRP Route Events or EIGRP packet debug
AMHERST#deb ip eigrp
IP-EIGRP Route Events debugging is on
AMHERST#deb ip eigrp neighbor 1 10.9.5.38
IP Neighbor target enabled on AS 1 for 10.9.5.38
IP-EIGRP Neighbor Target Events debugging is on
Amherst#
2w3d: IP-EIGRP: 10.1.254.0/24 - do advertise out Serial0/0.10
2w3d: IP-EIGRP: Int 10.1.254.0/24 metric 281600 - 256000 25600
2w3d: IP-EIGRP: 10.9.5.0/30 - do advertise out Serial0/0.10
2w3d: IP-EIGRP: Int 10.9.5.0/30 metric 40512000 - 40000000 512000
2w3d: IP-EIGRP: 10.9.5.4/30 - do advertise out Serial0/0.10
2w3d: IP-EIGRP: Int 10.9.5.4/30 metric 40512000 - 40000000 512000
2w3d: IP-EIGRP: 10.9.5.8/30 - do advertise out Serial0/0.10
2w3d: IP-EIGRP: Int 10.9.5.8/30 metric 40512000 - 40000000 512000
2w3d: IP-EIGRP: 10.9.5.12/30 - do advertise out Serial0/0.10
2w3d: IP-EIGRP: Int 10.9.5.12/30 metric 40512000 - 40000000 512000
```

Figure 5-13   Output of the debug ip eigrp neighbor command

Since the **debug ip eigrp** command displays packet information, it can produce a lot of output and put a heavy load on a busy router. You should take care not to use this command on a busy network. The **debug ip eigrp summary** command summarizes EIGRP activity, providing information about neighbors and route redistribution.

Troubleshooting Neighbor Problems

Some of the tools to examine EIGRP neighbor relationships include the **show ip eigrp neighbor** command and the **debug ip eigrp neighbor** command. Figure 5-13 shows output from the **debug ip eigrp neighbor** command. You will notice that first you must use the **debug ip eigrp** command before you can use the **debug ip eigrp neighbor** command to examine a neighbor relationship in more detail. In Figure 5-13, you can see the networks advertised to a particular neighbor, along with their metrics. The **show ip eigrp neighbor** command can also be useful in troubleshooting neighbor problems. In Figure 5-14, you can see typical output from this command. The column with the heading Q gives a count of all the packets queued up to be sent to that particular neighbor.

```
Amherst#show ip eigrp neighbor
IP-EIGRP neighbors for process 1
H  Address        Interface  Hold   Uptime   SRTT  RTO   Q    Seq
                             (sec)   (ms)            Cnt  Num
0  10.9.5.38      Se0/0.10   14     00:01:18  0     5000  1    0
2  10.9.5.26      Se0/0.7    10     00:35:16  65    2280  0    4
1  10.9.5.30      Se0/0.8    14     00:35:41  72    2280  0    4
```

Figure 5-14   Output of the show ip eigrp neighbor command

One method of detecting problems with neighbor relationships is to use the **eigrp log-neighbor-changes** command in router configuration mode. This command will turn on console messages describing changes in an EIGRP router's neighbor relationship. In particular, it can help you learn about neighbors in the SIA state. Additionally, you can configure your router to send the console messages as **syslog** messages to a remote server. This allows you to keep a record of events on your routers, which you can examine after a problem. You can use console or syslog messages about EIGRP neighbor changes to gauge the stability of your network, as well as troubleshoot problems with routers in SIA mode.

In addition to showing neighbors stuck in the active state, logging neighbor changes may tell you about other problems. Following, you can see output from Amherst, which cannot establish a neighbor relationship with Boston, an adjacent router. Amherst keeps marking its neighbor 10.9.5.38 down and then up again.

```
Amherst(config)#router eigrp 1
Amherst(config-router)#eigrp log-neighbor-changes
Amherst(config-route)#^Z
Amherst#
2w3d: %SYS-5-
CONFIG_I: Configured from console by vty1 (10.225.117.11)
2w3d: %DUAL-5-NBRCHANGE: IP-
EIGRP 1: Neighbor 10.9.5.38 (Serial0/0.10) is down: retry
limit exceeded
2w3d: %DUAL-5-NBRCHANGE: IP-
EIGRP 1: Neighbor 10.9.5.38 (Serial0/0.10) is up: new
adjacency
```

```
2w3d: %DUAL-5-NBRCHANGE: IP-
EIGRP 1: Neighbor 10.9.5.38 (Serial0/0.10) is down: retry
limit exceeded
2w3d: %DUAL-5-NBRCHANGE: IP-
EIGRP 1: Neighbor 10.9.5.38 (Serial0/0.10) is up: new
adjacency
2w3d: %DUAL-5-NBRCHANGE: IP-
EIGRP 1: Neighbor 10.9.5.38 (Serial0/0.10) is down: retry
limit exceeded
2w3d: %DUAL-5-NBRCHANGE: IP-
EIGRP 1: Neighbor 10.9.5.38 (Serial0/0.10) is up: new
adjacency
Amherst#ping 10.9.5.38
Type escape sequence to abort.
Sending 5, 100-
byte ICMP Echos to 10.9.5.38, timeout is 2 seconds:
!!!!!
Success rate is 100 percent (5/5), round-
trip min/avg/max = 72/74/76 ms
```

On Boston, however, the console message tells us that the two routers are not on the same subnet, yet they can still communicate with each other; the IP address Boston gives for the neighbor is 192.168.254.1, which is not on the same subnet as 10.9.5.38.

```
Boston#show ip int brief
Interface   IP-Address   OK?   Method Status   Protocol
Ethernet0   10.19.28.1   YES   NVRAM  up         up
Serial0     unassigned   YES   unset  administratively down d
own
Serial1     unassigned   YES   unset  up         up
Serial1.1   10.9.5.38    YES   NVRAM  up         up
Boston#
22w4d: IP-EIGRP: Neighbor 192.168.254.1 not on common
subnet for Serial1.1
22w4d: IP-EIGRP: Neighbor 192.168.254.1 not on common
subnet for Serial1.1
22w4d: IP-EIGRP: Neighbor 192.168.254.1 not on common
subnet for Serial1.1
22w4d: IP-EIGRP: Neighbor 192.168.254.1 not on common
subnet for Serial1.1
22w4d: IP-EIGRP: Neighbor 192.168.254.1 not on common
subnet for Serial1.1
```

Figure 5-15 shows the reason why – Amherst's serial 0.10 subinterface is configured with a secondary address. A **secondary address** is an additional address applied to an interface. Although depreciated by Cisco, you can configure an interface on a router with multiple secondary addresses in order to allow the interface to be on two or more networks at the same time. For instance, a router's interface might have a primary IP address of 172.16.1.1 and a secondary address of 10.1.1.1. Secondary addresses are often used when discontiguous subnets cannot communicate under classful routing protocols.

However, EIGRP can only communicate over the primary IP address on an interface. As a result, Amherst keeps receiving hello packets from Boston, but it can't form an adjacency because Boston's hello packets don't contain an address on the same network as its primary address. In this case, configuring another subinterface on Amherst would have made more sense than a secondary IP address.

```
Amherst#show ip int s0/0.10
Serial0/0.10 is up, line protocol is up
  Internet address is 192.168.254.1/24
  Broadcast address is 255.255.255.255
  Address determined by setup command
  MTU is 1500 bytes
  Helper addresses are 10.117.254.26
                      10.117.254.20
  Directed broadcast forwarding is disabled
  Secondary address 10.9.5.37/30
  Multicast reserved groups joined: 224.0.0.10 224.0.0.9
  Outgoing access list is not set
  Inbound  access list is not set
  Proxy ARP is enabled
  Security level is default
  Split horizon is enabled
[Output omitted]
```

Figure 5-15   Output of the show ip interface command on Amherst

Troubleshooting EIGRP Topology

In order to troubleshoot EIGRP topology, you can use the **show ip eigrp topology** command. This command shows you all feasible successors in a router's topology database, along with the feasible distance and the advertised distance. You can look at all the links in the topology database by using the **all–links** keyword, or you can look at an individual path in more detail by using a route number after the **show ip eigrp topology** command. See Figure 5-16 for sample output from this command.

```
Cleveland#show ip eigrp topo
IP-EIGRP Topology Table for AS(10)/ID(10.123.11.1)

Codes: P - Passive, A - Active, U - Update, Q - Query, R - Reply,
       r - Reply status

P 10.77.95.192/30, 0 successors, FD is Inaccessible
        via 10.123.11.39 (2172416/2169856), FastEthernet0/0.1
P 10.77.95.194/32, 1 successors, FD is 2172416
        via 10.123.11.39 (2172416/2169856), FastEthernet0/0.1
P 10.30.254.0/24, 1 successors, FD is 28160
        via Connected, FastEthernet0/0.2
P 10.123.11.0/24, 1 successors, FD is 28160
        via Connected, FastEthernet0/0.1
P 10.30.61.4/30, 1 successors, FD is 297244416
        via Connected, Tunnel1
P 10.30.60.0/28, 1 successors, FD is 128256
        via Connected, Loopback0
P 10.30.61.0/30, 1 successors, FD is 297244416
        via Connected, Tunnel0
P 10.30.32.0/24, 1 successors, FD is 28160
        via Connected, FastEthernet0/0.3
--More--
```

Figure 5-16   Output from the show ip eigrp topology command

Other Troubleshooting Commands

Other useful troubleshooting commands include:

- The **show ip protocols** command. This shows you whether or not EIGRP is running on a router, its K-values, information about route summarization, and its neighbors (referred to as "Routing Information Sources").

- The **show ip route eigrp** command. This lists all the routes a router learned through EIGRP.

- The **show ip eigrp traffic** command. You can use this command to find out how many hello, update, query, reply, and acknowledgement packets have been sent and received by the router. Typical output of this command is shown in Figure 5-17.

- The **debug ip eigrp summary** command. This command shows a summary of EIGRP activity, including information about neighbors, metrics, and route redistribution.

```
BowlingGreen#show ip eigrp traffic
IP-EIGRP Traffic Statistics for process 10
  Hellos sent/received: 8758163/8478865
  Updates sent/received: 12342/9126
  Queries sent/received: 14/10
  Replies sent/received: 10/14
  Acks sent/received: 4928/1520
  Input queue high water mark 3, 0 drops
```

Figure 5-17   Output from the show ip eigrp traffic command

CHAPTER SUMMARY

❐ Enhanced Interior Gateway Routing Protocol (EIGRP) is a routing protocol with characteristics of both distance vector and link-state routing protocols. Like distance vector routing protocols, EIGRP routers only share information with their neighbors; however, they only send incremental updates when necessary, resulting in significantly lower bandwidth usage. Like link-state routing protocols, EIGRP routers keep track of network topology, but only for their neighbors' routing tables. This allows them to use less memory and CPU time, while simultaneously converging quickly after topology changes. EIGRP also uses protocol-dependent modules to route traffic on networks using Apple's AppleTalk and Novell's Internetwork Packet Exchange protocols.

❐ EIGRP routers use hello packets to establish adjacencies with their neighbors. Many EIGRP packets are sent reliably using the Reliable Transfer Protocol (RTP), requiring an acknowledgement (sometimes implicit) from the destination router. Each EIGRP router keeps track of its neighbors in its neighbor table, and its neighbors' routes in its topology table. It puts the best routes in its routing table, and keeps others in its topology table. After a topology change, an EIGRP router first looks in its topology table; if the metric advertised by the neighboring router for a route to the same destination (called the advertised distance) is less than the metric for the old route, the router installs this route (known as a feasible successor). If the router can't find a feasible successor in its topology table, it goes into active mode on that route and queries its neighbors. Each neighbor receiving a query packet queries its neighbors until a new route is found, or it is determined that the neighbors don't have any knowledge of a route.

❑ If a router fails to reply to a query, the neighbor that sent the query enters the stuck-in-active (SIA) state and puts all of the routes for that neighbor in active mode. Controlling querying and preventing routers from entering the stuck-in-active (SIA) state are necessary to make EIGRP scalable. You can control query scope with careful use of route summarization.

❑ In order to troubleshoot EIGRP, you can use the **show ip eigrp neighbors** and the **debug ip eigrp neighbors** commands to troubleshoot neighbor problems. The **eigrp log-neighbor-changes** command can help you determine when neighbors enter the stuck-in-active (SIA) state. The **show ip eigrp topology** command shows you a router's topology table.

KEY TERMS

ACK packet — Acknowledgement packet sent by an EIGRP router to acknowledge a packet sent using reliable transmission, such as an update packet.

active state — The state an EIGRP router enters when it must recalculate its routing table because it can't find a feasible successor for a failed route.

active state timer — The timer EIGRP uses to wait for replies to query packets sent to neighboring routers; if a router doesn't receive a response before the active state timer expires, it enters the stuck-in-active (SIA) state and resets that neighbor.

advertised distance (AD) — The EIGRP metric advertised by a neighboring router to a destination.

AppleTalk — The protocol developed by Apple to allow Macintoshes and other Apple computers to communicate with each other.

diffusing update algorithm (DUAL) — The algorithm used by EIGRP to build loop-free routing tables while allowing only those routers affected by a topology change to update their routing tables.

Enhanced Interior Gateway Routing Protocol (EIGRP or Enhanced IGRP) — A routing protocol proprietary to Cisco that combines the features of link-state and distance vector routing protocols, and offers support for the IPX and AppleTalk protocols.

fast switching — A method used by Cisco routers to forward packets; instead of creating a completely new packet header as in process switching, the router uses the packet header stored in the fast-switching cache without interrupting the system processor.

fast-switching cache — A cache used to store the headers of packets so that the next packet to a particular destination can use that header and be sent faster to the same destination.

feasible — In EIGRP, this describes a route that will be added to a router's routing table.

feasible distance (FD) — The sum of the EIGRP metrics for each link to reach a destination network.

feasible successor (FS) — The next hop router for the back-up route, selected by the DUAL algorithm, and kept in the EIGRP topology table.

finite state machine — A program that starts at a given state and uses information it receives in the form of input variables to go to the next state; EIGRP's DUAL algorithm is an example.

handle (H) — The number EIGRP assigns to each neighbor for tracking purposes.

High-level Data Link Control (HDLC) — A communication protocol used over serial lines.

hold time — The interval that a router waits to receive packets from a neighboring router before declaring it down; generally, the hold time is three times the hello interval.

Init bit — A bit set in EIGRP update packets indicating whether or not a router is first establishing a neighbor relationship with the router to which it is sending the update packets.

Internetwork Packet Exchange (IPX) — The protocol developed by Novell to allow Netware servers to communicate with each other and their clients.

K-values — The constants used by EIGRP (and IGRP) to calculate the metric of a route.

maximum transmission unit (MTU) — The maximum packet size supported on a network segment.

Media Access Control (MAC) address — Data Link layer address consisting of a unique 48-bit number assigned to each network interface card.

neighbor table — A table maintained by each EIGRP router that contains information about its neighbors.

NetWare — A network operating system designed by Novell that uses IPX and/or IP as its transport protocol(s).

null interface — A software-only interface (generally numbered as Null 0) that discards all packets that reach it.

null route — A route to a null interface, which discards all packets sent to it.

passive state — The state of an EIGRP router when it does not need to recalculate its routing table.

Point-to-Point Protocol (PPP) — A communication protocol used over serial links.

process switching — The slowest switching method used in Cisco routers; when a packet arrives, the system processor is interrupted while the packet is copied into memory and the packet header is rewritten (and copied into the fast-switching cache).

protocol dependent module (PDM) — A module used by EIGRP to route a specific protocol, such as AppleTalk or IPX.

query — *See* query packet.

query packet — A packet sent to request information about a route when a router doesn't have a feasible successor in its topology table for a particular destination, which requires acknowledgement from the receiving router.

query range — The possible paths that a query made in an EIGRP Autonomous System could travel.

query scoping — Efforts made to limit the query range in an EIGRP Autonomous System.

queue count — The number of packets in the queue waiting to be sent to a particular EIGRP neighbor.

Reliable Transport Protocol (RTP) — The protocol used by EIGRP routers to communicate with each other, which sends routing updates using reliable transmission.

reply — *See* reply packet.

reply packet — A unicast packet sent in response to a query packet, requiring acknowledgement from the receiving router.

reset — When a neighboring router fails to send an acknowledgement to a query packet, a router puts all of its routes through that neighbor into active mode in order to verify that they are still valid.

retransmission list — The list of packets sent by RTP that a neighboring router has yet to acknowledge; each packet is retransmitted if an acknowledgement isn't received up to 16 times or the hold time (whichever is longer).

retransmit timeout (RTO) — The length of time (in milliseconds) an EIGRP router waits before retransmitting a packet, determined by the size of the smooth round trip timer.

secondary address — An additional IP address added to an interface in order to allow an interface to be on more than one network at a time; Cisco routers support multiple secondary IP addresses.

smooth round trip timer (SRTT) — The interval (measured in milliseconds) between the time a router sends an EIGRP packet requiring acknowledgement, and the time the router receives the ACK packet from the other router.

split horizon — In order to avoid routing loops, a router won't send routing updates learned through an interface back out that interface again.

Stuck-in-active (SIA) state — The state an EIGRP router enters when it sends out query packets and it does not receive a response before the active state timer expires (three minutes by default); an EIGRP router responds to this by resetting any neighbor that doesn't respond.

successor — A neighboring router with the lowest loop-free path to a particular destination.

Switched Multimegabit Data Service (SMDS) — A public packet-switched data communications service.

syslog — A facility used to send log messages to a remote server; in Cisco routers, the syslog facility is used to send console messages to a server where they can be logged.

topology table — In EIGRP, the topology table contains all destinations advertised by neighboring routers.

update packet — An EIGRP packet containing updated information about routes.

uptime — The amount of time in seconds since a router first heard from a neighbor.

variance — A parameter used by EIGRP to configure load balancing over unequal paths; the variance is taken into account when choosing feasible successors.

REVIEW QUESTIONS

1. Which of the following statements best describes how EIGRP shares properties of both distance vector and link-state routing protocols?

   a. EIGRP routers know the topology of the entire network (like a link-state routing protocol), but only send routing updates to their neighbors (like a distance vector routing protocol).

   b. EIGRP routers only know about connected networks (like a distance vector routing protocol), but support VLSMs and route summarization (like a link-state routing protocol).

   c. EIGRP routers keep topology tables with routes advertised by their neighbors (like a link-state routing protocol), and only send routing updates to neighboring routers who need the updates (like a distance vector routing protocol).

   d. EIGRP routers only send routing updates to routers who need the updates (like a link-state routing protocol), and keep topology tables with routes advertised by their neighbors (like a distance vector routing protocol).

2. Why doesn't RTP send hello packets reliably? (Choose all that apply.)

   a. RTP doesn't send any packets reliably.

   b. RTP only needs to send routing updates reliably.

   c. EIGRP doesn't use hello packets to send routing information.

   d. Each router receiving a hello packet sends another one back to the sender in five seconds anyway.

3. Since EIGRP is proprietary to Cisco, routers from other vendors don't support it. True or false?

4. When a router running EIGRP sends a routing update or another reliably transmitted packet, how does it set the retransmission timeout (RTO) to decide how long to wait before sending another packet?

   a. The RTO is always the same as the hello interval.

   b. The RTO is determined using the smooth round trip timer.

   c. The RTO is always the same as the hold time.

   d. The RTO is set to three minutes by default.

5. What parameters need to be the same in a hello packet in order for two EIGRP routers to become neighbors? (Choose all that apply.)

   a. Autonomous System

   b. hello interval and hold time

   c. K-values

   d. area number

6. When do EIGRP routers send routing updates to their neighbors? (Choose all that apply.)

   a. every 30 seconds

   b. every 30 minutes if a route hasn't been refreshed in that interval

   c. when a new router comes online

   d. after a network topology change

7. Why do EIGRP routers put back-up routes into their topology tables?

   a. so that each EIGRP router has full knowledge of the topology of the network

   b. in order to allow EIGRP routers to quickly find a new router in case the primary route fails

   c. for load balancing between multiple paths

   d. to restrict the possible query scope

8. If the bandwidth is the same throughout an EIGRP Autonomous System (if all interfaces are 10 Mbps Ethernet, for example), by default, what parameter will have the most effect on the metrics in the Autonomous System?

   a. cumulative delay along the path

   b. worst reliability along the path

   c. interface bandwidth

   d. highest load along the path

9. Why is it important to manually configure the bandwidth on serial interfaces?

   a. If bandwidth is configured too low, the interface is unable to use more than that bandwidth.

   b. EIGRP is unable to complete the metric calculation and won't route packets through that interface.

   c. Routes through a serial interface with unconfigured bandwidth are more likely to become stuck in the active state.

   d. EIGRP uses 1.544 Mbps as the bandwidth on serial interfaces, by default, which may be too low or too high for the interface.

10. RouterA has a path to the 172.16.138.0/26 network with a metric of 128256. Its neighbor, RouterB, is the only neighbor advertising a route to this network; the metric to get to the neighbor is 28160, and the neighbor's advertised distance for the route is 2169856. If RouterA's path to 172.16.138.0/26 fails, what happens?

a. RouterA installs the path through RouterB into its routing table with a metric of 2169856.

b. RouterA rejects the path through RouterB since RouterB's advertised distance is greater than the current metric for the path to 172.16.138.0/26, and queries its neighbors.

c. RouterA installs the path through RouterB into its routing table with a metric of 2298112.

d. RouterA installs a back-up route from one of its other neighbors into its routing table.

11. Which of the following problems on RouterA would cause a route to enter the stuck-in-active (SIA) state? (Choose all that apply.)

a. RouterA's CPU is too busy and the router is unable to reply to query packets within three minutes.

b. Packets over the link between RouterA and a neighbor it queried are being dropped.

c. RouterA doesn't have a feasible successor for that route.

d. A neighboring router's CPU is too busy and it is unable to reply to query packets within three minutes.

12. What effect does tripling the variance have on an EIGRP router's topology and routing tables?

a. A router adds fewer paths to both its topology and routing tables.

b. A router adds more paths to both its topology and routing tables.

c. A router adds paths with poorer metrics to its routing table, and uses them for load balancing.

d. A router adds paths with poorer metrics to its topology table, but no additional paths to its routing table.

13. Why does a router, by default, use a longer hello interval and hold time on a serial interface (60 and 180 seconds) instead of the five and 15 seconds used on an Ethernet interface? (Choose all that apply.)

a. because a router can often detect the outage of a serial interface through the loss of the carrier

b. so that EIGRP hello packets do not go over the maximum bandwidth allowed on an interface

c. to conserve bandwidth

d. so that EIGRP properly calculates the metric on serial links

14. Why does EIGRP put a null route into the routing table when you configure a summary route on a router? (Choose all that apply.)

    a. in order for the router to advertise the summary route to other routers

    b. so that the router will drop packets sent to destination addresses with the same prefix as the summary route while routing packets to subnets with longer prefixes

    c. so that the router can advertise routes to subnets of the summary route with longer prefixes

    d. so that the router will drop packets sent to subnets of the summary route with longer prefixes while routing packets to destination addresses with the same prefix as the summary route

15. How can you restrict the scope of queries a router might send out when it puts a route into the active state? (Choose all that apply.)

    a. by segmenting your network into multiple EIGRP Autonomous Systems

    b. by turning off automatic route summarization

    c. by summarizing routes

    d. by reducing the number of redundant paths

16. You are unable to reach one discontiguous subnet from another subnet on an EIGRP network. However, you know that EIGRP supports VLSMs and should also be able to handle discontiguous subnets. What are the possible causes of this problem? (Choose all that apply.)

    a. EIGRP doesn't send the subnet mask with routing updates.

    b. EIGRP automatically summarizes routes along classful boundaries.

    c. Poor metrics prevent these routes from entering the routing table.

    d. You've configured summary routes that include the discontiguous subnets.

17. Which of the following commands would show you information about redundant paths on an EIGRP network that aren't feasible successors?

    a. show ip route eigrp

    b. show ip eigrp neighbor

    c. show ip eigrp topology

    d. show ip eigrp topology all-links

18. Which of the following commands would give you information about an EIGRP router's relationships with its neighbors? (Choose all that apply.)

    a. show ip eigrp

    b. show ip protocols

    c. show ip eigrp neighbor

    d. debug ip eigrp neighbors

19. Which of the following commands or series of commands would configure a summary route for the 10.172.16.0/20 network in AS 21 on interface Ethernet 0?

   a. int eth 0
      ip summary-address eigrp 21 10.0.0.0 255.0.0.0

   b. int eth 0
      ip summary-address eigrp 21 10.172.16.0 255.255.240.0

   c. router eigrp 21
      no auto-summary
      int eth 0
      ip summary-address eigrp 21 10.172.16.0 255.255.240.0

   d. router eigrp 21
      no auto-summary
      int eth 0
      eigrp 21 summary-route 10.172.16.0 255.255.240.0

20. You want to configure EIGRP on RouterA. RouterA has a multipoint frame relay subinterface with a CIR of 1.544 Mbps. It connects to RouterB (128 Kbps CIR), RouterC (128 Kbps CIR), and RouterD (768 Kbps CIR). How can you configure RouterA in order to make sure that EIGRP uses the proper metric for each link?

   a. Configure bandwidths of 1.544 Mbps on RouterA, 128 Kbps on RouterB and RouterC, and 768 Kbps on RouterD.

   b. Configure bandwidths of 128 Kbps on all four routers to prevent RouterB and RouterC from being overloaded.

   c. Configure the connection between RouterA and RouterD as a point-to-point link with a bandwidth of 768 Kbps, configure the multipoint subinterface on RouterA at 256 Kbps, and the bandwidths on RouterB and RouterC at 128 Kbps.

   d. Configure the connection between RouterA and RouterD as a point-to-point link with a bandwidth of 768 Kbps, configure the multipoint subinterface on RouterA at 128 Kbps, and the bandwidths on RouterB and RouterC at 128 Kbps.

23. RouterA and RouterB are on the same Ethernet segment but cannot become EIGRP neighbors after you activate EIGRP on both routers. However, if you configure RIP on the two routers, they can exchange routing information without any problems. What are possible reasons why RouterA and RouterB cannot become neighbors? (Choose all that apply.)

   a. RouterA and RouterB have different hello intervals and hold timers.

   b. RouterA and RouterB are in different Autonomous Systems.

   c. Neither RouterA nor RouterB is configured to be ineligible to become the designated router on that segment.

   d. RouterA's address on that Ethernet segment is a secondary IP address.

24. How does EIGRP compare to IGRP? (Choose all that apply.)

   a. Both are pure distance vector routing protocols.

   b. EIGRP can learn IGRP routes.

   c. EIGRP and IGRP have nearly the same metric.

   d. EIGRP is a link-state protocol, while IGRP is a distance vector protocol.

CASE PROJECTS

Case 1

You are hired by an insurance company with a large network at its corporate headquarters in Milwaukee, WI. The company has over one thousand routers on its corporate network, and over 500 more routers connected to its main office through frame relay links. The company has been slow to move away from IGRP, even though large routing tables are a problem and convergence is slow; your boss, the CTO, likes the ease of configuration of IGRP, as well as the fact that it requires less CPU and memory than routers running link-state protocols, such as OSPF. With the frame relay network to the remote offices, network administrators use static routes instead of IGRP to save on bandwidth. However, this has become an administrative nightmare, and they'd like to use the same dynamic routing for both the corporate LAN and the frame relay links to the remote office. The CTO wants you to investigate the possibility of using EIGRP for the entire network. Compare and contrast EIGRP to RIP, IGRP, and OSPF in terms of convergence, ease of configuration, and the amount of traffic used, both during stable use and during routing updates. Can the company use EIGRP over frame relay links while using only minimal bandwidth for routing updates? Additionally, what advantages does EIGRP offer when migrating from IGRP?

Case 2

You work for an international manufacturing company and you just migrated from RIP to EIGRP on your network. Your network is highly redundant and includes at least two paths to every destination. Also, you configured each router with a high variance in order to allow for unequal load balancing between destinations. However, some of the WAN links to overseas offices are unstable. Periodically, after one of the links goes down, users throughout the company have trouble reaching certain destinations for up to several minutes at a time. While troubleshooting the problem, you discovered that the other links to these destinations remain up. However, while logging neighbor changes, you noticed that many of your routers had routes in the stuck-in-active state. What are the likely causes of this problem? How do you go about troubleshooting this? What steps can you take to reduce the frequency of the problem?

Case 3

You are brought in as a consultant to the Famous Flower Company. It's network administrator, Todd Smith, is having trouble with OSPF on their network and wants to look at EIGRP. Todd tells you that CPU usage on all but the most powerful routers in the core is too high, and many of the routers inside and outside the core have been crashing. He has split the Autonomous System into as many different areas as possible, and uses route summarization as much as possible, but most routers in the Autonomous System are older, and have relatively little memory and slower CPUs. However, he can't summarize routes within areas. All but a handful out of approximately 500 routers are Cisco routers, and all non-Cisco routers are in remote offices. Todd wants you to thoroughly compare the two routing protocols for him, and he wants you to describe how using EIGRP might help reduce memory and CPU usage on his routers.

Case 4

You are brought in as a consultant for Benite Industries, Inc. Benite has a national frame relay network with 23 remote offices that they use for billing and inventory traffic. Each PVC has a CIR of 128 Kbps. The network topology is a star running EIGRP, with each remote office having a single PVC to the main office; they use a modem for dial backup if the PVC goes down. However, the CIR for the main office is only 1.544 Kbps so there isn't enough bandwidth for each remote office to use the full CIR at the same time (for example, they're oversubscribed). Benite's CTO reports that they've had some performance problems over the whole frame relay network related to some problems with a couple of the PVCs. When one of these links goes down, several other offices also have trouble reaching the main office. He's sure it's related to the fact that the main office is oversubscribed, but none of his staff has been able to figure out what they must do to solve the problem. How would you go about troubleshooting the problem in order to confirm or deny what the CTO told you? How do you go about configuring the bandwidths on the hub router and on each spoke router so that each interface is advertised with the proper metric, and each interface devotes enough bandwidth to routing updates?

6

ROUTE FILTERING AND POLICY ROUTING

After reading this chapter and completing the exercises you will be able to:

♦ Describe and configure several methods to filter routes

♦ Use any of several methods to filter and control routing updates

♦ Describe and configure policy routing

In this chapter, you'll learn how to control routing updates. Controlling routing updates is important when you need to use two or more routing protocols, or if a routing protocol isn't working (the way you want it to). Especially on complex networks, by default, a routing protocol may not do what you require. However, you can control routing updates in order to route packets through your network as needed.

Additionally, you will learn how to configure policy routing. Policy routing allows you to change how a packet is forwarded based on its source address. This means that you can offer different levels of service depending on the customer. Policy routing is also a tool you can use to fine-tune routing within your Autonomous System.

REASONS TO CONTROL ROUTING UPDATES

Because many networks are more complex than you'd like, you will often find that you must control routing updates in order to maximize efficiency and scalability. Some of the situations where you might need to control routing updates include:

- When redistributing routes between your Autonomous System and that of another organization. This often happens when two organizations merge, for example. You will learn about redistribution in Chapter 7.

- When reducing the number of redundant paths between routers. Too many paths between routers can increase the size of routing tables and cause routing problems; you may find it helpful to restrict traffic to one or two paths.

- When allowing another organization (such as a vendor or partner) to connect to your network to access some of your servers or other network resources, while maintaining control over which portions of your network are accessible.

- When reducing the routing update traffic on particular WAN interfaces.

Cisco IOS offers you several tools to control routing updates. They include route filtering and policy routing.

FILTERING ROUTING UPDATES

One mechanism to control routing updates is to control the amount of information that a router advertises to other routers. You may wish to do this for a variety of reasons, including reducing the size of routing tables, preventing routing update traffic over WAN links, and preventing routers from learning about suboptimal paths.

Passive Interfaces

One technique to filter routing information sent by a router is to configure routers not to send routing updates out particular interfaces. You can do this by configuring interfaces that you do not want to advertise routing updates as passive interfaces. In routing protocols like RIP or IGRP, a **passive interface** listens for routing updates from other routers but does not send routing updates itself. In routing protocols like OSPF or EIGRP, which require routers to become neighbors before they share routing information, a passive interface does not send hello packets, and that interface cannot become a neighbor with another router; additionally, it neither sends nor listens for protocol updates.

You can configure a passive interface with the **passive-interface** command in router configuration mode. You use this command to make an individual interface passive, or you can use **passive-interface default** to make all interfaces passive except where specifically configured otherwise. For example, to make interface serial 1 a passive interface in EIGRP Autonomous System 112, you would type the following:

```
Router(config)#router eigrp 112
Router(config-router)#passive-interface serial 1
```

In OSPF, you have fine-grained control over which interfaces you can use to send routing updates. However, you do not have such control with other routing protocols. When you configure a network to be advertised by RIP, IGRP, or EIGRP, the routing protocol also advertises all other interfaces with networks falling within the same classful boundaries. For instance, using the network statement **network 10.21.56.0** in router configuration mode for RIP, IGRP, or EIGRP activates not only the interface with an address on the 10.21.56.0/24 network, but all interfaces whose addresses fall within the 10.0.0.0/8 block. This might include an interface with an address of 10.172.16.1, for example, or an interface with an address of 10.1.45.1. You can use passive interfaces to prevent routing protocols from activating unwanted interfaces.

 When configuring passive interfaces in OSPF, OSPF treats attached networks as stub networks unattached to another router. While a router advertises these networks, it does not send or receive routing information through a passive interface.

On networks with WAN links, configuring passive interfaces can eliminate routing update traffic. For example, in Figure 6-1, routers in the hub-and-spoke WAN topology are configured to eliminate routing update traffic over the WAN links. Each hub router is configured to use a default route through its serial interface so that it forwards all packets without a local route to the hub router. The hub router configured each of the interfaces attached to the spoke routers as passive interfaces; it uses static routes to get to the networks attached to each spoke router, which it redistributes back into EIGRP. As a result, no routing update traffic travels over the WAN. Using default routes, the spoke routers can reach the rest of AS 78. By redistributing static routes, the hub router can still advertise routes to the rest of the AS. This can be particularly useful with low-speed serial links, or in cases where a service provider charges for bandwidth used.

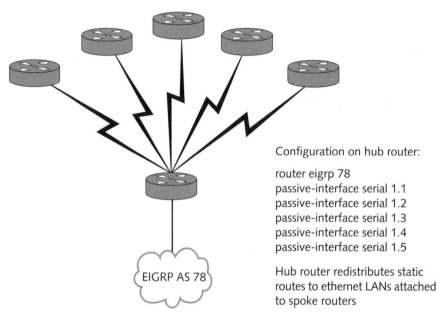

Each spoke is a router configured without a dynamic routing protocol and with a default route:

ip route 0.0.0.0 0.0.0.0 serial 0

Configuration on hub router:

router eigrp 78
passive-interface serial 1.1
passive-interface serial 1.2
passive-interface serial 1.3
passive-interface serial 1.4
passive-interface serial 1.5

Hub router redistributes static routes to ethernet LANs attached to spoke routers

EIGRP AS 78

Figure 6-1   Hub-and-spoke topology using passive interfaces and default routes to eliminate routing updates

Null Routes

One way to prevent packets from being routed improperly is to use null routes. As you learned in Chapter 5, a null route is a route to a software interface that simply discards any packets sent to it. As a result, while null routes allow you to change routing behavior on your network, they act more as packet filters than route filters. However, if its routing table contains a more specific route for a packet, a router will select the more specific path instead of the null route.

For example, you might wish to prevent routes to or from private IP address space (such as 10.0.0.0/8) from leaving your Autonomous System and going out onto the Internet. You might configure null routes like these on any border routers connected to the Internet:

```
Router(config)#ip route 10.0.0.0 255.0.0.0 null 0
Router(config)#ip route 172.16.0.0 255.240.0.0 null 0
Router(config)#ip route 192.168.0.0 255.255.0.0 null 0
```

For any destination network inside this address space that the border router must reach, its routing table must contain a route with a longer prefix. In order to send packets to the 10.21.0.0/16 network, for instance, the router must have a path to this network in its routing table. Otherwise, the packets are matched by the null route and discarded.

Route Filters

You can also use route filters to control routing updates. In a **route filter**, an access list is applied to the routing updates sent out on an interface in order to filter out unwanted routes. An **access list** is a list used to identify packets or addresses to be filtered. Different features of Cisco IOS software may use an access list to perform different tasks. For example, an access list can be used by a route filter to prevent certain routes from being advertised, while an access list applied to an interface can prevent packets from certain source IP addresses or packets using certain protocols from entering or leaving that interface.

Access Lists

In order to filter routes or packets, you must first specify routes or packets. An access list merely lists what you want to filter. While you can use access lists to filter a wide variety of protocol types, in this chapter, you'll learn about how to use IP access lists. While most of what you will learn applies to packet filtering, most also applies to any situation where access lists are used.

Access List Processing   An access list consists of a list of statements telling a router to permit or deny packets depending on the attributes in the access list. When a router decides whether or not it will filter a particular packet, it goes through the access list in order to see if the packet matches the statements in the access list:

- If a statement in the access list doesn't match the contents of a packet, the router goes on to the next statement (in order).

- If a statement does match a packet's contents, the router permits or denies the packet depending on what the statement says.

- If a packet reaches the end of the access list without a match, the router denies the packet. This is known as **implicit denial**.

Because of the manner in which routers process access lists, you should keep two things in mind. First, you must be careful about the order of access list statements. A router uses the first matching statement to decide what to do with a packet. If a packet you wish to deny with the fifth statement in an access list is permitted by the second statement, the packet will go through. Secondly, since an access list automatically denies any packet that doesn't match any statements, you will often want to end an access list with a statement permitting all packets. Otherwise you may block traffic you intended to let through.

Finally, access lists on Cisco routers are also sensitive to the order in which you enter commands. You must keep the following in mind when attempting to change an access list:

- Any statement added to an access list goes to the end of the list.

- An attempt to remove a statement in an access list deletes it.

As a result, you must be very careful when changing access lists. Depending on the situation, when you change an access list, you may wish to:

- Configure an entirely new access list with the changes you need, and then replace the old access list with the new access list in configuration statements.

- Delete the existing access list and then configure a new one with the changes you need.

You may find it useful to write the access list in a text editor such as Microsoft Notepad, and cut and paste it into the terminal window when needed.

Standard IP Access Lists A **standard IP access list** uses the source address to filter. In addition to using numbers to name access lists, Cisco IOS also uses numbers for the types of access lists. For instance, standard IP access lists can be any number from 1 to 99. You can configure a standard IP access list with the **access-list** command in configuration mode:

```
access-list [1-99] [permit|deny] [ip-address]
[wildcard-mask]
```

The wildcard mask allows you to specify a range of addresses. Like the wildcard mask used to specify networks in OSPF, the wildcard mask used by an IP access list consists of zeroes, which match any bit, and ones, which are don't care bits. In order to deny addresses on the 10.21.147.0/24 network in standard IP access list 88, for example, you would enter the following in configuration mode:

```
Router(config)#access-list 88 deny 10.21.147.0 0.0.0.255
```

In this example, every bit in the first three octets of the source address of a packet must match in order for a router to deny it. The router does not care about the bits in the last octet.

Since a router looks through an access list to determine which packets to deny and which packets to permit, the order in which you place access list statements determines whether or not packet lists are filtered. In general, you should place specific access list configuration statements first, and then more general statements last. For example, if you wish to configure standard IP access list 77 to allow traffic through from the host 10.63.16.89 and from subnets 10.198.115.0/24 and 10.22.114.0/24, deny traffic from other subnets in 10.0.0.0/8 and allow all other traffic through, you would configure your access list like this:

```
Router(config)#access-list 77 permit 10.65.16.89 0.0.0.0
Router(config)#access-list 77 permit 10.198.155.0
0.0.0.255
Router(config)#access-list 77 permit 10.22.114.0 0.0.0.255
Router(config)#access-list 77 deny 10.0.0.0 0.255.255.255
Router(config)#access-list 77 permit any
```

Since the list is processed in order, packets with source addresses of 10.65.16.89, or on the 10.198.155.0/24 and 10.22.114.0/24 networks, are allowed through because they are matched by one of the first three statements. Other packets on the 10.0.0.0/8 network, however, match the fourth statement and are denied. Keep in mind that without that last statement permitting all traffic, the router denies all other traffic.

Additionally, you can use the keywords **host** or **any** in place of the address and wildcard mask. The host keyword allows you to specify a host name afterward (instead of using an IP address and a wildcard mask of 0.0.0.0), while the any keyword matches any IP address (so a wildcard mask isn't necessary). In place of the host keyword, you can also use a single IP address (the router assumes the wildcard mask is 0.0.0.0 in either case). For example, to configure standard IP access list 21 to deny traffic to the hosts 10.212.56.87 and 172.16.138.12 while allowing all other traffic, you could type the following in configuration mode:

```
Router(config)#access-list 21 deny host 10.212.56.87
Router(config)#access-list 21 deny 172.16.138.12
Router(config)#access-list 21 permit any
```

In general, you should be careful when applying wildcard masks to make sure that the wildcard mask actually specifies the range of IP addresses you want. This is particularly important when a wildcard mask doesn't fall along octet boundaries. For example, you might need to use an access list to match addresses on the network 192.168.241.0/29. You might think that this access list statement would match:

```
Router(config)#access-list 21 permit 192.168.241.0 0.0.0.8
```

However, this statement will not do what you want. In binary, the last octet of the wildcard mask is 00001000, so this access list statement matches any packet with a source address whose first three octets are 192.168.241, and whose last octet cannot contain bits in any position except the fourth from the end. As a result, this statement only matches 192.168.241.0 (where all bits in the last octet are zeroes) and 192.168.241.8 (where the last octet is 00001000).

Extended IP Access Lists   If you need to filter packets based on something other than the source address, however, you must use an extended IP access list. **Extended IP access lists** allows you to filter packets based on source and destination address, IP protocol type, and port number, among other packet attributes.

In general, the syntax for extended IP access lists is:

```
access-list [100-199] [permit|deny] [protocol|
protocol-key-word] [source address] [source-wildcard-mask]
[destination-address] [destination-wildcard-mask]
```

In order to distinguish between extended IP access lists and other types of access lists, you must identify extended IP access lists with a number between 100 and 199. Depending on the protocol you're configuring, this command may also have other options (such as TCP port numbers, if a statement in an extended IP access list permits or denies specific TCP protocol packets). You can block or allow a variety of protocols by keyword (including IP, TCP, UDP, EIGRP, IGRP, and OSPF) or by the protocol number, which appears in the IP packet header.

In order for a packet to match a line in a standard access list, only its source address must match. For extended access lists, however, every option must match. The process a router goes through when it looks at a packet to see if it matches an extended access list goes like this:

1. The router compares the source address of the packet to the source address and mask in the top line of the access list not yet processed. If it does not match, it repeats this process beginning at Step 1 for the next line of the access list. If it does match, the router goes on to the next step.

2. The router compares the destination address of the packet to the destination address and wildcard mask in the line from the access list. If the router doesn't find a match, it repeats this process for the next line.

3. The router compares the protocol listed in the line of the access list with the protocol of the packet. The keyword **ip** matches every IP protocol. If the router doesn't find a match, it repeats this process for the next line.

4. The router compares protocol options (if any) for the line in the access list to the packet. If these match, the router permits or denies the packet depending on what that line in the access list says. If these don't match, then the router begins the process all over again.

5. If this is the last line in the access list and the router hasn't found a match yet, the router uses implicit denial to deny the packet.

In order to use extended IP access list 115 to block IP packets with a source address on the 10.127.14.0/24 network and a destination address on the 172.16.142.16/29 network, you would type the following in configuration mode:

```
Router(config)#access-list 115 deny ip 10.127.14.0
0.0.0.255 172.16.142.16 0.0.0.7
```

You can also use the host and any keywords, as you can with standard access lists. As with standard access lists, you should be careful to make sure that your wildcard mask matches the IP address range you actually wish to filter. The fact that extended IP access lists are more complex makes this even more important.

The options that allow you to match on other packet attributes vary depending on the protocol. For example, in order to filter based on the TCP port number, you first use the **tcp** keyword, and then you specify the port numbers after the destination address with either the **eq** (equal), **gt** (greater than), or **lt** (less than) keywords. In order to use extended IP access list 177 to filter packets with a source address on the 192.168.1.0/24 network, a source port greater than 1023, a destination address of 172.16.1.10, and a destination port of 80, and allow all other IP traffic, you would type the following in configuration mode:

```
Router(config)#access-list 177 deny ip 192.168.1.0
0.0.0.255 gt 1023 host 172.16.1.10 eq 80
Router(config)#access-list 177 permit ip any any
```

In many cases, you'll also be able to use keywords for TCP port names (and other protocol parameters you can filter with an access list). For example, TCP port 80 can also be specified with the **www** keyword.

Named Access Lists   Introduced in Cisco IOS 11.2, **named access lists** remove some of the problems associated with access lists identified by numbers (often called **numbered access lists**). Named access lists have these advantages:

- They allow you to create more than 100 access lists for a particular type or protocol on a router.

- They allow you to create access lists with descriptive names so you can easily identify their purposes.

- They allow you to selectively delete entries from an access list without deleting the whole list and starting over again.

- They can be used with both standard and extended access lists.

However, named access lists also have several disadvantages:

- They cannot be used on versions of Cisco IOS before 11.2.

- They cannot be used for all the same purposes as traditional standard and extended access lists (although they can be used for route filters and packet filters).

- Although you can delete entries from a named access list, any new entries in a named access list go to the end of the list.

To configure a named standard access list, first you define the access list with the **ip access-list** command in configuration mode. You must then use the **standard** keyword to identify this as a standard access list; while a router can use the number of a traditional access list to tell what kind of access list it is, with a named access list, you must specifically configure the type of access list. To begin a standard access list named RouteFilter, you would type the following in configuration mode:

```
Router(config)#ip access-list standard RouteFilter
```

The name of the access list can use most alphanumeric characters, including punctuation marks such as ? or @, although the names must begin with a letter. Additionally, access list names are case sensitive (so RouteFilter would be a different list than routeFilter).

At this point, the router enters named access list configuration mode and you can enter permit and deny statements. You do not need to begin each statement with the name of the access list. However, each statement must begin with the **permit** or **deny** keywords. Additionally, you can use the **remark** keyword to enter a comment into the access list about the purpose of the access list itself, or a particular line. A remark is any comment up to 100 characters long.

In order to continue configuring your standard access list named RouteFilter, you begin to enter permit and deny statements. In order to block the 172.16.212.0/24 network, allow the 172.16.0.0/16 network, and deny all other traffic, you would type the following in named access list configuration mode:

```
Router(config-std-nacl)#remark Block route to
172.16.212.0/24
Router(config-std-nacl)#deny 172.16.212.0 0.0.0.255
Router(config-std-nacl)#remark Allow other routes to
172.16.0.0/16
Router(config-std-nacl)#permit 172.16.0.0 0.0.255.255
```

Configuring a named extended access list works much the same way. You first activate and name the access list with the **ip access-list extended** command, and then you enter permit, deny, or remark statements, as necessary. In order to create an extended access list that blocks traffic originating on the 198.168.0.0/16 network from reaching TCP port 23 (telnet) on the 172.16.198.0/24 network, allows all other IP traffic, and contains a comment in the access list to indicate the purpose, you would enter the following in configuration mode:

```
Router(config)#ip access-list extended BlockTelnet
Router(config-ext-nacl)#remark Block telnet from
192.168.0.0/16 to 172.16.198.0/24
Router(config-ext-nacl)#deny tcp 192.168.0.0 0.0.255.255
172.16.198.0 0.0.0.255 eq telnet
Router(config-ext-nacl)#permit ip any any
```

Applying Access Lists   Generally, in order to use an access list you must apply it. How you actually apply it depends on how you are using the access list. For example, in order to apply an access list as a packet filter on an interface, you must apply it to the interface with the **ip access-group** command using the name or number of the access list as an argument. You must also apply the access list to outgoing or incoming packets with the **in** or **out** keywords. In order to apply the named access list BlockPing to incoming packets on the serial 0 interface, you would type the following beginning in interface configuration mode:

```
Router(config)#int s 0
Router(config-if)#ip access-group BlockPing in
```

When maintaining access lists on your routers, you should be careful not to apply a non-existent access list. Generally, applying a non-existent access list is equivalent to not applying an access list at all. This can happen easily with a typo, especially with named access lists; if you type BLockPing instead of BlockPing when applying an access list onto the serial 0 interface in the example above, it is the same as not applying an access list at all. However, in some circumstances, applying a non-existent access list may have unpredictable results, and should generally be avoided.

Editing Access Lists   Because access lists are sensitive to the order in which you enter permit or deny statements, changing a long access list can be a lot of work. You either need to delete the access list and retype it from scratch, or build and apply another access list with a new name or number. Named access lists allow you to delete some lines, but with long access lists, you still wind up doing a lot of typing.

However, you can get around this by keeping a copy of each access list on your network in a text file. If you need to change an access list, you can edit the copy on a laptop or a PC, and then apply it. The text file contains the steps you would take to manually:

1. Remove the access list from the interface (or wherever it was applied) in order to prevent unpredictable problems.

2. Delete the existing access list.

3. Re-create the access list as needed.

4. Re-apply the access list.

The commands should be the exact same commands you would use to manually configure the access list on a router. You can also add comments to the text file even in numbered access lists by starting a line with an exclamation point. While the router will ignore these lines and won't save them in the configuration, it will help you identify the purpose of an access list in a particular text file. See Figure 6-2 for an example of an access list kept in a text file.

```
! File is named acl.txt.
! Comments (lines which will not be included in the access list) begin with a !
!
! Access list for Router interface serial 0/0.1 to allow 172.16.1.1 and
172.16.198.24
! and block other hosts in 172.16.0.0/24
!
interface serial 0/0.1
no ip access-group 72 in
exit
no access-list 72
access-list 72 permit host 172.16.1.1
access-list 72 permit 172.16.198.24
access-list 72 deny 172.16.0.0 0.0.0.255
access-list 72 permit any
interface serial 0/0.1
ip access-group 72 in
```

Figure 6-2   Text file containing an access list

Finally, you will want to apply the access list changes in the text file to the router. You can do this in one of two ways:

- Put the router into configuration mode and cut and paste the entire text file into the terminal or telnet session. This is just like manually entering the configuration commands, except that you can edit them at your leisure beforehand.

- Use Trivial File Transfer Protocol (TFTP) to merge the text file into the router's running configuration.

In order to use TFTP to merge the text file containing the access list into the router's running configuration, you must have a working TFTP server, and you must use either the **config net** command with older versions of Cisco IOS, or the **copy tftp** command with newer versions. Free TFTP servers are available for Windows and UNIX operating systems.

In either case, you should use a template you know works. If any configuration statement in the text file containing the access list is wrong, the router will give you an error and ignore the statement. Depending on the configuration statement and how you're using the access list, this could cut you off from the router. Overall, you should be extremely careful when making changes to access lists on routers.

Order of Access List Entries   In general, you should place more specific entries at the beginning of an access list and more general entries later. For example, if you wish to block access to 192.168.233.12, allow packets from the rest of the 192.168.0.0/16 network, and deny all other packets, you first need a statement denying 192.168.233.12. Otherwise, any statement allowing packets from the 192.168.0.0/16 network also allows packets from that host through. You configure that particular list as follows:

```
Router(config)#access-list 11 deny 192.168.233.12 0.0.0.0
Router(config)#access-list 11 permit 192.168.0.0
0.0.255.255
```

In this case, all other packets are denied by the implicit denial at the end of the access list.

Often network administrators will explicitly include the denial at the end of the access list as follows:

```
Router(config)#access-list 11 deny any
```

This has the advantage of making the implicit denial at the end obvious to anyone who reads the access list. However, you can no longer add statements to the access list since the denial at the end would match packets before any additional statements could. You would have to delete and rebuild the access list instead.

Additionally, you should place statements in access lists so that packets are matched as soon as possible. If you want to allow packets from both 172.16.0.0/16 and 192.168.54.0/24, and deny all other packets, and you expect most of your traffic to arrive from 192.168.54.0/24, you would place the statement allowing that network before the statement allowing 172.16.0.0/24:

```
Router(config)#access-list 75 permit 192.168.54.0
0.0.0.255
Router(config)#access-list 75 permit 172.16.0.0
0.0.255.255
Router(config)#access-list 75 deny any
```

Since the majority of your traffic is matched by the first statement, the router also processes the access list faster in most cases.

Verifying Access List Configuration   While verifying that access lists were configured properly depends in large part on what you're doing with them and how you applied them, you can easily verify that each access list was configured as you intended with the **show access-lists** command. You can use it to show all access lists configured on a router, or you can use it to view individual access lists by name or number. Figure 6-3 shows typical output of the **show access-lists** command. Note that this command does not show you comments in a named access list; however, you can view those by using the **show running-config** command.

```
Standard IP access list 96
    permit 172.16.224.0, wildcard bits 0.0.0.255
    permit 206.83.0.0, wildcard bits 0.0.0.255
    permit 213.169.18.0, wildcard bits 0.0.127.255
Extended IP access list 111
    deny tcp host 201.14.129.4 any eq smtp log
    permit ip any any
Extended IP access list 161
    deny udp 10.198.178.0 0.0.0.255 any eq snmp log
    permit udp any any eq snmp log (1627882 matches)
    permit ip any any (2163566239 matches)
Extended IP access list LOCAL-IP
    permit ip 10.206.0.0 0.0.127.255 any (1564401549 matches)
    permit ip 138.104.25.0 0.0.0.255 any (26169909 matches)
    permit ip 209.115.40.0 0.0.7.255 any (635217019 matches)
    permit ip 209.115.48.0 0.0.7.255 any (348722297 matches)
    permit icmp any any (1471789 matches)
    deny ip any any (1477979 matches)
```

Figure 6-3   Typical output of the show access-lists command

Additionally, you can tell the router to indicate how often a particular line in an access list was matched with the **log** keyword at the end of a permit or deny statement in an access list. If you do, the router shows you the number of times it saw packets matching that statement every time you use the show **access-lists** command. This can help you identify whether or not you applied an access list correctly, or whether or not the access list is doing what you expect it to do. For example, each entry in both extended access list 161 and named access list LOCAL-IP in Figure 6-3 was configured with the **log** keyword. Keep in mind that you do not need to use this keyword on every line in an access list. You only need it where you troubleshoot, or where you want to keep track of the number of hits against an access list.

Disadvantages of Access Lists Because each packet requires additional processing if an access list is applied to an interface, access lists can slow down a router. Extended access lists require more processing than standard access lists and have a greater impact on performance. Additionally, access lists may prevent a router from using some of the faster methods of packet switching that a Cisco router uses to forward packets to their destinations. For each line in an access list a router must check a packet against, the router must use a little more CPU time. Additionally, it will take slightly longer to deliver the packet. This does not necessarily mean that long access lists use a lot of resources since a router stops checking after the first match. A long access list that matches most packets early is still relatively efficient. However, the resources used depends in part on how the access list is used by the router.

How Route Filters Work

In order to filter routing updates, route filters use access lists to decide which routes they will accept and which routes they will reject. Route filters can work on both incoming and outgoing routing updates. In other words, you can filter both the routes a router will advertise, and incoming routes accepted from other routers. In general, a router goes through the following process when it receives a routing update, or when it is about to send one out:

1. The router examines the interface affected by the routing update to see whether or not there is a routing filter applied to that interface.

2. If there isn't a route filter for that interface, the packet is processed normally. If there is, the router examines its access list to determine whether or not it should drop routes in the update.

3. If a statement in the access list matches a route inside the update, the router processes the route according to the access list. If a deny statement matches, the route is dropped; if a permit statement matches, the route is kept.

4. If a route doesn't match any of the statements in a route filter, the route is dropped by implicit denial at the end of the access list. If this is not what you want, you must configure a permit statement at the end of the route filter to allow any route.

While an access list used to filter packets increases the amount of CPU time a router must use when it forwards packets, and causes a router to forward packets more slowly, a route filter has little effect on a router's performance.

Configuring Route Filters

In order to configure a route filter, you should follow these steps:

1. Create an access list to match the routes you wish to filter.

2. Determine which interface or interfaces you wish to apply the route filter to, and whether you wish to apply it to incoming or outgoing routing updates.

3. Apply the route filter with the **distribute-list** command.

The syntax for the **distribute-list** command differs depending on whether you're filtering incoming or outgoing updates. In addition to configuring the access list used, you can configure the interface to which the filter will be applied; if you don't apply it to a specific interface, it will be applied to all interfaces. For instance, suppose you want to filter incoming routes from the 10.0.0.0/8 block received by EIGRP in Autonomous System 65000 on interface serial 0. You want to allow all other routes. To use access list 67 to filter these routes, you would enter the following in configuration mode:

```
Router(config)#access-list 67 deny 10.0.0.0 0.255.255.255
Router(config)#access-list 67 permit any
Router(config)#router eigrp 65000
Router(config-router)#distribute-list 67 in serial 0
```

Configuring route filters on outgoing interfaces is slightly more complicated. In addition to specifying an access list and an interface, you can also select a specific routing process, including static and connected routes, and the Autonomous System of the routing process, if necessary. Table 6-1 summarizes the options for the **distribute-list out** command.

Table 6-1   Options for the **distribute-list out** command

Command	Description
distribute-list	Activates the route filter.
[access list number or name]	Assigns an access list to the route filter.
out	Indicates that the filter will apply to outgoing updates.
[interface name]	Optional. Indicates the name of an interface where the route filter will be applied.
[routing process]	Optional. Gives the name of a routing process (such as RIP or EIGRP) or the keywords **static** or **connected**. You can use this to filter routing updates redistributed from a specific source of routing information.
[Autonomous System or process ID]	Optional. Gives the name of an Autonomous System or the process ID for a routing process.

In order to use named access list RouteFilter out of all interfaces for EIGRP AS 781, you would type the following in router configuration mode:

```
Router(config-router)#distribute-list out RouteFilter
eigrp 781
```

Depending on the routing protocols in use on your network, route filters may have some restrictions. For example, because OSPF depends on each router having complete knowledge of the network's topology, route filters in OSPF apply only to external routes. Additionally, you can't apply a route filter in OSPF to a single interface. You must apply it to all interfaces.

Verifying Route Filters

To verify use of route filters, you must first determine whether or not the interface was applied as you intended. Then you can look at the routing table or use debug commands to determine whether or not the proper routes are being filtered.

You can use the **show ip interface** command to see whether or not a route filter was applied to a particular interface. You can also use the **show access-list** command to verify that the route filter was configured properly.

You can use debug commands to look at the actual routing updates sent and received in order to see if routes are being filtered properly. For example, you can use the **debug ip rip** command to see the routes RIP sends with its updates.

However, in protocols such as OSPF or EIGRP, updates only occur after a topology change. In these cases, you may find it more helpful to look directly at the routing tables. If the route filter was applied to incoming routes, you can look directly at a router's routing table to determine whether or not a route filter is working as anticipated. If the route filter was applied to outgoing routes, however, you cannot use the routing table on that router. You can, however, look at the routing table on any routers receiving those routes.

If a router's routing table contains routes in addition to those you expected, you may need to clear the routing table with the **clear ip route** command. You can specify an individual route, or you can clear all routes with the **clear ip route *** command. You may also specify debug commands at this time in order to examine the updates sent and received. Obviously, this should be done with caution on a busy router, as it may cause problems. For instance, in OSPF, this command forces a router to recalculate its routing table.

Filtering Based on Administrative Distance

On networks where multiple routing protocols are running, and a router learns about routes from different sources, you can also filter based on administrative distance. A Cisco router does this automatically based on the default administrative distances assigned by a router. Table 6-2 lists the default administrative distances assigned by the source of routing information. Routes with lower administrative distances are preferred over those with higher administrative distances. For instance, a route learned through IGRP has an administrative distance of 100. It is preferred over a route learned through RIP (administrative distance of 120), while a route learned through EIGRP (administrative distance of 90) is preferred over both.

Table 6-2 Default administrative distances used by Cisco routers

Source	Administrative Distance	Description
Connected	0	Routes known through connected interfaces
Static	1	
EIGRP summary route	5	
External Border Gateway Protocol (BGP)	20	You will learn about BGP in Chapters 7 and 8
EIGRP	90	
IGRP	100	
OSPF	110	
Intermediate System-to-Intermediate System (IS-IS)	115	A link-state routing protocol somewhat similar to OSPF
RIP	120	
EIGRP external route	170	
Internal BGP	200	
Unknown routing source	255	Maximum possible administrative distance

In order to set the administrative distance of a particular route, you go into router configuration mode for the routing protocol for which you wish to change administrative distances, and use the **distance** command. The basic form of the **distance** command is:

```
Router(config-router)#distance weight [address
wildcard-mask [access-list]]
```

In addition to specifying the administrative distance, you can also specify a route for it to apply to, or an access list, including a range of routes.

For example, in order to change the administrative distance of OSPF routes learned to be 95 (and hence preferred over IGRP routes), you would type the following in configuration mode:

```
Router(config)#router ospf 1
Router(config-router)#distance 95
```

If you wish to change only the administrative distance of routes to the 192.168.1.0/24 network, you would type the following instead:

```
Router(config-router)#distance 95 192.168.1.0 0.0.0.255
```

For EIGRP, you can specify the administrative distance for both internal and external routes. The command takes the form:

```
Router(config-router)#distance eigrp internal-distance
external-distance
```

To set the administrative distance of internal EIGRP routes to 100 and external EIGRP routes to 180, you would type the following in router configuration mode:

```
Router(config-router)#distance eigrp 100 180
```

In general, you should be careful using this command. Using routes learned from multiple sources of routing information can lead to routing and convergence problems. However, in some situations, you cannot use only one routing protocol, and changing the administrative distance may be an effective way of manipulating the routing tables to select the best routes. For example, you might use administrative distance to select the best route when you're redistributing routing protocols, which you'll learn about later in Chapter 7.

Another use of administrative distance is a floating static route. A **floating static route** is a static route with an administrative distance set so that the router prefers it only when the primary route (generally one learned through a dynamic routing protocol) goes down. A static route with an administrative distance of 220, for example, is preferred over none of the sources of routing information in Table 6-2, except unknown sources. As a result, this floating static route is only used if all other sources of routing information fail.

Network administrators often use floating static routes as backups. For example, if the primary route to a destination fails, you want the router to use an alternate route (such as through dial backup with a modem). However, if you advertise the dial back-up route with a dynamic routing protocol, it may be activated when the primary route is still functioning. If the dial back-up route requires a long-distance or international call, for example, this can be quite expensive. Using a floating static route, the dial back-up route is activated only when the primary route fails.

In order to configure a floating static route, you must configure a static route and give it an administrative distance greater than the primary route. For example, in order to configure a floating static route to the 10.212.0.0/20 network through a next hop of 10.210.54.1, and an administrative distance of 220, you would enter the following in configuration mode:

```
Router(config)#ip route 10.212.0.0 255.255.240.0
10.210.54.1 220
```

USING ROUTE MAPS TO IMPLEMENT ROUTING POLICY

Route maps allow you to configure policy-based routing (also called **policy routing**). First introduced in Cisco IOS 11.0, **policy-based routing** allows you to route packets differently based on properties of the packets. For example, you can send packets through different paths based on the source address; this means that you can route less important traffic, such as Web browser traffic, over a lower-speed link, while sending high-priority traffic, such as interactive traffic for a billing system, through a higher-speed link.

One of the potential uses of policy-based routing is to use route maps to mark each packet with a precedence, or TOS value, at the edge of the network, allowing routers at the core to prioritize traffic. This means that you can provide different **Quality of Service (QOS)** to different types of traffic. QOS is often used to ensure that interactive traffic arrives on time. For example, some organizations run voice traffic over their IP networks; it allows them to save money on long-distance bills. However, if voice packets arrive late or out of order, then the quality of phone calls deteriorates and they may not be usable. However, using Quality of Service can help ensure the quality of voice traffic over IP networks. In addition to using route maps to set the precedence of different types of packets you can use these values in a queueing policy. **Queueing** allows routers to reorder packets, so that certain types of packets may have greater priorities than others. Otherwise you would have to explicitly set the precedence of the packets at each WAN interface in the core.

Another potential use of route maps is for service providers to route packets from different sources through different paths. This allows you to route packets from different customers through different paths depending on the level of service paid for; it can also allow you to route packets from suspect destinations on the Internet away from high-security areas on your internal network.

You can also use route maps to filter the routes you redistribute from one routing protocol into another. Route maps allow you a finer degree of control over the routes redistributed versus normal route filters.

How Route Maps Work

In a route map, you can use these attributes of a packet to make policies:

- The source address of a packet
- The protocol
- The application
- Packet size

Like an access list, you must first create a route map and then apply it to an interface, or use it in a **redistribution** command when redistributing routing protocols (which you will learn about in Chapter 7). A route map consists of a series of permit and deny statements. Each statement has one or more conditions (or **match** statements), which the router attempts to match the packet against, and then it may have one or more actions (or **set** statements), which it runs against the packet. Unlike an access list, however, route maps are processed in an order specified by a sequence number. By specifying the sequence number, you can specify the order in which the route map runs each statement.

In effect, a route map works like a computer program you added to the router's configuration. Each permit or deny statement works like an if/then statement; if a packet matches the **match** statement, then the router applies the **set** command to the packet. While this does potentially make a router's configuration more complex, it can also be a powerful tool to manipulate routing tables.

When processing a route map, a router goes through the following process:

1. The router looks at the statement with the lowest number not yet checked.

2. It sees if the packet fits the conditions listed in the match statement.

3. If the packet matches a deny statement in a route map, then the packet is processed normally.

4. If the packet matches a permit statement, then the router performs any **set** commands listed in this route map statement.

5. If the packet doesn't match the statement, the router goes back to Step 1 until the packet matches a statement in the route map. If this is the last statement in the route map, then the packet is treated as if it matched a deny statement. How this effects the packet depends on how the route map is being used.

 Since a packet that doesn't match any statements in a route map is denied, you may wish to add a statement at the end of the route map matching all packets. You can then have a **set** statement with some default action, such as sending all packets to a null interface (which discards them), or routing them all normally.

Configuring Route Maps

To configure a route map, you must first use the **route-map** command to define a route map statement:

```
Router(config)#route-map map-tag [permit | deny]
[sequence-number]
```

The keywords of this command are:

- *map-tag*. This is the name of the route map, which generally should describe the purpose of the route map.

- **permit**. If a packet matches the **match** conditions for a permit statement, then the router processes the packet according to any **set** statements that are part of this statement.

- **deny**. If a packet matches the **match** conditions for a deny statement, then the packet is no longer processed through the **set** command in the route map. When doing policy-based routing, if a packet isn't matched by any of the **match** commands, then the packet is processed normally.

- *sequence number.* This determines the order in which a router attempts to match a packet against the statement. The sequence number can be any number from 0 to 65,535. This command is optional and will default to 10.

 Since a router, by default, makes the sequence number of a route map statement 10, you should always manually configure sequence statements. If you don't, when you attempt to add new route map statements, you may instead be adding statements to statement number 10.

Adding Match Statements to a Route Map

After defining the route map statement, you add **match** and **set** statements that determine which packets or routes match the route map statement, and what happens when they do match. The rules for matching are:

- A packet matches a particular **match** statement if any of the conditions in it matches. Each **match** statement may have several different conditions. For example, one **match** statement may have three different access lists. If a packet matches any one of those access lists, then it also matches that **match** statement.

- In order to match a route map statement, a packet must match every **match** statement line in the route map. If there are two lines with **match** statements in a route map statement, then the packet must match both lines. Since a packet must match each **match** statement, the order you configure them in doesn't matter.

To configure a route map statement after you define it, you use the **match** command in route map configuration mode:

```
Router(config-route-map)#match conditions
```

You can use a wide variety of matching conditions. These include:

- **ip address** *access-list* [*access-list* ...]. This matches any destination network or packet matched by the access list or lists specified.

- **ip next-hop** *access-list* [*access-list* ...]. This statement matches any next hop router that is allowed by the access list or lists specified.

- **ip route-source** *access-list* [*access-list* ...]. Here the router advertising the route matches if it is matched by the access list or lists configured.

- **interface** *interface-type interface-number.* If a route forwards packets out of the interface or interfaces configured, then this statement matches.

- **length** [*min* | *max*]. This statement matches a packet based on whether or not it is equal to or greater than minimum packet length configured, or less than or equal to the maximum packet length configured. Packet length can be any value from 0 to 2147483647, and refers to the Layer 3 packet length (excluding headers from lower-level protocols).

- **metric** *metric-value.* This matches any packet with a metric equal to the value configured, which can be any value from 0 to 4294967295.

- **Route-type [internal | external [type-1 | type –2] local].** Matches either internal or external routes (including OSPF type 1 and type 2 external routes), as well as locally generated routes (such as connected or static routes). Matches any type of route if the route-type is left off.

- **tag** *tag-value.* This matches any route with the tag value configured. You can configure a particular route with a tag using a **set** statement in a route map, or by setting it during protocol configuration; you can give a static route a map tag, for example, with the **ip route** command.

These aren't the only possible matching values; others exist for other protocols, such as BGP, which you'll learn about in Chapters 7 and 8.

Note that the context of the **match** statement in some cases affects how or if it is interpreted. Applying a route map to redistribution between two routing protocols, for example, makes a statement matching packet length useless.

Adding Set Statements to a Route Map

You can configure the **set** command in much the same way you configure the **match** command. You can configure multiple **set** commands; each **set** command listed in a matching route map statement is performed.

Just like the match command, the basic form of the **set** command is:

```
Router(config-route-map)#set conditions
```

Also like the **match** command, the conditions following the **set** command can vary widely. These affect the destination address or interface:

- **set ip next-hop** *ip-address.* Sets the IP address of the next hop. The IP address must be the address of an adjacent router. This command always takes precedence over whatever the router may have in its routing table for packets to all destinations, known or unknown. If you configure more than one IP address, the router uses the first one that happens to be up.

- **set interface** *interface-type interface-number.* A router uses this command to select the outgoing interface for packets. If you configure more than one interface with this command, the router selects the first interface that happens to be up. However, the router does not use this command unless a packet's destination network is in its routing table; otherwise, it is ignored. This prevents the router from forwarding broadcast packets out the interface. If you need to forward packets with unknown addresses, you can use the **set default interface** or the **set ip default next-hop** commands. In general, you should use this with point-to-point links.

- **set default interface** *interface-type interface-number.* This command sets the default interface, which is only used if the router doesn't have a specific route to the destination network. You can select more than one interface, in which case the router selects the first interface in the list that happens to be up. In general, you should use this with point-to-point interfaces.

- **set ip default next-hop** *ip-address.* Sets the default next hop address. The router also only uses this command to route packets when there isn't a specific destination for a packet in its routing table. If you configure more than one IP address with this command, the router attempts to use them in the order they were configured.

When configuring **set** commands in a route map, you should keep in mind that the context helps determine the effect a **set** command has on a packet. For example, **set ip default next-hop** and **set default interface** only apply if a router doesn't already have a specific route for a packet. On the other hand, a router always uses the **set ip next-hop** command to select a path for a packet. Additionally, once a router selects the destination address or interface with the first applicable **set** command, it ignores later ones.

Configuring Quality of Service with Route Maps

In addition to or instead of setting a packet's destination address, you can set the metric of redistributed routes, the tag value (useful for matching by other route maps), or values related to the Type of Service (TOS). The **Type of Service** is an 8-bit field in an IP packet header that can be used to set the priority of an IP packet. It contains two fields that you can set with **set** commands on a route map, the **IP Precedence** field and the **IP TOS** field (also known as the **Class of Service (COS) field**). According to RFC 1349, the IP Precedence field determines the priority of a packet, while routers should use the IP TOS field to make trade-offs between throughput, delay, reliability, and cost. The Type of Service field also contains a third, unused field, the 1-bit **Must Be Zero (MBZ field)**, which routers ignore; this field is sometimes considered part of the IP TOS or COS field.

 While all IP packet headers contain the TOS field, not all vendors interpret or mark it in the same way. Additionally, often the IP TOS field and the IP Precedence field are used interchangeably. This means that routers from other vendors may not honor the way Cisco routers set these fields, and vice versa.

To set the IP TOS field in IP packets, you use the **set ip tos** command. This command takes either a number from 0 to 15 as its argument, or one of the names in Table 6-5. To set the IP TOS field so that routers attempt to maximize reliability, you can use the **max-reliability** keyword:

```
Router(config-route-map)#set ip tos max-reliability
```

Alternately, you can use the corresponding value from Table 6-3:

```
Router(config-route-map)#set ip tos 2
```

Table 6-3   IP TOS values that can be set with the set ip tos command

Keyword	Number	Description
normal	0	Makes packet TOS normal (unsets TOS value)
min-monetary-cost	1	The router should handle the packet with minimum monetary cost.
max-reliability	2	The router should handle the packet as reliably as possible.
max-throughput	4	The router should handle the packet to maximize throughput.
min-delay	8	The router should forward the packet as quickly as possible.

In order to set the IP Precedence field, you can use the **set ip precedence** command in route map configuration mode. Like the **set ip tos command**, you can use either a keyword or a number (between 0 and 7) with this command; Table 6-4 contains a list of all the possible values and the corresponding names you can use with this command.

Table 6-4   Possible keywords and values you can set with the set ip precedence command

Keyword	Value
routine	0
priority	1
immediate	2
flash	3
flash-override	4
critical	5
internet	6
network	7

In order to configure the IP precedence in a route map, you would enter the following in route map configuration mode:

```
Router(config-route-map)#set ip precedence critical
```

Alternately, you could use the numeric value:

```
Router(config-route-map)#set ip precedence 5
```

You can use the **set tag** command to set a route tag. The tag is a numeric value between 0 and 4294967295. You generally use this to mark a route so that it can be matched elsewhere with the **match tag** command during redistribution. To configure a tag of 150 in a route map, you would type the following in router configuration mode:

```
Router(config-route-map)#set tag 150
```

Activating Policy-Based Routing

How you activate policy-based routing depends on how you plan to use it. You'll learn how to activate it on an interface so that a route map applies to the packets received on that interface. You'll also see examples of how you might use route maps in applying quality of service.

Configuring Policy-Based Routing on an Interface

In order to configure policy routing for packets received on a particular interface, you can use the **ip policy route-map** *map-tag* command in interface configuration mode. Policy routing is only done on incoming packets. In order to apply a route map named RerouteTelnet to the serial 0/0 interface, you would enter the following:

```
Router(config)#int serial 0
Router(config-if)#ip policy route-map RerouteTelnet
```

Routing Packets through Different Static Routes   One situation where you might configure policy-based routing on an interface is when you wish to use different static routes based on the source address of a packet. For example, the network in Figure 6-4 has end users and a Web server farm on the 172.30.20.0/24 network reachable through RouterB, and two links connecting the end users and administrators (on the 172.30.16.0/24 network) on networks attached to RouterA. Suppose you want to reserve the high-speed link solely for Web traffic bound for the Web server farm, which originates from customers, and administrative traffic on port 8080. You want all other traffic to use the lower-speed link since other traffic will be used for file sharing and other, less critical applications.

If you tried to do this with static routes or a dynamic routing protocol alone, you'd fail. Traditional sources of routing information don't allow you to route based on source address or TCP port number. However, a route map will allow you in effect to have different static routes for different packets based on the content of the packets.

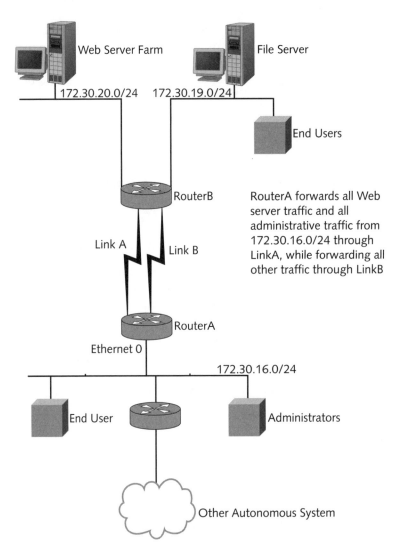

Figure 6-4   Routing packets through different static routes

In order to configure a route map, you first need to configure an access list to identify the packets you wish to use in the route map. First, you want to allow Web traffic over TCP port 80 for the destination network 172.30.20.0/24 to go over the high-speed link. In order to match protocol characteristics within an access list, you must use an extended access list. Let's make one numbered 110 that allows traffic for destination port 80 originating from any source address:

```
RouterA(config)#access-list 110 permit tcp any 172.30.20.0
0.0.0.255 eq 80
```

That statement will match a packet with any source address bound for a destination address inside the 172.30.20.0/24 network with a destination TCP port of 80.

In order to match administrative traffic, you must specify the source network as well as the destination network in the next line of the access list:

```
RouterA(config)#access-list 110 permit tcp 172.30.16.0
0.0.0.255 172.30.20.0 0.0.0.255 eq 8080
```

Now you can configure the route map itself. First, define a route map statement with a name of WebFilter and a sequence number of 10:

```
RouterA(config)#route-map WebFilter permit 10
```

The sequence number 10 is a good starting point since if you decide to add additional route map statements before this one, you've left room to do so.

Now must define a matching statement so that the route map looks at access list 110 before forwarding packets:

```
RouterA(config-route-map)#match ip address 110
```

If you want packets to match any additional conditions before the router processes the set command, you can add additional match statements.

The route map now looks for packets that match access list 110. You can now use the **set ip next-hop** command to specify the next hop for those packets. Since you have two links, you should configure the router so that it uses the back-up link in case the primary link fails. You can do this by specifying more than one next hop address, with the primary link first followed by the secondary link. Here, 172.30.18.1 is the next hop for the primary link, and 172.30.17.1 is the next hop for the secondary link:

```
RouterA(config-route-map)#set ip next-hop 172.30.18.1
172.30.17.1
```

If the **match** command matches a packet, the router first tries to forward it to 172.30.18.1, and then to 172.30.17.1 if the primary link is down.

Next, you must decide how to handle other traffic. One way is to simply end the route map here; a route map also ends with implicit denial so that any packets not matched by sequence number 10 in the route map are processed normally. In this case, you must have a route for those packets in the routing table using 172.30.17.1 as the next hop. You can do that with static routes:

```
RouterA(config)#ip route 172.30.19.0 255.255.255.0
172.30.17.1
RouterA(config)#ip route 172.30.20.0 255.255.255.0
172.30.17.1
```

In this way, all traffic that doesn't match the route map is forwarded to the next hop address of 172.30.17.1 over the slower link. Another way to forward other traffic over the slower link is to use the **set ip default next-hop** command to set the next hop.

First, you must configure another statement in the route map. Since you should leave space between the two route map statements in case you want to add additional statements later, you'll configure this statement as sequence number 20. You would do that as follows:

```
RouterA(config)#route-map WebFilter permit 20
```

Since you want all other traffic to match this statement, you can create an access list matching all traffic, and then create a **match** statement that uses this access list. Alternately, you can just leave out the **match** statement; all packets would still be matched, and you simplified the configuration.

Next, you must set the default next-hop address. You can do this with:

```
RouterA(config-route-map)# set ip default next-hop
172.30.17.1
```

Now, all traffic that doesn't either match access list 110, or have a specific route in the routing table, is forwarded through the slower link. As with any default route, you must make sure that any other destinations reachable from this router through other next hop addresses have the appropriate routes in the routing table. In this case, this isn't a concern.

Once you're done configuring the route map, you must apply the route map to the Ethernet 0 interface. You can do that by typing the following in configuration mode:

```
RouterA(config)#int eth 0
RouterA(config-if)#ip policy route-map WebFilter
```

Configuring Quality of Service with Route Maps In addition to using route maps to set routing policy, you can use then to set Quality of Service. Just as you can send packets through different links depending on qualities of each packet, you can specify a different priority for each packet depending on qualities of the packet, such as the source address or the protocol.

Suppose that you work for the company whose network is pictured in Figure 6-5. Your company has a mainframe used for billing, which all remote offices use over T-1 links. However, as they also use these T-1s for other traffic, the Accounting Department experiences trouble keeping its interactive mainframe sessions running. As a result, they want you to give their traffic a higher priority.

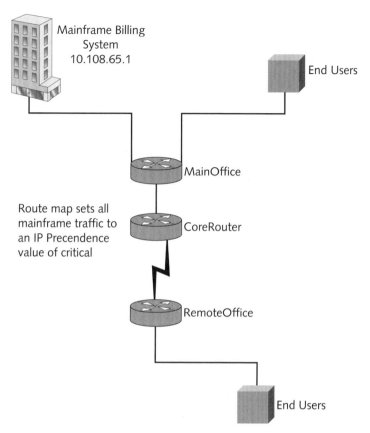

Figure 6-5   Using a route map to configure IP Quality of Service

In order to do this, you want to set up policy-based routing on the RemoteOffice and MainOffice routers. The route map on RemoteOffice will assign an IP Precedence value of five (critical) to all traffic destined for the mainframe, while the route map on MainOffice will assign the same IP Precedence value to all traffic originating from the mainframe. You then configure a queueing scheme that uses these precedence values. However, this is outside the scope of this book. Since the IP Precedence values are already set by the time they reach CoreRouter, it does not require a route map (although you do need to configure queueing on it).

Again, the first step is to create an access list identifying the traffic you want to match. On MainOffice, this is any traffic with a source address of 10.108.65.1; you can use a standard access list to match this address:

```
MainOffice(config)#access-list 11 permit host 10.108.65.1
```

On RemoteOffice, you must match the destination address 10.108.65.1; since a standard access list only matches source addresses, you must use an extended access list:

```
RemoteOffice(config)#access-list 120 permit ip any host
10.108.65.1
```

Next, you must define route maps and create **match** statements that use these access lists. You'll name it "Mainframe" on both routers. On MainOffice, you would use these commands:

```
MainOffice(config)#route-map Mainframe permit 10
MainOffice(config-route-map)#match ip address 11
```

On RemoteOffice, you would use these commands:

```
RemoteOffice(config)#route-map Mainframe permit 10
RemoteOffice(config-route-map)#match ip address 120
```

On both routers, after matching the packets whose IP Precedence values you want to change, you then must set the values. This can be done with the **set ip precedence** command:

```
MainOffice(config-route-map)#set ip precedence critical
```

You would use the same command on RemoteOffice.

Since you don't want to set the IP Precedence value in any other packets, you can now end the route map. Since a route map ends in an implicit denial, every packet that doesn't match the access list indicated in the **match** command is processed normally, and its IP Precedence value is left as is.

Finally, you must activate the route map on the appropriate interfaces on each route. On MainOffice, for example, suppose that traffic destined for the mainframe arrives on interface Ethernet 0. You would then activate the route map on that interface:

```
MainOffice(config)#int eth 0
MainOffice(config-if)#ip policy route-map Mainframe
```

You then configure policy routing on the interface on which RemoteOffice mainframe traffic will arrive.

Verifying and Troubleshooting Policy Routing

In order to verify that you configured policy routing, you have several options available to you. You can quickly verify that you applied a route map to an interface with the **show ip policy** command. Typical output from this command is shown in Figure 6-6.

```
Madrid#show ip policy
Interface       Route map
Serial0/0.1     PriorityTraffic
```

Figure 6-6   Output of the show ip policy command

In order to look at a route map to make sure that you created it as intended, you can use the **show route-map** [*map-name*] command. You can use this to look at an individual route map by using its name, or you can look at all route maps on a router by omitting a route map name. Figure 6-7 shows typical output from the **show route-map** command. One thing you can use to determine whether or not traffic is matching the route map as you anticipated is the counter at the bottom of each statement in the route map, which tells you how many packets each line matched. For the route map PriorityTraffic in Figure 6-7, you can see that only sequence number 10 matched any traffic. This may indicate that either the **match** statements don't work, or that the traffic you're trying to match is not arriving at the interface to which you applied the route map.

```
Madrid#show route-map
route-map PriorityTraffic, permit, sequence 10
  Match clauses:
    ip address (access-lists): 20
  Set clauses:
    ip precedence critical
  Policy routing matches: 83 packets, 10776 bytes
route-map PriorityTraffic, permit, sequence 20
  Match clauses:
    ip address (access-lists): 21
  Set clauses:
    ip precedence immediate
  Policy routing matches: 0 packets, 0 bytes
```

Figure 6-7   Output of the show route-map command

You can also use the **debug ip policy** command to see what the router does to traffic going through your route maps. Unfortunately, this command looks at packets on an individual basis, so it can generate a lot of output. You must be very careful when using it; you should either use it when the router isn't very busy, or if you can't, you should try to minimize the debugging output by applying an access list to it. The command **debug ip policy 98**, for example, lets you see debugging output only for those packets matched by access list 98. Figure 6-8 shows typical output from the **debug ip policy** command. In this example, you can see that some of the packets are matched and some of the packets are rejected; depending on how you configured the routing map, this may or may not be expected behavior. You can look at the output to see if the route map is behaving as you expected.

```
4d19h: IP: s=10.1.1.2 (Serial0/0.1), d=10.1.254.26, len 144, policy match
4d19h: IP: route map PriorityTraffic, item 10, permit
4d19h: IP: s=10.1.1.2 (Serial0/0.1), d=10.1.254.26 (Ethernet0/0), len 144,
policy rejected -- normal forwarding
4d19h: IP: s=10.1.1.2 (Serial0/0.1), d=10.1.254.26, len 200, policy match
4d19h: IP: route map PriorityTraffic, item 10, permit
4d19h: IP: s=10.1.1.2 (Serial0/0.1), d=10.1.254.26 (Ethernet0/0), len 200,
policy rejected -- normal forwarding
4d19h: IP: s=10.1.1.2 (Serial0/0.1), d=10.1.254.26, len 196, policy match
4d19h: IP: route map PriorityTraffic, item 10, permit
4d19h: IP: s=10.1.1.2 (Serial0/0.1), d=10.1.254.26 (Ethernet0/0), len 196,
policy rejected -- normal forwarding
4d19h: IP: s=10.1.1.2 (Serial0/0.1), d=10.1.254.26, len 86, policy match
4d19h: IP: route map PriorityTraffic, item 10, permit
4d19h: IP: s=10.1.1.2 (Serial0/0.1), d=10.1.254.26 (Ethernet0/0), len 86,
policy rejected -- normal forwarding
4d19h: IP: s=10.1.1.2 (Serial0/0.1), d=10.1.254.26, len 144, policy match
```

Figure 6-8   Output of the debug ip policy command

Finally, you should make sure to use the **ping**, **traceroute** and **show ip route** commands to verify that packets are going where you expect them to go. You will find it useful to use these from different locations within your network since route redistribution and policy routing may have different effects on different parts of your network. Additionally, when using the **ping** and **traceroute** commands to troubleshoot issues with route maps, access lists, or route redistribution, you may find it useful to use the extended commands. These can allow you to specify the source address or interface that the commands will use. Since many routing decisions may be made differently depending on the source address of a packet, this feature can be invaluable in troubleshooting problems. Figure 6-9 shows the use of the extended **ping** and **traceroute** commands.

```
Madrid#ping
Protocol [ip]:
Target IP address: 10.1.10.1
Repeat count [5]:
Datagram size [100]:
Timeout in seconds [2]:
Extended commands [n]: y
Source address or interface: 10.1.254.2
Type of service [0]:
Set DF bit in IP header? [no]:
Validate reply data? [no]:
Data pattern [0xABCD]:
Loose, Strict, Record, Timestamp, Verbose[none]:
Sweep range of sizes [n]:
Type escape sequence to abort.
Sending 5, 100-byte ICMP Echos to 10.1.10.1, timeout is 2 seconds:
!!!!!
Success rate is 100 percent (5/5), round-trip min/avg/max = 60/60/60 ms
Madrid#trace
Madrid#traceroute
Protocol [ip]:
Target IP address: 10.1.10.1
Source address: 10.1.254.2
Numeric display [n]:
Timeout in seconds [3]:
Probe count [3]:
Minimum Time to Live [1]:
Maximum Time to Live [30]:
Port Number [33434]:
Loose, Strict, Record, Timestamp, Verbose[none]:
Type escape sequence to abort.
Tracing the route to 10.1.10.1

  1 Seville (10.0.1.14) 40 msec *  40 msec
Madrid#
```

Figure 6-9   Extended ping and traceroute commands

CHAPTER SUMMARY

❏ Controlling routing updates becomes important when your network contains multiple routing protocols. For instance, this is the case when you need to connect your network to another, and equipment on your network does not understand more advanced routing protocols. The methods used to filter routing updates include passive interfaces, null routes, and route filters.

❏ Most methods of filtering routes use access lists. Access lists are used to match packets. A router checks a packet against an access list line by line, performing the action specified by the first matching line. Standard access lists match only against a packet's source address, while extended access lists match against both a packet's destination address and protocol-specific features of a packet.

❐ Route filters are access lists that you can use to specify which routes an interface should include in its routing updates, or which routes it should ignore when receiving routing updates from other routers. You can also change the administrative distance associated with routes so that a router will prefer the routes you select.

❐ You can use policy-based routing to finely control routing behavior, as well as configure Quality of Service. In order to use policy-based routing, you configure a route map that uses a series of permit or deny statements. These work like if/then statements; if a permit or deny statement in a route map matches certain conditions, then the route map sets other conditions that you specified. You can use route maps to send packets through different paths depending on the source address of the packet, the protocol of the packet, or other characteristics of the packet. You can also use route maps to set IP Precedence or IP TOS values in packets to use with queueing schemes, or you can use route maps to set the metrics of individual routes during redistribution, among other things.

6

KEY TERMS

access list — A list used to restrict access to a router or interface to control routing updates and a variety of other tasks; access lists may filter based upon source address, destination address, protocol type, port number, or other packet attributes.

address resolution protocol (ARP) — The protocol that a router or host uses to associate a MAC address with an IP address.

Class of Service (COS) field — *See* IP TOS field.

default gateway — The next hop used by a router when it doesn't have another route for a packet.

extended IP access list — An access list that can filter based upon source address, destination address, protocol type, or port number, among other packet attributes; extended access lists can be identified using a name or numbers between 100 and 199.

floating static route — A static route with an administrative distance set high so that it is not used unless the primary route to a destination (generally learned through a dynamic routing protocol) fails.

gateway of last resort — *See* default gateway.

implicit denial — By default, a Cisco router assumes that any access list ends with a statement denying all traffic; this can be prevented by ending the access list with a statement permitting all traffic.

Must Be Zero (MBZ) field — Unused 1-bit field in the Type of Service (TOS) field in an IP packet.

named access list — An access list identified by a name rather than a number; IP named access lists can be both standard or extended.

numbered access list — An access list identified by a number instead of a name.

IP Precedence field — According to RFC 1349, this is the sub-field in the Type of Service field of an IP packet header that determines the relative importance of an IP packet.

IP TOS field — According to RFC 1349, this is the sub-field in the Type of Service field of an IP packet header that determines trade-offs between throughput, delay, reliability, and cost.

Quality of Service (QOS) — Favoring different types of traffic over others, generally to ensure that certain kinds of traffic (often interactive traffic) arrive in a timely enough fashion to be useful.

queueing — A scheme that allows routers to reorder packets to ensure that certain types of traffic arrive in a timely manner, or aren't overwhelmed by other types of traffic.

passive interface — An interface that accepts routing updates from other routers, but does not send routing updates itself.

policy routing — *See* policy-based routing.

policy-based routing — Routing based on source, Quality of Service, load sharing, or other packet characteristics; routers use route maps to match various criteria in the packets, and then route the packets as desired.

proxy arp — When a router uses the Address Resolution Protocol for a host on an attached network to find the MAC address of a host (and hence where to send it).

route filter — A method of filtering routing updates that uses an access list to select which routes to filter.

route map — A series of permit or deny statements used to match packets based on source address, protocol used, or other packet characteristics; if a statement is marked as permit, and the packet matches the conditions for that particular statement, the route map then does additional processing on the packet, as specified after the match statements.

standard IP access list — An access list that filters primarily based on source address; standard access lists may be identified using a name or a number between 1 and 99.

Trivial File Transfer Protocol (TFTP) — A file transfer protocol that you can use to transfer router configurations and access lists and Cisco IOS images; TFTP does not support authentication.

Type of Service (TOS) — An 8-bit field in an IP packet header that is used to determine the priority of a particular packet; it includes a 4-bit field, also known as the IP TOS field, and a 3-bit field, known as the IP Precedence, as well as a 1-bit Must Be Zero (MBZ) field that isn't used.

REVIEW QUESTIONS

1. A running router learns one route to the network 172.23.16.0/24 from EIGRP and another route to the same destination network through OSPF. Based on the administrative distance, the router will choose the route learned through _____.

2. Which of the following are situations where you might want to use the **passive-interface** command? (Choose all that apply.)

   a. You have three interfaces on a router running EIGRP with IP addresses of 10.1.11.1, 10.1.12.1, and 10.20.1.1, and 24-bit netmasks, but you don't want to include the interface with the 10.1.12.1 address in the EIGRP Autonomous System.

   b. You have a WAN link attached to a router running RIP, and you don't want RIP routing update traffic to go over the WAN.

   c. You have a WAN link attached to a router running OSPF, and you want the router to listen for OSPF update traffic and hello packets, but you don't want it to send OSPF update traffic or hello packets.

   d. You have interfaces on a router running EIGRP with IP addresses of 10.150.221.1, 10.150.222.1, and 172.20.25.1, with 24-bit netmasks, but you don't want to include the interface with the 172.20.25.1 IP address in the EIGRP Autonomous System.

3. How does OSPF use the **passive-interface** command?

   a. The **passive-interface** command is invalid in OSPF because each router must know the status of every interface in the area.

   b. A passive interface is treated as a stub network, although routing information may be received through that interface.

   c. A passive interface is treated as a stub network, and no routing information is sent or received through that interface.

   d. The **passive-interface** command is invalid because you can specify precisely which interfaces should be included in an OSPF area.

4. You configured the following static routes on RouterA:

   ip route 0.0.0.0 0.0.0.0 10.121.14.1
   ip route 10.0.0.0 255.0.0.0 null 0
   ip route 10.226.14.0 255.255.255.0 10.121.16.1

   Which of the following statements is true about a packet forwarded to RouterA? (Choose all that apply.)

   a. Any packets sent to network 172.16.105.0/24 will be discarded.

   b. Any packets sent to network 10.226.14.0/24 will be discarded.

   c. Any packets sent to network 10.226.14.0 will be forwarded to 10.121.16.1.

   d. Any packets sent to 172.16.105.0/24 will be forwarded to 10.121.14.1.

6

5. Which of the following access lists would block packets sent to the 172.16.16.0/20 network, and allow all other packets to go through?

   a. **access-list 11 permit 172.16.0.0 0.0.255.255**
      access-list 11 deny 172.16.16.0 0.0.15.255
      access-list 11 permit any

   b. **access-list 15 deny 172.16.16.0 0.0.16.255**
      access-list 15 permit any

   c. **access-list 17 deny 172.16.16.0 0.0.15.255**
      access-list 17 permit 172.16.0.0 0.0.255.255

   d. **access-list 19 deny 172.16.16.0 0.0.15.255**
      access-list 19 permit any
      access-list 19 deny any

6. Which of the following is a disadvantage of numbered access lists? (Choose all that apply.)

   a. All unmatched packets are implicitly denied at the end of the access list.

   b. There are limited numbered access lists possible for each protocol.

   c. Statements cannot be deleted from the end of a numbered access list.

   d. Statements can only be added to the end of a numbered access list.

7. Which of the following is a disadvantage of named access lists? (Choose all that apply.)

   a. Named access lists cannot be used everywhere numbered access lists can be used.

   b. Named access lists cannot be used as extended access lists.

   c. Statements cannot be deleted from the end of a named access list.

   d. Statements can only be added to the end of a named access list.

8. How can you verify whether or not an access list has been matching the packets you intended?

   a. Verify access list configuration with the **show running-config** command.

   b. Use the **show access-list** command.

   c. Configure each statement in the access list with the **log** keyword and use the **show access-list** command.

   d. Use the **show ip interface** command to look at the packet counters.

9. Which of the following access lists would, if applied as a route filter with the **distribute-list** command, permit all networks in the range from 10.198.0.0/16 to 10.207.0.0/16, and block all other networks?

   a. **access-list 1 permit 10.198.0.0 0.9.255.255**

   b. **access-list 1 permit 10.198.0.0 0.7.255.255**
      access-list 1 permit 10.206.0.0 0.1.255.255

   c. **access-list 1 permit 10.198.0.0 0.15.255.255**

   d. **access-list 1 permit 10.198.0.0 0.2.255.255**
      access-list 1 permit 10.200.0.0 0.7.255.255

10. You configured the following access list:

ip access-list RouteFilter deny 10.121.14.0 0.0.0.255
ip access-list RouteFilter deny 10.121.15.0 0.0.0.255
ip access-list RouteFilter permit any

How would you configure RouterB with this access list so that EIGRP does not advertise networks 10.121.14.0/24 and 10.121.15.0/24 out of its serial 0 interface?

a. RouterB(config)#**router eigrp 1**
RouterB(config-router)#**distribute-list 1 in serial 0**

b. RouterB(config)#**interface serial 0**
RouterB(config-if)#**distribute-list 1 serial 0**

c. RouterB(config)#**router eigrp 1**
RouterB(config)#**distribute-list 1 out**

d. RouterB(config)#**router eigrp 1**
RouterB(config-router)#**distribute-list 1 out serial 0**

11. How can you confirm whether or not a route filter is properly filtering routes? (Choose all that apply.)

a. Use the **show ip route-filter** command.

b. Look at the routing table on the effected routers (possibly after clearing the routing table with the **clear ip route** command).

c. Use a debug command, such as **debug ip rip**, to examine updates sent.

d. Use the **show access-list** command in combination with the **log** keyword.

12. You want to configure a floating static route on the Cleveland router as a back-up route to the 172.16.100.0/24 network in case the primary route to a network goes down. If the next hop for the floating static route is 172.16.99.1, how can you configure Cleveland so that this route only comes up when the primary route goes down, and so that OSPF process ID 11 also learns about this route?

a. Cleveland(config)#**ip route 172.16.100.0 255.255.255.0 172.16.99.1 floating-static**

b. Cleveland(config)#**ip route 172.16.100.0 255.255.255.0 172.16.99.1**

c. Cleveland(config)#**ip route 172.16.100.0 255.255.255.0 172.16.99.1 80**

d. Cleveland(config)#**ip route 172.16.100.0 255.255.255.0 172.16.99.1 200**

13. On CoreRouterA, you configured both OSPF and EIGRP. Its serial 0 interface has the IP address 172.16.171.1/24; both routing protocols learned the route, but you want only the OSPF Autonomous System to advertise the route. Which of the following methods can you use to prevent EIGRP from advertising the route? (Choose all that apply.)

a. Set the administrative distance of the OSPF route lower than the EIGRP route.

b. Use a route filter to remove that route from EIGRP routing updates.

6

    c. Use the **passive-interface serial 0** command in router configuration mode when configuring OSPF.

    d. Use the **passive-interface serial 0** command in router configuration mode when configuring EIGRP.

14. You want to advertise a route to an international office in your EIGRP Autonomous System. However, you want to save money by not sending routing update traffic over the WAN link. How can you use EIGRP to advertise routes to this office without sending routing updates or hello packets over the link? (Choose all that apply.)

    a. Configure the WAN interface as a passive interface.

    b. Lower the administrative distance on the WAN links.

    c. Configure and apply a route filter to prevent the WAN interface from sending any routing updates.

    d. Use a route map to configure routing update traffic with the lowest priority.

15. How is filtering routes different in OSPF than in other protocols, such as EIGRP or RIP?

    a. OSPF does not allow route filtering of any kind.

    b. You can only filter external routes.

    c. You can only filter routes between areas.

    d. You can only filter routes within stub areas.

16. After you apply a routing map to an interface, what happens to packets that don't match any of the permit or deny statements?

    a. They're automatically discarded because of the implicit denial at the end of the route map.

    b. They're treated as if they matched a deny statement, and then processed normally.

    c. They're treated as if they matched a permit statement, and then discarded.

    d. They're treated as if they matched a permit statement, and then processed normally.

17. Which of the following can you do with policy-based routing and route maps? (Choose all that apply.)

    a. Route packets to different destinations based upon the source address.

    b. Route packets to different destinations based on the protocol and protocol parameters, such as TCP ports.

    c. Change the metrics of individual routes during route redistribution.

    d. Assign a packet an IP Precedence value that can be used later in Quality of Service schemes, based on its source address or the protocol.

18. RouterA has a route in its routing table for 172.16.105.0/24 with a next hop of 172.16.98.1. Which of the following route maps would forward packets for destination network 172.16.105.0/24 to a next hop router 172.16.101.2 if they matched both access lists 110 and 111?

    a. RouterA(config)#**route-map StaticA permit 10**
       RouterA(config-route-map)#**match ip address 110 111**
       RouterA(config-route-map)#**set ip default next-hop 172.16.101.2**

    b. RouterA(config)#**route-map StaticB permit 10**
       RouterA(config-route-map)#**match ip address 110**
       RouterA(config-route-map)#**match ip address 111**
       RouterA(config-route-map)#**set ip default next-hop 172.16.101.2**

    c. RouterA(config)#**route-map StaticB permit 10**
       RouterA(config-route-map)#**match ip address 110 112**
       RouterA(config-route-map)#**match ip address 98 99 111**
       RouterA(config-route-map)#**set ip next-hop 172.16.101.2**

    d. RouterA(config)#**route-map StaticC deny 10**
       RouterA(config-route-map)#**match ip address 110**
       RouterA(config-route-map)#**match ip address 111**
       RouterA(config-route-map)#**set ip next-hop 172.16.101.2**

19. When you apply a route map to an interface, the route map applies **set** commands to which type of packets?

    a. packets coming into any interface that are matched by the **match** commands in a permit statement

    b. packets leaving the interface to which you applied the route map, and that are matched by the **match** commands in a permit statement

    c. all packets coming into the interface to which you applied the route map

    d. packets arriving at the interface to which you applied the route map, and that are matched by the **match** commands in a permit statement

20. A match statement in a route map matches packets bound for the 10.14.101.0/24 network. The command applied after the match is **set default interface ethernet 0**. If the router has a route to 10.14.101.0/24 that would forward the packet out interface serial 0, how would the router handle this packet and why?

    a. It would forward the packet out interface serial 0 because the routing table takes precedence over the route map.

    b. It would forward the packet out interface serial 0 because the default interface is only used when a valid route does not exist.

    c. It would forward the packet out interface Ethernet 0 because it matched the statement in the routing map.

    d. It would forward the packet out interface Ethernet 0 because a default interface always takes precedence over a route in the routing table.

CASE PROJECTS

Case 1

You work as a network administrator for Advolus, a biotechnology firm. Your network connects to the Internet using a default route, and it uses EIGRP. Your company recently signed an agreement with Baker Biological Supplies to allow it to connect to portions of your network. Baker Biological Supplies distributes your company's products and needs access to your inventory, and to share files with your staff. Figure 6-10 shows your network and Baker's connection to it.

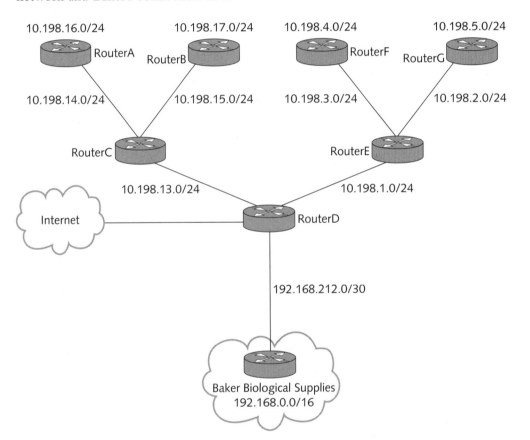

Figure 6-10 Redistributing between networks in California and Michigan

However, servers on some of the networks connected to RouterA, RouterB, and RouterC contain potentially sensitive information, and you want to restrict access to that information. Use the information in Figure 6-10 to:

❐ Build an access list to prevent devices on the Baker Biological Supplies network from accessing the restricted networks. Where should you place the access list?

❑ Build route filters to prevent devices on the Baker Biological Supplies network from communicating with devices on the restricted networks. How would this work, and what are the disadvantages of this approach?

❑ Build route maps to prevent devices on the Baker Biological Supplies network from communicating with devices on the restricted networks. How would this work, and how does it compare to using route filters?

❑ Build a route map to prevent devices on the Baker Biological Supplies network from accessing the Internet through Advolus' link.

Case 2

You are hired by a Web hosting company that is putting together a new offering for its customers. Your boss, the CTO, wants you to set up route maps so that packets on router CoreA will be treated like this:

❑ All customer traffic arriving on interfaces serial 0, serial 1, serial 2, or serial 3 on CoreA will be forwarded through the Gigabit Ethernet link with a next hop of 172.16.1.1, the Fast Ethernet link, and a next hop of 172.16.1.9 as a backup. Customer traffic can be identified because it will have TCP destination ports of 80 and 443.

❑ All other traffic arriving on interfaces serial 0, serial 1, serial 2, or serial 3 will be forwarded through the Fast Ethernet link to the next hop of 172.16.1.9.

❑ All traffic arriving on the Gigabit Ethernet interface will be assigned an IP Precedence value of critical. It is assumed that route maps on the other end of the Gigabit Ethernet link (CoreB) will only allow customer traffic through this link.

❑ Telnet traffic (TCP destination port 23) for the Web server at 172.16.2.12 will be discarded.

Configure route maps and any necessary access lists to accomplish these goals. Where would you apply each route map?

7

REDISTRIBUTION

After reading this chapter and completing the exercises you will be able to:

♦ Explain the benefits and potential pitfalls of route redistribution in a variety of scenarios

♦ Configure route redistribution between two routing protocols

♦ Prevent routing loops when redistributing routes in a variety of scenarios

♦ Monitor and troubleshoot redistribution

In this chapter, you will learn how to redistribute between routing protocols. Often you will find yourself unable to use a single routing protocol within an Autonomous System for various reasons. Some of your routers may not support your chosen routing protocol. Rather than replacing these routers, you can use redistribution to make sure that they can take part in your Autonomous System. Or you may find, for instance, that you must integrate routers running another routing protocol from another Autonomous System into yours. Rather than reconfigure all of those routers, you can instead redistribute routes between them.

BENEFITS AND DISADVANTAGES OF ROUTE REDISTRIBUTION

You may need to redistribute routes between different sources of routing information for a variety of reasons:

- You need to redistribute routes between your Autonomous System and that of another organization. This often happens when two organizations merge, for example.

- You are migrating from one interior gateway protocol to another. Until the migration is complete, you must redistribute from one protocol to another at various points in your Autonomous System.

- You must use multiple routing protocols on parts of your network. Some hosts may require a dynamic routing protocol, but only support a limited number of routing protocols (often only RIP). Alternately, you may want to use a Cisco proprietary protocol on your network while still communicating with other vendors' routers.

- In a hierarchical network design, you may wish to use different routing protocols on different sections of your network. For example, you might wish to use OSPF in the core and EIGRP in the distribution and access layers.

Redistributing Routes

In redistribution, a border router takes routes learned from one source of routing information and injects them into a second. Suppose your Autonomous System connects to a vendor's Autonomous System so that people at your company can use the vendor's inventory system. Figure 7-1 shows two Autonomous Systems connecting at two different spots. AS 25 runs OSPF and AS 1711 runs EIGRP, and both organizations connect to the Internet. The problem is connecting them.

You clearly cannot use a default route on either network. A router sends any packet whose destination network isn't in its routing table down its default route. While the routing protocols in each AS won't know about the routes in the other AS, they also won't know about routes to destination networks on the Internet. A default route from AS 1711 pointing at AS 25 would also send packets destined for the Internet into AS 25, which wouldn't work. A default route may be used, however, to connect each network to the Internet.

Another approach is to use static routes. For example, you might have static routes to the 10.100.0.0/16 and 10.200.0.0/16 networks from routers in AS 1711. However, configuring a static route on each router would result in a lot of administrative overhead, and increase the possibility that you'll make a mistake on one or more routers inside that AS. In this situation, you can redistribute the static routes into EIGRP to propagate them throughout AS 1711. Static routes are a valid source of routing information and work well in many situations.

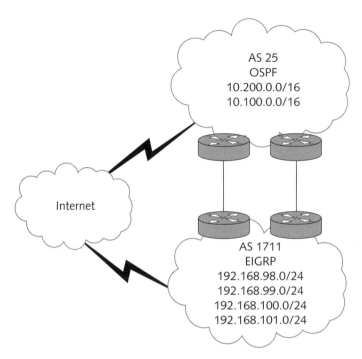

Figure 7-1   Two connected autonomous systems

However, static routes may not give routers in AS 1711 enough detail about routes in AS 25 for efficient routing. Routers may choose poor paths over slow, expensive WAN links, instead of the most optimal route (or even an acceptable route). In this case, you need one routing protocol to exchange routing information with the other routing protocol. You can do this through redistribution.

Potential Redistribution Problems

Since redistribution skips around the mechanisms that routing protocols normally use to ensure that routes are loop-free and use the best path, redistribution has several potential problems. These include:

- Routing loops. These can result when routers in one autonomous system re-learn routes that originated in that autonomous system. On the network in Figure 7-1, if one border router in AS 25 is redistributing a route for 10.200.0.0/24 into AS 1711, a routing loop might occur if the other border router for AS 25 learns the same route from EIGRP AS 1711.

- Poor path selection. Since different routing protocols use different metrics, information about metrics can be lost or distorted during redistribution.

■ Inconsistent convergence times. Each routing protocol converges at its own speed, depending on its own characteristics and the complexity of the Autonomous System where it is running. For example, OSPF networks generally converge more quickly than RIP networks; if OSPF is learning routes from RIP, it must wait for the RIP network to converge to get accurate information about a topology change.

Protocol Considerations

While Cisco routers support redistribution for all routing protocols, routers can only redistribute between routing protocols that support the same routed protocol stack. You can redistribute between any IP routing protocol and any other IP routing protocol, but you cannot redistribute between an IP protocol and an IPX protocol, or an AppleTalk routing protocol, even though all three protocols are fundamentally the same. Each routing protocol runs over incompatibly routed protocols (IP, IPX, and AppleTalk).

Additionally, how you redistribute routes between routing protocols depends on the protocols you're using. In the case of EIGRP, however, you may not need to redistribute at all. EIGRP automatically redistributes between EIGRP and IGRP in the same Autonomous System. The metrics for the two routing protocols are nearly identical (EIGRP metrics are equal to IGRP metrics multiplied by 256). If EIGRP and IGRP are in different autonomous systems, you must configure redistribution manually. On IPX and AppleTalk networks, EIGRP also redistributes automatically between its IPX and AppleTalk versions, and the most common routing protocols found on those networks.

Techniques to Solve Redistribution Problems

In effect, whenever you configure route redistribution between two different Autonomous Systems, you're performing the role that each of the routing protocols handles individually. You must make sure that each routing protocol has enough information about the other's routes in order to make the best decisions, while at the same time manipulating the routing tables in order to prevent routing loops. So far, you've learned about several methods you can use to manipulate routing tables:

■ Route filters

■ Administrative distance

■ Null routes

■ Passive interfaces

Later in the chapter, you'll see some examples where these methods are used to help solve routing problems with redistribution.

Additionally, you can set the **seed metric** of the routes redistributed into another routing protocol. Since one routing protocol rarely understands another routing protocol's metric, you can and should configure the seed (or initial) metric of redistributed routes.

Cisco recommends setting the metric for redistributed routes higher than any of the metrics used by routes in the Autonomous System receiving the routes.

This is done to prevent poor path selection or routing loops. If redistributed routes have high metrics, routes originating in the local Autonomous System are chosen over the redistributed routes. If a redistributed route is the only route to a particular destination, only then will it be chosen.

For example, in Figure 7-2, EIGRP in AS 2521 is redistributing routes into RIP at two different points. Las Vegas is redistributing routes from RIP into EIGRP. Meanwhile, the other border router, LA, is redistributing routes Las Vegas originally learned from RIP back into RIP. Since RIP's metric is a simple hop count that increases by one at every hop, Cupertino receives advertisements indicating that its neighbor Palo Alto has a route to San Fran with a metric of four hops. At the same time, Cupertino receives advertisements for a route to San Fran through LA with a metric equal to LA's seed metric, one hop. Since the route through LA has a shorter metric, Cupertino forwards packets destined for San Fran through LA instead of Palo Alto, even though this route results in an additional three hops.

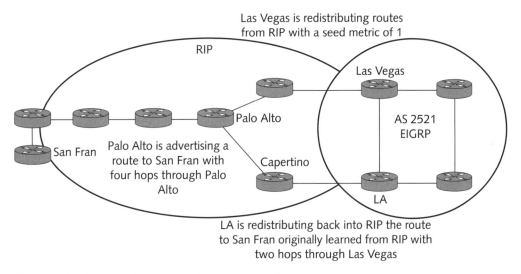

Figure 7-2 Routing loop caused by a low seed metric

Worse yet, this scenario could easily result in a routing loop. Cupertino forwards packets destined for San Fran to LA. Where will LA forward packets destined for SanFran? This depends in part on how redistribution and routing are configured inside the EIGRP Autonomous System. There are two possibilities:

- Towards LasVegas. LasVegas will most likely forward the packets back into the RIP AS for a route totaling eight hops from Cupertino to SanFran (as opposed to five hops for the route from Cupertino through PaloAlto).

- Towards Cupertino. This results in a routing loop since Cupertino simply forwards the packets back to LA.

Neither of these possibilities is desirable. With a routing loop, packets may never reach their destinations. Without a routing loop, packets are traveling through extra hops. This can be costly if any of the extra hops are expensive WAN links.

One way to solve this problem is to advertise a higher seed metric. For example, the highest metric possible between any two routers in the RIP AS is six. If Las Vegas redistributes the RIP routes it learns with a seed metric of six, then the route LA re-advertises back into the RIP AS will have a metric of seven. As a result, Cupertino will choose the route through Palo Alto instead of the route through LA. Setting the seed metric higher than any other metric in the AS prevents any routes from being learned by EIGRP, and sent back into RIP.

However, there are potential disadvantages to high seed metrics. For example, suppose you're redistributing EIGRP routes into RIP with a seed metric of ten. After these routes go five hops, the metric increases to 15 and the routes are considered unreachable. In general, you will probably use a mixture of techniques. For example, in Figure 7-2, you could also filter routing updates sent into the RIP AS by the LA Router. Careful selection of a routing filter prevents any routes originally learned through RIP from being redistributed by EIGRP back into RIP.

CONFIGURING ROUTE REDISTRIBUTION

In this section, you'll learn how to configure basic route redistribution, while later in the chapter, you'll learn how to analyze more complex scenarios. To configure basic, one-way route redistribution, you take the following steps:

1. Identify the border router or routers where you need to redistribute routes between routing protocols. Both routing protocols must be running on a border router in order for it to redistribute routes.

2. Decide which routing protocol will inject routes into the other routing protocol, and which routing protocol will learn routes.

3. Enter router configuration mode for the routing protocol that will learn routes.

4. Configure route redistribution between the two routing protocols (which will vary depending on the protocol you're configuring). Perform any additional tasks, such as setting the metric for redistributed routes or filtering routes.

Additionally, you may need to redistribute one instance of a routing protocol into another. This is possible, although you should take special care when doing this to avoid confusing the two protocols. You might need to do this, for example, when redistributing between two different EIGRP Autonomous Systems, or two different OSPF Autonomous Systems.

The actual process of redistribution, however, varies slightly depending on how the protocol handles its metric, and the topology of the network. In this section, you will first learn how to set metrics for redistributed routes, and then how to configure route redistribution in OSPF, EIGRP, IGRP, and RIP.

Setting Default Metrics

Depending on whether you need to configure **default metrics** for one protocol or for several, you can set a default (or seed) metric in one of two ways.

The first method is with the **default-metric** command. You can use this in router configuration mode to set the default metrics for every source of routing information that might inject routes into a particular routing protocol. For example, suppose you're configuring route redistribution on a border router that is routing for an EIGRP Autonomous System. This router also has an Ethernet interface attached to a network containing legacy equipment that needs to use RIP. As a result, you must set default metrics for two routing protocols. You can set them to a cost of 500 for OPSF process ID 71, for example, by typing the following in router configuration mode:

```
Router(config)#router ospf 71
Router(config-router)#default-metric 500
```

The arguments for the **default-metric** command vary depending on the routing protocol learning the routes. For example, setting the default metric for EIGRP and IGRP routes and their more complex metrics uses syntax like this:

```
Router(config-router)#default-metric bandwidth delay
reliability loading mtu
```

For EIGRP and IGRP, the arguments of the **default-metric** command are:

- *bandwidth*. Minimum bandwidth in units of Kbps.

- *delay*. Delay in units of tens of microseconds.

- *reliability*. The reliability of the route from 1 to 255; if the reliability of the route is 255, then the route is 100% reliable.

- *loading*. Load on the route from 1 to 255, where 255 indicates that the route is 100% loaded.

- *MTU*. The MTU along the route in units of bytes.

While, by default, EIGRP and IGRP only use the bandwidth and the delay in calculation of the metric, you still must configure the loading, reliability, and MTU values.

The second method of setting the default metric is to use the **metric-value** keyword with the **redistribute** command. You can use this to set separate default metrics for different redistributed protocols.

7

Redistributing into OSPF

You use this command to redistribute routes into OSPF in router configuration mode:

```
Router(config-router)#redistribute protocol
[process-id | autonomous-system]
[metric metric-value] [metric-type type-value]
[route-map map-tag] [subnet] [tag tag-value]
```

The arguments to the **redistribute** command have the following meanings:

- *protocol*. This is the protocol (or other source of routing information) whose routes you're injecting into OSPF. Possible keywords here include **connected** (for connected networks), **static**, **eigrp**, **igrp**, **isis** (**Intermediate System-to-Intermediate System**), **bgp** (**Border Gateway Protocol**), **ospf**, **rip**, and other routing protocols.

- *process-id | autonomous system*. This number is for those routing protocols, such as IGRP or EIGRP, which use an Autonomous System number to identify themselves, or for routing protocols like OSPF, which use a process ID to identify themselves. For other protocols, or the **static** and **connected** keywords, this can be left off.

- **metric** *metric value*. This optional parameter sets the seed metric given to redistributed routes. By default, the seed metric for routes redistributed into OSPF is a cost of 20.

- **metric-type** *type-value*. With OSPF, the metric type indicates whether or not the route will be a type 1 external route or a type 2 external route; the values you can use are 1 or 2. The default is 2, specifying a type 2 external route.

- **map** *map-tag*. This optional parameter identifies a route map which is to filter the routes learned through redistribution.

- **subnets**. This optional keyword determines whether or not OSPF redistributes subnetted routes. Without this keyword, OSPF learns about a route to 172.16.0.0/16, but does not learn about this network's subnets, such as 172.16.100.0/24.

- **tag** *tag-value*. Another optional parameter, this is a 32-bit value that may be used to communicate between ASBRs, but isn't used by OSPF.

In OSPF, any router redistributing routes learned from a source of routing information outside the OSPF Autonomous System becomes an Autonomous System Border Router. This happens if the router is redistributing routes learned from an entire EIGRP Autonomous System, a handful of RIP routes, a static default route to the Internet, a static route to a stub network, or a single static route across a WAN link to a stub network. In some cases, you may need to verify that a router in a particular area can redistribute the routes; routers in all types of stub areas except not-so-stubby areas cannot learn about external routes.

Redistributing into EIGRP, IGRP, and RIP

In order to redistribute routes into EIGRP, IGRP, or RIP, the **redistribute** command takes the following form:

```
Router(config-router)#redistribute protocol [process-
id or autonomous system] [match  [internal |external 1 |
external 2] ] [metric metric-value] [route-map map-tag]
```

While the arguments are mostly the same as when redistributing routes into OSPF, there is one additional set of keywords. This is the **match** keyword and its arguments. This keyword is optional and only used when a protocol is redistributing routes from OSPF. You can match either internal routes (with the **internal** keyword), external type 1 routes (**external 1**), or external type 2 routes (**external 2**). You can also use any combination of the keywords, or you can match all three types of routes by leaving out keywords.

Static, Default, and Connected Routes

Despite the obvious benefits of using dynamic routing protocols, static routes (including default routes) can be quite useful. Some situations where you might want to use a static or default route in place of a dynamic routing protocol include:

- Stub networks with only one outgoing connection. For example, you might use a static route to connect a remote office in a star topology through a WAN connection to the rest of your network with a default route. However, you would also need a static route on the hub router to reach any network attached to the remote router's other interfaces.

- Internet connections. If a network has only one Internet connection, using a default route is the simplest way to connect an Autonomous System to the Internet.

- Back-up links. Floating static routes are a good way to configure back-up links over dial-up connections so that they'll only be used when the primary route fails.

However, in order for other routers in your Autonomous System to use static routes configured on a router, you must redistribute them.

Redistributing Static Routes

When configuring a static route, you can use the following command:

```
Router(config)#ip route prefix mask {address|interface}
[distance] [tag tag] [permanent]
```

You already learned how to set the distance on a static route. The **route tag** allows you to match a static route in route maps. The **permanent** keyword means that the router keeps the route in its routing table even if the associated interface goes down.

One important thing to note is that you can configure a static route to go through an interface instead of with a next hop. You may want to use this with stub routers with default routes; if a WAN link attached to a serial interface is the only route out of a stub network, then this is a simple way to make sure all packets destined for non-local networks go out that interface.

 You should be careful to use static routes to interfaces only over point-to-point links. If you configure a static route to an interface over an Ethernet link, for example, the router will not know the address of the next hop, and will use proxy ARP to find it. This can cause poor router performance.

Redistributing Connected Routes

Additionally, you can redistribute any connected networks with the **redistribute connected** command. If you want a dynamic routing protocol to advertise connected networks without sending any routing updates out of those interfaces, you can use this command to avoid adding them to the dynamic routing protocol. However, the **redistribute connected** command redistributes all connected networks; if this is not what you want, you should use a route filter to remove the networks you don't want to advertise.

For example, suppose that you're administering the network in Figure 7-3, and you don't want to include the WAN link, or any of the other networks attached to the RemoteOffice Router in the EIGRP Autonomous System, to minimize the traffic going across the WAN link. Most of the necessary configuration is done on HubRouter; RemoteOffice only needs a default route pointing to the IP of HubRouter's end of the WAN link. In this case, neither the WAN link (192.168.1.0/30) nor the 192.168.2.0/24 or 192.168.3.0/24 networks attached to RemoteOffice are included in the EIGRP Autonomous System with the **network 172.16.0.0** command. You must configure HubRouter so that the rest of the EIGRP Autonomous System reaches these networks:

- 192.168.1.0/30. Since this network is attached to the HubRouter, you inject it into the EIGRP AS with the **redistribute connected** command.

- 192.168.2.0/24 and 192.168.3.0/24. You first need to configure a static route from HubRouter to RemoteOffice for these networks. Then you inject them into the EIGRP AS with the **redistribute static** command.

Additionally, static routes can be useful when you need to redistribute routes between routing protocols. Rather than redistributing between both routing protocols, in many cases, you can redistribute routes into one protocol, and redistribute a handful of static routes into the other routing protocol. Depending on the network topology, this can simplify configuration and reduce the chances of creating routing loops.

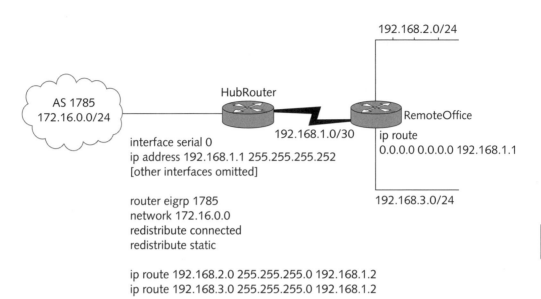

Figure 7-3   Redistributing static and connected routes

Redistributing Default Routes

Default routes are a special type of static route and are handled differently depending on the routing protocol you're using, and how you configure the default route. In general, you can use one of two ways to configure a default route:

- The **ip route 0.0.0.0 0.0.0.0** *next-hop* command. The 0.0.0.0 network matches any network unless a more specific route is found in the routing table.

- The **ip default-network** *network* command. This command specifies an existing route in the routing table to use as the default. If the network configured isn't in the routing table, this command won't have any effect. This command also helps a router choose its **default gateway** or **gateway of last resort**, which is the next hop when it doesn't have a route for a packet.

  Keep in mind that routers running classful routing protocols, such as RIP or IGRP, need to use the **ip classless** command to forward packets to default routes. This command is activated, by default, in routers beginning with Cisco IOS 12.0.

How these commands are used depends on the routing protocol used. For example, in Figure 7-4, BorderRouter is running RIP and must propagate a default route to Internal1 and Internal2. You can use the **ip default-network** command to configure a default route that will be redistributed to other RIP routers:

```
BorderRouter(config)#router rip
BorderRouter(config-router)#network 192.168.100.0
```

```
BorderRouter(config-router)#network 172.30.0.0
BorderRouter(config-router)#exit
BorderRouter(config)#ip-default network 192.168.100.16
BorderRouter(config)#ip classless
```

This injects a default route through BorderRouter into the routing tables of both Internal1 and Internal2, and allows it to forward packets to the default route.

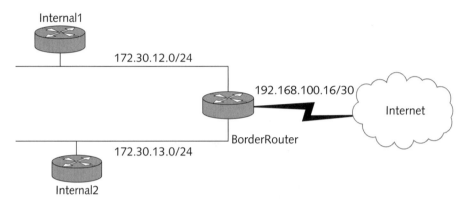

Figure 7-4   Redistributing a default network with RIP

In EIGRP and IGRP, a router won't automatically propagate a default route unless you configure a route to 0.0.0.0 and use the **ip default-network** command. You can also add the 0.0.0.0 network to EIGRP by using the **network 0.0.0.0** command if a route to 0.0.0.0 is already configured.

The **ip default-network** command should not be confused with the **ip default-gateway** command. While the **ip default**-network command helps a router choose its default gateway, you use the **ip default-gateway** command only when a router is used as an IP host and IP routing has been disabled.

In general, you should weigh the benefits of using static routes and default routes against the disadvantages. In situations where a static or default route will result in minimum configuration, and will minimize routing update traffic over WAN links, you should seriously consider using them. In situations where using static routes would result in a lot of extra configuration, you should consider using a dynamic routing protocol instead.

Redistributing into Classful Routing Protocols

Another potential pitfall of redistribution is redistributing between classless routing protocols with VLSMs, and classless routing protocols that do not support VLSMs. The problem is, of course, that the classless routing protocol may inject routes that aren't subnetted along classful boundaries into the classful routing protocol. Consequently, the classful routing protocol is unable to forward packets properly to the other Autonomous System.

For example, an Autonomous System running RIPv1 would have difficulty forwarding packets properly to routes in an OSPF Autonomous System subnetted to contain routes with 30-bit prefixes, 29-bit prefixes, 28-bit prefixes, and so on. RIP does not send the netmask with its updates, and any router learning these routes is unable to forward information about the netmask to other routers in the RIPv1 Autonomous System.

In general, there are two strategies for dealing with this issue. These are:

- Propagate a default route to the OSPF domain throughout the RIPv1 domain. This way, the RIPv1 routers don't have to learn anything about the routes in the OSPF domain or their netmasks.

- Summarize or filter routes injected from the OSPF domain so that the RIPv1 routers only learn about routes with classful netmasks. Depending on how you summarize routes or filter routes from the OSPF domain, this may require the use of the **ip classless** command so that RIPv1 routers are able to forward packets to supernetted summary addresses.

Cleaning Up Routing Tables Before Redistribution

In general, the more complex the topologies of Autonomous Systems you need to redistribute between, the more likely you are to encounter trouble. In order to prevent problems, you should attempt to simplify the topology each Autonomous System will present to other Autonomous Systems as much as possible before you begin redistribution.

While you may or may not be able to simplify either the logical or physical layout of an Autonomous System prior to redistribution, you can reduce the amount of routing information that each routing protocol will redistribute. Reduce the size of the routing tables that you must redistribute as much as possible before you attempt redistribution. This has the added benefit of reducing the routing table size in each Autonomous System after redistribution.

Two methods you can use to manipulate the routes being redistributed are route filters, which you learned about in Chapter 6, and route maps.

Using Route Maps with Redistribution

Route maps allow you to filter routes like route filters. However, route maps also allow you to set properties on redistributed routes, including the metric. A route map offers you much greater control over the metric of redistributed routes than setting a default metric. You can match groups of routes by creating multiple access lists, and then applying a different metric to each group.

Filtering Routes with Route Maps To use a route map to filter routes, first you need to build an access list to identify the routes to be permitted or denied. Then you must build a route map and apply it to the route distribution process.

In addition to matching routes with an access list, you can use a route tag to match routes. You can use the **set tag** command to apply a route tag to a group of routes in a route map. The tag is a numeric value between 0 and 4294967295. You can then use a **match tag** command in another route map during redistribution. To configure a tag of 150 in a route map, you type the following in route map configuration mode:

```
Router(config-route-map)#set tag 150
```

In order to match this tag in another route map, you use the following in route map configuration mode:

```
Router(config-route-map)#match tag 150
```

For instance, suppose you wanted to prevent routes on the 172.16.0.0/16 network and routes marked with the tag 70 from being redistributed from OSPF into EIGRP. All other routes should be permitted. Additionally, you want to tag all redistributed routes with a tag of 240. You first create an access list matching the 172.16.0.0/16 routes:

```
Router(config)#access-list 11 permit
172.16.0.0 0.0.255.255
```

Then you prepare the route map. First, you deny routes matching tag 70:

```
Router(config)#route-map FilterRoutes deny 5
Router(config-route-map)#match tag 70
```

Since this is a deny statement, any route matched with the match statement will not be processed by the route map (and will not be redistributed).

Then you deny routes matching the access list:

```
Router(config-route-map)#route-map FilterRoutes deny 10
Router(config-route-map)#match ip address 11
```

Then you match all other routes and set a tag of 240 on them. By leaving out a specific match statement, you match all other routes.

```
Router(config-route-map)#route-map FilterRoutes permit 15
Router(config-route-map)#set tag 240
```

Finally, you must configure the router to use the route map FilterRoutes when redistributing routes from OSPF into EIGRP. Assuming that the EIGRP Autonomous System is 65000 and the OSPF process ID, you enter the following:

```
Router(config)#router eigrp 65000
Router(config-router)#redistribute ospf 1 route-map
FilterRoutes
```

Changing Metrics with Route Maps As with any other type of route map, you must first identify the routes whose metrics you want to change. In Figure 7-5, RouterA and RouterB are redistributing between an OSPF Autonomous System (with process ID 62) and EIGRP Autonomous System 1114. By default, you want to redistribute routes from EIGRP into OSPF with a cost of 200. However, in order to improve poor path selection, you want to redistribute from RouterA the 10.68.16.0/24, 10.79.171.0/24, and 10.41.18.0/24 networks with a cost of 250. You also want to redistribute the 10.16.156.0/24 and 10.198.114.0/24 networks with a cost of 500.

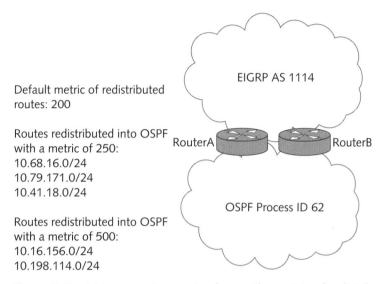

Default metric of redistributed
routes: 200

Routes redistributed into OSPF
with a metric of 250:
10.68.16.0/24
10.79.171.0/24
10.41.18.0/24

Routes redistributed into OSPF
with a metric of 500:
10.16.156.0/24
10.198.114.0/24

Figure 7-5   Using a route map to change the metric of redistributed routes

As you would expect, the first step is to write access lists identifying the routes to be matched. In order to match the routes you want to redistribute with a cost of 250, you make a standard access list on RouterA:

```
RouterA(config)#access-list 91 permit 10.68.16.0 0.0.0.255
RouterA(config)#access-list 91 permit 10.79.171.0
0.0.0.255
RouterA(config)#access-list 91 permit 10.41.18.0
0.0.0.255
```

And for the routes to be redistributed with a cost of 500:

```
RouterA(config)#access-list 92 permit 10.16.156.0
0.0.0.255
RouterA(config)#access-list 92 permit 10.198.114.0
0.0.0.255
```

Now you must define the route map, which you'll call OSPFMetric:

```
RouterA(config)#route-map OSPFMetric permit 10
```

In order to add the routes described in access list 91, you add them in a **match** statement:

```
RouterA(config-route-map)#match ip address 91
```

Next, you want to set the metric of these routes with the **set** command:

```
RouterA(config-route-map)#set metric 250
```

Next, you want to create another permit statement in the route map, which will match the routes described by access list 92 and set the metric to 500. You can do that with:

```
RouterA(config-route-map)#route-map OSPFMetric permit 20
RouterA(config-route-map)#match ip address 92
RouterA(config-route-map)#set metric 500
```

Finally, you must decide how to handle all other routes. As you might expect, there is more than one way to set the metric of other redistributed routes to a cost of 200. You can create a third permit statement in the route map without a **match** statement, which would match all routes, and then set the metric to 200 with a **set** statement. Or you can set the metric during redistribution; since all routes not matched with a **match** statement in the route map will be processed normally, this will set the metric properly for all other routes. In this case, we'll set the metric during redistribution.

You can activate redistribution, set the default metric, and activate the route map at the same time:

```
RouterA(config)#router ospf 62
RouterA(config-router)#redistribute eigrp 1114 metric 200
route-map OSPFMetric
```

ROUTE REDISTRIBUTION SCENARIOS

Many complex scenarios exist where you might need to use route redistribution. In order to configure two-way redistribution (where each routing protocol learns routes from the other routing protocol), for example, you repeat the steps given above for redistribution, reversing the roles of the two routing protocols. However, you should take great care when doing this since it can result in suboptimal routing or routing loops. Some of the strategies you may wish to use in more complex redistribution scenarios include:

- Filtering out unwanted routes from one or both routing protocols during redistribution

- Propagating a default route instead of redistributing routes from one of the protocols

- Propagating multiple static routes instead of redistributing routes from one of the protocols

- Changing the administrative distance of one of the routing protocols, as necessary, to make sure that each router chooses routes from the desired routing protocol

Additionally, when redistributing, you should take special care to think about what routers in each Autonomous System need to know about each other. You may find it helpful to think about redistribution from the perspective of the hierarchical design model. For example, routers on access layer networks don't need to know much beyond their local routes and how to route packets out of the access layer. You might choose to propagate a default route throughout the access layer. At the same time, you can redistribute routes local to the access layer into the distribution layer routers. This way, the access layer routers only know local routes and the default route, while the distribution layer routers know routes inside the access layer and can choose the best path.

One-Way Redistribution Through a Single Border Router

In this scenario, two Autonomous Systems are redistributing routes at a single router. For example, in Figure 7-6, an EIGRP Autonomous System and a RIP Autonomous System connect through a single border router. In turn, the EIGRP Autonomous System has a connection to the Internet.

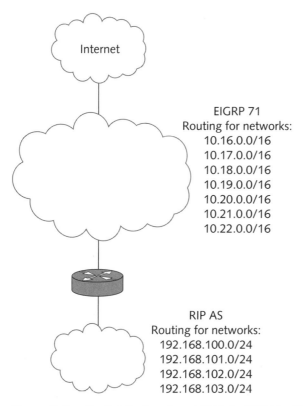

Figure 7-6   Redistributing from RIP into EIGRP with a default route for RIP

In terms of the hierarchical design model, you can describe this scenario as a two-layer network, with EIGRP AS as the core layer and RIP AS as the access layer. The fact that there is only one border router simplifies it even more; any packet traveling from one AS to the other must go through the border router, so metrics aren't important.

For the RIP domain, a default route is the most efficient way to route packets into the EIGRP AS. You will also need to redistribute the default route, and use the **ip classless** command. In RIP, default routes are automatically redistributed. Assuming that the next hop for BorderRouter in the EIGRP AS is 192.168.100.2, you can use the following commands in router configuration mode:

```
BorderRouter(config)#ip classless
BorderRouter(config)#ip route 0.0.0.0 0.0.0.0 192.168.100.2
```

For the EIGRP AS, you can configure redistribution so that each EIGRP router learns all of the routes local to the RIP Autonomous System. This can be accomplished with the following in configuration mode:

```
BorderRouter(config)#router eigrp 71
BorderRouter(config-router)#redistribute rip
```

You also configure a default route elsewhere in the EIGRP Autonomous System and have it propagated throughout the Autonomous System so that all of the EIGRP routers can get out to the Internet.

Finally, in this situation, instead of redistributing from RIP into EIGRP, you can use a static route to allow the EIGRP Autonomous System to learn about the routes in the RIP Autonomous System. For instance, suppose you configured a static route on the border router for 192.168.100.0/22 with a next hop of 192.168.1.1. In order for routers in the EIGRP AS to learn about these routes, you must redistribute static routes into the EIGRP AS. The configuration follows:

```
BorderRouter(config)#ip route 192.168.100.0 255.255.252.0
192.168.1.1
BorderRouter(config)#router eigrp 71
BorderRouter(router-config)#redistribute static
```

The disadvantage to this approach is that the EIGRP Autonomous System may not learn about new routes added to the RIP Autonomous System. For instance, suppose you add another network to the RIP AS, such as 192.168.254.0/24. Since this route is not matched by the static route configured above, the EIGRP domain does not learn about it unless you add another static route.

In general, in any redistribution scenario, you should plan carefully whenever making any changes. You must make sure that any change made either does not affect redistribution between the two Autonomous Systems, or that you've planned to compensate for any changes that will affect redistribution. Adding a second border router, for example, has the potential to cause routing problems if its effects aren't taken into account.

One-Way Redistribution Through Multiple Border Routers

While it simplifies redistribution, connecting two Autonomous Systems at a single border router allows the two Autonomous Systems to be partitioned if the border router fails, or if either of the two connecting links fails. To avoid this single point of failure, you must connect the two Autonomous Systems at multiple places.

Figure 7-7 shows an example of a network where you might need to redistribute between RIP and EIGRP at multiple points. BorderA and BorderB will both advertise default routes into the RIP Autonomous System; whether a RIP router forwards a packet destined for the EIGRP Autonomous System or the Internet through BorderA or BorderB will depend on the metric of its route to that router. On the other hand, BorderA and BorderB are injecting the routes from the RIP Autonomous System into the EIGRP Autonomous System. Unless done carefully, this can present problems.

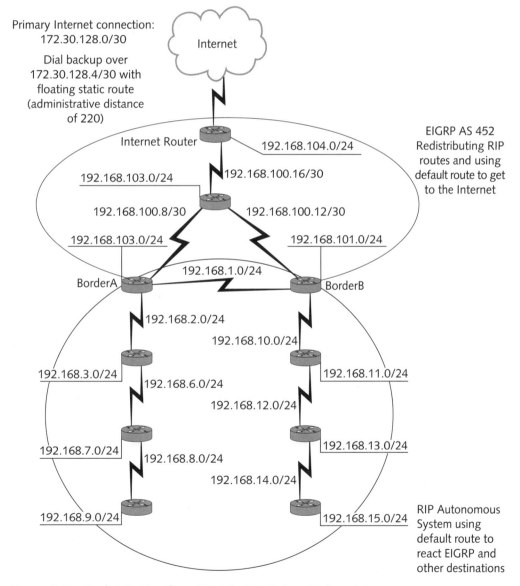

Figure 7-7   Redistributing from RIP into IGRP at multiple points

First, you must set the seed metric for RIP routes redistributed into EIGRP. The default route propagated through the RIP Autonomous System eliminates the potential problem of RIP trying to learn the routes with 30-bit prefixes in the EIGRP domain. However, you may still want to decrease the odds that the EIGRP routers will learn suboptimal routes to destinations in the RIP AS. If a router forwards a packet to the wrong border router, that border router will have to forward it to the other border router over a WAN link in order to get it to its destination. On networks with more complicated topologies than this example, suboptimal routing like this can both cost money and increase the latency of each packet forwarded to certain destinations. In this scenario, you could use route filters to prevent BorderA from advertising routes to destinations where it doesn't have an optimal path (such as the 192.168.10.0/24 network) with an outgoing route filter. However, if the 192.168.100.12/30 link fails, then BorderB is no longer directly connected to the EIGRP Autonomous System, and neither border router will advertise the 192.168.10.0/24 network and any other routes filtered on BorderA. In this case, it might make sense to include the 192.168.1.0/24 link in the EIGRP AS instead of the RIP AS so that EIGRP routers have multiple paths to each border router.

In order to set the seed metric for routes redistributed into EIGRP, you'll assume that each WAN link on the network is at T-1 speed, or 1.544 Mbps. If you set the bandwidth and delay used to calculate the metric for redistributed routes to 768 Kbps and 40,000 microseconds, respectively, the resulting metric should be higher than for any other path in the EIGRP domain. By default, the other values set for the EIGRP metric don't matter; you can set the reliability, loading, and MTU to 100, 100, and 1500, respectively. You configure redistribution into EIGRP on BorderA like this:

```
BorderA(config)#router eigrp 452
BorderA(config-router)#redistribute rip metric
768 4000 100 100 1500
```

You repeat this on BorderB too. Note that the default delay is configured in units of 10 microseconds. Also, you want to make sure that the **subnets** keyword isn't necessary to redistribute routes properly. In this case, it isn't since none of the networks local to the RIP Autonomous System are subnetted.

The default route is a potential problem. Both EIGRP and RIP are propagating default routes. While RIP won't learn any routes from EIGRP since it uses the default route to go to both the EIGRP AutonomousSystem and the Internet, the default route from RIP could cause problems in the EIGRP Autonomous System in certain situations. The RIP default route is only a problem if the primary route to the Internet goes down. In that case, InternetRouter has a floating static route, which should come up when the main route fails. It should also propagate that route back to the other EIGRP routers, which will prefer the default back-up route propagated through the Autonomous System over the default route learned from RIP. However, InternetRouter itself chooses the default route learned from RIP because it has a smaller administrative distance than the floating static route. As a result, it receives packets bound for the Internet as expected, but it tries to forward them back into the EIGRP Autonomous System because of the default route learned from RIP. Routers in the EIGRP AS forward the packets back to InternetRouter, and so on. As a result, all packets sent to destinations on the Internet enter a routing loop even though InternetRouter has a valid default route out to the Internet.

What might make this problem particularly difficult to troubleshoot is the fact that it only occurs when the primary route to the Internet is down. Instead of troubleshooting redistribution, you might be tempted to troubleshoot the back-up link instead. You should keep in mind that changes on apparently unrelated parts of the network can cause problems related to redistribution, especially on more complex networks.

One way to get around this is to simply filter the default route so that the EIGRP Autonomous System doesn't learn about it. You can create a route filter with a standard access list numbered 19 and then apply it to any routes advertised by either of the border routers. Assuming that serial interface 0 and Ethernet interface 0 are the interfaces inside the EIGRP AS, you do that as follows:

```
BorderA(config)#access-list 19 deny 0.0.0.0 0.0.0.0
BorderA(config)#access-list 19 permit any
BorderA(config)#router eigrp 452
BorderA(config-router)#distribute-list 19 out ethernet 0
```

You then repeat this on BorderB.

Two-Way Redistribution at Multiple Points

This is the most complicated redistribution scenario you have encountered so far. The greater the complexity of the redistribution scenario, the more possibilities exist to create routing loops or other routing problems. You must avoid these with a combination of the default metric and route filters.

Figure 7-8 shows an example where an EIGRP Autonomous System is connected to an OSPF Autonomous System at two different points. Neither Autonomous System can use a default route to get to the other since each already uses a default route to get to the Internet. This is common when networks for two different organizations connect; in many cases, neither organization wants the other to send traffic out its Internet connection for political reasons, or simply to avoid the cost of excessive traffic over any WAN links connecting the two organizations. As a result, each Autonomous System must learn routes from the other.

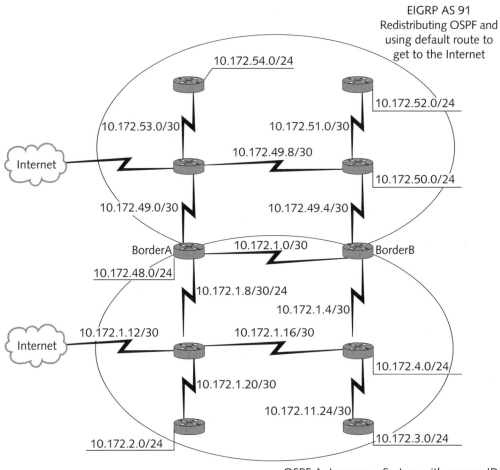

EIGRP AS 91
Redistributing OSPF and
using default route to
get to the Internet

10.172.54.0/24

10.172.52.0/24

10.172.53.0/30

10.172.51.0/30

10.172.49.8/30

Internet

10.172.50.0/24

10.172.49.0/30

10.172.49.4/30

BorderA

10.172.1.0/30

BorderB

10.172.48.0/24

10.172.1.8/30/24

10.172.1.4/30

10.172.1.12/30

10.172.1.16/30

Internet

10.172.4.0/24

10.172.1.20/30

10.172.11.24/30

10.172.2.0/24

10.172.3.0/24

OSPF Autonomous System with process ID
of 64 Redistributing EIGRP and using default
route to get to the Internet

Figure 7-8   Two-way redistribution between EIGRP and OSPF

First, you must set seed metrics for routes redistributed into each routing protocol. Assuming that each WAN link has a bandwidth of 1.544 Mbps, in OSPF, each link would have a cost of 63. Setting the default OSPF metric to 128, for example, ensures that the metric of each route redistributed into OSPF from EIGRP is higher than the metric for any link in the OSPF domain. Conversely, setting the bandwidth at 768 Kbps and the delay at 40,000 microseconds for each route redistributed into EIGRP ensures that the metric of each route redistributed into EIGRP from OSPF is higher than the EIGRP metric for any link in the Autonomous System. As before, load, reliability, and MTU won't be used in metric calculations unless you change the K-values, but these must be configured anyway; you can set these to 100, 100, and 1500 as before.

Additionally, redistributing OSPF into EIGRP allows you the option of matching only certain types of routes (internal, type 1 external or type 2 external routes). By default, OSPF marks external routes as type 2 external routes. The default route to the Internet is a type 2 external route, as well as any of the routes redistributed into the OSPF Autonomous System from the EIGRP Autonomous System. As a result, by using the **match** keyword when configuring redistribution from OSPF into EIGRP, you can avoid learning the default route and re-learning any of the routes OSPF injected into EIGRP.

Finally, you want to use the **subnets** keyword to make sure that each routing protocol injects information about subnets into the other routing protocol.

You can configure these on BorderB with the following commands:

```
BorderB(config)#router ospf 64
BorderB(config-router)#redistribute eigrp 91 metric
768 4000 100 100 1500 subnets
BorderB(config-router)#router eigrp 91
BorderB(config-router)#redistribute ospf 64 metric 128
match internal subnets
```

You must repeat this on BorderB.

Since the **redistribution** command doesn't allow you to control the type of routes injected into OSPF as it does with EIGRP, you must control the information EIGRP injects into OSPF. For example, since the route for 10.172.1.16/30 originated within the OSPF Autonomous System, allowing the EIGRP domain to advertise it back into the OSPF AS may lead to problems. You can eliminate this problem easily enough with a route filter. First, you must identify the networks to be filtered and make an access list, which you will apply with the **distribute-list out** command. The access list will also include the default route. You can configure this for an access list numbered 24 as follows:

```
BorderA(config)#access-list 24 deny 0.0.0.0 0.0.0.0
BorderA(config)#access-list 24 deny 10.172.1.0 0.0.0.255
BorderA(config)#access-list 24 deny 10.172.2.0 0.0.0.255
BorderA(config)#access-list 24 deny 10.172.3.0 0.0.0.255
BorderA(config)#access-list 24 deny 10.172.4.0 0.0.0.255
BorderA(config)#access-list 24 permit any
BorderA(config)#router ospf 64
BorderA(config-router)#distribute-list 24 out eigrp 91
```

Alternately, you can use an access list summarizing all of the network statements to be filtered (such as **access-list 24 deny 10.172.0.0 0.0.0.7.255**). However, you must be careful not to let this overlap with any of the routes you wish to redistribute. For example, if you use this statement in the route filter above and then add the network 10.172.6.0/24 to the OSPF Autonomous System without changing the access list, you do not redistribute a route to that network into the EIGRP Autonomous System.

MONITORING AND TROUBLESHOOTING REDISTRIBUTION

You have two ways to verify that you've configured route redistribution. The first way is to look at the router configuration with the **show running-config** command and look for redistribution statements. The second way is to use the **show ip protocols** command. In addition to summarizing information about which routing protocols you are running on a particular router, it shows you whether or not a protocol is redistributing routes learned from another source.

When you look at the output from the **show ip protocols** command, the entry for a particular protocol will usually say that the router is learning routes from itself. For example, it will say that OSPF 1 is redistributing routes from OSPF 1. This simply means that, as part of an Autonomous System using OSPF, the router itself is learning routes from OSPF 1.

The **show ip route** command allows you to actually examine routing tables in each Autonomous System. You should use this command to check the routing tables of routers besides the border routers. The border router should have the routes in its routing table regardless of whether redistribution is occurring properly. Using the **show ip route** command, you can determine whether or not routers in each Autonomous System are learning the proper routes (or unwanted routers) from the other Autonomous System.

In general, troubleshooting redistribution problems requires you to:

1. Carefully examine the topology of each Autonomous System involved. This may be the most important step. The better you know the topologies involved, the more likely you are to spot problems. Additionally, a thorough knowledge of the network topology makes you less likely to cause other problems while you're in the process of fixing the original set of problems.

2. Examine the routing tables of any border routers involved to see if you can find the routes you expect to see.

3. Examine the routing tables of routers inside each Autonomous System to see if you can find the routes you expect to see. How many routers you must look at depends on the nature of the problem, the routing protocol used, and how you configured summarization. For instance, each router in a single-area OSPF Autonomous System should have knowledge of the entire AS. On the other hand, a router in an EIGRP AS may have dramatically different routing information than other routers in the AS because of route summarization.

4. Use the **ping** and **traceroute** (also called **trace**) commands for routes crossing the boundary between Autonomous Systems to see if they succeed, and which paths packets are actually taking. Do this from border routers and from internal routers in both Autonomous Systems.

5. Use **debug** commands on any router where you appear to have a problem to look at the information contained in routing updates.

To see if you've applied a route map to redistribution between two routing protocols, you generally must look at the router configuration. In versions of Cisco IOS after 12.0, you can use the | character and the **include** keyword to show only part of the configuration. The | character and the **include** keyword are **output modifiers**, which filter or modify the output of a **show** command. The **include** keyword will show only lines containing the word or words that follow it. Other output modifiers are **exclude** (which shows every line in the configuration that doesn't match the following text) and **begin** (which shows every line in the configuration beginning with the following text). For example, in order to see all lines in the configuration including the word **redistribute**, you type the following in enable mode:

```
Router#show runn | include redistribute
```

This shows you every line in the configuration that includes the word **redistribution**. As shown in Figure 7-9, since it's case sensitive, it misses the word **redistribution** if it appeared in the router configuration (in the comments configured for an interface with the **description** command, for example).

```
Madrid#show runn ?
  interface  Show interface configuration
  |          Output modifiers
  <cr>

Madrid#show runn | include redistribute
 redistribute rip metric 200 route-map OSPF
 redistribute eigrp 1114
 redistribute connected
 redistribute static
Madrid#show runn | include route-map
 ip policy route-map PriorityTraffic
 redistribute rip metric 200 route-map OSPF
route-map OSPF permit 10
route-map OSPF permit 20
route-map PriorityTraffic permit 10
route-map PriorityTraffic permit 20
```

Figure 7-9   Show command output filtered by output modifiers

CHAPTER SUMMARY

❏ Redistribution is used when you need to inject routes from one routing protocol into another. You can redistribute from any source of routing information into a dynamic routing protocol, including other dynamic routing protocols and static routes. When redistributing routes, however, you must plan very carefully to avoid routing loops. One way to do this is to specify the seed metric so that if redistributed routes are injected back into the routing protocol from which they originally came, then the redistributed routes will have poorer metrics than the original routes and won't be used. Another way of avoiding routing loops is to filter the routes redistributed into another protocol.

❏ In general, simpler redistribution scenarios are less likely to cause routing loops than more complex scenarios. If possible, redistribute routes into only one routing protocol, and use a default route instead of redistributing into the other protocol. When it is not possible to use a default route, you should carefully filter routes to prevent routing loops. The **show ip protocols** command is one method you can use to verify that redistribution has been configured on a router. In order to verify that routes are being redistributed between routing protocols, you can use the **show ip routes** command on non-border routers.

KEY TERMS

default metric — The metric initially assigned to redistributed routes.

gateway of last resort — *See* default gateway.

Intermediate System-to-Intermediate System (ISIS) — A link-state routing protocol.

output modifiers — The | character and the include, exclude, or begin keywords, which filter the output of **show** commands.

proxy ARP — When a router uses the Address Resolution Protocol for a host on an attached network to find the MAC address of a host (and hence where to send it).

redistribution — The process of injecting routing information from one routing protocol or source of routing information into another.

route filter — A method of filtering routing updates that uses an access list to select which routes to filter.

route map — A series of permit or deny statements used to match packets based on source address, protocol used, or other packet characteristics; if a statement is marked as permit and the packet matches the conditions for that particular statement, the route map does additional processing on the packet, as specified, after the match statements.

route tag — A numeric value assigned to a route in a route map, which can be used in other route maps to match particular routes.

seed metric — The initial metric for routes redistributed into another routing protocol.

REVIEW QUESTIONS

1. What are some of the potential problems you might encounter as a result of route redistribution? (Choose all that apply.)

   a. increased routing table size

   b. routing loops

   c. poor path selection

   d. discontiguous subnets

2. Which of the following is a potential disadvantage of setting a high seed metric?

   a. It might filter too many routes.

   b. In routing protocols such as RIP or IGRP, a high seed metric might lead to redistributed routes being marked as unreachable because of high metrics.

   c. Redistributed routes might be chosen over local routes.

   d. High seed metrics can cause routing loops.

3. Which of the following commands would properly set the metric for routes redistributed from OSPF into EIGRP?

   a. Router(config-router)#**default-metric 100**

   b. Router(config-router)#**default-metric cost 1500**

   c. Router(config-router)#**default-metric 64 100 100 100 1500**

   d. Router(config-router)#**default-metric eigrp 64**

4. When redistributing routes from OSPF into another protocol, what types of routes can you redistribute? (Choose all that apply.)

   a. stub area routes

   b. type 1 external routes

   c. type 2 external routes

   d. internal routes

5. Which of the following statements is true when redistributing routes into OSPF from another routing protocol? (Choose all that apply.)

   a. An OSPF router redistributing routes cannot be in the backbone area.

   b. An OSPF router redistributing routes cannot be in any type of stub area.

   c. An OSPF router redistributing routes cannot be in any stub area except a not-so-stubby area.

   d. An OSPF router redistributing routes automatically becomes an Autonomous System Border Router.

6. What is a potential disadvantage of using an Ethernet interface as the next hop on a static route?

   a. These routes cannot be redistributed into dynamic routing protocols.

   b. The router cannot determine the destination address from the static route and must perform proxy ARP to find the address of the next hop, causing performance problems.

   c. The router cannot determine the destination address and drops packets sent to that route.

   d. The router cannot determine the destination address from the static route and must perform DHCP to find the address of the next hop, causing performance problems.

7

7. You configured a default route on a router using the **ip default-network 172.16.19.0** command. However, the router discards packets unless it has a specific route. What might be a possible reason?

   a. Another default route was configured on the router.

   b. The 172.16.19.0 network is not in the routing table.

   c. The route to 172.16.19.0 is a summary route.

   d. This command can only set the gateway of last resort.

8. Why does redistribution between two or more routing protocols increase the odds of a routing loop or poor path selection? (Choose all that apply.)

   a. Redistribution requires excessive route summarization.

   b. Redistribution removes routing information, such as metrics, which helps routers choose the best paths and avoid loops.

   c. Redistribution increases the odds of creating a discontiguous subnet.

   d. Redistribution works around the mechanisms that routing protocols use to prevent routing loops.

9. The **ip default-gateway 10.131.14.1** command sets the default route on a router to be 10.131.14.1. True or false?

10. You began to redistribute EIGRP routes into OSPF, but routers in the OSPF Autonomous System are having trouble getting to many networks. When you look at the routing tables, you see major networks, but you don't see any routes for subnets with longer prefixes. What might be the problem here? (Choose all that apply.)

    a. routing loops caused when EIGRP injects routes it learned from OSPF back into OSPF

    b. A route filter is blocking many of the EIGRP routes at the border routers.

    c. routing loops caused by a poor seed metric

    d. Subnets aren't being redistributed into the OSPF Autonomous System with the **subnets** keyword to the **redistribute** command.

11. Which of the following are methods you can use to redistribute routes from a classless routing protocol, such as OSPF, into a classful routing protocol, such as IGRP? (Choose all that apply.)

    a. Propagate a default route to the OSPF domain throughout the RIP domain.

    b. Filter routes from the OSPF domain with subnet masks that do not fall along classful boundaries.

    c. Propagate a default route to the RIP domain throughout the OSPF domain.

    d. Configure static routes to destinations in the OSPF domain and redistribute them throughout the RIP domain.

12. Router CoreB is redistributing routes from a RIP AS and from EIGRP AS 542. Which command or commands would you use to configure a default cost of 500 from each route redistributed into OSPF (process ID 11)?

    a. **router ospf 11**
       redistribute rip metric 500

    b. **router ospf 11**
       redistribute eigrp 542 metric 500

    c. **router ospf 11**
       redistribute metric 500

    d. **router ospf 1**
       default-metric 500

13. Why should you try to redistribute routes only in one direction (and use a default route in the other) whenever possible?

    a. to prevent one routing protocol from injecting routes it learned from the other protocol back into that protocol

    b. to simplify configuration

    c. so that both protocols learn the most current routing information

    d. to prevent poor path selection resulting from the route redistribution

14. How should you set the seed metric when redistributing routes, and why?

    a. You should set the seed metric low; otherwise redistributed routes will not be used by the routing protocol that learns them.

    b. You should configure metrics for all routes based on the metric in the router doing the redistribution so that each router has the information necessary to make optimal path selections.

    c. You should set the seed metric high so that if routes learned from one protocol are redistributed back into it, routers will prefer the original routes.

    d. You don't need to set the seed metric at all since the routing protocol will automatically set it, and routers have enough information to send packets through the best path.

15. When redistributing routes from OSPF into EIGRP, what are some ways you can make sure not to redistribute default or other external routes into EIGRP? (Choose all that apply.)

    a. Use a routing filter to remove all the external routes during redistribution.

    b. Change the administrative distance of the OSPF external routes so routers prefer EIGRP routes.

    c. Use the **match internal** keywords when redistributing routes from OSPF so that only internal routes are redistributed.

    d. Configure OSPF with passive interfaces for any external routes you don't want to redistribute into EIGRP.

7

16. Which of the following sets of commands could you use to redistribute routes from OSPF (process ID 17) into EIGRP (AS 2224)?

    a. **router eigrp 2224**
       redistribute ospf match internal route-map OSPF metric 500

    b. **router ospf 17**
       redistribute eigrp 2224 route-map EIGRP metric 500

    c. **router eigrp 2224**
       redistribute ospf match internal route-map OSPF metric 64 50 100 100 1500

    d. **router ospf 17**
       redistribute eigrp route-map EIGRP metric 64 50 100 100 1500

17. What is the purpose of a route tag in a route map? (Choose all that apply.)

    a. You can use a route tag to mark a group of routes so that you can match them in another route map.

    b. You can use a route tag in place of an access list.

    c. You can use a route tag to set parameters for a route with the set command.

    d. You can use a route tag in a route map to set a metric for matched routes.

18. You are redistributing routes between an OSPF and EIGRP Autonomous Systems. Each AS has its own default route to the Internet. How can you config-ure two-way redistribution between the two routing protocols so that routers in neither domain learn the default route from the other domain?

    a. Use a route filter to prevent each AS from learning about the other Autonomous System's default route.

    b. Redistribute only internal routes from the OSPF domain.

    c. Configure summary routes within each domain and redistribute them in the other domain.

    d. Configure a default route in one domain leading to the other domain.

19. When redistributing between a classful and a classless routing protocol, how are Variable-Length Subnet Masks handled during redistribution?

    a. The classless protocol automatically handles all VLSM issues during redistribution.

    b. The router automatically summarizes all routes from the classless protocol along classful boundaries so that the classful protocol understands them.

    c. You must use a default route because the classful routing protocol is unable to understand any of the routes from the classless routing protocol.

    d. You must use either a default route, or static routes summarizing routes with VLSMs, and a route filter to prevent the classful routing protocol from learning routes with VLSMs.

20. Router CoreA is redistributing between OSPF and EIGRP. However, the **trace-route** command shows that it is sending packets for certain destinations in the EIGRP domain through the OSPF network. You think the problem is the administrative distance of the EIGRP routes. Which command could you use to verify this?

   a. **show ip protocols**

   b. **show ip interface eigrp** and **show ip interface ospf**

   c. **show ip route**

   d. **debug ip ospf** and **debug ip eigrp**

21. What commands can you use to determine whether or not you have configured route redistribution on a particular router? (Choose all that apply.)

   a. **show ip protocols**

   b. **show ip route**

   c. **show running-config**

   d. **show redistribution**

22. How can you determine whether or not route redistribution is occuring properly inside an Autonomous System? (Choose all that apply.)

   a. Use the **show ip routes** command on a border router.

   b. Use the **show ip routes** command on a non-border router.

   c. Use the **ping** and **traceroute** commands to check connectivity and the paths taken by packets.

   d. Use the **show running-config** command on a border router.

CASE PROJECTS

Case 1

The Dentless Auto Body chain hires you to administer its network. Dentless recently acquired the RealFast Oil Change chain, and your first task as network administrator is to connect the two networks. Neither Autonomous System is addressed suitably for route summarization; both Autonomous Systems use a mixture of private IP addresses in the 10.0.0.0/8 block and the 172.16.0.0/16 block (although fortunately neither address space overlaps). Dentless Auto Body uses OSPF in one area, and it has several small pockets of RIP because of legacy equipment that doesn't understand OSPF. The network numbers used in OSPF by Dentless fall between 172.16.100.0/24 and 172.16.200.0/24, and between 10.0.0.0/16 and 10.15.0.0/16, with the RIP networks using network addresses in 10.27.0.0/16. RealFast Oil Change uses EIGRP; it uses networks falling between 172.16.0.0/16 and 172.16.80.0/24, between 172.16.220.0/24 and 172.16.250.0/24, and between 10.100.0.0/16 and 10.200.0.0/16. However, the net-

7

works are numbered somewhat randomly. Each AS also has a default route to the Internet. Finally, you must redistribute at two border routers between each AS. Assuming that you can't use route summarization and that you don't want Internet traffic from one AS to travel through the other AS, how would you handle the issues of redistribution between the two Autonomous Systems? What would the configuration for redistribution look like on the two border routers? Remember that neither Autonomous System wants to learn about its own routes from the other AS, and you don't want to redistribute the default route to the Internet.

Case 2

You are brought in as a consultant to help Darren's Discount Brokerage migrate from IGRP to OSPF. You can see the current network in Figure 7-10. The CTO tells you that she wants you to accomplish this migration with an absolute minimum of downtime; brief outages of one to two minutes at off periods are acceptable, but no outages would be preferred. Additionally, she prefers that you don't activate two routing protocols at the same time on any one interface, which means you must work your way through the network redistributing between OSPF and IGRP. Given those requirements, what is your plan for migrating between the two routing protocols?

Case 3

You are hired as the new network administrator for a small auto parts manufacturer. The company has factories and offices in Michigan and California. The facilities in Michigan have been networked together for years, and the facilities in California for almost as long, but the networks in Michigan and California have never been connected before. Each network also has a default route to the Internet. You have been charged by your boss, the CTO, with the job of connecting the networks in the two states. As you can see in Figure 7-11, the network in California is using EIGRP, and the network in Michigan is using OSPF. The basic plan is to redistribute at the two border routers in Figure 7-11, CoreA and CoreB. The CTO wants you to create three plans describing how you would redistribute routes between the two routing protocols, looking at each of three scenarios:

❑ Using default routes or static routes to redistribute between the two routing protocols

❑ Propagating a default route throughout one AS, and then redistributing routes for the other AS

❑ Two-way redistribution between each routing protocol

What are the strengths and weaknesses of each approach? Show how you would prevent routing loops in two-way redistribution.

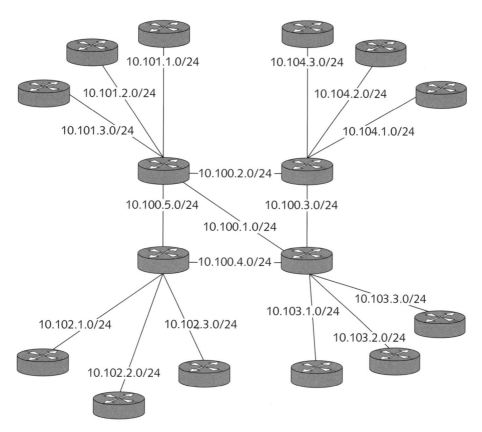

Figure 7-10   Darren's Discount Brokerage's IGRP network

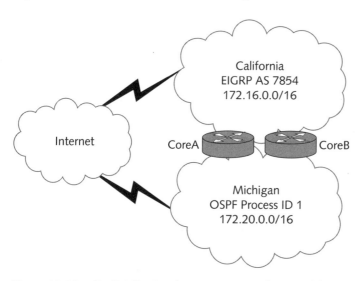

Figure 7-11   Redistributing between networks in California and Michigan

BORDER GATEWAY PROTOCOL

**After reading this chapter and completing the exercises
you will be able to:**

♦ Explain when and where you would use BGP, and how you can
avoid using BGP

♦ Describe how BGP operates

♦ Explain how BGP aggregates routes

In previous chapters, you learned about routing protocols used inside a net-work. In this chapter, you will learn about **Border Gateway Protocol
(BGP)**, which is the protocol used when you want your Autonomous
System to talk to other organizations' Autonomous Systems. BGP is used
throughout the Internet so that thousands of other Autonomous Systems in
different topologies and running a variety of different routing protocols can
exchange routing information and communicate with each other.

Network administrators are asked to perform tasks beyond the capabilities
of traditional link-state and distance vector routing protocols. For example,
OSPF and EIGRP would have trouble handling connections to multiple
Internet providers or multiple Autonomous Systems, as well as routing other
traffic through a service provider's Autonomous System. In this chapter and
the next two, you will learn how to do these things.

BGP BACKGROUND

BGP is an **Exterior Gateway Protocol (EGP)** used to route packets *between* Autonomous Systems. Interior Gateway Protocols (IGPs), such as EIGRP and OSPF, route packets *within* Autonomous Systems. Both EGP and BGP are based on distance vector routing protocols. BGP does not require a hierarchical design as OSPF does. BGP is also the successor to the EGP.

 The protocol name (Exterior Gateway Protocol) and the acronym (EGP) are identical to the generic term *exterior gateway protocol*, which is confusing.

The current version of BGP (BGP version 4 or BGP-4) contains a number of enhancements over EGP, is more stable, and uses less bandwidth and CPU time. RFC 1771 defines BGP-4. However, several other RFCs add on to or further describe BGP-4, including RFCs 1772, 1773, 1774, 1863, 1965, 1966, 1997, 1998, 2042, 2283, 2385, and 2439. BGP is now the only EGP in wide use and, in essence, fills the Internet routing table. Any router whose routing table contains the full Internet routing table runs BGP.

Additionally, you should expect BGP-4 to continue to be added onto or modified, especially as the size of the Internet routing table grows. At over 100,000 routes, routers with less memory and slower CPUs will have trouble keeping the entire BGP Internet routing table. As the size of the Internet routing table increases, it may become more difficult to stay ahead of it, necessitating further changes in the protocol in order to make it even more scalable.

BGP can be used both inside and outside an Autonomous System. Inside an Autonomous System, BGP can be used to exchange information about external Autonomous Systems. BGP can also be used to exchange routing information between different portions of very large Autonomous Systems. To distinguish between the two uses of BGP, people use the term **Internal BGP (IBGP)** when BGP is used between routers inside an Autonomous System and **External BGP (EBGP)** when BGP is used between Autonomous Systems. In general, the term BGP refers to EBGP.

Routing Between Autonomous Systems

An Exterior Gateway Protocol such as BGP was designed to route packets *between* Autonomous Systems. An EGP does not care about the routing protocols within an Autonomous System. To review, an Autonomous System is a set of routers under the same administration with the same routing policies. In fact, some Autonomous Systems may run two or more routing protocols. From the point of view of an EGP like BGP, the important thing is that it sees an Autonomous System as a cohesive unit with a clear definition of the routes it contains. From this point of view, you can see that an Autonomous System must be contiguous, or an EGP will be unable to route packets to all of its sections.

BGP uses Autonomous System numbers to avoid routing loops. In order for this to work successfully, however, public AS numbers must be controlled just like public IP addresses. The same organizations that allocate public IP addresses also allocate Autonomous System numbers. The **Internet Assigned Numbers Authority (IANA)** is ultimately responsible for these allocations, although it did delegate this responsibility to regional organizations. These include the American Registry for Internet Numbers (ARIN) in North and South America, the Carribean, and sub-Saharan Africa; the Asia Pacific Network Information Center (AP-NIC) in the Asia-Pacific region; and the Reseaux Europeennes-Network Information Center (RIPE-NIC) in Europe, the Middle East, and northern Africa.

Like IP addresses, IANA and its member organizations can allocate only a limited number of AS numbers. The AS Number field is 16 bits long, which limits the total number of Autonomous Systems possible to 65,535. Also like IP addresses, a range of private AS numbers has been set aside. This includes all AS numbers from 64,512 to 65,535. See RFC 1930 for more information on the allocation of AS numbers.

BGP stores the Autonomous Systems that a route passes through. It uses this information to avoid routing loops. For this reason, BGP is sometimes referred to as a **path vector routing protocol**.

Using BGP

Because of the additional complexity BGP can add to routing in your Autonomous System, and because a mistake in BGP on one of your routers could potentially affect the entire Internet, the decision to use BGP or not should be considered carefully.

Reasons to Use BGP

After you have a good understanding of how BGP works, and the possible effects it might have on your Autonomous System and on other Autonomous Systems, you might wish to use BGP because:

- Your AS is **multihomed** (that is, it has multiple connections to other Autonomous Systems) and you must perform load balancing between these connections.

- Other Autonomous Systems use your AS as a **transit AS**. That is, they pass traffic through your AS as if you were a service provider.

- You must control traffic entering and leaving your AS. An IGP does not allow you to influence traffic arriving from external Autonomous Systems, and only gives you minimal influence over outgoing traffic.

Reasons to Avoid BGP

As helpful as BGP can be, there are some instances when you should avoid BGP:

- Your AS has a lone connection to the Internet or to another AS.

- Your routers do not have enough memory or a CPU to handle tens of thousands of routes.

- You do not need to worry about routing policy or controlling traffic as it enters and leaves your AS.

- You do not have much bandwidth between Autonomous Systems.

You should also avoid BGP if you do not understand it well, or if you do not have an appreciation of the consequences of poor BGP configuration on your routers.

You may be able to avoid using BGP even in situations where you are multihomed. For example, if you have two Internet connections, but only a relatively small amount of Internet traffic, you may be able to use default routes instead of BGP. You will not be able to load balance across the two Internet connections, but with a small amount of traffic this is not really important.

How to Avoid Using BGP

In general, you can avoid using BGP by using static or default routes, and then redistributing them into your IGP, as discussed in Chapter 7. This is how most organizations connect to the Internet. Their service providers may also use static routes, which they may or may not need to explicitly advertise with BGP. If the address block fits within a larger block they are advertising, then it is advertised with that larger block. If not, they may have to specifically advertise it.

For example, in Figure 8-1, you can see how a customer connects to the Internet through an ISP. The customer uses a default route, which it propagates throughout its OSPF AS with the **default-information originate always** command. The **always** keyword ensures that the route is always propagated even when the next hop interface might be down. The ISP itself uses a static route to get to the customer's AS, which it redistributes into its IGP. It advertises the customer's block of IP addresses as part of its larger block of IP addresses, 192.168.0.0/16. You learned about how to propagate default routes into IGPs in earlier chapters.

For the majority of organizations connecting to the Internet, this scenario is enough. However, since you have only one connection to the Internet, you will not have any redundancy. If your Internet connection fails, you may be out of luck (or saturating a low-bandwidth dial back-up line). Depending on the nature of your organization, this may or may not be acceptable.

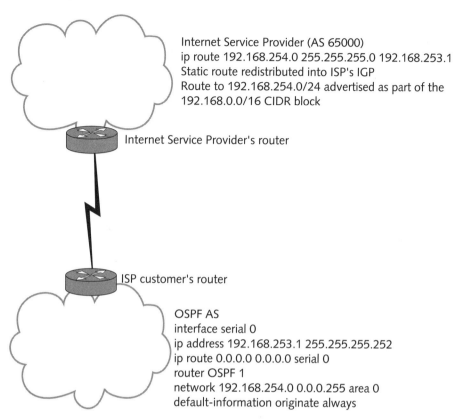

Internet Service Provider (AS 65000)
ip route 192.168.254.0 255.255.255.0 192.168.253.1
Static route redistributed into ISP's IGP
Route to 192.168.254.0/24 advertised as part of the
192.168.0.0/16 CIDR block

Internet Service Provider's router

ISP customer's router

OSPF AS
interface serial 0
ip address 192.168.253.1 255.255.255.252
ip route 0.0.0.0 0.0.0.0 serial 0
router OSPF 1
network 192.168.254.0 0.0.0.255 area 0
default-information originate always

Figure 8-1   Connecting to an Internet Service Provider with a default route

Be careful about using default routes with classful routing protocols. You must also use the **ip classless** command in order for them to honor default routes. This command is on by default in Cisco IOS 12.0 and later.

For a more complex example, look at Figure 8-2. Here, two routers in EIGRP AS 65117 connect to two different Internet Service Providers. One approach to using two simultaneous Internet connections is to redistribute default routes for both links into EIGRP. This approach has the disadvantage of creating asymmetric routing. **Asymmetric routing** occurs when packets to a particular destination take different routes, depending on which direction they are going. For example, if you redistribute two default routes into the EIGRP Autonomous System, one packet can be sent to Cisco's Web site through one ISP, and the next packet can be sent through the other ISP.

While TCP was designed to handle this sort of problem, nonetheless, some applications (particularly phone and voice applications) cannot handle packets arriving out of order, which may happen if there is any difference in the round trip time of a packet to a destination. Additionally, asymmetric routing can make troubleshooting more difficult simply by preventing you from clearly seeing what is going on. However, asymmetric routing is common on the Internet since you generally have little or no control over a packet once it leaves your AS.

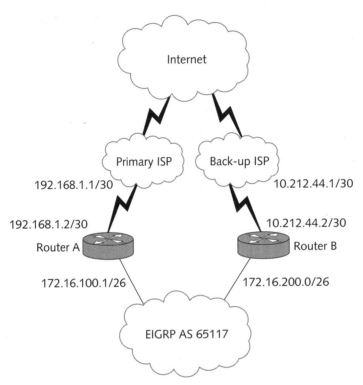

Figure 8-2 Connecting to two different Internet Service Providers with default routes

To avoid asymmetric routing as packets leave your AS, you can instead use one ISP as the primary ISP and the other as the back-up ISP. The simplest way to do this is to use a floating static route. For example, to set RouterA's Internet connection as the primary link, you configure a default route with a next hop of 192.168.1.1, activate EIGRP on the router, and redistribute the default route into EIGRP. You can do that as follows in configuration mode:

```
RouterA(config)#ip route 0.0.0.0 0.0.0.0 192.168.1.1
RouterA(config)#router eigrp 65117
RouterA(config-router)#network 172.16.0.0
RouterA(config-router)#redistribute static
```

On RouterB, on the other hand, you instead must create a floating static route. An administrative distance of 200, for example, ensures that the floating static route is not added to RouterB's routing table. Hence, it is not propagated to the rest of AS 65117 unless the default route it learned from RouterA through EIGRP (with its administrative distance of 170) is down. You would type the following in configuration mode:

```
RouterB(config)#ip route 0.0.0.0 0.0.0.0 10.212.44.1 200
RouterB(config)#router eigrp 65117
RouterB(config-router)#network 172.16.0.0
RouterB(config-router)#redistribute static
```

While this scenario will work quite well for you in many situations, it may not provide the flexibility you need. First, what happens if you need to do load balancing because of high outbound traffic? Since one link is always down, you clearly cannot do any load balancing at all. Additionally, you cannot do any load balancing based on the traffic coming into this AS because you do not have any mechanism to influence it. RouterA and RouterB also cannot choose the best path to destinations on the Internet. They can only forward packets through the Internet connection that happens to be active. In order to get around the limitations of this particular scenario, you will probably have to use BGP instead.

8

BGP PROTOCOL OPERATION

Like any other routing protocol, BGP routers must communicate with each other, establish neighbor relationships, and exchange routing information. When two BGP routers exchange routing information, they are called neighbors or **peers**.

BGP literature usually refers to "peers", while Cisco commands refer to "neighbors".

BGP Neighbor Relationships

BGP routers, also known as **BGP speakers**, communicate using TCP port 179. This means that all communication between two BGP speakers will be reliable and that, because BGP does not have to worry about making sure that communication between routers is reliable, the protocol itself is simpler.

When two BGP peers exchange routing information, they send one of several different types of messages. Each BGP message has a header, which consists of a 16-byte Marker field, a 2-byte Length field, and a 1-byte Type field. The header may or may not be followed by data, depending on the message type. Figure 8-3 shows the BGP message header format.

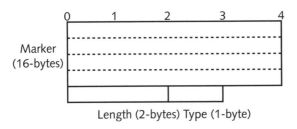

Figure 8-3   BGP message header format

BGP uses the Marker field to authenticate messages from other routers (which is beyond the scope of this book). If a router is not using any form of authentication, the Marker field will be all ones. If the router is using authentication, then the value of the Marker field will depend on the type of authentication in use. If the message type is open (also discussed later in the chapter), the field will be all ones. As you would expect, the Length field indicates the length of the entire BGP message. BGP messages are between 19 bytes (if they contain only the message header) and the maximum of 4096 bytes. The Type field includes the message type. BGP uses four types of messages:

- **Open**. Open messages are used to initiate neighbor relationships and negotiate BGP parameters.

- **Notification**. A notification message is used to reset the peer relationship between two routers.

- **Update**. This message is used to send information about a single route, or to withdraw one or more invalid routes. Both may be done simultaneously.

- **Keepalive**. These messages are used to indicate that a router accepted an open message, as well as to make sure that its peers are still responding (much like a hello packet in OSPF or EIGRP).

Establishing Neighbor Relationships

When establishing a neighbor relationship with a potential BGP peer, a BGP router sends an open message after opening a TCP connection. BGP routers use the open message to establish the peer relationship and negotiate BGP parameters.

Unlike other routing protocols, BGP peers do not necessarily have to be adjacent to each other. Peers running IBGP within an Autonomous System can be anywhere within that AS, while peers in different Autonomous Systems typically are adjacent to each other. Non-adjacent EBGP peers require additional configuration.

Figure 8-4 shows the format of the open message, which typically includes several mandatory and optional fields. Fields in the open message include:

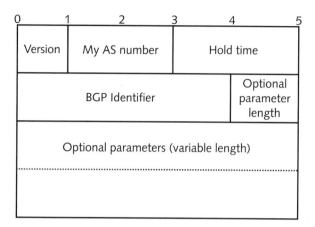

Figure 8-4   Format of the open message

8

- **Version.** This 1-byte field contains the version of BGP used by the sending router. If two routers do not support the same version, they reset the BGP session and resend open messages with different versions until they find one supported by both routers. Each router starts with the highest version that it supports. With Cisco routers, you can explicitly configure the version of BGP in order to avoid this negotiation. Typically, most vendors use a default of BGP-4 since it offers several performance advantages over earlier versions of BGP.

- **My AS number.** This 2-byte field contains the Autonomous System number of the router which sent the open message.

- **Hold time.** The hold time is the maximum amount of time in seconds that a router will wait between receiving keepalive or update packets. When a router receives either type of packet, it resets its **hold timer**, which it uses to track the hold time. After the hold timer expires, a router declares the neighbor that has not been sending keepalives. Cisco routers set the hold timer to 180 seconds, and the interval between keepalive packets to 60 seconds, by default. You can, however, configure this as low as 3 seconds, or you can tell a router to ignore the hold time altogether by setting it to 0 seconds. While BGP peers negotiate this parameter with each other, as they do the version number, two routers will not reset their BGP sessions if the hold time does not match. The maximum hold time is 65,535 seconds.

- **BGP Identifier.** The BGP Identifier is a 4-byte field that identifies a BGP router to other BGP peer routers. This parameter is much like the router ID in OSPF. If a router has loopback interfaces, it uses the highest IP address for a loopback interface, or else it uses its highest IP address configured on a physical interface. Also like OSPF, the BGP Identifier does not change after a BGP session has begun, for the sake of stability.

- **Optional parameter length**. If this 1-byte field has a value of zero, then the open message contains no additional parameters. Otherwise, this field gives the length in bytes of the next field, the Optional parameters field.

- **Optional parameters**. The length and contents of this field depend on the number of optional parameters sent in the open message. Each optional parameter consists of a triplet containing a 1-byte Parameter Type field, a 1-byte Parameter Length field, and a variable-length Parameter Value field. Currently, the only optional parameter defined is authentication. However, that may change in the future as additional capabilities are added to the BGP.

If a router accepts an open message, it begins sending keepalive messages. Since the default interval is relatively high and the packet size is small, keepalive messages use little bandwidth. Additionally, the keepalive interval can be increased, or the hold time disabled completely, preventing the exchange of keepalives.

States During Neighbor Negotiation

During the process of becoming neighbors, BGP routers pass through several states. RFC 1771 describes these states from the perspective of the BGP finite state machine:

- **Idle**. At this state, a BGP router refuses all incoming BGP connections until either the system itself, or an operator, initiates a **Start event**. In Cisco routers, you can initiate a Start event by configuring a router, or by resetting an existing BGP session. After the Start event, the BGP process on the router initializes its resources and resets the **ConnectRetry** timer. Additionally, it attempts to start a TCP connection to its peer, while at the same time listening for one initiated by its peer. In the event of an error at any point during this process, the router will generally go back to the Idle state. The router may automatically generate a Start event, of course, and attempt to begin another connection. Depending on the nature of the error that put the router back into the Idle state, automatic generation of Start events may result in flapping.

- **Connect**. In the Connect state, the router waits for the TCP connection to complete. If the TCP connection completes successfully, a BGP router clears its ConnectRetry timer, finishes its initialization, sends an open message to its neighbor, and enters the OpenSent state. If the ConnectRetry timer fails, the router resets it while attempting to initiate a TCP connection to the peer. At the same time, the router continues to listen for TCP connection attempts from its peer. If the TCP connection fails, the router restarts the ConnectRetry timer and enters the Active state, while continuing to listen for TCP connections from its peer. Other events or errors, such as a **Stop** event from you or someone on the router, will cause the router to send a notification message (if it already established a TCP connection), and put it back into the Idle state.

- **Active**. In the Active state, a BGP router attempts to initiate a BGP connection with its peer while listening for TCP connection attempts from its peer.

If it succeeds, it clears its ConnectRetry timer, finishes its initialization, sends an open message to its neighbor, and enters the OpenSent state. If the ConnectRetry timer fails, then the router restarts it and goes back to the Connect state. The router will go back into the Idle state for most other events or errors, although it will ignore Start events.

- **OpenSent**. In this state, the router has already sent an open message in either the Active or Connect states, and is waiting for a reply from its neighbor. When it does receive an open message from a peer, a BGP router checks through it for errors, such as mismatched version numbers, or unexpected AS numbers. If it finds errors, the router sends a notification message and goes back to the Idle state. If not, it begins sending keepalive messages. The router and its peer negotiate the hold timer. If the two routers disagree on the hold timer, then they select the smaller value. If the hold timer is zero, however, the routers do not send keepalive messages or use the hold timer. The router also determines whether or not this is an IBGP or EBGP session by comparing its AS number to the AS number contained in its peer's open message. If the router encounters a TCP connection error, it goes back into the Active state. Other errors or events will cause the router to send a notification message and go back to the Idle state.

- **OpenConfirm**. The OpenConfirm state indicates that a BGP router is waiting for a keepalive or notification message from its neighbor. If it receives a keepalive, this signals the end of neighbor negotiation, and the router enters the Established state. If it receives a notification message, it goes back into the Idle state (just as it would at any other time). The router also resets the hold timer if it was not set to zero. Any errors or other events will cause the router to send a notification message with the appropriate error code, and put it back into the Idle state.

- **Established**. In the Established state, a router has completed negotiation with its peer. It may now exchange update messages (and hence routing information) with its neighbor. The router sends keepalive packets periodically if the hold timer is not set to zero. Errors or events, such as a Stop event or the expiration of the hold timer, will generally cause the router to send a notification message, and put it back into the Idle state.

If a router continues to jump between the Connect and Active states, this is generally a good indication of a communication problem between two routers. For example, this may be caused by heavy packet loss on the link between the two routers, or simply because the two routers cannot reach each other. You can resolve this by correcting the problem preventing the two routers from making a TCP connection.

One other point to keep in mind is that although BGP is a dynamic routing protocol, it does not allow for dynamic discovery of neighbors. You must manually configure them. While inconvenient, this adds to network stability by preventing unwanted (and possibly misconfigured) routers from being dynamically discovered and injecting routes into your BGP routing tables. Since the entire Internet might feel any mistakes made in your BGP configuration, manual configuration of neighbors helps make the Internet more stable. If a remote router attempts to start a BGP session to a local router in the Connect or Active states, and you haven't configured it as a BGP neighbor on the local router, the local router will reject the connection and restart its ConnectRetry timer.

Notification Messages

During and after the process of establishing a peer relationship, a BGP router may encounter an error or an event requiring a notification message (such as a Stop event). After sending the notification message, the router closes its TCP connection to its peer.

A notification message consists of a 1-byte Error Code field, a 1-byte Error subcode field, and a variable-length Data field. As you would expect, the Data field may contain additional information about the particular error encountered. Figure 8-5 shows the format of a notification message. Additionally, Table 8-1 shows BGP error codes you might encounter. Some of the error codes describe properties of BGP that you will learn about later in the chapter.

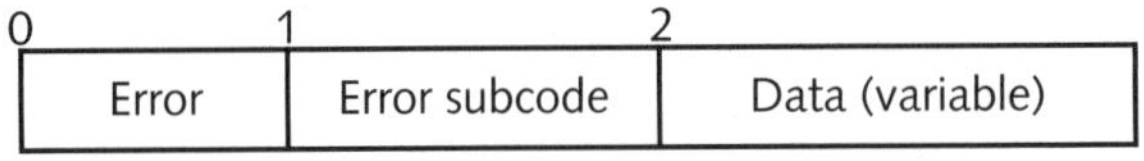

0	1	2
Error	Error subcode	Data (variable)

Figure 8-5   Notification message format

Table 8-1   BGP Error codes

Error Code	Description of Error Code	Error Subcodes
1	Error in message header	1 Connection not synchronized 2 Bad message length 3 Bad message type
2	Error in open message	1 Unsupported version number 2 Bad peer AS number 3 Bad BGP Identifier 4 Unsupported optional parameter 5 Authentication failure 6 Unacceptable hold timer 7 Unsupported capability
3	Error in update message	1 Malformed attribute list 2 Unrecognized well-known attribute 3 Missing well-known attribute 4 Attribute flags error 5 Attribute length error 6 Invalid origin attribute 7 AS routing loop 8 Invalid NEXT_HOP attribute 9 Optional attribute error 10 Invalid Network field 11 Malformed AS_PATH

Table 8-1   BGP Error codes (continued)

Error Code	Description of Error Code	Error Subcodes
4	Hold timer expired	None
5	Error detected by finite state machine (such as a response inappropriate to the state of the connection)	None
6	Cease (for fatal errors not listed)	None

Exchanging Routing Information

After two BGP peers enter the Established state, they begin to exchange routing information. Like EIGRP or OSPF, the only time two BGP peers exchange their full routing tables is when they first become peers. Afterwards, BGP routers send incremental routing updates. This is a significant advantage of BGP over the earlier EGP (and over traditional distance vector routing protocols such as RIP), considering the size of the Internet routing table.

Update Messages

BGP routers use update messages to exchange routing information. As you learned earlier, each update message contains information either about a single route, or about one or more withdrawn routes that are **unfeasible**, or no longer reachable. These routes are called **withdrawn** routes since their inclusion in an update message indicates a router is no longer advertising them. Additionally, update messages may contain **Network Layer Reachability Information (NLRI)** and **path attributes** (often called BGP attributes or just attributes). NLRI indicates the network being advertised, and consists of a prefix and its length. An example of NLRI is the prefix 172.16.0.0 and the prefix length 16 bits. Path attributes include information about a route. The NEXT_HOP attribute indicating the next hop for a route is a typical example of a path attribute. Figure 8-6 shows the format of an update message.

Unfeasible routes length (2 bytes)	Withdrawn routes (length/prefix)
Total path attribute length (2 bytes)	Path attributes (variable)
NLRI (length/prefix)	

Prefix length (1 byte)	Prefix (1-4 bytes)

Length/prefix format

Figure 8-6   Update message format

NLRI was added to BGP-4 to better support CIDR. Each NLRI entry consists of a 1-byte field showing the length of the prefix, followed by the prefix itself. The length of the prefix itself is variable. A router must include only enough bits to fully describe the prefix, followed by enough trailing bits so that the prefix ends on an octet boundary. For example, suppose a router includes NLRI about the 10.198.4.0/22 network. The prefix length is 22. The prefix itself consists of 22 bits (10.198.4.0 in binary), followed by two trailing bits so that the prefix ends on an octet boundary. According to RFC 1771, the value of the trailing bits is irrelevant. The router does not look at any bits beyond the end of the prefix. A router can only advertise one route in an update message. However, the message may contain multiple path attributes.

Withdrawn routes appear in the same format of a 1-byte Length field followed by a route prefix. However, the router must include the Length field of the withdrawn routes. It must also include the Length field of the path attributes.

According to RFC 1771, not all of these fields must be in a packet. For example, if a router sends an update message withdrawing certain routes, then it may set the Length field of the path attributes to zero and not include any path attributes. It may also leave the NLRI field empty. If it includes information about a particular route, an update packet may also have an unfeasible route Length field set to zero, and not include any withdrawn routes. In theory, the minimum size of an update message packet is 23 bytes (19 for the header plus two each for the unfeasible route Length field and the path attribute Length field). However, without either routes to withdraw or routers to advertise, there is no point to sending such a packet.

Path Attributes

BGP routers use path attributes to decide which routes to include in the routing table and which routes to filter. Numerous path attributes exist, and different implementations of BGP may include different path attributes. However, all BGP-4 routers agree on some path attributes.

Figure 8-7 shows the format of path attributes included within an update message.

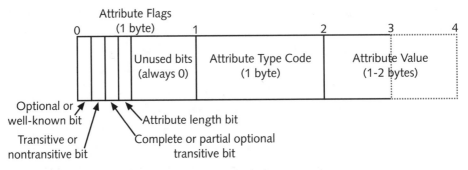

Figure 8-7 Format of path attributes included in an update message

Each attribute includes three parts: the attribute type, the attribute length, and the attribute value. The attribute type itself consists of two parts, a 1-byte attribute flag and a 1-byte attribute type code. The first two bits of the Attribute Flags field determine which of the following four possible classes each attribute is in:

- **Well-known mandatory attributes**. Each update message packet must include each well-known mandatory attribute. Additionally, each BGP implementation must also recognize these. A router receiving an update packet without each of these attributes generates a notification message and goes back into the Idle state. The AS_PATH, for example, is a well-known mandatory attribute. Each BGP router uses this attribute to determine whether or not a particular path is a routing loop. The other two well-known mandatory attributes include the ORIGIN and NEXT_HOP attributes. All three are defined in RFC 1771. If a well-known mandatory attribute is missing from an update for a route, or if a router does not understand a well-known mandatory attribute included in an update, a router generates a notification message and resets the BGP session.

- **Well-known discretionary attributes**. Every implementation of BGP must recognize these attributes. However, they need not be sent in an update message. Two examples of well-known discretionary attributes are the LOCAL_PREF and ATOMIC_AGGREGATE attributes.

- **Optional transitive attributes**. Optional attributes do not need to be supported by all implementations of BGP. The transitive flag indicates whether or not an optional attribute should be propagated to other BGP speakers regardless of whether or not a router understands that particular flag. For example, if a Cisco router includes a Cisco-only optional transitive attribute is inside an update message, routers from other vendors would include this attribute within their update messages even though they do not support that attribute. Only optional non-transitive attributes may be marked as partial. The AGGREGA-TOR path attribute is an example of an optional transitive attribute.

- **Optional nontransitive attributes**. If a router receives this type of attribute in an update message and it does not support this particular attribute, it simply ignores it. A Cisco-only optional nontransitive attribute is completely ignored by routers from other vendors instead of being passed on in update messages. The MULTI_EXIT_DSC (MED) path attribute is an example of an optional nontransitive attribute.

Table 8-2 shows the meaning of each bit in the Attribute Flags field, while Table 8-3 shows a summary of the possible attribute type codes.

8

Table 8-2   Bits in the Attribute Flags field of an update message

Bit	Meaning if set to 0	Meaning if set to 1
0	Attribute is well known	Attribute is optional
1	Attribute is nontransitive	Attribute is transitive
2	Information in the optional transitive attribute is complete	Information in the optional transitive attribute is partial
3	Attribute length is 1 byte	Attribute length is 2 bytes
4-7	Unused (always set to zero)	Unused (always set to zero)

Table 8-3   Attribute type codes

Attribute Number	Attribute Name	Type Code	Category	Source
1	ORIGIN	1	Well-known mandatory	RFC 1771
2	AS_PATH	2	Well-known mandatory	RFC 1771
3	NEXT_HOP	3	Well-known mandatory	RFC 1771
4	MULTI_EXIT_DISC (MED)	4	Optional nontransitive	RFC 1771
5	LOCAL_PREF	5	Well-known discretionary	RFC 1771
6	ATOMIC_AGGREGATE	6	Well-known discretionary	RFC 1771
7	AGGREGATOR	7	Optional transitive	RFC 1771
8	COMMUNITY	8	Optional transitive	RFC 1997
9	ORIGINATOR_ID	9	Optional nontransitive	RFC 1966
10	Cluster List	10	Optional nontransitive	RFC 1966
11	DPA	N/A	Destination point attribute for BGP	Expired Internet Dract
12	Advertiser	N/A	BGP/IDRP route server	RFC 1863
13	RCID_PATH/CLUSTER_ID	N/A	BGP/IDRP route server	RFC 1863
14	Multiprotocol Reachable NLRI	14	Optional nontransitive	RFC 2283
15	Multiprotocol Unreachable NLRI	15	Optional nontransitive	RFC 2283
16	Extended Communities	N/A	N/A	Internet Draft
256	N/A	N/A	Reserved for development	N/A

BGP Table

In addition to its routing table, a BGP router keeps track of various protocol-specific parameters in its **BGP table**. This table includes information about the attributes of each path. A router also keeps track of the **BGP table version**, which it increases by one every time the table changes. You can use this to give you an idea of the stability of BGP sessions on your routers. However, the BGP table version on a router with the full Internet BGP routing table will increase frequently because of changes on the Internet that you cannot control.

Types of Path Attributes

Since BGP routers make routing decisions and filter routes based on path attributes, you will learn about the most common BGP attributes in more detail.

ORIGIN Attribute The **ORIGIN attribute**, or **origin attribute**, is a well-known mandatory attribute that indicates the source of a particular route. It has three possible values:

- **EGP**. This indicates that a route was learned from another AS through an Exterior Gateway Protocol. In a router's BGP table, routes with an ORIGIN attribute of EGP will appear as an **e**.

- **IGP**. A route was learned from the same AS as the BGP router through an Interior Gateway Protocol such as EIGRP or OSPF. This is indicated with an **i** in a router's BGP table.

- **Incomplete**. This means that the route's source is either unknown, or was learned through some other means. One way in which a BGP router can learn a route with an ORIGIN value of incomplete is through redistribution of the route from an IGP into BGP. A router's BGP table indicates an ORIGIN attribute of incomplete with a question mark (?).

8

AS_PATH Attribute As you would expect, the **AS_PATH attribute** (also known as the **AS path attribute**) indicates the path that a particular route took to reach a router. Since routers use the AS_PATH attribute to determine whether or not a particular route is loop free, this attribute is both well known and mandatory.

After a route travels through an AS, that AS places its own AS number at the beginning of that particular route's AS_PATH (sometimes called **prepending** its AS number). As a result, the AS_PATH gives a list of all the Autonomous Systems a particular route must travel through, starting with the next AS, and ending with the originating AS. If a router is advertising a route to an IBGP router (that is, a router inside its own AS), it does not prepend its AS number. A router only does that when advertising a route through EBGP to a neighboring router in another Autonomous System.

In Figure 8-8, you can see an example of how a router calculates the AS_PATH. Router3 advertises a route to the 10.72.114.0/24 network in AS 65003. To its external BGP peer, Router2, it prepends its own AS number to the AS_PATH attribute. As this is the first entry in the AS_PATH, the AS_PATH Router3 advertises to Router2 is 65003. Any packet sent from Router2, or any other router in AS 65002, must go through AS 65003 to get to the 10.72.114.0/24 network. If Router3 has any IBGP peers, it advertises an empty AS_PATH for this route since the route is internal to the AS.

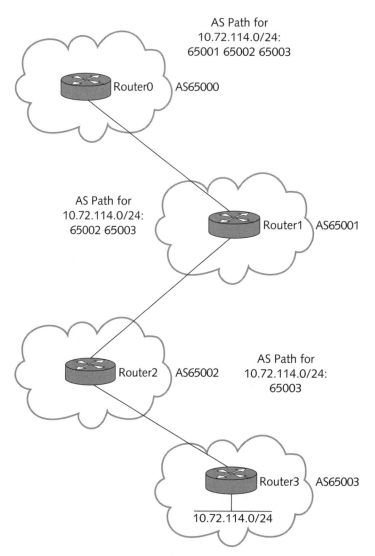

Figure 8-8 BGP routers adding AS numbers to the AS_PATH attribute

In turn, Router2 prepends its AS number (65002) to the AS_PATH when it advertises this route to its other BGP peer, Router1. The AS_PATH advertised from Router2 to Router1 is 65002 65003 since a packet from Router1 must travel first through AS 65002 and then AS 65003 in order to get to the 10.72.114.0/24 network. If Router2 has any IBGP peers in AS 65002, it won't prepend its AS number to the AS_PATH it advertises. Instead, it advertises an AS_PATH of 65003 because its IBGP peers in AS 65002 only have to go through AS 65003 to get to the 10.72.114.0/24 network. As you would expect, Router1 prepends its AS number to the AS_PATH when advertising the route to Router 0, so it advertises an AS_PATH of 65001 65002 65003. Any packets sent from Router0 or any other router in AS 65000 must travel through AS numbers 65001, 65002, and 65003, in that order.

However, suppose that Router1 receives an update message from Router0 containing an AS_PATH attribute of 65000 65001 65002 65003. It looks at the AS_PATH, sees that it contains its own AS number, and rejects the route since it is a loop. A packet sent through this AS_PATH first goes from a router in AS 65001, through AS 65000, and then back to AS 65001 where it started—the classic symptoms of a routing loop.

Additionally, the AS_PATH attribute can contain information about summarized routes, which you will learn about later in the chapter.

NEXT_HOP Attribute The **NEXT_HOP attribute** (also known as the **next hop attribute**) is the third of the well-known mandatory attributes. In EBGP, the NEXT_HOP attribute is the next hop router. While this seems straightforward, there are several factors that can complicate this process.

First, EBGP routers consider the next hop to be the peer that sent the update containing that particular route. However, IBGP routers must keep the NEXT_HOP attribute for routes learned from EBGP even when advertising them to IBGP peers. In Figure 8-9, each router is running BGP. Router4 is an IBGP peer of Router3, while the other routers are running EBGP. For EBGP, the NEXT_HOP attribute works much as you would expect. Router1, for example, advertises a route to the 10.168.21.0/24 network with 172.30.14.2 as the next hop. Router2 uses that path and includes 172.30.14.2 (Router1's address) as the NEXT_HOP attribute since it learned that route through Router1. In the same way, Router3 uses 172.30.13.1 (Router2's address) as the NEXT_HOP attribute for its route to the 10.168.21.0/24 network since it learned the route from Router2.

As you might expect, Router3 includes 172.30.13.1 as the NEXT_HOP attribute in its advertisement of the 10.168.21.0/24 network to Router4. However, because Router4 is an IBGP peer, it also uses 172.30.13.1 as the next hop! This remains true even though Router4 is not adjacent to 172.30.13.1. If Router4 does not have a route to 172.30.13.1, then it is unable to get to 10.168.21.0/24. Any packets forwarded to that network are dropped. You must verify that Router4 either has a static route to the 172.30.13.0/30 network, or a route through any IGP running in AS 65050.

8

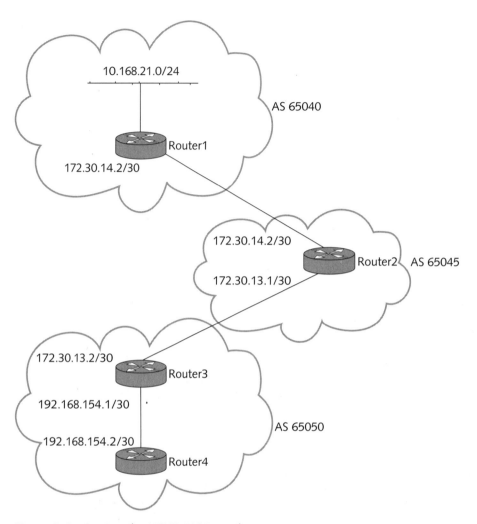

Figure 8-9   Setting the NEXT_HOP attribute

How BGP determines the next hop on multiaccess networks is another potential problem. In Figure 8-10, Alpha, Beta, and Gamma are on a frame relay network. Alpha advertises a route to 10.20.14.0/24 with a NEXT_HOP attribute of 10.20.15.2, even though this is the address of Beta. Since both routers are on a multiaccess network, packets can avoid having an extra hop by going directly to Beta instead of going first to Alpha. Avoiding an extra hop by directly specifying the destination router is called a **third-party next hop**. On Ethernet networks, for example, this should not pose any problems since reach router on a properly functioning Ethernet segment should be able to reach every other router. On NBMA networks, however, you cannot automatically guarantee that two routers will be able to communicate directly with each other. Suppose, for example, that Gamma and Beta cannot communicate directly through a PVC. While Gamma could reach 10.20.14.0/24 by sending packets directly to Alpha (which would in turn forward them to Beta), Alpha instead advertises Beta as the next hop. Gamma is unable to reach Beta, and is therefore unable to forward packets to the 10.20.14.0/24 network. In this case, the simplest way to work around this is to configure Alpha to advertise the route with a next hop of 10.20.15.1 (its address).

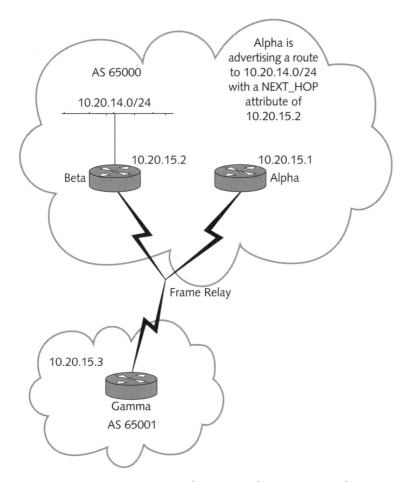

Figure 8-10   NEXT_HOP attribute on multiaccess networks

MED Attribute The **MULTI_EXIT_DISC attribute**, usually abbreviated as **MED**, and also called the **BGP metric**, is used to help routers distinguish between multiple connections to the same external AS. In show commands on Cisco routers, the MED attribute is simply called "the metric". Like metrics in other protocols you learned about, lower MEDs indicate better routes. The MED is an optional, nontransitive attribute defined in RFC 1771. It may be propagated to neighboring Autonomous Systems, but not beyond. Routers outside an AS may use this attribute to decide how to enter it, but routers inside an AS do not use it to decide where to leave.

Figure 8-11 shows how the MED attribute might be used. Both AS 65050 and AS 65030 are attempting to use the MED attribute to influence how RouterC sends packets back into those Autonomous Systems. For example, the MED attribute shows RouterC that the best path back into AS 65050 is through RouterB. It also tells RouterC that the best path into AS 65030 is through RouterD. However, RouterC will not pass the MED for routes from either AS when it advertises routes to other Autonomous Systems. When advertising destination networks in AS 65030 to RouterA and RouterB in AS 65050, RouterC sets the MED attribute to zero. The reason for this is fairly simple. Neither RouterA nor RouterB is adjacent to AS 65030. Although none are shown in Figure 8-11, either router might have multiple paths to AS 65030, going through multiple Autonomous Systems. Since the MED attribute must be configured manually, MED attributes advertised for paths through different Autonomous Systems do not necessarily compare easily. A network administrator in another AS could set the MED attribute for an inferior path so that your router chooses the inferior route through that AS.

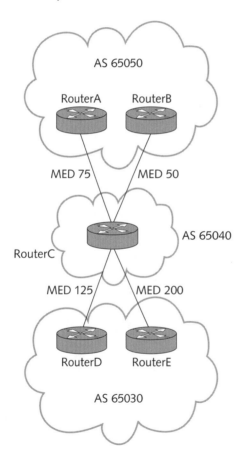

Figure 8-11   Advertisement of the MED attribute between Autonomous Systems

While Cisco routers assign a value of zero to routes missing the MED attribute, the IETF has decided that BGP routers should instead have a value of infinity. This means that a route with a MED attribute of any value is preferred over any routes without the MED attribute. You can, however, manually configure this behavior on your routers.

Cisco routers do not use the MED attribute, by default, when comparing routes through different Autonomous Systems. However, you can manually configure them to do this in situations where it might be beneficial.

The advantage of using the MED attribute is that it allows you the opportunity to influence how traffic leaves your Autonomous System. You can set the MED attribute on your border routers so that higher bandwidth links are preferred over lower bandwidth links for traffic coming into your AS from another AS, for example.

- **LOCAL_PREF Attribute** The **LOCAL_PREF attribute**, also known as the **local preference attribute**, is a well-known discretionary attribute that routers inside an AS use to choose an exit route. The LOCAL_PREF attribute is propagated inside an AS only by IBGP. Routers should not propagate it through EBGP (although if they do, it will be ignored by any EBGP peer that receives it).

  Like the MED attribute, the LOCAL_PREF attribute works just like a metric passed by an IGP. Unlike the MED attribute, however, routers prefer higher LOCAL_PREF attribute values over lower values. You can use this value to influence the routes taken by packets leaving your AS.

- **ATOMIC_AGGREGATE Attribute** The **ATOMIC_AGGREGATE** attribute, also known as the **atomic aggregate attribute**, is a well-known discretionary attribute used in BGP's handling of CIDR address blocks. When a BGP router chooses a summary route over a more specific route, it advertises the summary route with the ATOMIC_AGGREGATE attribute. This attribute tells the router's peers not to advertise more specific routes to destination networks within the summary route.

- **AGGREGATOR Attribute** The **AGGREGATOR attribute**, or **aggregator attribute**, is an optional transitive attribute that a router may add to summarized routes. The AGGREGATOR attribute consists of the address and AS number of any BGP router that summarizes (or aggregates) a block of routes.

- **COMMUNITY Attribute** The **COMMUNITY attribute** gives BGP routers a mechanism to filter routes. Setting the COMMUNITY attribute on a particular path is the same as **tagging the route**. BGP routers can use the **community** set in the COMMUNITY attribute to decide which routes to filter.

In general, you use the COMMUNITY attribute to tag a group of routes with the same community. It allows you to group any number of routes into a BGP community. You can then manipulate groups of routes by community, rather than individual routes.

8

Without the COMMUNITY attribute, if you needed to filter a group of 500 routes, you would have to filter each one based on the network number, which may or may not be done simply. If each route was configured with a BGP community value, you could then filter them all based on the community instead. Potentially, the use of BGP communities may significantly simplify the configuration of an individual BGP router.

Defined in RFC 1997, the COMMUNITY attribute is an optional transitive attribute. Routers with BGP implementations that do not understand this attribute should pass it along with their updates to other routers. The COMMUNITY attribute itself consists of one or more community values. Each community value consists of a 32-bit field. A particular route can therefore have multiple community values. Individual BGP routers can use any combination of a path's community values when deciding how to act upon that particular path, including none or all.

Each community value may be either well known or private. The ranges from hexadecimal values 0x00000000 through 0x0000FFFF and 0xFFFF0000 and 0xFFFFFFFF are reserved for well-known community values. These include the NO_EXPORT community value (0xFFFFFF01), which tells BGP routers not to advertise a particular path outside an AS, and NO_ADVERTISE (0xFFFFFF02), which tells BGP routers not to advertise a route at all.

Additionally, you can configure private community values that may have significance only inside your AS. One convention for defining private community strings is to use the first two bytes of a community value to specify the AS number, and the third and fourth bytes to specify a value that you can set, as necessary. The community strings are then written as two values separated by a colon. For example, a service provider might tag its routes with any one of several BGP community values, depending on the source or purpose of the routes. Assuming the AS number is 65000, it might use community values of 65000:400 for internal routes, 65000:401 for customer routes, and 65000:402 for routes learned from peers.

Weight Attribute   Cisco routers use the proprietary **weight attribute** to set local routing policy. You can configure the weight of routes on an individual router to influence path selection on that router only. Routers do not propagate the weight attribute to any BGP peer, internal or external.

Like the LOCAL_PREF attribute, the weight attribute operates like a metric, with higher values preferred over lower values. By default, each path has a weight of 32,768. You can configure a route to have any weight value from 0 to 65,535. Cisco routers use the weight value when choosing between routes to the same destination. As higher weight values are preferred, the path with the higher weight will be chosen. This allows you to force routing decisions on individual routers in cases where using other attributes to influence routing is either ineffective or more complex. As you will learn shortly, Cisco routers look at the weight attribute before looking at the LOCAL_PREF attribute.

BGP Routing Decisions

After it receives update messages from its peers, a BGP router selects only one route per destination network. Route selection is based upon path attributes. However, the rules for sharing routes between IBGP and EBGP also play a role.

BGP Synchronization

Because BGP is usually not run on all routers within an Autonomous System, IBGP peers often learn routes inside the Autonomous System via redistribution from an IGP. For example, an IBGP router may learn about the paths within an AS from a RIP or OSPF routing process. However, in some cases, an IBGP router may learn about a route before the IGP does, even if the IGP converges relatively quickly, like OSPF or EIGRP. Suppose, for example, that an IBGP peer learns a route to the 172.16.27.0/24 network from one of its IBGP peers. Because the AS is large and traffic must travel over many slow links, however, the OSPF routing process used as the IGP did not converge yet, and OSPF does not have a route to the 172.16.27.0/24 network. If the IBGP peer advertises that route to its EBGP peers, any packets forwarded from the EBGP peers would not reach their destinations. Even though IBGP learned a route to the destination, not all of the IGP routers inside the AS learned it.

As a result, an IBGP peer does not advertise a route unless it is local (on an attached interface, for example), or the IBGP peer receives the route from an IGP. The process of waiting until the routes are received from the IGP is called **synchronization**. Synchronization helps each route ensure that it will be able to properly forward any traffic received for Autonomous Systems it advertised to other Autonomous Systems, thus preventing black hole routes. A **black hole** occurs when a router advertises routes it cannot reach. Synchronization also helps routers within an AS maintain consistent routing information.

If the synchronization rules are turned on in routers, the rules BGP uses to decide whether or not to propagate routes depend on the source of routing information:

- **Local origin**. Since a router can guarantee that it can reach any route it learned locally, routes originating locally are propagated to all peers, both EBGP and IBGP.

- **EBGP peers**. Any route learned from an EBGP peer is forwarded to all peers.

- **IBGP peers**. Any route learned from an IBGP peer is propagated to EBGP peers.

Since routes learned from IBGP peers are not sent to other IBGP peers, you must have a full mesh between BGP peers in the same AS, or each router will not have the same routing information.

However, you can safely turn off BGP synchronization in certain situations:

- When all transit routers in your AS are running BGP

- When your AS is not serving as a transit point between two or more Autonomous Systems

For example, a service provider might use BGP on all of its routers. As a result, any route a BGP peer learns through IBGP is also learned by all its other BGP peers. Any router along the way has a route to any destination network advertised to EBGP peers in other Autonomous Systems, and a BGP peer cannot advertise a path it cannot reach. In the other situation, if your AS is not serving as a transit AS, then all local routes (static and connected routes, as well as those learned through the local IGP) should appear in each IBGP router's routing table anyway.

In Figure 8-12, routers CoreA, CoreB, and CoreC are each running IBGP between them, as well as EIGRP. If EIGRP is not configured to learn routes from BGP through redistribution, it will not learn about either the 10.155.0.0/16 route or the 10.198.0.0/16 route. Even though it learned the 10.198.0.0/16 route through IBGP CoreB will not include it in its routing table since the IGP does not have that route. CoreC will not include the 10.155.0.0/16 route in its routing table for the same reason. CoreA will not put either route into its routing table since it learned both routes from IBGP peers, and neither route appears in its routing table. As a result, even though AS 65000 is connected to both AS 65100 and AS 65200, neither of those Autonomous Systems is able to reach the other (and most of AS 65000 will have trouble reaching one or both of those Autonomous Systems too).

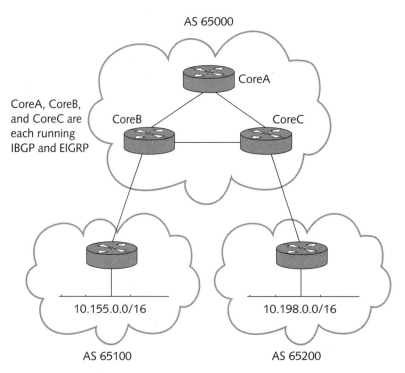

Figure 8-12 Example showing BGP synchronization

One way to get around this is to redistribute BGP routes into EIGRP. This way, the routes will appear in the IGP, and CoreA, CoreB, and CoreC will be able to put the appropriate routes into their routing tables. However, this increases the size of your EIGRP routing tables, as well as the load on your router. If you inject tens of thousands of routes learned from BGP into your IGP, your IGP may have performance problems. You could leave them in the core and use a route filter to filter them at the border between the core and distribution layers, but this increases the complexity of your configuration.

Another approach is to turn off synchronization. Since CoreA, CoreB, and CoreC are in a full mesh, each has the same routing information. When you turn off synchronization, each router installs the routes it learns through IBGP from its peers. This means that CoreB installs the 10.198.0.0/16 network in its routing table, CoreC installs the 10.155.0.0/16 network in its routing table, and CoreA installs both networks in its routing table. Each router in AS 65000 is then able to reach AS 65100 and AS 65200, while those two Autonomous Systems are also able to communicate with each other.

Route Selection

The following process gives a somewhat simplified version of how Cisco routers choose the best path out of several routes to the same destination:

1. The router ignores routes learned from IBGP if synchronization is on and the route is not in the IGP routing table.

2. The router ignores routes with unreachable next hops.

3. The router chooses the route with the highest weight.

4. For routes to the same destination with the same weight attribute, the router chooses the route with the highest LOCAL_PREF attribute.

5. If each route also has the same LOCAL_PREF value, then the router chooses any of the routes it originated.

6. If none of the routes originates locally, then the router chooses the route with the shortest AS_PATH attribute.

7. If each route also has the same AS_PATH length, then the router chooses the route with the lowest ORIGIN attribute. An ORIGIN attribute of IGP is the lowest, followed by EGP, and then incomplete.

8. If each route also has the same ORIGIN attribute, the router chooses the path with the lowest MED attribute. Unless configured to do otherwise, the router will only look at the MED attribute for paths that go through the same neighboring AS.

9. If each route also has the same MED, the router chooses external paths over internal paths (EBGP over IBGP).

10. If each path is internal and synchronization was turned off, the router chooses the shortest path through the AS to reach the next BGP peer.

11. If the destination network is in an external AS, the router chooses the oldest path (since this is also the most stable path).

12. Otherwise, the router chooses the route that goes through the BGP peer with the lowest BGP Identifier.

13. If each path goes through the same BGP peer, the router chooses the path that goes through that peer's lowest IP address.

While this process probably does not apply in all situations, you should have a good idea of how Cisco routers choose routes when they have multiple paths to the same destination. Perhaps more importantly, you should have a good idea of which values are more significant in influencing BGP routing decisions. You should see that, for example, the weight attribute configurable in Cisco routers overrides any other attribute (unless synchronization or a bad next hop prevents the router from putting the route into its routing table in the first place).

Cisco routers do, however, add multiple paths to the same destination into their routing tables with the **maximum-paths** command. This applies only with routes to the same external Autonomous System. However, a Cisco router still follows BGP and includes only one route in its BGP table as the best route.

BGP, CIDR, AND AGGREGATE ADDRESSES

BGP-4 added support for both CIDR and summary routes (usually referred to as aggregate addresses in BGP terminology). Neither previous versions of BGP nor EGP supported CIDR. Because of the growth of the Internet routing table over the last decade or so, any technique that can reduce the size of the Internet routing table is desperately needed.

In order to support CIDR, BGP update messages now carry both the route prefix and the length of the prefix. Earlier versions of BGP did not include the prefix length in update messages. Instead, they determined the length of a route's prefix by looking at the class of the route. BGP routers can now advertise aggregate addresses, allowing for the summarization of many routes with long prefixes into one route with a shorter prefix.

Additionally, instead of a simple sequence of Autonomous Systems that a particular route passes through, the AS_PATH can include an unordered list of all Autonomous Systems that the individual routes inside a particular aggregated route pass through. An AS_PATH attribute consists of a triplet containing the path segment type, the path segment length, and the path segment value. The path segment type is a 1-byte field that may include either:

- **AS_SEQUENCE**. This is a list of all the Autonomous Systems an individual route passes through, as you learned earlier in the chapter.

- **AS_SET**. This is an unordered list of all the Autonomous Systems that the individual routes inside an aggregated route pass through.

The path segment length is a 1-byte field containing the number of Autonomous Systems included in the path segment value, while the path segment value simply contains the number of 2-byte Autonomous System numbers indicated by the path segment value.

A router can use an AS_SET value in the same way it uses the AS_SEQUENCE value to find routing loops. If a router finds its own AS number inside an aggregated route's AS_SET value, it can assume that the aggregate route is a loop.

By default, however, a BGP router receives an aggregate route in an update message with the ATOMIC_AGGREGATE attribute set, and an AS_SEQUENCE value instead of an AS_SET value. The ATOMIC_AGGREGATE attribute tells the router receiving the update that the route was summarized, and information about the AS path may be incomplete. However, you can configure a router to include the AS_SET value in its AS_PATH attribute.

In Figure 8-13, you can see an example of an aggregate route. RouterA advertises the routes 10.2.0.0/24 through 10.2.3.0/24 as an aggregate route of 10.2.0.0/22 to its peer RouterB in AS 65500. By default, the AS_PATH included in update messages sent to RouterB includes AS 65495. If you configure RouterA to include an AS_SET value as its AS_PATH attribute, the AS_PATH advertised to RouterB includes AS 65495, as well as each of the individual Autonomous Systems whose routes are included in this aggregate route (65000, 65001, 65002, and 65003).

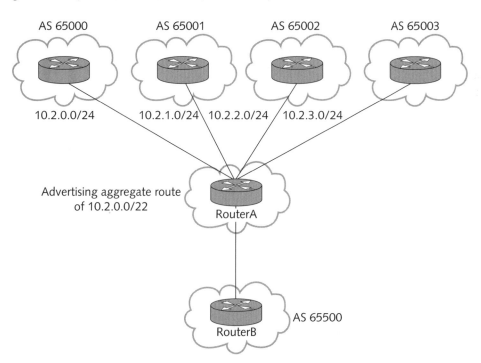

Figure 8-13   Aggregate route example

Like summarization done inside an IGP, route aggregation in BGP can also result in sub-optimal path selection. It can also cause routing problems if done incorrectly. If you attempt to summarize a group of routes that overlaps with someone else's routes, then large sections of the Internet might have trouble reaching those routes. For example, if another Autonomous System has control over the 10.2.3.0/24 network in Figure 8-13, and if this route is several AS hops away from RouterA, then advertising an aggregate route to 10.2.0.0/22 from RouterA would mean that RouterA is advertising a route it does not have. Other routers receiving the aggregate route would forward packets towards RouterA and its Autonomous System to reach this network. The net result would be that the packets would not reach the 10.2.3.0/24 network.

While you can advertise summarized routes learned from within your AS, these will not necessarily appear as aggregate routes to BGP. If BGP learns of a route to 172.24.0.0/16 from an IGP without learning about any of the individual routes summarized within that block, then this route will not appear as an aggregate route to BGP since BGP has not done anything to summarize it. If you have multiple customers who have Autonomous Systems contained within summarizable blocks, you may want to summarize these. A service provider, for example, may want to summarize blocks of addresses from several different customers. Assuming these are public addresses, this has the advantage of decreasing the size of the Internet routing table.

One reason that you may not want to aggregate routes is multihoming. If your AS has connections to multiple ISPs, you probably want to make sure that both ISPs advertise routes to your AS. If one ISP advertised your AS as part of an aggregate route, its BGP routers send update messages containing the ATOMIC_AGGREGATE attribute, which tells the routers that receive it not to advertise less specific routes to those destinations. For example, suppose your AS contains addresses on the 10.156.128.0/18 network and is connected to ISP 1 and ISP 2. If ISP 1 advertises your block of addresses as part of an aggregate route to 10.156.0.0/16, then it sends out update messages with the ATOMIC_AGGREGATE attribute telling other routers not to advertise the more specific route to 10.156.128.0/18, which ISP 2 would advertise. A BGP peer in another AS may receive both routes in update messages. If it receives the ATOMIC_AGGREGATE attribute, it will not advertise the more specific route. While the ATOMIC_AGGREGATE attribute is discretionary, and is not always propagated along with the route, in general, only one route to your AS is advertised through the Internet. Unfortunately, this has the disadvantage of increasing the size of BGP tables throughout the Internet.

CHAPTER SUMMARY

❑ BGP is an Exterior Gateway Protocol used to route packets between Autonomous Systems. It is the primary routing protocol used on the Internet. BGP routers, also known as BGP speakers, communicate using TCP to reliably exchange routing information. Two BGP neighbors use an open message to initiate a connection and negotiate parameters. If an error occurs at any point during a BGP session, a router sends a notification message to terminate the session. BGP speakers use update messages to exchange information about advertised or withdrawn routes. An update message advertising a route contains network layer reachability information about the route, as well as the path attributes for that route. Path attributes may be well-known mandatory, well-known discretionary, optional transitive, or optional non-transitive. An example of a path attribute is the AS path attribute, which BGP speakers use to avoid routing loops.

❏ Routers running Internal BGP (IBGP) cannot learn routes from other IBGP routers until the router learns the route from another source. This is known as synchronization, and it may be disabled in certain situations. When choosing routes, Cisco routers first decide if synchronization will allow them to choose a route, then look at the Cisco proprietary weight attribute, followed by the local preference, the length of the AS path, the origin attribute, and the MED attribute. BGP route aggregation supports Classless InterDomain Routing. To help avoid routing loops, the AS path attribute can include all Autonomous Systems a route passes through.

8

KEY TERMS

Active state — The state in the BGP finite state machine in which a router actively attempts to establish a TCP connection with a neighboring BGP router in order to establish a peer relationship.

AGGREGATOR attribute — An optional transitive path attribute that allows the BGP peer aggregating a route to specify its identity as the router that did the aggregation.

AS path attribute — *See* AS_PATH attribute.

AS_PATH attribute — A well-known mandatory path attribute that lists all the Autonomous Systems a route crosses; this attribute is used to prevent routing loops.

AS_SEQUENCE value — One type of AS_PATH attribute, which lists all the Autonomous Systems a particular route crosses.

AS_SET value — One type of AS_PATH attribute, which lists all the Autonomous Systems each individual route inside an aggregated route passes through, in no particular order.

asymmetric routing — Routing where packets take different paths on their way to and returning from a destination network.

ATOMIC_AGGREGATE attribute — A well-known discretionary path attribute used to tell BGP peers not to advertise subnets of an aggregate route.

Border Gateway Protocol (BGP) — An External Gateway Protocol and a path vector routing protocol designed to route packets between Autonomous Systems throughout the Internet.

BGP community — *See* community attribute.

BGP Identifier — A 4-byte number used to identify a BGP speaker; Cisco routers generally select either their highest loopback address or their highest interface address as their BGP Identifier.

BGP metric — *See* MULTI_EXIT_DISC attribute.

BGP speakers — Routers that run Border Gateway Protocol.

BGP table — A table each BGP router keeps in addition to its routing table, containing information such as path attributes.

BGP table version — The version number of a BGP router's BGP table, which increases by one after every change in the BGP table.

black hole — A route advertised by a router, which the router cannot reach.

community attribute — The value set with the BGP community attribute, which allows routers to tag routes and filter them based upon the community value.

Connect state — The state in the BGP finite state machine in which a BGP router waits for a TCP connection to complete.

ConnectRetry timer — A timer that controls how long a BGP router will wait to establish a TCP connection as it attempts to establish a peer relationship with a neighboring BGP router.

Established state — The state in the BGP finite state machine in which a router finished neighbor negotiation with its peer; this is the state in which two routers can begin to share routing information.

Exterior Gateway Protocol (EGP) — A routing protocol designed to route packets between Autonomous Systems. It is also the name of the first EGP, the predecessor to BGP.

External Border Gateway Protocol (EBGP) — BGP when used as an Exterior Gateway Protocol between multiple Autonomous Systems.

hold time — The length of time in seconds a BGP router will wait before declaring a neighbor down; defaults to 180 seconds in Cisco routers.

hold timer — The timer used to keep track of the hold time.

Idle state — The state in the BGP finite state machine in which a router has not yet begun to establish a peer relationship with a neighboring router. A router begins the process after receiving a Start event, and falls back to this state after most errors or events during the neighbor negotiation process.

Interior Gateway Protocol (IGP) — A routing protocol designed to route packets within an Autonomous System.

Internal Border Gateway Protocol (IBGP) — BGP when used between routers in the same Autonomous System.

keepalive message — A message consisting solely of a BGP message header, which a router uses to tell its neighbors that it is still up and functioning.

LOCAL_PREF attribute — A well-known discretionary attribute passed between IBGP peers to help them select an exit path from their Autonomous System.

local preference attribute — *See* LOCAL_PREF attribute.

MULTI_EXIT_DISC (MED) attribute — Sometimes called "the metric", this optional nontransitive path attribute is used like a metric to help external BGP neighbors select the best path into an Autonomous System.

multihomed — Having multiple connections to other Autonomous Systems.

next hop attribute — *See* NEXT_HOP attribute.

NEXT_HOP attribute — A well-known mandatory path attribute indicating the next hop for the path.

notification message — A message used by BGP routers to indicate that an error of some sort occurred; after receiving a notification message, a BGP router resets its connection with the peer that sent it.

OpenConfirm state — The state in the BGP finite state machine where a router has sent and received open messages to and from its peer, and is waiting for a keepalive or notification message.

open message — A message used by BGP routers to establish a peer relationship and negotiate parameters.

OpenSent state — The state in the BGP finite state machine where a router has sent an open message to a potential peer and is waiting for it to send an open message in response.

optional nontransitive attribute — An optional attribute that does not need to be recognized by every implementation of BGP; if a router does not recognize this attribute, it can ignore it.

optional transitive attribute — An optional attribute that does not need to be recognized by every implementation of BGP; if a router does not recognize this attribute, it must include it in its update messages so that it is propagated to other routers.

origin attribute — A well-known mandatory path attribute indicating the origin of the path's routing information, such as an Interior Gateway Protocol or an Exterior Gateway Protocol.

path vector — A list of Autonomous Systems a route passes through.

path vector routing protocol — A protocol that keeps track of the Autonomous Systems a route passes through; if a router receives a route containing its own AS, it assumes that a routing loop exists, and it ignores the route. BGP is an example of a path vector routing protocol.

peer — A BGP neighbor.

prepending — When a router places its own AS number at the beginning of a route's AS_PATH attribute.

routing domain — Another term for Autonomous System.

Start event — An event sent manually or automatically that tells a BGP router to attempt to establish a peer relationship with one of its neighbors.

Stop event — An event that tells a BGP router to reset its relationship with a peer.

synchronization — The process of not advertising routes learned through IBGP unless the routes are either local, or also advertised through an IGP.

8

tagging routes — Identifying routes with the COMMUNITY attribute in order to allow filtering based on BGP communities.

third-party next hop — When a BGP router specifies the NEXT_HOP attribute of a route as another router on a multiaccess network in order to prevent packets from taking an extra hop.

transit Autonomous System — An Autonomous System used to transmit traffic between two or more external Autonomous Systems; a service provider's Autonomous System is typically a transit AS.

unfeasible routes — Routes that are no longer reachable by a BGP peer, and that it no longer advertises; a BGP router notifies its peers of these in update messages.

update message — A message used by BGP routers to exchange information about either a single route, or one or more unfeasible routes.

weight attribute — A path attribute proprietary to Cisco, which is used on local routers to help a router choose a path; this attribute is not advertised to other BGP peers, internal or external.

well-known discretionary attribute — A BGP attribute that must be recognized by all BGP implementations, but which a router does not need to include in its update messages.

well-known mandatory attribute — A BGP attribute that must both be recognized by all BGP implementations and included in all update messages.

withdrawn routes — *See* unfeasible routes.

REVIEW QUESTIONS

1. What protocol do two BGP neighbors use when communicating with one another to ensure that they reliably exchange routing information?

   a. TCP over port 179

   b. Reliable Transport Protocol (RTP)

   c. TCP over port 79

   d. UDP

2. What sort of topology requirements does BGP have?

   a. BGP requires a hierarchical topology with a core and outlying areas.

   b. BGP requires a hierarchical topology with core, distribution, and access layers.

   c. BGP has no topology requirements.

   d. BGP networks must have a hub-and-spoke topology.

3. Which of the following situations requires the use of BGP? (Choose all that apply.)

   a. You work for a service provider and your AS is used to transmit traffic for other Autonomous Systems.

   b. Your AS has only one connection to the Internet and no connections to other Autonomous Systems.

   c. Your AS has four connections to the Internet, and you want to load balance between each of them.

   d. Your AS has two connections to the Internet, one used as the primary link, and the other used only as a backup in case the primary link fails.

4. Which of the following methods could be used to avoid using BGP to connect to the Internet? (Choose all that apply.)

   a. Propagate a default route to an Internet Service Provider's router throughout your AS.

   b. Propagate a non-default static route to an Internet Service Provider's router throughout your AS.

   c. Propagate a default route to one Internet Service Provider's router and a floating static default route to a second Internet Service Provider's router throughout your AS.

   d. Redistribute routes from an Internet Service Provider's IGP into your AS.

5. When initiating a BGP connection with a neighbor, how do BGP routers negotiate the version of BGP to be used?

   a. They set the version number dynamically during the BGP session.

   b. No negotiation is required since BGP-4 is backwards-compatible with earlier versions of BGP.

   c. Each router sends the latest version of BGP it will support in update messages, decreasing the version number, if necessary, until both peers agree on a particular version.

   d. If the version sent in each router's open message doesn't match, the routers resend the connection and send lower version numbers until one matches.

6. How does a BGP router determine whether or not a potential route is free of loops?

   a. Each BGP router can avoid loops because it knows the topology of all connected Autonomous Systems.

   b. If the weight of a route increases, a BGP router assumes that the route is in a loop.

   c. A BGP router assumes that any route containing its own AS in the AS_PATH is in a loop.

   d. If a BGP router detects that the metric of a route has increased, it assumes that the route is in a loop.

8

7. When does a BGP router send its routing table to its peers? (Choose all that apply.)

   a. A BGP router sends its entire routing table at each keepalive interval.

   b. when two routers first become BGP peers

   c. after a network topology change

   d. after a BGP connection has been reset

8. A BGP router receives an update for a route containing a well-known mandatory attribute. Which of the following is true for that attribute?

   a. A BGP router must both understand the attribute, and include it in its own updates for that route.

   b. A BGP router must understand the attribute, but does not need to include it in its own updates for that route.

   c. A BGP router does not need to either understand the attribute or include it in its own updates for that route.

   d. A BGP router does not need to understand the attribute, but does need to pass it along in its own updates for that route.

9. A BGP router receives an optional transitive attribute in an update for a route. Which of the following is true for that attribute?

   a. A BGP router must both understand the attribute, and include it in its own updates for that route.

   b. A BGP router must understand the attribute, but does not need to include it in its own updates for that route.

   c. A BGP router does not need to either understand the attribute or include it in its own updates for that route.

   d. A BGP router does not need to understand the attribute, but does need to pass it along in its own updates for that route.

10. What sort of information might be included in a BGP update message? (Choose all that apply.)

   a. network layer reachability information for a particular path

   b. path attributes for a particular path

   c. unreachable routes withdrawn by the router sending the update message

   d. unreachable Autonomous Systems withdrawn by the router

11. What does a router keep track of in its BGP table?

   a. the number of times path attributes for a particular path change

   b. path attributes for each path the router learned through BGP

   c. path attributes for each path the router learned through both BGP and any IGP running in the AS

   d. routing table entries learned through BGP

12. In what state does a BGP router need to be in before it can exchange routing information with a peer?

    a. Connect

    b. OpenConfirm

    c. Active

    d. Established

13. You just configured a router to be a BGP peer with a second router. However, the neighbor state has been cycling between Idle, Connect and Active. What is the most likely cause of the problem?

    a. The two peers are unable to agree on a version number.

    b. The two peers are unable to establish a TCP connection.

    c. The two peers cannot agree on a keepalive interval.

    d. The two peers can establish a neighbor relationship but cannot exchange routing information.

14. Which of the following are ways route aggregation can change the AS_PATH attribute for a path? (Choose all that apply.)

    a. A router can include only its own AS number as the AS_PATH attribute.

    b. A router can include all of the Autonomous Systems of the aggregate routes within the AS_PATH attribute.

    c. A router can leave the AS_PATH attribute out of its updates for aggregate routes.

    d. A router can send update messages for aggregate routes with the AS_PATH attribute blank.

15. EBGP requires a router to include its own address as the NEXT_HOP attribute for all paths included in its update messages. True or false?

16. How is the MED attribute used?

    a. The MED attribute overrides other attributes during the selection of the best route.

    b. A router uses the MED attribute to choose between different paths out of an Autonomous System.

    c. A router uses the MED attribute to choose between different paths into an Autonomous System.

    d. A router uses the MED attribute to choose between different paths into each neighboring Autonomous System.

8

17. How is the LOCAL_PREF attribute used?

    a. A router uses the LOCAL_PREF attribute to choose between different paths out of an Autonomous System.

    b. A router uses the LOCAL_PREF attribute to choose between different paths into an Autonomous System.

    c. A router uses the LOCAL_PREF attribute to filter paths.

    d. The LOCAL_PREF attribute overrides other path attributes during the selection of the best route.

18. Which of the following is true about the weight attribute? (Choose all that apply.)

    a. All BGP routers use the weight attribute to override other path attributes during route selection.

    b. Cisco routers use the weight attribute to override all path attributes except the LOCAL_PREF attribute.

    c. Cisco routers use the weight attribute to choose between different paths out of an Autonomous System.

    d. Cisco routers use the weight attribute to override other path attributes.

19. Which of the following is true about BGP synchronization?

    a. Synchronization prevents a router from re-advertising information about a path back to the router that originally advertised it.

    b. Synchronization prevents a BGP router from advertising any route that is not already in its routing table.

    c. Synchronization prevents a router from learning a route from an IBGP peer before it learns the route locally or from an IGP peer.

    d. Synchronization allows a BGP router to advertise routes learned from an IGP.

20. In which of the following situations can you disable BGP synchronization? (Choose all that apply.)

    a. when an AS is a transit AS

    b. when an AS does not allow transit traffic from other Autonomous Systems

    c. when all routers in an Autonomous System are using BGP

    d. when all routers within the transit path are using BGP

21. One of your core routers has been receiving updates from an EBGP peer on the Internet with an AS_PATH attribute containing AS number 65173. Why might this be a problem?

    a. The highest AS number possible in BGP-4 is 32767.

    b. The AS_PATH attribute does not actually contain AS numbers.

    c. AS numbers between 64512 and 65535 are reserved for future use.

    d. AS numbers between 64512 and 65535 are reserved for private use and are not unique.

22. What is the purpose of the BGP community attribute?

    a. to allow routers to choose between different paths out of an Autonomous System

    b. to override other attributes during path selection

    c. to allow administrators to group paths with similar characteristics for the purpose of filtering routes

    d. to allow administrators to simultaneously configure policies for a group of routers

CASE PROJECTS

Case 1

You were recently hired as a network administrator for Serrance Scientific, Inc. in Toledo, Ohio. Serrance recently acquired three smaller firms. The chief information officer and your supervisor, Laura Pettitbone, put you in charge of integrating Serrance's network with those of the three smaller firms so that each firm can exchange laboratory data. Each firm uses a different IGP. Serrance Scientific itself uses OSPF within its own AS, and the other firms use RIP, IGRP, and EIGRP. Initially, you will connect the individual Autonomous Systems of Serrance and each of the three smaller firms with a frame relay network at a single core router in each AS. Laura tells you that later she plans to add redundant connections between each AS, and do load balancing. Compare and contrast the merits of using BGP to connect these four Autonomous Systems versus the merits of redistributing default routes into each AS. Which would you prefer to use? How does the fact that Serrance will eventually do load balancing over multiple links between each AS affect your decision?

Case 2

You are the network administrator for Wiley Pharmaceuticals in Research Triangle Park, North Carolina. You recently used BGP to connect Wiley Pharmaceutical's AS, AS 65318, to the Autonomous Systems of two vendors and a partner. All three firms also have offices in the same office park in Research Triangle Park, and need to use various resources on Wiley Pharmaceutical's network. You also connected your AS to that of an Internet Service Provider. Wiley Pharmaceuticals will charge the three smaller firms for Internet access through this ISP. Figure 8-14 shows Wiley Pharmaceutical's AS and those of its partner, vendors, and ISP.

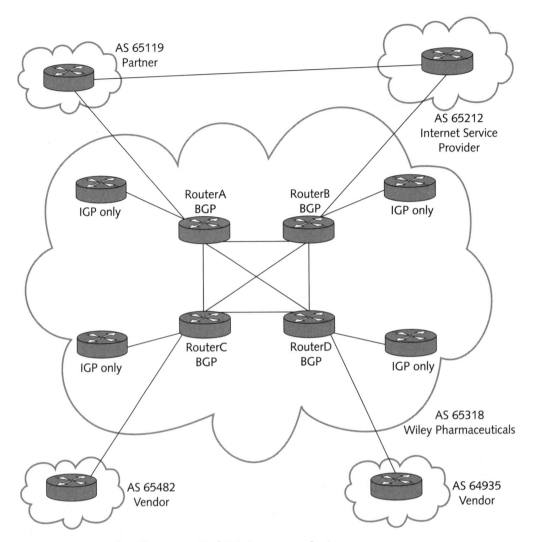

Figure 8-14   Wiley Pharmaceuticals' Autonomous System

Inside the AS, you choose to run EIGRP. However, only the four routers in the core run BGP. Given the network diagram in Figure 8-14, can you safely turn off synchronization? Explain your reasoning. Would your answer be the same if instead of allowing the other firms to use your connection to the ISP, you instituted policies to prevent them from using this connection?

Case 3

You are brought in as a consultant for the Wisconsin Fund For Teachers (WFFT). WFFT has a connection to a sister organization, Milwaukee Teachers' Fund, which uses resources on WFFT's network. The Milwaukee Teachers' Fund also uses WFFT for

Internet access. WFFT just added a second Internet connection. Figure 8-15 shows its AS and those of both ISPs, and the Milwaukee Teachers' Fund.

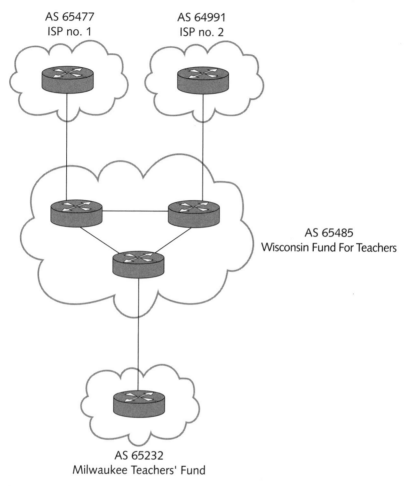

Figure 8-15   Wisconsin Fund For Teachers' Autonomous System

Currently, WFFT is using OSPF as its IGP. However, because of the second Internet connection, its chief technology officer wants you to investigate the possibility of using BGP. Currently, network traffic through the link to ISP no. 1 peaks at 15% of total bandwidth, while no significant traffic flows through the other link. Would you recommend that WTTF use BGP? How could they use both links without using it? Additionally, how would your recommendations change if:

❑ The first Internet link was completely saturated and the other link still had very little traffic?

❑ WTTF decided to host a publicly accessible Web site on its network?

9

CONFIGURING AND
TROUBLESHOOTING BGP

After reading this chapter and completing the exercises you will be able to:

♦ Configure BGP in simple scenarios
♦ Troubleshoot BGP

In the last chapter, you learned how the Border Gateway Protocol operates. In this chapter, you will learn how to configure and troubleshoot BGP in your autonomous system. Additionally, you will learn how to control BGP sessions, when necessary. Unlike IGPs, you learned about in previous chapters, you probably will not have control over the EBGP peers of your routers. In some situations, you may need to stop a BGP session. Also, restarting a BGP session is often necessary in order for a router to update some configuration parameters.

CONFIGURING BGP

Basic BGP configuration can be relatively simple. However, the protocol is so flexible that it allows you to use many different options, and configuring BGP can quickly become quite complex. You should also keep in mind that, because BGP serves a different role than IGPs, there are some key differences in the way BGP is configured.

Activating BGP

In order to activate BGP, first activate BGP on the router with the **router bgp** *autonomous-system-number* command, and then configure its neighbors. Because BGP has no mechanism to discover neighbors dynamically, *each* BGP neighbor must be manually configured. To configure each neighbor, use the following **neighbor** command with the following syntax:

```
Router(config-router)#neighbor [ip address | peer-group-
name ] remote-as autonomous-system-number
```

Configure a neighbor by identifying it with an IP address. Additionally, you can configure a peer group as the neighbor. A **peer group** is a group of routers under the same set of policies. Each member of a peer group receives policies from the group, while the group generates updates as a group instead of as individual BGP peers.

The *autonomous-system-number* configured is the AS number of the neighboring router. As you might expect, the value of the remote Autonomous System configured with the **neighbor** command determines whether or not the router will conduct an IBGP session or an EBGP session. If the neighbor has the same AS number, then the router will start an IBGP session. If the AS numbers are different, then it will start an EBGP session. You may have multiple IBGP and EBGP sessions on the same router.

At this point, a BGP router can receive updates from its peers, but it can't advertise routes to other BGP peers. To advertise a route to a peer, use the **network** command. The syntax of the network command is:

```
Router(config-router)#network network-number [ mask
network-mask ]
```

The **mask** keyword is optional. Without it, BGP will assume that the network being advertised has a netmask falling along traditional classful boundaries. Any sort of mask needed can be used, as BGP fully supports classless routing. Generally, you should include the **mask** keyword and the netmask when advertising networks, unless the netmask falls along a classful boundary. The critical differences between advertising a route in BGP and in IGPs are:

- BGP will not advertise a route included in a network statement unless it fits an existing route in the routing table.

- If a route in a **network** statement does not exactly match a route in a routing table, then BGP will not advertise the route in the **network** statement.

- Routes advertised with a **network** statement can be anywhere in your AS, in addition to those networks directly attached to the router.

- The **network** command does not activate BGP on an interface, as it does with an IGP.

With older releases of Cisco IOS, you were limited to 200 **network** commands on an individual router. Beginning with Cisco IOS 12.0, however, the only limits on the number of **network** statements you can use on a particular router are the router's RAM or NVRAM. For instance, a router with a limited amount of NVRAM could fill up its NVRAM with **network** statements.

Additional BGP Neighbor Configuration

Because BGP does not have the same requirements for its neighbors as an IGP, there are more options for configuring BGP neighbors. A BGP peer does not have to be adjacent, for example. However, this flexibility is at the expense of additional configuration and complexity.

Configuring Unadjacent Neighbors

While BGP allows you to configure unadjacent routers as neighbors, you must specifically configure this in EBGP in order for the BGP peer relationship to work properly. By default, EBGP assigns a **Time to Live (TTL)** value of one to EBGP packets, which means that they expire after reaching the first hop. In IBGP, however, the TTL is set to 255, so IBGP peers do not need to be adjacent. Since IBGP peers are generally under the same administration and EBGP peers are not, a network administrator is more likely to ensure that two IBGP peers are able to communicate than two EBGP peers.

However, you can configure Cisco routers to increase the TTL for EBGP connections to 255. Use the **neighbor ebgp-multihop** command to do this. The syntax is:

```
Router(config-router)#neighbor { ip-address | peer-group-
name } ebgp-multihop [ttl]
```

As long as the TTL is long enough for packets to reach the neighbor configured, this command can also be used to set the TTL, as necessary.

Figure 9-1 shows an example of a situation where using the **neighbor ebg-multihop** command is necessary. RouterA and RouterC are connected through RouterB, which does not have sufficient memory to store the BGP table and the many routes in the BGP routing table. The **neighbor ebg-multihop** command allows RouterA and RouterC to be EBGP peers even though they are not directly connected. However, this command requires that the router has a route to its neighbor besides the default route.

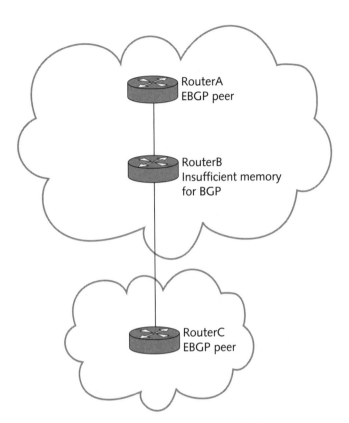

Figure 9-1   EBGP peers requiring multiple hops

Using Loopbacks as the BGP Identifier

In IBGP, loopbacks are used as BGP Identifiers for the same reasons they are used as router IDs in OSPF. As a software interface, a loopback will not go down unless the whole router goes down. So if you use a loopback as the address that supplies the BGP Identifier, the IBGP network will be more stable. In that case, BGP connections will not go down, even if the interface used to reach a neighbor goes down (as long as each neighbor still has at least one path to the other).

Another potential use of a loopback address is for load balancing over multiple links between EBGP peers, while still maintaining a single source IP address for routing updates. In order to do this, use static routes to make sure that each router can reach the loopback interface of the other.

However, you must specifically configure a BGP router to use a loopback interface as the source of routing updates with the **neighbor update-source loopback** command. The syntax is:

```
Router(config-router)#neighbor {ip-address | peer-group-
name } update-source loopback interface-number
```

After configuring a loopback interface, activating BGP, and manually configuring a neighbor, tell the neighbor to use the loopback interface to initiate its BGP connection. For example, in order to configure a peer at 172.16.1.1 to receive BGP messages from interface loopback 0, use the following command in router configuration mode:

```
Router(config-router)#neighbor 172.16.1.1 update-source
loopback 0
```

Variations of this command can be used to specify other interfaces instead. For example, the command **neighbor 172.16.1.1 update-source serial 0** configures interface serial 0 as the source of BGP updates.

Figure 9-2 shows an example of a network where two IBGP peers are configured to use loopback interfaces as the source of update messages.

Physical interfaces on RouterA:

Ethernet 0/0: 10.1.1.1
Ethernet 0/1: 10.1.2.1
Ethernet 0/2: 10.1.3.1

9

RouterA(config)#**int loopback 0**
RouterA(config-if)#**ip address 172.16.1.1 255.255.255.255**
RouterA(config-if)#**outer bgp 65000**
RouterA(config-router)#**neighbor 172.16.2.1 remote-as 65000**
RouterA(config-router)#**neighbor 172.16.2.1 update-source loopback 0**

RouterB(config)#**int loopback 0**
RouterB(config-if)#**ip address 172.16.2.1 255.255.255.255**
RouterB(config-if)#**outer bgp 65000**
RouterB(config-router)#**neighbor 172.16.1.1 remote-as 65000**
RouterB(config-router)#**neighbor 172.16.1.1 update-source loopback 0**

Physical interfaces on RouterB:

Ethernet 0/0: 10.1.1.2
Ethernet 0/1: 10.1.2.2
Ethernet 0/2: 10.1.3.2

Figure 9-2   IBGP peers using loopback as source of updates

Changing the Next Hop Attribute for Advertised Routes

In frame relay or other NBMA environments, you may need to require a router to advertise itself as the next hop for routes sent to a peer. As you learned in Chapter 8, you may need to do this because BGP will advertise a neighbor as the next hop on multiaccess networks. If a peer does not have a PVC to the router advertised as the next hop on a particular route to a destination, packets forwarded to that destination will not reach it. This command can be used in router configuration mode to configure a BGP router to advertise itself as the next hop:

```
Router(config-router)#neighbor { ip-address | peer-group-
name } next-hop-self
```

Cisco recommends that you avoid this command unless you have a single connection to the neighboring AS. As you might expect, changing the next hop can result in poor path selection if there are multiple paths to a destination. In many cases, adding the necessary PVCs so that the **neighbor next-hop-self** command is not necessary may be a better long-term solution to the problem (although it will be more expensive).

Figure 9-3 shows an example of a situation where the **neighbor next-hop-self** command would be useful. RouterA has PVCs to both RouterB and RouterC, but RouterB and RouterC do not have a PVC connecting each other. By default, RouterA advertises the 10.252.0.0/16 route with RouterB as the next hop. Because RouterB and RouterC are not directly connected, RouterC is unable to reach that network. However, RouterC is directly connected to RouterA. If RouterA advertises itself as the next hop for that route, RouterC will be able to reach the 10.252.0.0/16 network.

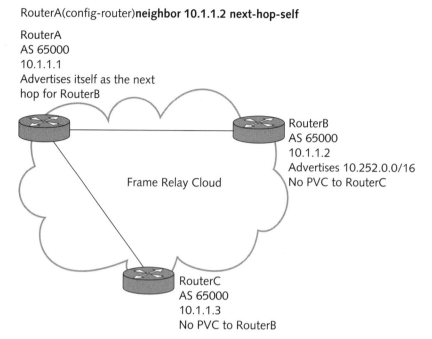

RouterA(config-router)**neighbor 10.1.1.2 next-hop-self**

RouterA
AS 65000
10.1.1.1
Advertises itself as the next
hop for RouterB

RouterB
AS 65000
10.1.1.2
Advertises 10.252.0.0/16
No PVC to RouterC

Frame Relay Cloud

RouterC
AS 65000
10.1.1.3
No PVC to RouterB

Figure 9-3   Changing the next hop attribute

Disabling Synchronization

To disable synchronization, use the **no synchronization** command in router configuration mode, or the **synchronization** command to reenable it. You should be careful to ensure that your AS does not need synchronization. This is the case when an AS does not carry transit traffic for other autonomous systems, or if all the routers in the transit path through your Autonomous System are running BGP. If enabled, synchronization requires routes advertised by BGP to be first learned through an IGP or other source of routing information. If you disable synchronization, you may be able to reduce the number of routes carried in your IGP (since they will not need to appear in both the BGP and IGP routing tables). Additionally, BGP may converge more quickly without synchronization.

To use the **no synchronization** command, simply enter it in router configuration mode:

```
Router(config-router)#no synchronization
```

Figure 9-4 shows an example of an Autonomous System where you might disable synchronization. AS 65000 could be used as a transit AS connecting autonomous systems 64990 and 64995. The transit path between these two autonomous systems consists of RouterA, RouterB, and RouterC. These routers are fully meshed IBGP peers. Although other routers inside AS 65000 are only running IGPs, none of these routers is in the transit path. If synchronization is disabled and the topology of AS 65000 is changed to add another router into the transit path, IBGP must run on that router.

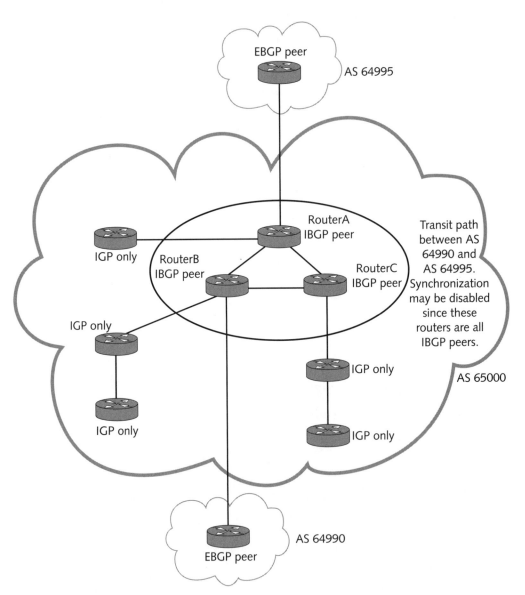

Figure 9-4   Disabling synchronization

Resetting and Disabling BGP Sessions

Unlike in an IGP, from time to time, you may need to suddenly stop a BGP session between two BGP peers. Since you are unlikely to have control over a session with an external BGP peer, the peer may cause problems that cannot be fixed. In this case, the only way to work around the problem may be to shut down the BGP connection. In order to do this quickly and efficiently without losing any configuration information, use the **neighbor shutdown** command in router configuration mode, which will disable a session with a particular neighbor or peer group. The syntax of the command is:

```
Router(config-router)#neighbor { ip-address | peer-group-
name} shutdown
```

To disable a BGP session in AS 65535 with peer 172.30.1.1, enter the following:

```
Router(config)#router bgp 65535
```

```
Router(config-router)#neighbor 172.30.1.1 shutdown
```

To enable a session disabled with this command, use the **no** version of the command:

Router(config-router)#**no neighbor 172.30.1.1 shutdown**

 If done carelessly, disabling a BGP session can disrupt routing within your AS, or between other autonomous systems.

Additionally, a Cisco router running BGP will not necessarily update all of its peers after configuration changes. For example, if path attributes, such as the WEIGHT, BGP timers, or other parameters change, you must reset BGP connections, in full or in part, for the changes to take effect. You also must reset a BGP session if you change filtering policy (covered in the next chapter). Depending on the version of Cisco IOS your routers use, you may have several options for resetting a BGP session:

- **Hard reset.** This is equivalent to sending a notification message and restarting the BGP session from scratch. As a result, the router loses all the information in its BGP table and routing table from that neighbor. You should avoid this whenever possible.

- **Inbound soft reset.** This resets all routes received from a particular peer, requiring it to resend all of its routes. Without prior configuration (see below), this requires Cisco IOS 12.1, or better. This is also sometimes called a dynamic soft inbound reset.

- **Outbound soft reset.** This resets all routes sent to a particular peer. It does not require any prior configuration.

- **Soft reset.** A soft reset is equivalent to doing both soft inbound and soft outbound resets. This requires Cisco IOS 12.1, or later.

- **Configured soft inbound reset.** Use this when two peers do not have the ability to automatically refresh routes. This requires using the **neighbor soft-reconfiguration** command and clearing all BGP sessions. The router stores all of the updates sent by its neighbors. By storing all of its neighbors' updates, it does not have to request them later if you need to do a soft inbound reset. However, this does use quite a bit of memory and should be avoided whenever possible.

In order to reset a BGP session, you use the **clear ip bgp** command in EXEC mode. The syntax of the command is:

```
Router#clear ip bgp { * | autonomous-system-number |
peer-address } soft { in | out }
```

Using the **clear ip bgp** command with the * symbol clears all BGP sessions, while using an IP address or an Autonomous System number clears sessions only for that neighbor or that Autonomous System. Using the **soft** keyword does a soft reset, while using the **soft in** or **soft out** key phrases does a soft inbound reset or a soft outbound reset.

In order to do a configured soft inbound reset, first use the **neighbor soft-reconfiguration inbound** command. To configure a router in AS 655535 to do a configured soft inbound reset for neighbor 10.1.1.1, enter the following:

```
Router(config)#router bgp 65535
Router(config-router)#neighbor 10.1.1.1 soft-reconfiguration
inbound
```

Then reset the session with that neighbor so that it sends all of its routing updates:

```
Router#clear ip bgp 10.1.1.1
```

Any kind of reset will have an effect on both router performance and on routing. Routes external to an Autonomous System learned through BGP, for example, might be unavailable if you reset all BGP sessions on a particular router. In general, try to avoid doing this on a production network, except during off-hours.

Route Aggregation

Route aggregation is another term for route summarization. In BGP, you can configure a router to advertise an aggregate route by itself. You can also configure a router to advertise both the aggregate route and the more specific routes summarized by the aggregate routes.

In order to create an aggregate route in the BGP table, use the **aggregate-address** command in router configuration mode. The syntax is:

```
Router(config-router)#aggregate-address ip-address mask
[summary-only] [as-set]
```

In order for this command to work, the router must already have these routes in its BGP table.

The default **aggregate-address** command without any keywords will advertise both the summary route and the individual routes included in the summary route. With the **summary-only** keyword, the router advertises only the summary route. The AS_PATH attribute will include only the AS that summarized the route.

If you use the **as-set** keyword instead, the AS_PATH attribute will be of the AS_SET type, which will include each AS for each individual route contained within the summary route. This version of the command will also overwrite the **aggregate-address** command used with the **summary-only** keyword.

However, you may use both keywords together. If so, the router will advertise only the summary route, but the AS_PATH attribute will be of the AS_SET type.

BGP Example

Figure 9-5 provides an example of a slightly more complex configuration scenario. Here, RouterB and RouterC must be configured as multihop EBGP peers since the router that connects them (RouterA) is not running BGP. In AS 65535, you must configure a summary route for 10.200.0.0/16. Synchronization between the IBGP peers also must be turned off since no IGP is running between the routers even though it is a transit AS, and since all the routers in this AS are running BGP. Otherwise, peers will be unable to learn routes from each other through IBGP. Finally, RouterE cannot reach RouterG's 192.168.2.2 address, so in AS 65300, RouterF must be configured to advertise itself as the next hop for routes learned from RouterG.

9

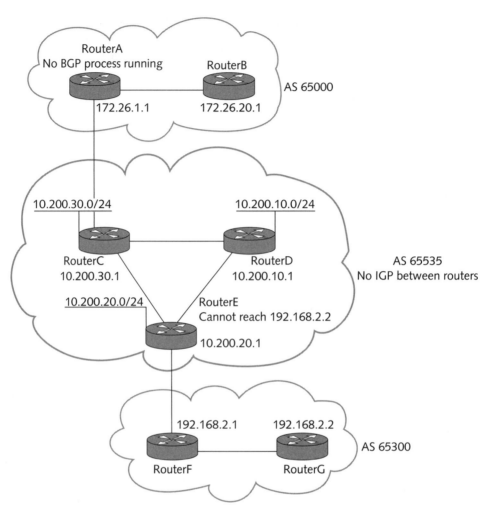

Figure 9-5 More complex BGP example

Configuring Neighbor Relationships

To configure RouterB and RouterC as mulithop EBGP peers, first configure the two routers as BGP peers. On RouterB in AS 65000, activate BGP, establish RouterC in AS 65535 as a neighbor, and then use the **neighbor ebgp-multihop** command to allow them to become neighbors even though they are not directly connected:

```
RouterB(config)#router bgp 65000
RouterB(config-router)#neighbor 10.200.30.1 remote-as 65535
RouterB(config-router)#neighbor 10.200.30.1 ebgp-multihop
```

On RouterC, use the same commands, but use RouterB's IP address and reverse the AS numbers:

```
RouterC(config)#router bgp 65535
RouterC(config-router)#neighbor 172.26.20.1 remote-as 65535
RouterC(config-router)#neighbor 172.26.20.1 ebgp-multihop
```

On RouterC, configure RouterD and RouterE as its IBGP peers. As IBGP peers, the AS number of each router is the same.

```
RouterC(config-router)#neighbor 10.200.10.1 remote-as 65535
RouterC(config-router)#neighbor 10.200.20.1 remote-as 65535
```

Advertising Networks

Next, make sure that RouterC advertises the 10.200.30.0/24 network:

```
RouterC(config-router)#network 10.200.30.0 mask
255.255.255.0
```

Before continuing, configure RouterE and RouterD as IBGP peers of RouterC, and make sure that they advertise their routes with the appropriate **neighbor** and **network** commands. RouterE as an EBGP peer of RouterF in AS 65300 also must be configured. Afterwards, add a summary route for the 10.200.0.0/16 network with the **aggregate-address** command in router configuration mode:

```
RouterC(config-router)#aggregate-address 10.200.0.0
255.255.0.0
```

Since the 10.200.0.0/16 network does not fall along traditional classful boundaries, make sure to use the mask to properly specify the aggregate route. Leave off the **summary-only** keyword so that the individual routes inside the summary route are still advertised.

 For the purposes of this example, assume that there are no other routes inside the aggregate route that are controlled by other autonomous systems. Before summarizing routes to be advertised by BGP, make sure that you are not attempting to advertise routes that are actually found in another Autonomous System.

Disabling Synchronization and Changing the Next Hop

Now you can disable synchronization. Since no IGP is running in AS 65535, none of the routers will learn routes from each other because with synchronization on, BGP will not add routes learned from IBGP peers to the routing table. Since all peers in AS 65535 are running BGP, it can be turned off on RouterC with this command in router configuration mode:

```
Router(config-router)#no synchronization
```

This also must be done on both RouterD and RouterE.

Several configuration changes were made since BGP was initially activated, so reset each BGP session. Assume that you are performing the configuration at an off-hour in order to affect as little traffic as possible. Reset all BGP sessions to both internal and external peers:

```
RouterC#clear ip bgp *
```

Repeat this on RouterD and RouterE.

Finally, configure RouterF and RouterG as IBGP neighbors. Then configure RouterF so that it advertises itself as the next hop to peer RouterE in routes learned from RouterG (since RouterE does not know how to reach RouterG's 192.168.2.2 address). Use the following command in router configuration mode:

```
RouterF(config-router)#neighbor 10.200.20.1 next-hop-self
```

VERIFYING AND TROUBLESHOOTING BGP

In BGP, show and debug commands provide you with information in three primary areas: neighbor relationships, the exchange of routing information, and the routing information itself.

Troubleshooting Neighbor Relationships

When troubleshooting neighbor relationships, use the **show ip bgp neighbor** command to provide the status of a router's connections with each of its peers. This command is used to look at all neighbors or a specific neighbor. This command also provides detailed information about each neighbor, including the remote AS, the BGP state, the hold time, the keepalive interval, the number of messages sent and received, and the last time the connection was reset (and the reason).

Additionally, the **show ip bgp summary** command shows the status of each peer. Other information provided by the **show ip bgp summary** command includes the number of messages sent and received, the BGP state, the remote AS, and the number of messages in the input and output queues waiting to be transmitted to each peer. Typical output from this command follows:

```
Cork#show ip bgp summary
BGP router identifier 10.200.200.1, local AS number 2
BGP table version is 8, main routing table version 8
3 network entries and 3 paths using 399 bytes of memory
2 BGP path attribute entries using 120 bytes of memory
1 BGP AS-PATH entries using 24 bytes of memory
0 BGP route-map cache entries using 0 bytes of memory
0 BGP filter-list cache entries using 0 bytes of memory
BGP activity 5/14 prefixes, 5/2 paths, scan interval 15 secs

Neighbor       V    AS MsgRcvd MsgSent TblVer  InQ OutQ Up/Down  State/PfxRcd
10.1.254.2     4     1      26      29      8    0    0 00:06:33           2
```

Note One important fact to keep in mind is that if a peer is in any state other than Established, a router is either attempting to establish a connection, or is unable to establish one. In particular, remember that peers in the Active state have not yet established a connection. Despite the name, a router cannot share routing information with a peer in the Active state.

When a neighbor's state cycles between the Idle, Connect, and Active states, typically the router cannot establish a TCP connection. If this happens, it is also indicated in the output of the **show ip bgp neighbors** command for that neighbor. After identifying this as the problem, use the **ping** and **traceroute** EXEC mode commands and the appropriate show commands (such as **show ip route**) to identify why the two routers cannot form a TCP connection.

Following is some typical output from the **show ip bgp neighbors** command:

```
Dublin#show ip bgp neigh
BGP neighbor is 10.0.1.18, remote AS 2, external link
 Index 1, Offset 0, Mask 0x2
BGP version 4, remote router ID 0.0.0.0
  BGP state = Active, table version = 0
  Last read 00:07:57, hold time is 180, keepalive interval
is 60 seconds
  Minimum time between advertisement runs is 30 seconds
  Received 0 messages, 0 notifications, 0 in queue
  Sent 0 messages, 0 notifications, 0 in queue
  Prefix advertised 0, suppressed 0, withdrawn 0
  Connections established 0; dropped 0
  Last reset never
  0 accepted prefixes consume 0 bytes
  0 history paths consume 0 bytes
  No active TCP connection
```

The Dublin router was never able to establish a connection with this particular neighbor. The session remains in the Active state, and the last line of the output indicates that an active TCP connection has not yet been established.

After a neighboring router is in the Established state, the **show ip bgp neighbor** command shows more information about the peer relationship between the two routers:

```
BGP neighbor is 10.1.254.9,  remote AS 2, external link
 Index 2, Offset 0, Mask 0x4
  BGP version 4, remote router ID 10.200.200.1
  BGP state = Established, table version = 1, up for
00:00:22
  Last read 00:00:21, hold time is 180, keepalive interval
is 60 seconds
  Minimum time between advertisement runs is 30 seconds
  Received 23 messages, 10 notifications, 0 in queue
  Sent 23 messages, 0 notifications, 0 in queue
```

9

```
Prefix advertised 2, suppressed 0, withdrawn 0
Connections established 2; dropped 1
Last reset 00:00:49, due to User reset
1 accepted prefixes consume 32 bytes
0 history paths consume 0 bytes
Connection state is ESTAB, I/O status: 1, unread input
bytes: 0
Local host: 10.1.254.2, Local port: 11738
Foreign host: 10.1.254.9, Foreign port: 179

Enqueued packets for retransmit: 0, input: 0   mis-
ordered: 0 (0 bytes)

Event Timers (current time is 0xC8ED6AEC):
Timer          Starts    Wakeups        Next
Retrans        4         0              0x0
TimeWait       0         0              0x0
AckHold        4         3              0x0
SendWnd        0         0              0x0
KeepAlive      0         0              0x0
GiveUp         0         0              0x0
PmtuAger       0         0              0x0
DeadWait       0         0              0x0

iss:  406760149  snduna:  406760217  snd nxt:  406760217
sndwnd:  16317
irs: 1392943914  rcvnxt: 1392944050  rcvwnd:       16249
delrcvwnd:      135

SRTT: 710 ms, RTTO: 4442 ms, RTV: 1511 ms, KRTT: 0 ms
minRTT: 0 ms, maxRTT: 300 ms, ACK hold: 200 ms
Flags: higher precedence, nagle

Datagrams (max data segment is 1460 bytes):
Rcvd: 7 (out of order: 0), with data: 4, total data
bytes: 135
Sent: 8 (retransmit: 0), with data: 3, total data bytes: 67
```

The information includes the connection state (now Established), the table version, the number of prefixes advertised, and the number of messages sent since the session began.

If a neighbor reaches the OpenSent or OpenConfirm states before the session is reset, or if a session is reset after entering the Established state, it may be necessary to find out why the connections are failing. To watch a BGP router attempt to build a peer relationship with a neighboring router, it is useful to use one of the following debug commands:

- **debug ip bgp events.** This command shows you how a router attempts to form a peer relationship with its neighbors, among other things.

■ **debug ip bgp keepalives.** This command can help you identify problems with the keepalives between two routers. Since the two routers may be configured with different hold time and keepalive intervals, this can sometimes be useful in determining problems.

One potential problem that prevents two routers from becoming BGP peers is an incorrect Autonomous System number. As part of the **neighbor remote-as** command, the neighboring router's AS number must be identified correctly during configuration. If the remote AS is configured incorrectly on one router or the other, then the two cannot become peers until the remote AS number is configured correctly on both routers.

Finally, you may find it useful to track neighbor state changes with the **bgp log-neighbor-changes** command (used in router configuration mode). If logged to a central server, you can use the output produced by this command to help troubleshoot problems after the fact.

Problems with the Exchange of Routing Information

When debugging problems with routing updates, you can use the **debug ip bgp update** command to take a detailed look at the exchange of routing information.

```
Dublin#deb ip bgp update
BGP updates debugging is on
Dublin#clear ip bgp *
5w4d: BGP: 10.1.254.9 computing updates, neighbor version
0, table version 1, starting at 0.0.0.0
5w4d: BGP: 10.1.254.9 update run completed, ran for 0ms,
neighbor version 0, start version 1, throttled to 1,
check point net 0.0.0.0
5w4d: BGP: 10.1.254.9 rcv UPDATE w/ attr: nexthop
10.1.254.9, origin i, metric 0, path 2
5w4d: BGP: 10.1.254.9 rcv UPDATE about 10.200.200.0/24
5w4d: BGP: nettable_walker 10.200.200.0/24 calling
revise_route
5w4d: BGP: revise route installing 10.200.200.0/24 ->
10.1.254.9
5w4d: BGP: nettable_walker 10.1.250.0/24 route sourced
locally
5w4d: BGP: nettable_walker 10.1.254.0/24 route sourced
locally
5w4d: BGP: 10.1.254.9 computing updates, neighbor version
1, table version 4, starting at 0.0.0.0
5w4d: BGP: 10.1.254.9 NEXT_HOP part 2 net 10.1.250.0/24,
next 10.1.254.2
5w4d: BGP: 10.1.254.9 send UPDATE 10.1.250.0/24, next
10.1.254.3, metric 0, path 1
5w4d: BGP: 10.1.254.9 send UPDATE 10.1.254.0/24, next
10.1.254.2, metric 0, path 1
5w4d: BGP: 10.1.254.9 2 updates enqueued (average=52,
maximum=52)
```

9

```
5w4d: BGP: 10.1.254.9 update run completed, ran for 0ms,
neighbor version 1, start version 4, throttled to 4, check
point net 0.0.0.0
```

Verifying Routing Information

The BGP table is the primary source of routing information used by BGP. The **show ip bgp** command takes a summary of the path attributes for each network from the BGP table, as well as the BGP table version. The following shows output from this command:

```
Cleveland#show ip bgp
BGP table version is 11062217, local router ID is
12.0.1.28
Status codes: s suppressed, d damped, h history, * valid,
> best, i - internal
Origin codes: i - IGP, e - EGP, ? - incomplete

     Network      Next Hop          Metric LocPrf Weight Path
* 3.0.0.0        12.123.1.236        0 7018 701 80 i
*                12.123.137.124      0 7018 701 80 i
*                12.123.142.124      0 7018 701 80 i
*>               12.123.25.245       0 7018 701 80 i
*                12.123.33.249       0 7018 701 80 i
*                12.123.145.124      0 7018 701 80 i
*                12.123.37.250       0 7018 701 80 i
[Output omitted]
```

In this case, the output shows the next hop, metric, local preference, and AS path for a single path to 3.0.0.0. Because routers running BGP may contain over 100,000 routes, the full output of this command may be quite large. The output in this example was cut short.

The **show ip bgp** command can also be used to look at individual paths by using the path as a keyword. For instance, you can see each possible path to the 3.0.0.0 network as follows:

```
Cleveland#show ip bgp 3.0.0.0
BGP routing table entry for 3.0.0.0/8, version 9399347
Paths: (18 available, best #4)
  Not advertised to any peer
  7018 701 80, (received & used)
    12.123.1.236 from 12.123.1.236 (12.123.1.236)
      Origin IGP, localpref 100, valid, external
      Community: 7018:5000
  7018 701 80, (received & used)
    12.123.137.124 from 12.123.137.124 (12.123.137.124)
      Origin IGP, localpref 100, valid, external
      Community: 7018:5000
  7018 701 80, (received & used)
    12.123.142.124 from 12.123.142.124 (12.123.142.124)
      Origin IGP, localpref 100, valid, external
      Community: 7018:5000
[Output omitted]
```

Here, you can see, in detail, the next hop, the peer advertising each path, the AS path, and other information (including the BGP community). You can also use the prefix length to more precisely specify the route to view. For instance, you could use the command **show ip bgp 3.0.0.0/8** if a routing table contained multiple routes with the prefix 3.0.0.0.

Finally, the **show ip route** command can be used to see which routes a router actually chose, and whether or not these match your expectations. The **bgp** keyword shows you routes learned through BGP, while using the **show ip route** command with a network number or IP address will show you detailed information about that route. For instance, you can verify that Cleveland is using 12.123.25.245 as the next hop to 3.0.0.0 with this command:

```
Cleveland#show ip route 3.0.0.0
Routing entry for 3.0.0.0/8
  Known via "bgp 65000", distance 20, metric 0
  Tag 7018, type external
  Last update from 12.123.25.245 1w4d ago
  Routing Descriptor Blocks:
  * 12.123.25.245, from 12.123.25.245, 1w4d ago
      Route metric is 0, traffic share count is 1
      AS Hops 3, BGP network version 9399347
```

CHAPTER REVIEW

Configuration of BGP requires you to manually configure each peer. In order to advertise a route through BGP with the **network** command, a route that exactly matches must already be present in a router's routing table. You may also configure load balancing between two BGP neighbors, configure External BGP (EBGP) routers as peers when they are not adjacent, alter the next hop attribute for advertised routes, and disable synchronization. When configuring an aggregate route, at least one of the routes to be summarized must already exist in a router's routing table. In order for new attributes or configuration changes to take effect, you may need to do either a soft or hard reset.

While EBGP peers normally are directly connected, you can also configure EBGP peers when they are not. This is not an issue for IBGP peers. You may also configure the next hop advertised for a route in some situations.

You may use several show and debug commands to troubleshoot and monitor BGP. You can use the **show ip bgp neighbor** command to examine peer relationships. The **show ip bgp summary** command shows summary information about BGP, as well as the status of each peer. You can debug BGP problems with the **debug ip bgp events** command, which shows BGP events, and **debug ip bgp keepalives**, which show you information about keepalives sent and received between two routers. The **debug ip bgp update** command helps you troubleshoot the exchange of routing information between two peers, while the **show ip bgp** command lets you look at information in the BGP table.

KEY TERMS

AS path attribute — A well-known mandatory path attribute that lists all the autonomous systems a route crosses; this attribute is used to prevent routing loops.

AS_SEQUENCE value — One type of AS path attribute, which lists all the autonomous systems a particular route crosses.

ATOMIC_AGGREGATE attribute — A well-known discretionary path attribute used to tell BGP peers not to advertise subnets of an aggregate route.

black hole — A route advertised by a router, which the router cannot reach.

Border Gateway Protocol (BGP) — An External Gateway Protocol and a path vector routing protocol designed to route packets between Autonomous Systems throughout the Internet.

BGP Identifier — A 4-byte number used to identify a BGP speaker; Cisco routers generally select either their highest loopback address or their highest interface address as their BGP Identifier.

BGP table — A table each BGP router keeps in addition to its routing table, containing information such as path attributes.

BGP table version — The version number of a BGP router's BGP table, which increases by one after every change in the BGP table.

External Border Gateway Protocol (EBGP) — BGP when used as an Exterior Gateway Protocol between multiple Autonomous Systems.

hard reset — An action taken to reset the BGP connection; a notification message is sent to one or more peers and the BGP connection starts over.

Interior Gateway Protocol (IGP) — A routing protocol designed to route packets within an Autonomous System.

Internal Border Gateway Protocol (IBGP) — BGP when used as an Interior Gateway Protocol between routers in the same Autonomous System.

next hop attribute — A well-known mandatory path attribute indicating the next hop for the path.

peer — A BGP neighbor.

peer group — A group of BGP peers that uses the same policies; the members of a peer group receive configuration options and policies of the peer group, which they can override to a limited extent, and the members generate routing updates as a group.

soft inbound reset — An event that requires a BGP router to request all of the update messages from one or more peers without completely resetting the BGP connection.

soft outbound reset — An event that requires a BGP router to resend all of the update messages from one or more peers without completely resetting the BGP connection.

soft reset — An event that requires a BGP router to resend all its update messages, and request all of the update messages from one or more of its peers without completely resetting the BGP connection.

third-party next hop — When a BGP router specifies the NEXT_HOP attribute of a route as another router on a multiaccess network in order to prevent packets from taking an extra hop.

Time to Live (TTL) — A timer that is increased by one after each hop on a network; a router discards packets if the TTL has expired.

REVIEW QUESTIONS

1. What effect does the command **network 192.168.0.0 mask 255.255.128.0** have in router configuration mode after activating BGP?

   a. It activates BGP on any interface on the router included within 192.168.0.0/17.

   b. It advertises any network included within 192.168.0.0/17.

   c. It adds 192.168.0.0/17 to the routing table and advertises it with BGP.

   d. It advertises 192.168.0.0/17 if that route is already in the routing table.

2. You configured a router with BGP. Which of the following routes can you advertise using BGP? (Choose all that apply.)

   a. routes that appear in the routing table, but originate outside your Autonomous System

   b. routes that appear in the routing table, and originate elsewhere in your Autonomous System

   c. routes that do not appear in the routing table, and originate elsewhere in your Autonomous System

   d. routes that are local to the router

3. Which of the following sets of commands would you use to configure 10.1.1.1 as an IBGP peer?

   a. Router(config)#**router bgp 65000**

   Router(config-router)#**neighbor 10.1.1.1 remote-as 65001**

   b. Router(config)#**router bgp 65000**

   Router(config-router)#**neighbor 10.1.1.1 autonomous-system 65000**

   c. Router(config)#**router bgp 65000**

   Router(config-router)#**neighbor 10.1.1.1 65000**

   d. Router(config)#**router bgp 65000**

   Router(config-router)#**neighbor 10.1.1.1 remote-as 65000**

4. Which of the following are limitations on the number of network statements you can use to advertise routes through BGP on an individual router? (Choose all that apply.)

a. In Cisco IOS releases prior to 12.0, you are limited to 200 network statements.

b. In all releases of Cisco IOS, you are limited to 200 network statements.

c. Beginning with Cisco IOS 12.0, you are limited only by the memory of your router.

d. Beginning with Cisco IOS 12.0, you are limited to 2000 network statements.

5. Why do EBGP neighbors require extra configuration if they are not directly connected to each other, while IBGP neighbors do not?

a. EBGP routers assign a TTL value of 255 to BGP messages, while IBGP routers assign a TTL of one.

b. All BGP neighbors, EBGP and IBGP, must be directly connected in order for BGP to function properly.

c. EBGP routers assign a TTL value of one to BGP messages, while IBGP routers assign a TTL value of 255.

d. EBGP peers must use the **neighbor next-hop-self** command if they are not directly connected to a peer.

6. How does using a loopback interface as the source of BGP messages allow you to load balance over multiple connections?

a. It automatically connects each IBGP peer in an AS in a full-mesh topology.

b. Unless the loopback address is used as the source address of BGP messages, update messages from that router will appear to come from multiple sources.

c. Unless the loopback address is used as the source address of BGP messages, update messages from that router will appear to come from other IBGP peers.

d. The loopback address allows a router to use fewer network statements.

7. In which of the following situations is the **neighbor next-hop-self** command useful?

a. when two EBGP peers do not have a direct connection with each other

b. when a BGP peer on a frame relay network is a peer to two routers that are not connected with a PVC

c. when you have disabled synchronization in an Autonomous System

d. after a hard reset

8. Which of the following commands would cause a BGP router to advertise the 10.152.0.0/18 network (assuming that the route already exists in its routing table)?

a. Router(config-router)#**network 10.152.0.0**

b. Router(config-router)#**network 10.152.0.0 255.255.192.0**

c. Router(config-router)#**network 10.0.0.0**

d. Router(config-router)#**network 10.152.0.0 mask 255.255.192.0**

9. Which of the following are disadvantages of doing a soft reset on a connection between two BGP peers? (Choose all that apply.)

   a. It may disrupt routing.

   b. It clears the BGP table.

   c. A soft inbound reset requires configuration in advance, and the router must store all of the updates from its neighbors.

   d. Soft resets are not supported in older releases of Cisco IOS.

10. Which of the following must be true in order for a router to advertise an aggregate route of 172.20.0.0/17?

   a. The router must have already learned this route from an IGP, or the route must be connected or static.

   b. The router must already have one of the routes contained within the aggregate route in its routing table before it can advertise the aggregate route.

   c. The router must already have all of the routers contained within the aggregate route in its routing table before it can advertise the aggregate route.

   d. The router must not be using synchronization.

11. Why should you avoid doing a hard reset on a BGP session if at all possible?

   a. It will prevent the router from reestablishing a connection with the peer.

   b. A hard reset will cause the router to lose all of the information in its BGP table and all of the routes learned from BGP through that peer.

   c. A hard reset will cause the router to lose all of the information in its BGP table and all of the routes learned from BGP through all peers.

   d. A hard reset will cause the router to lose all of the information in its BGP table and rebuild its routing table from scratch.

12. Why does a configured soft inbound reset require so much memory?

   a. because it requires a router to store all of its neighbors' update messages, in addition to its own, so that it can reprocess them later, if necessary

   b. because it requires a router to store its neighbor's entire BGP table

   c. because it requires a router to store its neighbor's entire configuration, including network statements

   d. because it requires a router to use a more recent version of Cisco IOS

13. Which of the following situations requires you to reset a BGP connection with a peer? (Choose all that apply.)

   a. after you change path attributes

   b. after you change filtering policy

   c. after you remove a route

   d. after you shut down a BGP session with another peer

14. You just made a change to the path attributes for a route in your AS advertised by BGP. Which of the following commands would you use so that the changes are propagated to all BGP peers, with minimum effect on existing BGP sessions?

    a. Router#**clear ip bgp ***

    b. Router#**clear ip bgp * soft in**

    c. Router#**clear ip bgp soft out**

    d. Router#**clear ip bgp * soft out**

15. Which of the following commands could you use to show the status of a BGP peer? (Choose all that apply.)

    a. **show ip bgp summary**

    b. **show ip bgp peer**

    c. **show ip bgp neighbor**

    d. **debug ip bgp neighbor**

16. RouterA has routes to 172.16.0.0/17 and 172.16.128.0/17 in its routing table. If you use the command **aggregate-address 172.16.0.0 255.255.0.0 summary-only** to summarize these two routes, which one of the following statements is true?

    a. RouterA will advertise 172.16.0.0/17, 172.16.128.0/17, and the summary route.

    b. RouterA will advertise 172.16.0.0/17 and 172.16.128.0/17, but not the summary route because it isn't in RouterA's routing table.

    c. RouterA will advertise 172.16.0.0/17, 172.16.128.0/17, and the summary route, and the AS path attribute will be of the AS_SET type.

    d. RouterA will advertise only the summary route

17. You are attempting to establish a peer relationship between RouterY and RouterZ. Running the **show ip bgp neighbors** command on RouterY shows that the BGP session between the routers cycles between the Idle, Connect, and Active states. What is the most likely cause of the problem?

    a. There is no problem since the neighbor relationship is fully established at the Active state.

    b. RouterZ is rejecting the open message sent by RouterY.

    c. RouterY and RouterZ cannot establish a TCP connection.

    d. RouterY and RouterZ use incompatible versions of the BGP protocol.

18. You configured RouterA (at 10.1.1.1) as follows:

```
RouterA(config)#router bgp 65499
RouterA(config-router)#neighbor 10.1.1.2 remote-as 65531
```

What would you expect to happen after you configure RouterB (10.1.1.2) with the following:

```
RouterB(config)#router bgp 65531
RouterB(config-router)#neighbor 10.1.1.1 remote-as 65531
```

a. The two routers would become IBGP peers.

b. The two routers would not become BGP peers because the IP addresses do not match.

c. The two routers would become EBGP peers.

d. The two routers would not become BGP peers because the AS numbers do not match.

19. Which of the following commands would you use to examine updates between BGP peers as they occur?

a. **debug ip bgp update**

b. **show ip bgp update**

c. **show ip bgp**

d. **debug ip bgp update-messages**

20. Which of the following commands could you use to see detailed information about the 192.168.16.0/20 route, including path attributes? (Choose all that apply.)

a. **show ip route 192.168.16.0**

b. **show ip bgp 192.168.16.0**

c. **show ip bgp 192.168.16.0/16**

d. **show ip bgp 192.168.16.0/20**

CASE PROJECTS

Case 1

You are the new network administrator for Sarnia Wicket. Figure 9-6 shows its network. Your first project is to configure Sarnia Wicket's routers so that its Autonomous System (AS 64981) can connect to the autonomous systems of two of its chief suppliers (AS 64787 and 64991). How would you configure each of Sarnia Wicket's routers? What sort of configuration is needed on each of the supplier's routers?

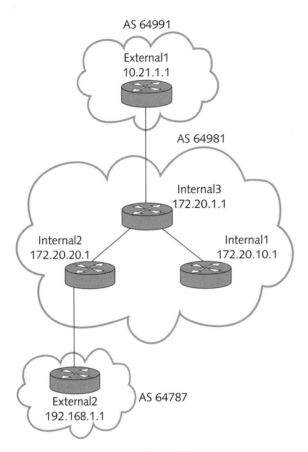

Figure 9-6 Sarnia Wicket's AS

Case 2

You are a network administrator at Thames Networks in Sandusky, Ohio. Figure 9-7 shows your AS (65050), as well as those of two customers. Your AS serves as a transit AS for the two customer autonomous systems, AS 65000 and AS 65100. You have been trying to remove EIGRP from inside your network, as your routers do not have enough memory or a fast enough processor to run both routing protocols simultaneously. However, when you attempted to do this during your scheduled maintenance window, AS 65000 and AS 65100 were unable to communicate with each other. What's the nature of the problem, and how would you go about troubleshooting it? How would you configure each router in AS 65000 to use BGP without using an IGP? Show the full configuration of each router.

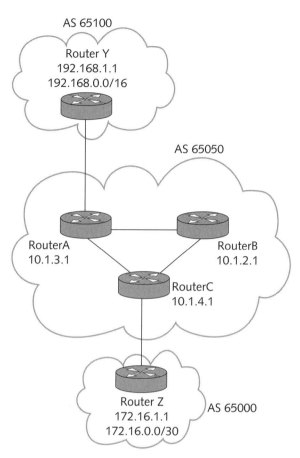

AS 65100

Router Y
192.168.1.1
192.168.0.0/16

AS 65050

RouterA
10.1.3.1

RouterB
10.1.2.1

RouterC
10.1.4.1

Router Z
172.16.1.1
172.16.0.0/30

AS 65000

9

Figure 9-7 Thames Networks' AS

Case 3

You are the new network administrator at Gallic Industries. As shown in Figure 9-8, Gallic Industries has its headquarters and a factory in Boston. Additionally, Gallic Industries connects to its parent company in New York. Both Boston locations are in one AS (AS 65003), and the network of the parent company in New York is in another (AS 64990). Develop BGP configurations for the routers at each location. BostonHQ and BostonFactory will be IBGP peers, while BostonHQ and New York will be EBGP peers.

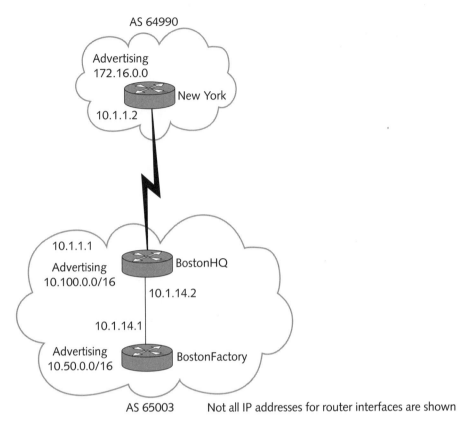

Figure 9-8 Gallic Industries

ADVANCED BGP

After reading this chapter and completing the exercises you will be able to:

♦ Describe and configure methods to make BGP more scalable in large Autonomous Systems

♦ Configure BGP routing policy and prefix lists

♦ Explain how BGP interacts with Interior Gateway Protocols

♦ Configure a multihomed Autonomous System

In the last chapter, you learned how to configure and troubleshoot BGP. As you might expect from the protocol largely responsible for routing traffic between Autonomous Systems on the Internet, BGP is both quite powerful and flexible. In this chapter, you will learn how to make BGP more scalable, and how to take advantage of that flexibility.

Because IBGP peers must be in a full mesh, in Autonomous Systems with many IBGP peers, scalability can be a problem. You will learn how to increase the scalability of BGP inside your Autonomous System. You will also learn the finer points of how BGP interacts with Interior Gateway Protocols.

You will also see some of the ways you can control routing policy with BGP. Because of its flexibility, and because BGP is designed to route packets between Autonomous Systems, BGP has mechanisms for policy routing, in addition to those you learned about in previous chapters.

Finally, you will learn how to use BGP to multihome your Autonomous System.

BGP SCALABILITY

In Autonomous Systems with many IBGP peers, BGP can have problems with scaling. The primary reason is the **BGP split horizon rule**. This rule prevents routers from propagating routes they learn through IBGP, in order to prevent routing loops inside an AS.

Figure 10-1 shows an example of a network where the BGP split horizon rule causes a problem. In this case, BGP peer sessions in Figure 10-1 follow the physical topology, so unconnected routers do not peer. RouterA in AS 65535 learns the route to 172.28.0.0/16 from its EBGP peer, RouterZ in AS 65500. Since it learned this route from EBGP, RouterA propagates the route to 172.28.0.0/16 to RouterB.

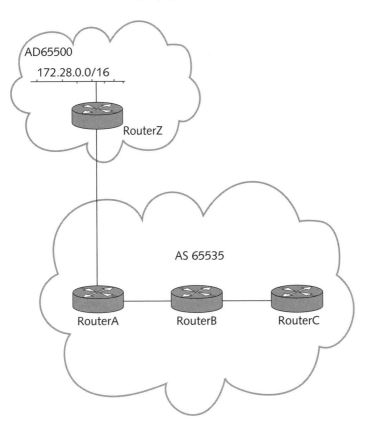

Figure 10-1   IBGP Autonomous System without a full mesh

Unfortunately, RouterB learns the route to 172.28.0.0/16 through IBGP and cannot propagate that route to RouterC. As a result, RouterC is unable to reach destinations on the 172.28.0.0/16 network.

In order for RouterC to learn routes through IBGP from RouterA, RouterC must be an IBGP peer of RouterA. Figure 10-2 shows RouterC as an IBGP peer of RouterA.

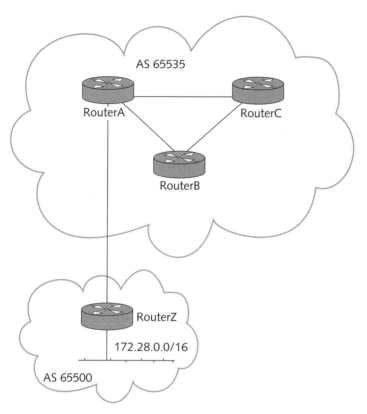

Figure 10-2   IBGP Autonomous System with a full mesh

10

As a result, in order for IBGP peers to exchange routing information, all IBGP peers in an AS must be in a full mesh. This does not necessarily mean that each router must have a physical connection, or a PVC, to all of the other routers. However, each router must establish a BGP session with each of the other routers.

As the number of IBGP peers increases, so does the number of BGP sessions each router is required to have (and the number of **neighbor** statements configured on each router). The number of IBGP peers in a mesh is determined by the formula $n(n - 1)/2$, where n is the number of peers in the mesh. For instance, an IBGP mesh with 25 peers requires 300 BGP sessions between the peers to create a full mesh. The number of connections required for an IBGP mesh increases exponentially as the number of peers increases. An IBGP mesh with 100 peers requires 4950 connections, while a mesh with 500 peers requires 124,750 connections.

Additionally, large numbers of IBGP peers may use a significant amount of bandwidth exchanging routing information. In WAN environments, this can increase the cost of using WAN links.

Finally, the large number of **neighbor** statements required on a router can lead to problems. If you configure several hundred neighbors on a BGP router, you may easily miss one or more neighbors. This may be difficult to find simply because of the sheer number of neighbors. Depending on the model of router and the number of peers, you may also find it difficult to successfully save a router's configuration because of its sheer size.

While the BGP split horizon rule requires IBGP peers to be in a logical full mesh, it does not require each IBGP peer to have a direct physical connection with every other IBGP peer. However, each IBGP peer must be able to maintain a TCP connection with each of its IBGP peers in order to establish BGP sessions with them.

Two techniques to avoid the problem of the IBGP mesh are route reflectors and **confederations**. A **route reflector** acts like a route server for multiple **route reflector clients,** allowing you to concentrate BGP sessions so that one or a handful of routers maintains BGP sessions while passing routes on to the client routers. To use confederations, you divide your Autonomous System (AS) into multiple sub-Autonomous Systems and run EBGP between them. However, your AS still appears as one unified AS to external Autonomous Systems.

Route Reflectors

Because route reflectors simply propagate routes learned to client routers, using route reflectors provides several advantages in an Autonomous System with many IBGP peers. These include:

- Fewer BGP sessions since route reflector clients may only peer with their route reflectors
- Fewer BGP **neighbor** statements in router configurations
- Minimal configuration on route reflectors and route reflector clients
- Simple migration path to using route reflectors

However, route reflectors do have some potential drawbacks. These include:

- Greater CPU usage on route reflectors
- Routing loops may result in poorly designed route reflector topologies

Because of these limitations, you should only use route reflectors when you have many IBGP peers. For instance, route reflectors often provide significant benefit for Internet Service Providers since they typically have many IBGP peers in their Autonomous Systems.

Route Reflector Operation

A route reflector works like a route server for one or more clients. A route reflector and its clients are known as a **cluster**.

A route reflector may also have one or more ordinary IBGP peers, which are known as **nonclients**. Because of the BGP split horizon rule, route reflectors must be in a full mesh with their nonclient peers. Nonclients do not need to be peers with route reflector clients. In fact, you should not configure route reflector clients as IBGP peers with any routers besides the route reflector in their cluster. Route reflector clients may have external EBGP peers, however.

A route reflector uses the **originator ID**, an optional, non-transitive attribute, to avoid routing loops. The originator ID contains the router ID of the router inside the AS that initially learned the route. If a router receives an update from a peer containing its own router ID as the originator ID for a particular route, it ignores that route.

You may use multiple route reflectors within a particular cluster to provide redundancy in case one of the route reflectors fails. To allow a client to receive updates from multiple route reflectors, you must configure each route reflector with a cluster ID. The **cluster ID** identifies a route reflector as belonging to a particular cluster. A route reflector uses the cluster ID to recognize updates received from the other route reflectors in the cluster.

10

Additionally, route reflectors include the **cluster list** attribute in their update messages to nonclient IBGP peers. The cluster list is an optional, non-transitive attribute that contains a list of all the clusters the route passes through. If a route has an empty cluster list, a route reflector creates one. Route reflectors use the cluster list in the same way that they use the AS_PATH attribute. If a route reflector examines the cluster list for a route and discovers that it contains its own cluster ID, the route reflector assumes that the route is a loop and ignores the advertised route.

Route Reflector Updates

When a route reflector receives an update, it decides what to do with the update based on what sort of peer sent it. Route reflectors may receive updates from these types of peers:

- **EBGP peers.** A route reflector propagates any updates received from EBGP peers to all client and nonclient peers (excluding the EBGP peer that originally sent the update).

- **Client peers.** Updates received from client peers are forwarded to all nonclient peers, and to all client peers except the client peer that originally sent the update message.

- **Nonclient peers.** These update messages are forwarded to all clients, but not to any peers outside the cluster.

Route reflectors and their clients send updates to any EBGP peers. As you would expect, the split horizon rule prevents route reflectors or their clients from sending any updates back to the routers that first sent them.

Route Reflector Topologies

To avoid routing loops, you should generally follow the physical topology of your Autonomous System, and ensure that route reflector clients are physically connected to the route reflectors for their clusters. If a client is not physically connected to its route reflector, a routing loop might result.

Avoiding Routing Loops   Figure 10-3 shows an example of a route reflector topology that does not follow the physical topology of the network. This topology may produce routing loops. The problem stems from the fact that while Router2 is attached to RouteReflectorA, it is actually a client of RouteReflectorB. At the same time, Router3 is attached to RouteReflectorB while it is a client of RouteReflectorA. Additionally, Router5 is a client of both route reflectors.

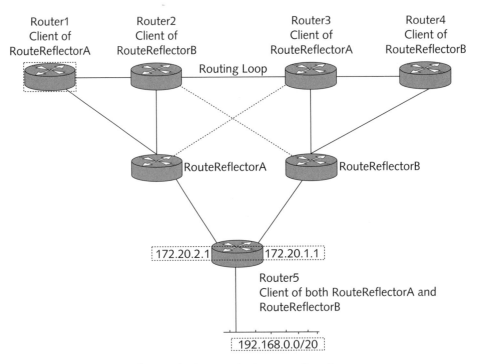

Figure 10-3   Route reflector design producing a routing loop

In order to reach the 192.168.0.0/20 network, Router2 learns that 172.20.1.1 is the next hop from RouteReflectorB. Since Router2 learns routes from RouteReflectorB, the best path from Router2 to 172.20.1.1 may be through Router3. At the same time, Router3 learns that 172.20.2.1 is the next hop for the 192.168.0.0/20 network from RouteReflectorA. If the best path from Router3 to 172.20.2.1 is through Router2, a routing loop results. Any packet from Router2 destined for the 192.168.0.0/20 network is sent to Router3, while any packet from Router3 destined for that network is sent to Router2.

At the same time, Router1 and Router4 will probably not run into routing loops. Router1 is a route reflector client of RouteReflectorA and is directly connected to it. As a result, it learns that the next hop for the 192.168.0.0/20 network is through 172.20.2.1. Its best path to 172.20.2.1 is through RouteReflectorA, avoiding a routing loop. The same principle applies for the path between Router4 and the 192.168.0.0/20 network.

You can avoid this problem by more closely following the topology of the Autonomous System. Figure 10-4 shows how you might do this. In Figure 10-4, each client router is now directly attached to its route reflector and Router5 is still a client of both route reflectors. Router2 now learns that the next hop to 192.168.0.0/20 is through 172.20.2.1. Packets are forwarded for that network to RouteReflectorA. At the same time, Router3 uses 172.20.1.1 as its next hop for 192.168.0.0/20, and forwards packets to RouteReflectorB. This avoids the routing loop found in Figure 10-3.

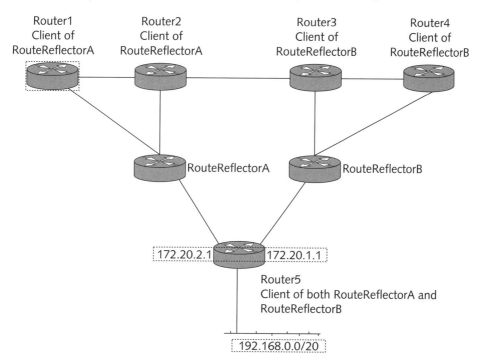

Figure 10-4   Route reflector design without a routing loop

Route Reflector Design   Besides following the physical topology, keep the following principles in mind when designing route reflector clusters:

- Route reflectors must be fully meshed with other IBGP peers.
- Multiple route reflectors within a cluster must also be fully meshed.
- Multiple route reflectors within a cluster must have the same list of clients.

- Use multiple route reflectors in a cluster for redundancy.
- Use an IGP for local routes.
- Use standalone IBGP peers, where necessary.
- Add EBGP peers, as necessary, to both route reflectors and route reflector clients.

Standalone IBGP peers may be used, where necessary, because of the network topology or design goals. However, this requires more connections. Because route reflector clients propagate updates from EBGP peers to their route reflectors, both route reflectors and clients may have EBGP peers.

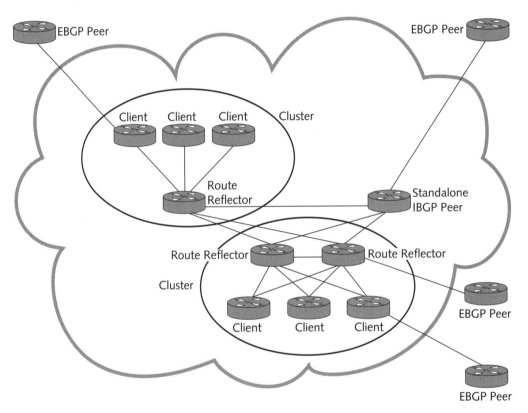

Figure 10-5   Example of a route reflector design

Figure 10-5 shows a more complicated example of an Autonomous System using route reflectors. Only the logical links (BGP sessions) between routers are shown. Two different clusters are configured. One uses redundant route reflectors, while the other uses a single route reflector. Figure 10-5 shows a total of 15 connections between routers in AS 65000. With a total of 10 routers, a full mesh between IBGP peers without route reflectors requires 45 connections, a difference of 30.

While adding multiple route reflectors to a cluster increases redundancy, the added complexity can cause problems in some topologies.

Migrating to Route Reflectors

In order to migrate from a fully meshed IBGP topology to a topology using route reflectors, you should:

1. Decide which routers should be route reflectors and which routers should be route reflector clients, following the physical topology of the AS.

2. Configure one route reflector at a time.

3. After configuring the route reflectors, delete redundant IBGP sessions between peers.

Configuring Route Reflectors

Route reflector configuration is done primarily on the route reflector itself and not on the clients. As a result, route reflector clients do not need any additional configuration (beyond the establishment of an IBGP session with the route reflector).

To configure a route reflector, you must first configure IBGP sessions with each of its clients. Then you must configure each neighbor as a client with the **neighbor route-reflector-client** command. The syntax of the command is:

```
Router(config-router)#neighbor { ip-address | peer-group-
name } route-reflector-client
```

While peer groups and route reflectors may be used together, they are not entirely compatible.

In order to use multiple route reflectors in a cluster, you must specify the cluster ID with the **bgp cluster-id** command as follows:

```
Router(config-router)#bgp cluster-id cluster-id
```

For example, suppose you want to configure RouterZ in AS 65500 as a route reflector and 10.155.41.1 and 10.155.126.1 as its clients. Additionally, you want to configure#10.66.27.1 as another route reflector in this cluster. Configure this router as an IBGP peer, and then configure RouterZ with cluster ID 145. Configuration on RouterZ would look like this:

```
RouterZ(config)#router bgp 65500
RouterZ(config-router)#neighbor 10.155.41.1 remote-as 65500
RouterZ(config-router)#neighbor 10.155.41.1
route-reflector-client
```

```
RouterZ(config-router)#neighbor 10.145.126.1
remote-as 65500
RouterZ(config-router)#neighbor 10.145.126.1
route-reflector-client
RouterZ(config-router)#neighbor 10.66.27.1 remote-as 65500
RouterZ(config-router)#bgp cluster-id 145
```

To properly configure the other neighbors, configure route reflector clients 10.155.41.1 and 10.155.26.1 to be IBGP peers of RouterZ. The configuration on the other route reflector in the cluster, 10.66.27.1, is very similar to the configuration above since it has the same list of clients. However, you must configure RouterZ as an IBGP peer.

Inside a route reflector cluster, you do not need to configure the route reflector and its clients in a full mesh. However, in some situations, you may find it desirable. In this case, the route reflector does not need to propagate routes to its clients. You can disable this with the **no bgp client-to-client reflection** command in router configuration mode.

You can use the **show ip bgp neighbors** command on a route reflector to identify its clients. Run on a route reflector client, this command does not show any information about the client's status as a route reflector, or about its route reflector. However, you can use the **show ip bgp** *network-address* command to show attributes for a route added by a route reflector (such as the cluster list or the originator ID).

BGP Confederations

Using BGP confederations is another way to make IBGP more scalable. Confederations break down an AS into several smaller sub-Autonomous Systems. Each of these uses a different AS number, generally taken from the range of private AS numbers, and each sub-AS communicates with the others through EBGP. As a result, the AS_PATH attribute is used to detect potential routing loops between the sub-Autonomous Systems. External Autonomous Systems, on the other hand, see a single AS instead of a collection of sub-Autonomous Systems. The group of sub-Autonomous Systems is called the confederation.

Inside the confederation, the sub-Autonomous Systems preserve the NEXT_HOP, MED, and LOCAL_PREF attributes when exchanging routes. Although they use EBGP to communicate with each other, in practice, routing between the sub-Autonomous Systems behaves like IBGP. Inside each sub-AS, IBGP peers must be in a full mesh.

Confederations offer these benefits:

- They reduce the number of IBGP connections between IBGP peers.
- They allow you to use either a single IGP or multiple IGPs in each sub-AS.

By segmenting an AS into multiple sub-Autonomous Systems, confederations can be used to help make IGPs more scalable in situations where IGP routing tables have become too large. For example, you can run different instances of EIGRP or OSPF in each sub-Autonomous System (or any other mixture of routing protocols).

However, confederations have several drawbacks as well. These include the following:

- Configuration of routers within each sub-AS is more difficult.

- Confederation design is more complicated and requires more planning.

- Policy routing within the confederation may be required to avoid poor path selection, thus further increasing the complexity of the configuration.

In general, Cisco recommends using route reflectors over confederations. However, confederations may be useful in some situations, such as when you need to segment your IGP inside an AS.

However, the two approaches are not mutually exclusive. Since a full IBGP mesh is required within each sub-AS, if you need to configure an AS as a confederation, you may find it useful to configure each individual sub-AS with route reflectors.

Routing Decision within Confederations

Without confederations, BGP prefers EBGP routes to IBGP routes, assuming all other attributes are the same. Inside confederations, BGP still prefers EBGP routes over IBGP routes, as well as any routes between sub-Autonomous Systems. However, BGP also prefers routes between sub-Autonomous Systems over IBGP routes.

So BGP chooses routes external to a sub-AS, wherever possible, with routes external to the confederation preferred over all others. You can alter this, however, by adjusting other path attributes (such as the LOCAL_PREF or weight attributes).

10

Confederation Design

In general, approach confederation design as you would approach any other hierarchical design. While the full, three-layered hierarchical design model may not be useful, you may use a two-layered approach with a backbone sub-AS (similar to an OSPF area design). However, you are not limited to any particular topology. Figure 10-6 shows the design.

Hierarchical designs typically offer advantages over randomly configured sub-Autonomous Systems. Since each sub-AS must use EBGP to exchange routing information, random or poor design of the sub-Autonomous Systems may result in poor route selection. Figure 10-6 shows an example of a hierarchical, two-layer confederation design.

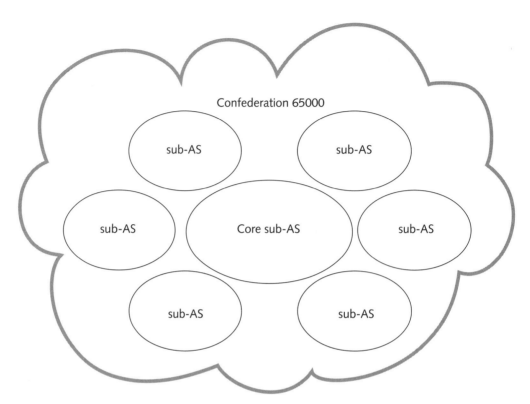

Figure 10-6   Example of a confederation design

Configuring Confederations

After deciding how to divide your Autonomous System into sub-Autonomous Systems, you may begin configuring the confederation. In order for EBGP peers to treat the confederation as one AS, each router in the confederation must be configured with a **confederation identifier**. EBGP peers see the confederation identifier as the AS number of the confederation. You can configure the confederation identifier in router configuration mode as follows:

```
Router(config-router)#bgp confederation-identifier
autonomous-system-number
```

Next, use the **bgp confederation peers** command in router configuration mode to tell the router which Autonomous Systems are also members of the confederation:

Router(config-router)#**bgp confederation peers** *AS-number* [*AS-number* …]

You may configure multiple Autonomous Systems as members of the confederation with this command. The AS numbers configured with this command should be the private AS numbers assigned to the individual sub-Autonomous Systems in the confederation.

Finally, configure the BGP peers in the other sub-Autonomous Systems with the **neighbor remote-as** command, just as you would any other BGP peers.

Route Dampening

Route dampening (sometimes called route damping) is a mechanism used in BGP to increase the stability of BGP routes, and decrease the bandwidth and CPU time used by frequent update messages. Route dampening is particularly important on the Internet. A flapping route can cause BGP routers to generate numerous update messages, as each router must repeatedly advertise and then withdraw the route. With over 100,000 routes in the BGP Internet routing table, flapping links can cause CPU usage on routers to increase dramatically, and can saturate lower-bandwidth links.

How Route Dampening Works

Route dampening works by tracking the stability of a route over time. Routes are categorized as either **well-behaved**, meaning that the route has been stable over a long period of time, or **ill-behaved**, meaning that the route has been unstable.

In order to categorize a route as well behaved or ill behaved, a BGP router assigns it a **penalty** each time it flaps. It keeps track of a route's flapping with a **history entry** for that route. If the penalty on a particular route reaches a certain threshold (known as the **suppress limit**), the route is **suppressed**. This means that the **suppressed route** is no longer advertised for a period of time, even if the route goes back up again.

If a suppressed route remains stable, the penalty decreases over time. The decrease in the penalty follows the rules of **exponential decay**. After each interval (known as the **half-life**) passes, the penalty is reduced by half. The half-life is, strictly speaking, not a timer since (unless the value of the penalty is one) half the penalty remains.

While the penalty decreases by half during each half-life, you should keep in mind that the penalty will decrease continuously (not just at the end of a half-life). The half-life is a measure of how fast the penalty decreases.

If the route is back up again, and the penalty is less than the **reuse limit**, the router begins advertising the route again. Like the half-life and the suppress limit, you can configure the reuse limit to adjust route dampening, as necessary. Table 10-1 contains a list of the default values for the flapping penalty, suppress limit, and reuse limit.

Since the penalty decreases over time, the more frequently a route flaps, the faster it is suppressed. Frequent and rapid flapping do not allow any time for the penalty to decrease. By contrast, occasional flapping allows the penalty time for that route to decrease. If the flapping is infrequent enough, the route may not be suppressed.

The penalty may also increase when the route is suppressed if the route continues to flap. If the penalty increases for a suppressed route, the route remains suppressed.

10

Table 10-1   Default values

Property	Default Value	Comments
Penalty	1000	Penalty incurred each time a route flaps
Suppress limit	2000	If the penalty for a route is above this limit, then the route is suppressed
Reuse limit	750	When the route is up, and the penalty falls below this level, the route is advertised again
Half-life	15 minutes	After each half-life, the penalty is reduced by half, regardless of the value of the penalty; if the penalty has a value of one, the value of the penalty is set to zero

 Route dampening only works for EBGP peers. With IBGP peers, the network administrator is assumed to have control over the links flapping, and can stop the link from flapping, or otherwise mitigate its effect.

Since EBGP can prevent the propagation of unstable routes to EBGP peers, route dampening can significantly reduce bandwidth and CPU usage on EBGP peers (and on any IBGP peers that might be learning the flapping routes). If your BGP routers receive the full Internet routing table, you may wish to activate route dampening.

Route Dampening Example

Suppose that RouterA in AS 65000 in Figure 10-7 is using route dampening. If the single link from RouterA to RouterC and the 10.172.0.0/16 CIDR block in AS 65200 flaps, causing it to be withdrawn by RouterA in AS 65000 and then updated again a minute later, the penalty on the route to 10.172.0.0/16 is the default penalty, 1000.

If the link remains stable for 15 minutes (or one half-life), then the penalty is reduced to 500. If the link then quickly flaps two more times, causing RouterA to withdraw and readvertise the route twice in a row, then RouterA applies the penalty to the route twice in a row for total penalty of 2500. As this is over the default suppress limit of 2000, the route to 10.172.0.0/16 is now suppressed. RouterA does not advertise this route to RouterZ, and hosts in AS 64999 cannot reach destinations in AS 65200, even though RouterB is reachable.

As a result, hosts and routers in AS 65000 cannot reach destinations in AS 65200 unless they have a route from another source (such as a static route or a route through an IGP). Additionally, if any packets from hosts in AS 65200 reach external Autonomous Systems, any packets sent in return are unable to reach the sending host since those packets do not have a route back. If the link from RouterA to RouterB is the only connection to the Internet for AS 65200, then AS 65200 is effectively cut off from the Internet until the penalty falls below the reuse limit.

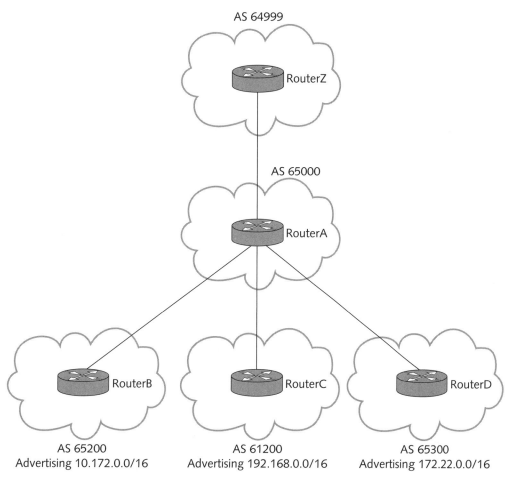

Figure 10-7 Route dampening example

Route Dampening and Your Autonomous System

In some situations, route dampening can effectively remove an AS from the Internet because of a flapping link. If your single link to the Internet flaps, BGP route dampening could, in essence, remove your AS from the Internet until you can prevent the link from flapping. At this time, the majority of organizations connect to the Internet through a single link.

It does not matter if your routers are running BGP. The penalty is applied to a route advertised by BGP, so the only requirement is that a BGP router must be advertising a route for dampening to affect it.

Figure 10-8 shows one way around this problem. Suppose that the routes advertised for Autonomous Systems 65100, 65200, and 65300 are part of a block that could be summarized at RouterA. In Figure 10-8, these routes could be advertised as a summary route to 10.168.0.0/13. If any of the single links to Autonomous Systems 65100, 65200, and 65300 flaps, the route to 10.168.0.0/13 is not withdrawn because the other routes in this summary route remain up. As a result, each individual AS is protected from the affects of route dampening if its single link flaps.

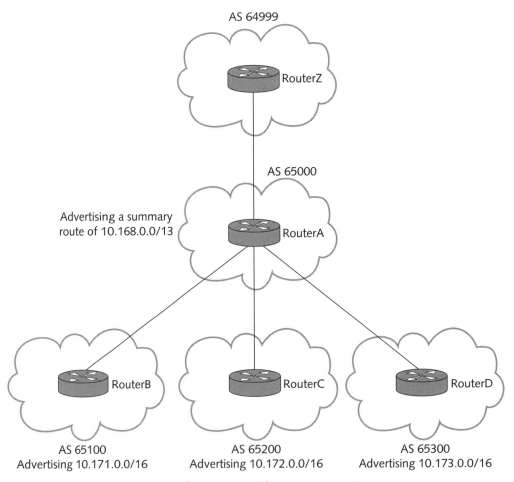

Figure 10-8   Preventing route dampening with aggregate route

The disadvantage of this is that it requires you to use IP addresses assigned from your service provider. In theory, your service provider could ask you to readdress or return some or all of the IP addresses assigned to you. However, if you have been assigned your own block of IP addresses outside of your service provider's address space, you may be vulnerable to route dampening if you have only a single link to your service provider.

Resetting a session with a BGP peer does not affect route flapping for any routes advertised by the peer. No BGP routes are suppressed as a result of a reset BGP session.

CONFIGURING BGP ROUTING POLICY

Because of its flexibility, BGP gives you a lot of control over routing policy. Using routing policy, you can control updates sent or received from your routers. One of the methods used to control routing policy in BGP is **prefix lists**.

Prefix Lists

You have already used one technique to filter routes: route filters applied with the **distribute-list** command, or **distribute lists**. Beginning with Cisco IOS 12.0, you can use prefix lists to filter BGP updates. Prefix lists offer several advantages over distribute lists:

- Incremental modifications. Because prefix lists include a sequence number (like a route map), you do not need to delete a prefix list and reconfigure it every time you need to make a change, as you do with distribute lists.

- Performance improvements.

- Greater flexibility.

In many ways, a prefix list works like an access list. Prefix lists contain permit and deny statements that indicate whether or not a particular route will be used. As you would expect, permitted routes are used and denied routes are not. Additionally, a prefix list has an implicit denial at the end. However, an empty prefix list allows all prefixes.

The sequence number makes a prefix list different from an access list. While routers still process prefix lists in order, they use the sequence number to determine the order. A router processes the prefix list statement with the lowest sequence number first, followed by the statement with the next lowest sequence number, and so on. At the first match, the router stops processing the list and performs the action in the matched line (permitting or denying the prefix).

Configuring Prefix Lists

Like an access list, you must first build a prefix list before applying it. To build a prefix list, use the **ip prefix-list** command as follows:

```
Router(config)#ip prefix-list [seq sequence-
number] [deny | permit] network/len [ge ge-value] [le le-
value]
```

Sequence Numbers in Prefix Lists   You do not need to specifically assign a sequence number to each statement in a prefix list. The router automatically adds them in increments of five. If the router automatically generates the sequence numbers, your first statement will have a sequence number of five, your second statement will have a sequence number of 10, and so on. However, if you need to add a statement to anywhere but the top of the list, you must specify the sequence number. Sequence numbers can range from one to 4294967294. However, if you place sequence numbers too close together, you may not be able to add additional statements between them. For instance, if you added a permit statement with a sequence number of six and a deny statement with a sequence number of seven, you would not be able to insert a statement between them.

You may disable the automatic generation of sequence numbers in a prefix list with the **no ip prefix-list sequence-number** command. You can enable it again with the **ip prefix-list sequence-number** command.

Specifying Ranges of Prefixes   Each statement in a prefix list must include either the **permit** or **deny** keywords, followed by a network number or prefix, and a prefix length (such as 172.30.0.0/16). If a network number and prefix length are specified without any other keywords, a route must exactly match the prefix and length chosen. For instance, 172.30.0.0/16 matches only routes with that network number and prefix length. Routes to 172.30.0.0/24 or to 172.30.0.0/18 are not matched.

You can use the optional **ge** and **le** keywords to specify routes that are more specific than the route chosen with the *network/len* option. The **ge** keyword specifies the bottom of the range, or the least specific prefix to be matched. The **le** keyword specifies the top of the range, or the most specific range to be matched. The router chooses from any routes that can be matched by the *network/len* configured. For instance, if you configure 10.0.0.0/8 as the *network/len*, then the *ge-value* and/or *le-value* configured will be applied against more specific routes in this block. These include 10.1.0.0/16, 10.2.0.0/16, 10.1.1.0/24, and so on.

The rules for the values you can select with the **ge** and **le** keywords are as follows:

- The *ge-value* selected must be greater than the length of the prefix in the statement.

- The *le-value* selected must be greater than the length of the prefix, and greater than or equal to the *ge-value* selected (if any).

- Both values must be less than or equal to the maximum prefix possible (32 bits).

You may use both keywords together, or you may use either keyword alone. If you use the **ge** keyword alone, routes with prefixes whose lengths are between the *ge-value* and 32 will be matched. If you use the **le** keyword alone, routes with prefixes whose lengths are between the *le-value* and the *len* value configured will be matched. If you use both keywords, prefixes whose length is between the *le-value* and the *ge-value* will be matched.

For instance, suppose RouterZ has the following routes:

```
172.30.0.0/16
172.30.0.0/17
172.30.128.0/17
172.30.5.0/24
172.30.6.0/24
172.30.5.16/28
172.30.5.32/28
```

If you want to permit only the 172.30.0.0/16 route, and deny all of the more specific routes, you could configure a prefix list called "Allowed" with:

```
RouterZ(config)#ip prefix-list seq 5 Allowed
permit 172.30.0.0/16
```

Since this statement does not use the **le** or **ge** keywords, only this route matches. Without any additional statements in the prefix list, the implicit denial at the end of the prefix list denies all other routes.

If you want to permit routes in the 172.16.0.0/16 block with prefixes of 17 or less bits, deny other routes in the 172.30.0.0/16 block with prefixes of 18 or more bits, and permit all other routes with a prefix length between eight and 24, you can configure a prefix list as follows:

```
RouterZ(config)#ip prefix-list seq 5 Allowed permit
172.30.0.0/16 le 17
RouterZ(config)#ip prefix-list seq 10 Allowed deny
172.30.0.0/16 ge 18
RouterZ(config)#ip prefix-list seq 15 Allowed permit
0.0.0.0/8 le 24
```

If you want to permit the route with the 16-bit prefix, deny routes with prefixes between 17 and 23 bits, permit routes with 24-bit prefixes, and deny routes with prefixes longer than 25 bits (all in the 172.16.0.0/16 block), while allowing other routes outside the 172.16.0.0/16 block with prefixes of 24 or less bits, you can configure a prefix list as follows:

```
RouterZ(config)#ip prefix-list seq 5 Allowed permit
172.30.0.0/16
RouterZ(config)#ip prefix-list seq 10 Allowed deny
172.30.0.0/16 ge 17 le 23
RouterZ(config)#ip prefix-list seq 15 Allowed permit
172.30.0.0/16 ge 24 le 24
RouterZ(config)#ip prefix-list seq 20 Allowed deny
172.30.0.0/16 ge 25
RouterZ(config)#ip prefix-list seq 25 Allowed permit
0.0.0.0/0 le 24
```

10

You can also use a prefix list to block the default route:

```
RouterZ(config)#ip prefix-list seq 5 Allowed deny
0.0.0.0/0
```

You can use a prefix list to block all routes with prefixes whose lengths are 25 or more bits:

```
RouterZ(config)#ip prefix-list seq 5 Allowed deny
0.0.0.0/0 ge 25
```

Or you can use a prefix list to completely deny a block of IP addresses. To deny every route in the 192.168.0.0/16 block, you can use:

```
RouterZ(config)#ip prefix-list seq 5 Allowed deny
192.168.0.0/16 le 32
```

This denies any route with a prefix between 32 bits and 16 bits, effectively denying the entire block.

Deleting Prefix Lists and Prefix List Entries

To delete a single entry in a prefix list, you use the no form of the **ip prefix-list** command. For example, suppose you need to delete the prefix list named "Allowed" that you created earlier. To do this, simply enter the following in configuration mode:

```
Router(config)#no ip prefix-list Allowed
```

To delete a single entry in a prefix list, use the no form of that particular statement. For example, to delete an entry in a prefix list, such as **ip prefix-list seq 5 Allowed deny 192.168.0.0/16 le 32**, you use the following in configuration mode:

```
Router(config)#no ip prefix-list seq 5 Allowed deny
192.168.0.0/16 le 32
```

You may also leave out the sequence number. A router gives an error if you try to configure a duplicate prefix list entry so there will be no ambiguity about which statement to delete. As you would expect, the entry must exist in the prefix list specified in order to delete it.

Applying a Prefix List

After building a prefix list, you must apply it. You may apply a prefix list with either the **neighbor prefix-list** command.

The **neighbor prefix-list** command is used in router configuration mode. Its syntax is as follows:

```
Router(config-router)#neighbor [ip-address | peer-group-
name] prefix-list prefix-list-name [in | out]
```

You may specify either a neighbor or peer group for the prefix list. The **in** and **out** keywords indicate whether the prefix list will be applied to incoming or outgoing updates from that peer or peer group.

Verifying Prefix Lists

You can use the **show ip prefix-list** command to look at prefix lists you configured. Typical output from this command follows:

```
Router#show ip prefix-list
ip prefix-list Allowed: 2 entries
    seq 5 deny 172.16.0.0/16 ge 25
    seq 10 permit 0.0.0.0/8 le 24
```

You can find out how many times the prefix list has been hit with the **detail** or **summary** keywords. The **detail** keyword shows you both the hitcount and the prefix list itself, while the **summary** keyword shows you only the hitcount.

```
Router#show ip prefix-list detail
Prefix-list with the last deletion/insertion: Allowed
ip prefix-list Allowed:
    count: 2, range entries: 2, sequences: 5 - 10,
refcount: 2
    seq 5 deny 172.16.0.0/16 ge 25 (hit count: 0,
refcount: 1)
    seq 10 permit 0.0.0.0/8 le 24 (hit count: 0,
refcount: 1)
```

In this case, the prefix list did not have any hits for either statement.

Other variations on the **show ip prefix-list** command you can use to view a prefix list or see if a particular route will match it include:

- **show ip prefix-list** *name network/len*. This shows you whether that particular route is permitted or denied by the named prefix list.

- **show ip prefix-list** *name network/len* **longer**. This shows you the entries in a prefix list that specify longer prefixes than the one given by *network/len*.

- **show ip prefix-list** *name network/len* **first-match**. This shows you the first entry in a prefix list matching *network/len* (if any).

- **show ip prefix-list seq** *name seq-number*. This shows you a particular sequence number in a prefix list.

For example, you can see which statement in a prefix list (if any) first matches a particular route:

```
Router#show ip prefix-list Allowed 172.16.0.0/23
first-match
```

```
Router#show ip prefix-list Allowed 172.16.0.0/25 first-
match
   seq 10 deny 172.16.0.0/16 ge 24 (hit count: 0,
refcount: 0)
```

In this case, the prefix list Allowed matches 172.16.0.0/25 (in a deny statement), but does not match 172.16.0.0/23. Since prefix lists have an implicit denial at the end like access lists, this could indicate a problem with the prefix list.

Finally, you can use the **clear ip prefix-list** *name* [*network/len*] command in enable mode to reset the hit count on a particular prefix list, or even a particular prefix in a prefix list.

Using Peer Groups to Simplify BGP Configuration

As described in the last chapter, a **peer group** is a group of BGP peers that have the same update policies. Peer groups offer the following advantages:

- Peer groups simplify the configuration of routing policy because you must configure it only once per group.

- Each peer group generates one update per peer group instead of one update per individual BGP peer. This update is then copied to the other routers, so they do not need to allocate CPU time to produce the update.

Figure 10-9 shows an example of an Autonomous System where you might configure peer groups. In AS 65501, you can configure routing policy for a peer group named AS65501 on RouterB. After adding RouterC and RouterD to that peer group, routing policy is the same throughout AS 65501.

Additionally, you can configure external peers as a member of a peer group. For example, it may be useful for a service provider to include its customers' routers in a peer group, even though they reside in other Autonomous Systems.

Configuring Peer Groups

In order to configure a peer group, you first configure a peer group on a router with the **neighbor peer-group** command in router configuration mode. The syntax for this command is:

```
Router(config-router)#neighbor peer-group-name peer-group
```

Next, configure routing policy for the peer group. Because all routing policy configuration for the peer group will be done on this router, it is known as the **peer group leader**.

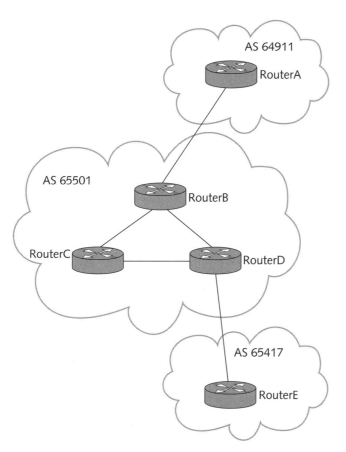

Figure 10-9   Peer groups

Routing policy configuration consists of configuring and applying route filters, route maps, and prefix lists. Routing policy commands can be configured with variations on the **neighbor** command, such as the **neighbor prefix-list** command. This allows you to configure different routing policies for each peer or peer group. Other forms of the neighbor command you can use in router configuration mode to configure routing policy include:

- **neighbor** {*ip-address* | *peer-group-name*} **distribute-list** {*distribute-list-name* | *number*} **in** | **out**. This command allows you to add a route filter for updates sent to or received from a particular neighbor or peer group.

- **neighbor** {*ip-address* | *peer-group-name*}**route-map** *route-map-name* **in** | **out**. This command allows you to apply a route map sent to or received from a particular neighbor or peer group.

Next, add other members to the peer group. On the peer group leader, add each router to the peer group. You can do this with the following command:

```
Router(config)#neighbor ip-address peer-group peer-
group-name
```

If the neighbor is an external BGP peer, first specify the remote AS with the **neighbor** *ip-address* **remote-as** command. If the neighbor is an IBGP peer, however, you can configure the remote AS on all members of the peer group with the **neighbor** *peer-group-name* **remote-as** *as-number* command.

On other routers in the peer group, perform the following tasks in router configuration mode:

1. Establish the peer group with the **neighbor** *peer-group-name* **peer-group** command.

2. If members of the peer group will be EBGP peers, use the **neighbor** *ip-address* **remote-as** *as-number* command to configure each of the router's EBGP peers.

3. If the members of the group will be IBGP peers, use the **neighbor** *peer-group-name* **remote-as** *as-number* command to configure the AS number.

4. Configure each neighbor as a part of the peer group with the **neighbor** *ip-address* **peer-group** *peer-group-name* command.

However, you only need to configure routing policy on the peer group leader.

For instance, suppose you want to configure RouterA, RouterB, and RouterC in a peer group named "InternalPeers". Apply prefix list Outbound to outbound updates, prefix list Inbound to inbound updates, and route map External to the peer group. Assuming that each router is in AS 65000, and RouterB and RouterC have IP addresses of 172.16.10.2 and 172.16.10.3, respectively, your configuration on RouterA looks like this:

```
RouterA(config)#router bgp 65000
RouterA(config-router)#neighbor InternalPeers peer-group
RouterA(config-router)#neighbor InternalPeers remote-as
65000
RouterA(config-router)#neighbor InternalPeers prefix-
list Outbound out
 RouterA(config-router)#neighbor InternalPeers prefix-
list Inbound in
RouterA(config-router)#neighbor InternalPeers route-map
External out
RouterA(config-router)#neighbor 172.16.1.2 peer-group
InternalPeers
RouterA(config-router)#neighbor 172.16.1.3 peer-group
InternalPeers
```

On RouterB, assuming RouterA's address is 172.16.1.1, your configuration looks like this:

```
RouterB(config)#router bgp 65000
RouterB(config-router)#neighbor InternalPeers peer-group
RouterB(config-router)#neighbor InternalPeers remote-as
65000
RouterB(config-router)#neighbor 172.16.1.1 peer-group
InternalPeers
RouterB(config-router)#neighbor 172.16.1.3 peer-group
InternalPeers
```

Configuration on RouterC would be similar to RouterB.

The configuration is the same for a peer group among external peers, except the AS of each EBGP peer should be explicitly configured. For instance, suppose you want to configure RouterA in a peer group named "ExternalPeers" with RouterZ. Routing policy consists of an outbound prefix list named "ExternalAS", while routerZ is in AS 65077 and has an address of 172.20.1.1. On RouterA, use the following commands to configure the peer group:

```
RouterA(config)#router bgp 65000
Router1(config-router)#neighbor ExternalPeers peer-group
Router1(config-router)#neighbor ExternalPeers prefix-list
ExternalAS out
Router1(config-router)#neighbor 172.20.1.1 remote-as 65077
Router1(config-router)#neighbor 172.120.1.1 ExternalPeers
peer-group
```

Since a peer group sends out a single update, you cannot change outgoing routing policy on an individual member of a peer group without removing it from the peer group. However, you can override incoming routing policy.

Route reflector clients cannot be members of a peer group unless you use the **no bgp client-to-client reflection** command.

Verifying Peering Groups

In order to verify and troubleshoot peer groups, you can use the **show ip bgp peer-group** command. This command shows you to which peer group a router belongs, as well as the peer group leader.

On the peer group leader, you can also see information about the routing policy configured. Output from the **show ip bgp peer-group** command on a peer group leader follows:

```
Madrid#show ip bgp peer-group
BGP peer-group is Peers, peer-group leader 10.1.254.9,
internal, remote AS 1
 Index 1, Offset 0, Mask 0x2
  BGP version 4
  Minimum time between advertisement runs is 5 seconds
  Outgoing update prefix filter list is Outbound
  Route map for outgoing advertisements is SetMetric
```

However, the same command does not show information about routing policy on other routers in the peer group:

```
Toledo#show ip bgp peer-group
BGP peer-group is Peers, remote AS 1
  BGP version 4
  Default minimum time between advertisement runs is 5
seconds
 For address family: IPv4 Unicast
  BGP neighbor is Peers, peer-group internal, members:
        10.1.254.2
  Index 1, Offset 0, Mask 0x2
  Update messages formatted 2, replicated 0
```

You can also use the **show ip bgp neighbors** command to find information about peer groups.

Interacting with IGPs

Because BGP and an IGP in an Autonomous System have no way of automatically exchanging routes, you must specify some way for them to share routing information. This decision can dramatically affect the stability of both protocols.

Injecting Routes into BGP

You have three options for injecting routes from an IGP into BGP. The first is using the **network** command to select which routes BGP will advertise. Although this has the disadvantage of not being dynamic, it is quite stable.

The second option is redistributing routes from an IGP into BGP. However, instability in an IGP will also affect BGP. A flapping route could result in many update packets being sent to withdraw and readvertise the route, or it could result in route dampening. Another potential hazard is routing loops resulting from the redistribution of routes learned by the IGP from other Autonomous Systems through BGP. The resulting routing loops might prevent your AS from reaching the affected Autonomous Systems. In general, Cisco does not recommend the redistribution of IGP routes into BGP.

The third option for injecting routes into BGP is redistributing null routes, or static routes to interface Null 0. Using this technique, you can summarize several routes with longer prefixes. A router matches packets against the more specific routes in its routing table. Only if the router does not find a more specific match does it use the null route (and discard the packets).

For example, Figure 10-10 shows an Autonomous System where a router is redistributing null routes into BGP. You can summarize the routes to 172.16.0.0/24, 172.16.1.0/24, 172.16.2.0/24, and 172.16.3.0/24 with a null route to 172.16.0.0/22. If you redistribute static routes into BGP, then RouterB advertises this route to its peer, RouterA. When RouterA receives a packet intended for a host on the 172.16.1.0/24 network, it looks up the route to 172.16.0.0/22 in its routing table and forwards the packet to RouterB. RouterB sees that the route with the longest match was to 172.16.1.0/24. Then it uses that route to send the packet to the appropriate destination.

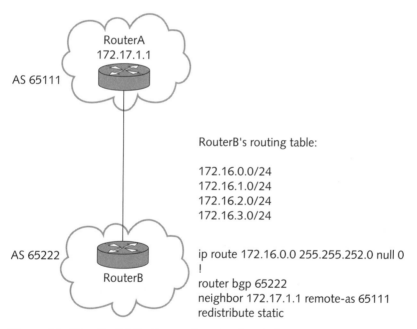

10

Figure 10-10   Redistributing null routes into BGP

However, RouterB continues to advertise this route even if all of the individual routes summarized by the null route are unavailable. If none of the routes with longer prefixes in Figure 10-10 is valid, RouterB cannot find routes with longer prefixes than the null route, and it discards all packets matched by it. This is particularly a problem if there are other paths to these networks through other routers. Some routers will continue to forward packets to RouterB, even though RouterB cannot reach these networks and other routers can.

If you summarized these routes with the **aggregate-address** command in BGP, then RouterB withdraws the aggregate route when the more specific routes summarized are no longer valid. As a result, you eliminate the risk of RouterB advertising a black hole route.

Injecting Routes into an IGP

When injecting routes from BGP into an IGP, determine how much routing information the IGP must learn. Since BGP routing tables can contain over 100,000 routes, this can have quite an effect on an IGP.

Situations where you do not need to redistribute BGP routes into an IGP include:

- The IGP can use default routes to reach routers running BGP. In some environments, this may result in poor path selection.

- The IGP can use static routes to reach routers running BGP. Since this requires manual configuration, it will likely result in an administrative headache if more than a handful of static routes is configured.

- All routers are running IBGP. In this case, you can disable synchronization. This is the strategy often chosen by Internet Service Providers. Since BGP does not need to wait for the IGP to advertise routes, it will also converge faster.

If you do choose to redistribute routes from BGP into an IGP, you should carefully filter unnecessary routes from BGP to minimize the number of routes injected into the IGP.

MULTIHOMING

Multihoming is the practice of connecting an Autonomous System to multiple Internet Service Providers. Multihoming offers two potential advantages:

- **Redundancy.** If the link to one Internet Service Provider fails, one or more of the additional links are likely to remain active.

- **Better path selection.** Packets sent to a particular destination may reach their destination faster if sent through one Internet Service Provider rather than another. Using multiple Internet Service Providers allows BGP to select from more paths, and many of these paths will be better than the paths available through a single Internet Service Provider.

If your Autonomous System is multihomed, each ISP should advertise paths to your AS. Suppose your organization owns the 172.16.0.0/20 block of addresses. If you have connections to two different Internet Service Providers, ISP A and ISP B, each ISP should advertise a route to 172.16.0.0/20. If only ISP A advertises this prefix, outgoing traffic might use either the link to ISP A or the link to ISP B. However, returning traffic only uses the link to ISP A.

As you might expect, many different scenarios are possible when you have a multihomed AS. The biggest factor distinguishing each scenario is generally the number of routes each ISP provides to a multihomed AS. Typically, an ISP provides either a default route, selected routes from other customers of that ISP, in addition to a default route, or all routes.

Multihoming with Default Routes

This is the simplest scenario. Because your AS only receives default routes from the connected ISPs, you do not need to run BGP within your AS.

The IGP decides which ISP link to use based on its metric. Routing decisions about incoming packets are made by BGP routers external to your Autonomous System. You cannot influence these routing decisions.

In Figure 10-11, AS 65499 uses OSPF as its IGP and does not use BGP. Both ISP A and ISP B advertise its address block, and both ISP links are redistributed into OSPF as default routes. If a host sends a packet destined for any address outside this AS, routing decisions are made based on the cost assigned by OSPF. RouterA, for instance, chooses to send packets through the link to ISP A.

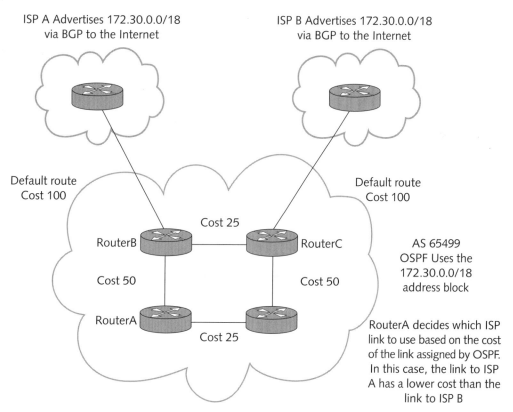

ISP A Advertises 172.30.0.0/18
via BGP to the Internet

ISP B Advertises 172.30.0.0/18
via BGP to the Internet

10

Default route
Cost 100

Default route
Cost 100

Cost 25

RouterB

RouterC

AS 65499
OSPF Uses the
172.30.0.0/18
address block

Cost 50

Cost 50

RouterA

Cost 25

RouterA decides which ISP
link to use based on the cost
of the link assigned by OSPF.
In this case, the link to ISP
A has a lower cost than the
link to ISP B

Figure 10-11   A multihomed AS receiving default routes only

> **Note** If you are using OSPF inside a multihomed AS, you should configure external routes as type 1 external routes. When calculating the cost of type 1 external routes, OSPF adds the cost of using the external link to the cost of each internal link. This allows OSPF to choose between multiple external routes or multiple default routes.

In addition to simple configuration, this scenario offers the advantage of using fewer additional resources on routers inside your AS because it does not require you to use BGP.

Multihoming with Customer Routes

In some cases, you may need to exchange limited routing information with each ISP. Suppose that you share large amounts of data with your customers, and many them are also customers of one of your ISPs. In order to select the best path to reach these customers, each ISP may need to send you the appropriate routes.

Figure 10-12 shows an example of this scenario. AS 65499 is connected to both ISP A and ISP B. ISP A has a link to CustomerA, while ISP B has a link to CustomerB. If RouterB and RouterC only advertises a default route to AS 65499, routers inside AS 65499 may choose poor paths. For instance, a router might choose to use ISP B to reach CustomerA. This requires sending packets for CustomerA through the Internet, even though CustomerA is directly connected to ISP A. However, if ISP A announces a route to CustomerA to AS 65499, then routers in that AS can choose the best path to reach CustomerA.

In general, BGP routing decisions are made based upon the AS path attribute. In the last example, a packet sent through the Internet to CustomerA might cross several Autonomous Systems. As a result, it would have a longer AS path than a packet sent through ISP A. However, you can force routers inside an AS to use a particular ISP for certain routes. You can set the local preference attribute higher for those routes on the link to the desired ISP.

For packets bound for other external destinations, the IGP again controls the link used based on the IGP metric. Additionally, you cannot influence routing decisions made by external routers about incoming packets.

This scenario does require the use of BGP. As a result, it requires your routers to have more memory and faster processors than the previous scenario. However, this scenario still requires significantly fewer resources than the next scenario.

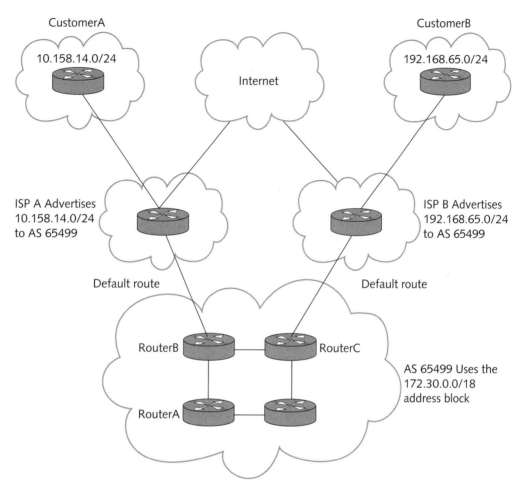

Figure 10-12   A multihomed AS receiving customer and default routes

Multihoming with Full Routes

In this scenario, routers inside your Autonomous System may choose the best path because they have complete routing information. However, they also must store significantly more routes than in either of the previous two scenarios. Full routes from an ISP may be equivalent to the entire BGP routing table, which at the time of this writing consists of over 100,000 routes.

Figure 10-13 shows an example of a multihomed AS (AS 65000). By default, it chooses paths based on the AS path. For example, when selecting paths to destination networks inside AS 65400 (which is also multihomed), routers in AS 65000 choose paths leading through AS 65200. These routes have a shorter AS path than routes leading through AS 65100. When choosing between routes with the same AS path length, BGP looks at other path attributes, as described in Chapter 8. To change the path packets take when leaving your AS, you may change the weight and the local preference.

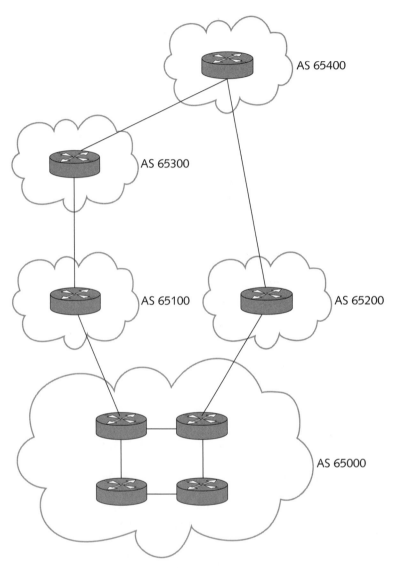

Figure 10-13   Path selection in a multihomed AS with full routes

Changing the Weight for a Neighbor

You can use the **neighbor weight** command in router configuration mode to change the weight assigned to routes from a particular neighbor. If synchronization is disabled, the weight is the first attribute a Cisco router uses when deciding among multiple routes for a particular destination. The weight attribute is only used on the router on which it is configured. The syntax of the command is as follows:

```
Router(config-router)#neighbor [ip address | peer-group-
name] weight weight
```

The weight assigned may be from 0 to 65,535. By default, routes originating on the router have a weight of 32,768, while non-local routes have a weight of zero.

To assign routes from a neighbor with an IP address of 10.1.10.1 a weight of 32,768, enter the following in router configuration mode:

```
Router(config-router)#neighbor 10.1.10.1 weight 32768
```

Changing the Local Preference

To change the default local preference, you can use the **bgp default local-preference** command in router configuration mode. When choosing between multiple routes to the same destination, Cisco routers first look for the route with the higher weight, and then for the route with the higher local preference. Unlike the weight, the local preference is propagated to other routers in the Autonomous System. By default, Cisco routers set the local preference to 100, although the actual value may be anywhere from 0 to 4,294,967,295.

The syntax of the **bgp default local-preference** command is as follows:

```
Router(config)#bgp default local-preference value
```

> After changing parameters that affect a neighbor (such as the path attributes for routes sent to that neighbor), you must run the **clear ip bgp** command for the updates to take effect.

You can also change the local preference for specific routes using a route map. For example, suppose you want to change the local preference to 1000 for the route 192.168.0.0/18. In order to do this, you can build a prefix list to match this route, and then use the **set local-preference** command inside the route map to set the local preference. Suppose you are a network administrator in AS 65535. You decide to name the prefix list local-routes and the route map local-pref. You configure the prefix list and route map as follows:

```
Router(config)#ip prefix-list local-routes permit
192.168.0.0/18
Router(config)#router bgp 65535
Router(config)#route-map local-pref permit 10
Router(config-route-map)#match ip address prefix-list
local-routes
Router(config-route-map)#set local-preference 1000
```

You can manipulate path attributes in BGP in many different ways, often through the use of route maps. A full list of these commands is beyond the scope of this book.

Configuring Multihomed Autonomous Systems

Configuring a basic multihomed Autonomous System simply requires you to configure BGP for routers within your Autonomous System, as you did in previous chapters. Figure 10-14 shows an example of a multihomed autonomous system. RouterA in AS 65100 advertises 192.168.0.0/16 to EBGP peers in AS 65200 and AS 65300.

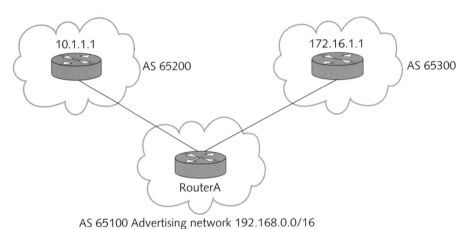

AS 65100 Advertising network 192.168.0.0/16

Figure 10-14   Multihoming example

To configure RouterA in a multihomed AS, first advertise 192.168.0.0/16 with a **network** statement and then configure its neighbors as EBGP peers. To do so, enter the following:

```
RouterA(config)#router bgp 65100
RouterA(config-router)#network 192.168.0.0 mask
255.255.0.0
RouterA(config-router)#neighbor 10.1.1.1 remote-as 65200
RouterA(config-router)#neighbor 172.16.1.1 remote-as 65300
```

Influencing the path chosen by packets leaving this Autonomous System requires additional configuration. The most direct method involves changing the weight attribute for each neighbor. Suppose that you prefer RouterA to forward packets through the 172.16.1.1 router in AS 65300, whenever possible. In this scenario, adjusting the weight of each neighbor is the simplest method. To adjust the weight of the 172.16.1.1 peer to 1000 and the weight of the 10.1.1.1 peer to 500, enter the following in router configuration mode:

```
RouterA(config-router)#neighbor 172.16.1.1 weight 1000
RouterA(config-router)#neighbor 10.1.1.1 weight 500
```

Since Cisco routers look at the weight attribute before other attributes when making routing decisions, RouterA will choose routes through the 172.16.1.1 router unless the 10.1.1.1 router is the only peer to advertise a route.

CHAPTER SUMMARY

❐ Because IBGP requires routers inside an Autonomous System to be in a full mesh, BGP can run into scalability problems in large IBGP environments. One method to overcome this is to use route reflector clusters. A route reflector acts as a route server for its route reflector clients. Another method is to use BGP confederations. In a confederation, you divide your Autonomous System into multiple sub-Autonomous Systems. Route reflectors tend to be easier to configure and implement than confederations.

❐ Flapping links cause another scalability problem. These can generate excessive traffic from update messages as they go up and down. Route dampening applies a penalty to flapping links, and suppresses them after they go above a certain threshold. The penalty decreases over time, and when the penalty is below the reuse limit, the route is no longer suppressed.

❐ You can use prefix lists to apply routing policy with BGP. While similar to an access list, a prefix list is more flexible and allows you to selectively delete entries. With a prefix list, you can also filter based on the length of a prefix. You can use peer groups to simplify the configuration of routing policy on multiple routers. After you configure a peer group, you must configure routing policy only on the peer group leader.

❐ The most stable way to advertise routes with BGP is by using the **network** statement. Redistribution requires less manual configuration, but can be less stable. You can also advertise a null route to make a manual summary route, although it is usually better to use an aggregate route instead. You may use static routes, default routes, or redistribution for an IGP to learn routes from BGP. In general, you should try to minimize the number of routes an IGP learns from BGP.

❐ Multihoming increases the redundancy of an Internet link and can improve path selection. A multihomed AS may receive only a default route, a default route and customer routes, or full routes from its Internet Service Providers. You may use the local preference and weight attributes to influence the selection of paths for packets leaving your autonomous system.

KEY TERMS

BGP split horizon rule — A router that learns routes from an IBGP peer cannot propagate those routes to other IBGP peers to avoid routing loops within an autonomous system.

cluster — One or more route reflectors and their route reflector clients.

cluster ID — A value assigned to a route reflector to identify its cluster, allowing a cluster to contain multiple route reflectors.

cluster list — An optional, non-transitive attribute that contains a list of clusters a particular route passes through; the cluster list is used to avoid routing loops.

confederation — An Autonomous System divided into a group of two or more sub-Autonomous Systems to make IBGP more scalable.

confederation identifier — A value assigned to each member of a confederation, which EBGP peers will see as the Autonomous System number of the confederation.

distribute list — An access list applied as a route filter.

exponential decay — Decrease of a value (such as the penalty given to a route by BGP route dampening) in a manner so that the value decreases by half every time an interval known as the half-life passes.

half-life — A value indicating the amount of time before the penalty on a route will be cut in half.

history entry — An entry used to store information about when and how often a route has flapped.

Ill-behaved route — A route that, according to BGP's route dampening algorithm, has proved to be unstable.

nonclient — An IBGP peer of a route reflector that is not one of its clients; IBGP nonclients must be in a full mesh.

null route — A route to a null interface, which discards all the packets sent to it.

originator ID — An optional, non-transitive BGP attribute used by route reflectors to indicate the originator of a particular route within the autonomous system.

peer group — A group of BGP peers that use the same policies; the members of a peer group receive configuration options and policies of the peer group, which they can override to a limited extent, and the members generate routing updates as a group.

peer group leader — The router in a peer group on which routing policy for the peer group is configured.

penalty — A value assigned to a route by BGP's route dampening algorithm each time it flaps.

prefix list — A list of prefixes used to filter BGP updates received or sent.

reuse limit — A value used to determine whether or not a suppressed route will be advertised when it comes up again; if the penalty is less than the reuse limit and the route is up, the route will be advertised again.

route damping — *See* route dampening.

route dampening — A mechanism that promotes stability in BGP by suppressing unstable routes after excessive flapping.

route reflector — A router that runs an IBGP session and passes routes onto its clients so that the clients do not need to be included in a full mesh with the other IBGP peers.

route reflector client — A router that receives routes from a route reflector.

suppress — To prevent a route from being advertised for a period of time by BGP route dampening because of excessive flapping, even if the route goes back up.

suppress limit — The maximum value of the penalty set on a route by BGP's route dampening algorithm before the route is suppressed.

suppressed route — A route suppressed for excessive flapping by BGP route dampening.

Well-behaved route — A route that, according to BGP's route dampening algorithm, has proved to be stable over an extended period of time.

REVIEW QUESTIONS

1. Which of the following are reasons why BGP has scalability problems in some situations? (Choose all that apply.)

   a. IBGP peers must be in a full mesh.

   b. Route aggregation increases the amount of memory and processor time used by BGP.

   c. Large numbers of IBGP peers increase the number of BGP sessions each router must establish.

   d. IBGP peers must also learn IGP routes from any existing EBGP peers.

2. Why must IBGP peers in an Autonomous System be in a full mesh?

   a. RFC 1778 requires this.

   b. This compensates for the fact that IBGP routers do not need to be directly connected to each other.

   c. This is a consequence of the BGP split horizon rule.

   d. This is a result of the redundancy requirements of IBGP.

3. Which of the following are methods you can use to avoid scalability problems with many IBGP peers? (Choose all that apply.)

   a. route dampening

   b. BGP confederations

   c. BGP communities

   d. route reflectors

4. Which of the following are advantages of route reflectors? (Choose all that apply.)

   a. Fewer BGP sessions are required within an Autonomous System.

   b. Fewer neighbor statements are required on BGP peers within an autonomous system.

   c. BGP connections are not required between route reflectors and route reflector clients.

   d. Only minimal configuration is required for route reflectors and route reflector clients.

10

5. A route reflector receives an update from an EBGP peer. Where will it send updates?

  a. only to its client peers

  b. to its client peers and its non-client peers

  c. to its client peers, its nonclient peers, and all of its EBGP peers

  d. to its client peers, its nonclient peers, and all of its EBGP peers except the peer that originally sent the update

6. Why should you follow the physical topology of the Autonomous System when you configure route reflector clusters?

  a. to minimize the number of BGP sessions required between routers in the autonomous system

  b. to prevent potential routing loops

  c. to increase redundancy

  d. to minimize the number of EBGP peers

7. Configuring BGP confederations in an Autonomous System makes BGP more scalable by:

  a. configuring multiple route reflectors

  b. dividing the Autonomous System into multiple sub-Autonomous Systems

  c. increasing the number of BGP sessions between routers

  d. dampening routes that flap excessively

8. Which of the following are disadvantages of using BGP confederations when compared to route reflectors? (Choose all that apply.)

  a. Configuration of confederations is more complex.

  b. Poor path selection may result.

  c. Routing loops may result from poorly designed confederations.

  d. Confederation design is more complex.

9. How does route dampening add to BGP stability?

  a. by decreasing the number of BGP sessions necessary between neighbors

  b. by removing the need to send updates for a particular route

  c. by not allowing flapping routes to be advertised, and preventing them from being repeatedly advertised and withdrawn

  d. by aggregating flapping routes and advertising the aggregate route instead

10. A flapping route is suppressed. If the route flaps again before the penalty is lifted, how does this affect the route?

  a. Since the route is already suppressed, this has no effect on the route.

  b. The penalty is decreased, shortening the amount of time that the route is suppressed.

    c. The penalty is increased, increasing the amount of time that the route is suppressed.

    d. The reuse limit is increased, also increasing the amount of time that the route is suppressed.

11. Prefix lists allow you to add and remove statements at any point, unlike access lists. True or false?

12. If you leave out the sequence number from a statement in a prefix list, what happens?

    a. Sequence numbers in increments of five are added for each new statement.

    b. The statements are invalid and generate an error.

    c. Each new statement cancels out the previous statement.

    d. The router prompts you for a sequence number.

13. At the end of a prefix list, there is an implicit denial. If you configure and apply an empty prefix list, all routes will be denied. True or false?

14. You configure the following prefix list statement:

```
Router(config)#ip prefix-list seq 5 permit 172.16.0.0/16
ge 20
```

Which of the following routes would be matched by this prefix list statement? (Choose all that apply.)

    a. 172.16.0.0/16

    b. 172.16.102.0/24

    c. 172.16.102.16/30

    d. 172.16.0.0/18

15. What would the **no ip prefix-list seq 15 LocalRoutes permit 172.16.0.0/16** command do in router configuration mode?

    a. nothing, because the syntax is incorrect

    b. delete the prefix list LocalRoutes

    c. delete sequence 15 from the prefix list LocalRoutes

    d. delete sequence 15, and all sequences with less value from the prefix list LocalRoutes

16. Which of the following commands will apply a prefix list named Filter to a router?

    a. Router(config-router)#**neighbor 192.168.1.1 prefix-list Filter in**

    b. Router(config-if)#**ip prefix-list Filter in**

    c. Router(config-router)#**neighbor 192.168.1.1 distribute-list Filter in**

    d. Router(config-router)#**neighbor 192.168.1.1 ip prefix-list Filter in**

10

17. Which of the following commands would you use to view the first entry in a prefix list named Filter matching network 172.16.0.0/20 (assuming that any entry matches)?

    a. Router#**show ip prefix-list seq Filter 5**

    b. Router#**show ip prefix-list 172.16.0.0/20 longer**

    c. Router#**show ip prefix-list 172.16.0.0/20 first-match**

    d. Router#**show ip prefix-list 172.16.0.0/20**

18. Peer groups increase the amount of resources dedicated to sending update messages by sending multiple update messages for each member of the peer group. True or false?

19. Where does configuration of routing policy occur in a peer group?

    a. on the route reflector for the peer group

    b. on each router in the peer group

    c. on the peer group leader

    d. on each router in the peer group that sends routing updates

20. Why does Cisco recommend using the **network** command to advertise routes with BGP instead of redistributing routes from an IGP into BGP? (Choose all that apply).

    a. Redistribution from an IGP is less stable.

    b. Redistribution requires more configuration.

    c. Redistribution can result in route dampening.

    d. Redistribution can cause routing loops.

21. Which of the following is a potential disadvantage of redistributing a null route summarizing several smaller routes into BGP?

    a. All packets matching the null route, or any of the routes summarized in the null route, would be dropped.

    b. This technique is less stable than using the **network** command.

    c. BGP will still advertise the null route even if all of the routes it summarizes become invalid.

    d. This technique prevents you from using aggregate routes on the same router.

22. In a multihomed AS, how are routes chosen when all path attributes are set to their default values?

    a. the local preference attribute

    b. the weight attribute

    c. the AS path attribute

    d. local routes

23. How does increasing the weight on a router for a particular neighbor affect path selection in a multihomed AS?

    a. The local router choose routes through that neighbor over routes through other neighbors if the local preference for that attribute is the same for both neighbors.

    b. Routers throughout the AS choose routes through that neighbor over routes through other neighbors with the default weight.

    c. Routers throughout the AS choose routes through that neighbor over routes through other neighbors if the local preference for that attribute is the same for both neighbors.

    d. The local router chooses routes through that neighbor over routes through other neighbors with the default weight.

24. The local preference attribute influences how EBGP peers select routes coming into an autonomous system. True or false?

25. Which of the following are advantages of multihoming? (Choose all that apply.)

    a. better path selection

    b. redundancy

    c. simple load balancing of incoming traffic over multiple connections

    d. simpler control over routing policy than with a single-homed AS

10

CASE PROJECTS

Case 1

Figure 10-15 shows the network topology in Autonomous System 65000. Each router in this Autonomous System is an IBGP peer. How many BGP sessions would each router require? Show how you would configure route reflector clusters in the Autonomous System to minimize the number of BGP sessions between IBGP peers. How many BGP sessions would be required after configuring route reflector clusters?

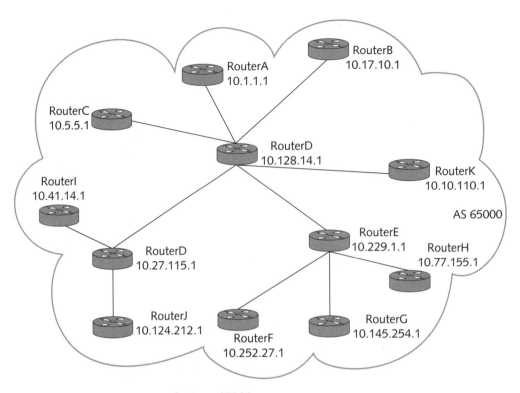

Figure 10-15   Autonomous System 65000

Case 2

You work as a network administrator for Solid Auto Parts in Detroit. Figure 10-16 shows its Autonomous System.

You currently have one Internet Service Provider, which is sending you default routes plus its customer routes. However, your ISP is sending you many routes (shown in Figure 10-16). Much of this is traffic you are not interested in. You want to examine your options for filtering these extra routes. How would you build prefix lists in order to:

❐ Filter out all routes with prefixes longer than 18 bits

❐ Filter out all routes with prefixes between 24 and 28 bits long

❐ Filter out all routes except the route to 172.16.128.0/17

Show how you would apply the prefix lists to your router.

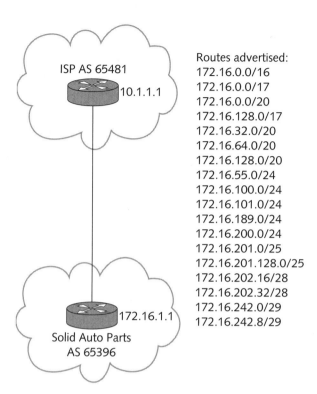

Routes advertised:
172.16.0.0/16
172.16.0.0/17
172.16.0.0/20
172.16.128.0/17
172.16.32.0/20
172.16.64.0/20
172.16.128.0/20
172.16.55.0/24
172.16.100.0/24
172.16.101.0/24
172.16.189.0/24
172.16.200.0/24
172.16.201.0/25
172.16.201.128.0/25
172.16.202.16/28
172.16.202.32/28
172.16.242.0/29
172.16.242.8/29

Figure 10-16   Cary Electronics

10

Case 3

You work as a network administrator for Cary Electronics, which has connections to two Internet Service Providers. Your R&D staff exchanges large amounts of data with several local firms that have Internet access through the same ISPs that Cary Electronics uses. Network administrators at these firms point out that traffic often takes an excessively long path when leaving your Autonomous System. For example, a packet destined for a customer using one ISP might leave your AS through the second ISP and pass through the Internet before arriving. Ideally the packets should leave your AS through the same ISP that the customer uses, resulting in a much shorter path.

Management asks you to ensure that traffic leaving the network uses the best paths possible. Based on the information given, recommend to management whether Cary Electronics should use default routes, request customer routes, or request all routes from its ISPs.

Case 4

You are brought in as a consultant for Craftwork Candlemakers. Craftwork Candlemakers currently uses its second Internet link only when the first link fails. Figure 10-17 shows its AS (AS 65100).

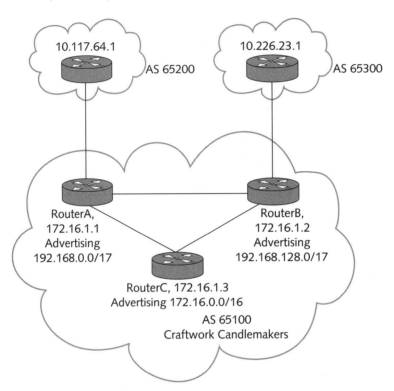

Figure 10-17   Craftwork Candlemakers

Show how you would configure each router in AS 65100. Additionally, how could you configure the routers in this AS so that:

◻ Traffic leaves through AS 65200 by default

◻ Traffic with a source address in the 172.16.0.0/16 block of addresses leaves through AS 65300, whenever possible

APPENDIX

A

CCNP GUIDE TO ADVANCED ROUTING EXAM REQUIREMENTS MATRIX

Topic	Objective	Chapter
Routing Principles	List the key information needed to route data	Chapter 1
	Describe classful and classless routing protocols	Chapter 2
	Compare distance vector and link-state protocol operation	Chapter 1
	Describe the use of fields in a routing table	Chapter 1
	Given a pre-configured laboratory network, discover the topology, analyze the routing table, and test connectivity using accepted troubleshooting techniques	Chapter 1
Extending IP Addresses	Given an IP address range, use VLSMs to extend the use of IP addresses	Chapter 2
	Given a network plan that includes IP addressing, explain if route summarization is or is not possible	Chapter 2
	Configure an IP helper address to manage broadcasts	Chapter 2
Configuring OSPF in a Single Area	Explain why OSPF is better than RIP on a large internetwork	Chapter 3
	Explain how OSPF discovers, chooses, and maintains routes	Chapter 3
	Explain how OSPF operates in a single-area NBMA environment	Chapter 3
	Configure OSPF for proper operation in a single area	Chapter 3
	Given an addressing scheme and other laboratory parameters, configure a single-area OSPF environment and verify proper operation (within described guidelines) of your routers	Chapter 3

Topic	Objective	Chapter
	Given an addressing scheme and other laboratory parameters, configure single-area OSPF in an NBMA environment and verify proper operation (within described guidelines) of your routers	Chapter 3
Interconnecting Multiple OSPF Areas	Describe the issues with interconnecting multiple areas and how OSPF addresses each	Chapter 4
	Explain the differences between the possible types of areas, routers, and LSAs	Chapter 4
	Explain how OSPF supports the use of VLSM	Chapter 4
	Explain how OSPF supports the use of route summarization in multiple areas	Chapter 4
	Explain how OSPF operates in a multiple-area NBMA environment	Chapter 4
	Configure a multiple-area OSPF network	Chapter 4
	Verify OSPF operation in multiple areas	Chapter 4
	Given an addressing scheme and other laboratory parameters, configure a multiple-area OSPF environment and verify proper operation (within described guidelines) of your routers	Chapter 4
Configuring EIGRP	Describe Enhanced IGRP features and operation	Chapter 5
	Explain how EIGRP discovers, chooses, and maintains routes	Chapter 5
	Explain how EIGRP supports the use of VLSM	Chapter 5
	Explain how EIGRP operates in a NBMA environment	Chapter 5
	Explain how EIGRP supports the use of route summarization	Chapter 5
	Describe how EIGRP supports large networks	Chapter 5
	Configure EIGRP	Chapter 5
	Verify EIGRP	Chapter 5
	Given a set of network requirements, configure an EIGRP environment and verify proper operation (within described guidelines) of your routers	Chapter 5
	Given a site of network requirements, configure EIGRP in a NBMA environment and verify proper operation (within described guidelines) of your routers	Chapter 5

Topic	Objective	Chapter
Configuring Basic Border Gateway Protocol	Describe BGP features and operation	Chapter 8
	Describe how to connect to another Autonomous System using an alternative to BGP, static routes	Chapter 8
	Explain how BGP policy-based routing functions within an Autonomous System	Chapter 10
	Explain how BGP peering functions	Chapter 8
	Describe BGP communities and peer groups	Chapter 8, Chapter 10
	Describe and configure external and internal BGP	Chapter 9
	Describe BGP synchronization	Chapter 8
	Given a set of network requirements, configure a BGP environment and verify proper operation (within described guidelines) of your routers	Chapter 9
Implementing BGP on Scalable Networks	Describe the scalability problems associated with internal BGP	Chapter 10
	Explain and configure BGP route reflectors	Chapter 10
	Describe and configure policy routing in BGP using prefix lists	Chapter 10
	Describe methods to connect to multiple ISPs using BGP	Chapter 10
	Given a set of network requirements, configure a multihomed BGP environment and verify proper operation (within described guidelines) of your routers	Chapter 10
Optimizing Routing Update Operation	Select and configure the different ways to control routing update traffic	Chapter 6
	Configure route redistribution on a network that doesn't have redundant paths between dissimilar routing processes	Chapter 7
	Configure route redistribution on a network that has redundant paths between dissimilar routing processes	Chapter 7
	Resolve path selection problems that result on a redistributed network	Chapter 7
	Verify route redistribution	Chapter 7
	Configure policy-based routing using route maps	Chapter 6

Topic	Objective	Chapter
	Given a set of network requirements, configure redistribution between different routing domains and verify proper operation (within described guidelines) of your routers	Chapter 7
	Given a set of network requirements, configure policy-based routing within your pod and verify proper operation (within described guidelines) of your routers	Chapter 6
Implementing Scalability Features in Your Internetwork	Given a set of network requirements, configure many of the features discussed in the course and verify proper operation (within described guidelines) of your routers	Lab Guide

Glossary

access layer — In a hierarchical network design, the access layer feeds traffic from end users into the distribution layer.

access list — A list used to restrict access to a router or interface to control routing updates and a variety of other tasks; access lists may filter based upon source address, destination address, protocol type, port number, or other packet attributes.

ACK packet — Acknowledgement packet sent by an EIGRP router to acknowledge a packet sent using reliable transmission, such as an update packet.

active state — The state an EIGRP router enters when it must recalculate its routing table because it can't find a feasible successor for a failed route.

Active state — The state in the BGP finite state machine in which a router actively attempts to establish a TCP connection with a neighboring BGP router in order to establish a peer relationship.

active state timer — The timer EIGRP uses to wait for replies to query packets sent to neighboring routers; if a router doesn't receive a response before the active state timer expires, it enters the stuck-in-active (SIA) state and resets that neighbor.

address aggregation — *See* Route Summarization.

address resolution protocol (ARP) — The protocol used in IP networks to associate and IP address with a Layer 2 address.

adjacency — A relationship between two neighboring routes in an OSPF area where each router shares its link-state database with the other router; not all routers in an area form adjacencies.

administrative distance — A value used by Cisco routers to decide between routes learned from different sources.

advertised distance (AD) — The EIGRP metric advertised by a neighboring router to a destination.

AGGREGATOR attribute — An optional transitive path attribute that allows the BGP peer aggregating a route to specify its identity as the router that did the aggregation.

AllDRouters — The multicast address 224.0.0.6, to which all designated and backup designated routers listen.

AllSPFRouters — The multicast address 224.0.0.5, to which all OSPF routers listen.

American Registry for Internet Numbers (ARIN) — The Regional Internet Registry for North and South America, the Caribbean, and Sub-Saharan Africa.

AppleTalk — The protocol developed by Apple to allow Macintoshes and other Apple computers to communicate with each other.

area — A unit into which an OSPF network can be divided.

Area Border Router (ABR) — A router with interfaces in multiple areas. An ABR must build link-state databases for each area it is connected to.

AS path attribute — A well-known mandatory path attribute that lists all the autonomous systems a route crosses; this attribute is used to prevent routing loops.

Asia Pacific Network Information Centre (APNIC) — The Regional Internet Registry for the Asia Pacific region.

asymmetric routing — Routing where packets take different paths on their way to and returning from a destination network.

401

asynchronous communication —
Communication method using start and stop bits; for example, used by modems over the public telephone network.

AS_PATH attribute — A well-known mandatory path attribute that lists all the autonomous systems a route crosses; this attribute is used to prevent routing loops.

AS_SEQUENCE value — One type of AS path attribute, which lists all the autonomous systems a particular route crosses.

AS_SEQUENCE value — One type of AS_PATH attribute, which lists all the autonomous systems a particular route crosses.

AS_SET value — One type of AS_PATH attribute, which lists all the autonomous systems each individual route inside an aggregated route passes through, in no particular order.

ATOMIC_AGGREGATE attribute — A well-known discretionary path attribute used to tell BGP peers not to advertise subnets of an aggregate route.

Autonomous System (AS) external link entry LSA — An LSA (of type 5) advertising an external route, sent by ASBRs and flooded throughout the entire Autonomous System with the exception of stub, totally stubby, and not-so-stubby areas.

Autonomous System — A group of routers under the same administrative control, using the same routing policies.

Autonomous System Border Router (ASBR) — A router with one or more interfaces connected to an OSPF area, and one or more interfaces connected to another Autonomous System. An ASBR can redistribute routing information between the OSPF Autonomous System and the external Autonomous System.

backbone area — On OSPF networks, the backbone area (Area 0) connects all other areas; all intra-area traffic must pass through the backbone area.

backbone router — A router with at least one interface inside the backbone area.

BGP community — *See* community attribute.

BGP Identifier — A 4-byte number used to identify a BGP speaker; Cisco routers generally select either their highest loopback address or their highest interface address as their BGP Identifier.

BGP metric — *See* MULTI_EXIT_DISC attribute.

BGP speakers — Routers that run Border Gateway Protocol.

BGP split horizon rule — A router that learns routes from an IBGP peer cannot propagate those routes to other IBGP peers to avoid routing loops within an autonomous system.

BGP table — A table each BGP router keeps in addition to its routing table, containing information such as path attributes.

BGP table version — The version number of a BGP router's BGP table, which increases by one after every change in the BGP table.

bit E — A field in an Autonomous System external LSA consisting of a single bit, which is used to determine the type of external route the LSA is advertising.

black hole — A route advertised by a router, which the router cannot reach.

Border Gateway Protocol (BGP) — An External Gateway Protocol and a path vector routing protocol designed to route packets between autonomous systems throughout the Internet.

broadcast domain — A group of devices receiving each other's broadcasts.

broadcast mode — A mode that can be used with OSPF on NBMA networks, in which OSPF emulates a broadcast multiaccess network and elects a designated router and backup designated router.

broadcast multiaccess topology — A network topology that can support more than two routers on a segment, and where routers can send broadcasts to all other devices on the segment.

CIDR block — A block of IP addresses allocated based on Classless Inter-Domain Routing; each block of addresses is described by a network number and a prefix.

Cisco Discovery Protocol (CDP) — A protocol Cisco routers use to share information about their hardware and interfaces.

Class of Service (COS) field — *See* IP TOS field.

classful routing — Routing that follows the traditional classful boundaries.

Classless Inter-Domain Routing (CIDR) — A strategy to allocate and aggregate IP addresses based on classless routing; IP addresses are allocated in CIDR blocks.

classless routing — Routing that ignores the traditional classful boundaries and uses VLSMs.

cluster — One or more route reflectors and their route reflector clients.

cluster ID — A value assigned to a route reflector to identify its cluster, allowing a cluster to contain multiple route reflectors.

cluster list — An optional, non-transitive attribute that contains a list of clusters a particular route passes through; the cluster list is used to avoid routing loops.

community attribute — The value set with the BGP community attribute, which allows routers to tag routes and filter them based upon the community value.

confederation — An autonomous system divided into a group of two or more sub-autonomous systems to make IBGP more scalable.

confederation identifier — A value assigned to each member of a confederation, which EBGP peers will see as the autonomous system number of the confederation.

congestion — Traffic on the network using most or all of the available bandwidth, or when the amount of traffic exceeds the available bandwidth.

Connect state — The state in the BGP finite state machine in which a BGP router waits for a TCP connection to complete.

ConnectRetry timer — A timer that controls how long a BGP router will wait to establish a TCP connection as it attempts to establish a peer relationship with a neighboring BGP router.

convergence — A process in which routers rebuild their routing tables to reflect a change on the network, such as a router going down.

core layer — In a hierarchical network design, the core layer switches packets between other sections of the network.

cost — The metric OSPF uses to decide between routes; in Cisco routers, cost is based on the bandwidth of a link, by default.

database description packet (DD, DBD or DDP) — The packets used in OSPF by two routers forming an adjacency to exchange their link-state databases.

dead interval — The interval between the time an OSPF router last receives a hello packet and the time it declares it unreachable; typically, this is four times the hello interval.

default gateway — The next hop used by a router when it doesn't have another route for a packet.

default metric — The metric initially assigned to redistributed routes.

default route — A route used to send traffic when no other destination is known; default routes are usually described as routes to 0.0.0.0 or 0.0.0.0/0.

dialer map — Configuration statement that associates a destination IP address with a dialer string or phone number.

diffusing update algorithm (DUAL) — The algorithm used by EIGRP to build loop-free routing tables while allowing only those routers affected by a topology change to update their routing tables.

discontiguous subnets — Subnets of a major network number separated by other networks.

distance vector routing protocol — A dynamic routing protocol in which routers periodically broadcast their entire routing tables to neighboring routers.

distribute list — An access list applied as a route filter.

distribution layer — In a hierarchical network design, the distribution layer funnels traffic from the access layer and aggregates it as it goes to the core network.

Djikstra algorithm — The algorithm used by OSPF to calculate routing tables.

don't care bits — Bits in the wildcard mask on an OSPF network configuration statement set to one, which matches all possible bits.

DROTHER — A router that isn't a designated router or a backup designated router.

Dynamic Host Control Protocol (DHCP) — A protocol that allows a network administrator to dynamically assign IP addresses to host machines.

Enhanced IGRP (EIGRP) — A hybrid routing protocol containing features of both link-state and distance vector routing protocols.

Enhanced Interior Gateway Routing Protocol (EIGRP or Enhanced IGRP) — A routing protocol proprietary to Cisco that combines the features of link-state and distance vector routing protocols, and offers support for the IPX and AppleTalk protocols.

Established state — The state in the BGP finite state machine in which a router finished neighbor negotiation with its peer; this is the state in which two routers can begin to share routing information.

exponential decay — Decrease of a value (such as the penalty given to a route by BGP route dampening) in a manner so that the value decreases by half every time an interval known as the half-life passes.

ExStart state — The state when two OSPF routers are about to form adjacencies with each other.

extended IP access list — An access list that can filter based upon source address, destination address, protocol type, or port number, among other packet attributes; extended access lists can be identified using a name or numbers between 100 and 199.

Exterior Gateway Protocol (EGP) — A routing protocol designed to route packets between autonomous systems. It is also the name of the first EGP, the predecessor to BGP.

External Border Gateway Protocol (EBGP) — BGP when used as an Exterior Gateway Protocol between multiple autonomous systems.

fast switching — A method used by Cisco routers to forward packets; instead of creating a completely new packet header as in process switching, the router uses the packet header stored in the fast-switching cache without interrupting the system processor.

fast-switching cache — A cache used to store the headers of packets so that the next packet to a particular destination can use that header and be sent faster to the same destination.

feasible — In EIGRP, this describes a route that will be added to a router's routing table.

feasible distance (FD) — The sum of the EIGRP metrics for each link to reach a destination network.

feasible successor (FS) — The next hop router for the back-up route, selected by the DUAL algorithm, and kept in the EIGRP topology table.

finite state machine — A program that starts at a given state and uses information it receives in the form of input variables to go to the next state; EIGRP's DUAL algorithm is an example.

flash update — When a router sends an update immediately after detecting an outage.

floating static route — A static route with an administrative distance set high so that it is not used unless the primary route to a destination (generally learned through a dynamic routing protocol) fails.

flooding — The process of sending updated link-state advertisements throughout an area in order to ensure that each router in the area has up-to-date knowledge of the network topology.

flushing a route — Completely removing a route from a routing table.

full mesh topology — Topology in which all routers are connected to all other routers.

Full state — When an OSPF router has exchanged its complete topology database with a neighbor and is ready to route packets.

gateway of last resort — The default gateway through which a router will send all traffic without another route.

group pacing — The practice of sending packets to refresh LSAs in small groups at intervals set by the group pacing interval, rather than all at once.

group pacing interval — The interval at which groups of refresh packets are sent in group pacing.

half-life — A value indicating the amount of time before the penalty on a route will be cut in half.

handle (H) — The number EIGRP assigns to each neighbor for tracking purposes.

haphazard growth — Growth on a network without following any plan or design.

hard reset — An action taken to reset the BGP connection; a notification message is sent to one or more peers and the BGP connection starts over.

hello interval — The interval between hello packets sent by an OSPF router; in multiaccess and point-to-point topologies, this is typically 10 seconds, while in nonbroadcast multiaccess topologies, the hello interval is typically 30 seconds.

hello packets — Packets sent out by a router using the Hello protocol in order to discover new neighbors, and identify the status of existing neighbors.

Hello protocol — The protocol responsible for establishing and maintaining neighbor relationships with other OSPF routers.

helper address — A specific IP address where Cisco routers will forward broadcasts without broadcasting them to the entire network segment.

hierarchical addressing — Addressing done in a layered, orderly fashion.

hierarchical design — A network design segmented into different parts with different functions.

High-level Data Link Control (HDLC) — A communication protocol used over serial lines.

history entry — An entry used to store information about when and how often a route has flapped.

hold time — The interval that a router waits to receive packets from a neighboring router before declaring it down; generally, the hold time is three times the hello interval.

hold timer — The timer user ID to keep track of the hold time.

holddown time — The period between the time a router receives a poison reverse update and the time it flushes that route from its routing table; the router will not place the route back into its routing table during this time.

hop count — The number of hops to a destination network, used as metric in some distance vector routing protocols.

Hub-and-spoke topology — *See* star topology.

hybrid routing protocol — A routing protocol combining the qualities of two or more types of routing protocols.

Idle state — The state in the BGP finite state machine in which a router has not yet begun to establish a peer relationship with a neighboring router. A router begins the process after receiving a Start event, and falls back to this state after most errors or events during the neighbor negotiation process.

Ill-behaved route — A route that, according to BGP's route dampening algorithm, has proved to be unstable.

implicit denial — By default, a Cisco router assumes that any access list ends with a statement denying all traffic; this can be prevented by ending the access list with a statement permitting all traffic.

Init bit — A bit set in EIGRP update packets indicating whether or not a router is first establishing a neighbor relationship with the router to which it is sending the update packets.

Interior Gateway Protocol (IGP) — A routing protocol designed to route packets within an autonomous system.

Interior Gateway Routing Protocol (IGRP) — A distance vector routing protocol designed by Cisco.

Intermediate System-to-Intermediate System (ISIS) — A link-state routing protocol.

Internal Border Gateway Protocol (IBGP) — BGP when used as an Interior Gateway Protocol between routers in the same autonomous system.

internal router — A router with all of its interfaces within the same area; all internal routers within an area have identical link-state databases.

Internet Engineering Task Force (IETF) — An organization devoted to the growth and operation of the Internet.

Internetwork Packet Exchange (IPX) — The protocol developed by Novell to allow Netware servers to communicate with each other and their clients.

invalid timer — The timer that controls how long a router will wait before declaring one of its neighbors unreachable (typically three times the update timer).

IP Precedence field — According to RFC 1349, this is the sub-field in the Type of Service field of an IP packet header that determines the relative importance of an IP packet.

IP TOS field — According to RFC 1349, this is the sub-field in the Type of Service field of an IP packet header that determines trade-offs between throughput, delay, reliability, and cost.

IP version 6 (IPv6) — The next version of the Internet Protocol, which has a 128-bit address space.

K-values — The constants used by EIGRP (and IGRP) to calculate the metric of a route.

keepalive message — A BGP message sent between two BGP peers to determine whether or not the connection is still alive; by default, keepalive messages on Cisco routers are sent every 60 seconds.

link-state acknowledgement (LSAck) packet — OSPF packet that acknowledges the receipt of another packet.

link-state advertisement (LSA) — Describes the state of a network or neighboring router; sent in routing updates during flooding, and used by routers to build their link-state databases.

link-state Aging timer — The timer set by each router to determine when it should attempt to refresh a LSA by flooding it out (after 30 minutes), and when it should discard the LSA (after 60 minutes).

link-state database — Contains a LSA for every router and network in an OSPF area so that a router has complete knowledge of the area's topology.

link-state routing protocol — A routing protocol in which routers learn the state of every link on the network, and use that information to build their routing tables.

Link-state update (LSU) — Packet containing a LSA; sent to update other routers' link-state databases during flooding.

local preference attribute — *See* LOCAL_PREF attribute.

LOCAL_PREF attribute — A well-known discretionary attribute passed between IBGP peers to help them select an exit path from their autonomous system.

longest match — When deciding between multiple routes to the same destination, routers choose the route with the longest prefix.

manageability — The degree to which network administrators can administer a network.

Maximum Transmission Unit (MTU) — The largest packet size usable on a particular network segment.

Media Access Control (MAC) address — Data Link layer address consisting of a unique 48-bit number assigned to each network interface card.

metric — A value used to distinguish between multiple routes to the same destination; for example, RIP uses the hop count to decide which route is the best route to a particular destination.

multihomed — Having multiple connections to other autonomous systems.

multipoint subinterfaces — Logical interfaces on the same subnet.

MULTI_EXIT_DISC (MED) attribute — Sometimes called "the metric", this optional non-transitive path attribute is used like a metric to help external BGP neighbors select the best path into an autonomous system.

Must Be Zero (MBZ) field — Unused 1-bit field in the Type of Service (TOS) field in an IP packet.

named access list — An access list identified by a name rather than a number; IP named access lists can be both standard or extended.

NBMA mode — A mode for the operation of OSPF on a nonbroadcast multiaccess network; the network is usually in a full mesh, uses the Hello protocol to discover neighbors, and selects a designated router and a backup designated router.

neighbor — A router sharing a common network segment.

neighbor table — A table maintained by each EIGRP router that contains information about its neighbors.

neighbors — Other routers with interfaces in the same area.

netmask — Subnet mask.

NetWare — A network operating system designed by Novell that uses IPX and/or IP as its transport protocol(s).

network address translation (NAT) — Translation of one or more of the private IP addresses defined in RFC 1918 into publicly routable IP addresses.

network link entry LSA — A LSA (of type 2) advertising a network, generated by a Designated Router and flooded throughout the area, including the network.

NEXT_HOP attribute — A well-known mandatory path attribute indicating the next hop for the path.

nonbroadcast multiaccess (NBMA) topology — A network topology that can support more than two routers on a segment, but which doesn't support broadcasts.

nonclient — An IBGP peer of a route reflector that is not one of its clients; IBGP nonclients must be in a full mesh.

not-so-stubby area (NSSA) — A stub area that accepts a limited number of external routes.

not-so-stubby area (NSSA) Autonomous System external link entry LSA — A LSA sent throughout a not-so-stubby area.

notification message — A message used by BGP routers to indicate that an error of some sort occurred; after receiving a notification message, a BGP router resets its connection with the peer that sent it.

null interface — A software-only interface (generally numbered as Null 0) that discards all packets that reach it.

null route — A route to a null interface, which discards all packets sent to it.

numbered access list — An access list identified by a number instead of a name.

open message — A message used by BGP routers to establish a peer relationship and negotiate parameters.

Open Shortest Path First (OSPF) — A link-state routing protocol.

OpenConfirm — The state in the BGP finite state machine where a router has sent and received open messages to and from its peer, and is waiting for a keepalive or notification message.

OpenSent state — The state in the BGP finite state machine where a router has sent an open message to a potential peer and is waiting for it to send an open message in response.

optional transitive attribute — An optional attribute that does not need to be recognized by every implementation of BGP; if a router does not recognize this attribute, it must include it in its update messages so that it is propagated to other routers.

origin attribute — A well-known mandatory path attribute indicating the origin of the path's routing information, such as an Interior Gateway Protocol or an Exterior Gateway Protocol.

originator ID — An optional, non-transitive BGP attribute used by route reflectors to indicate the originator of a particular route within the autonomous system.

output modifiers — The | character and the include, exclude, or begin keywords, which filter the output of **show** commands.

partial mesh topology — A topology in which many routers, but not all, are connected to each other, sometimes without a clearly defined central site.

passive interface — An interface that accepts routing updates from other routers, but does not send routing updates itself.

passive state — The state of an EIGRP router when it does not need to recalculate its routing table.

path vector — A list of autonomous systems a route passes through.

path vector routing protocol — A protocol that keeps track of the autonomous systems a route passes through; if a router receives a route containing its own AS, it assumes that a routing loop exists, and it ignores the route. BGP is an example of a path vector routing protocol.

peer — A BGP neighbor.

peer group — A group of BGP peers that uses the same policies; the members of a peer group receive configuration options and policies of the peer group, which they can override to a limited extent, and the members generate routing updates as a group.

peer group leader — The router in a peer group on which routing policy for the peer group is configured.

penalty — A value assigned to a route by BGP's route dampening algorithm each time it flaps.

permanent virtual circuit (PVC) — A logical connection in a nonbroadcast multiaccess network topology, such as frame relay or ATM; one port may have multiple such connections.

Point-to-multipoint mode — Operation of OSPF on nonbroadcast multiaccess networks, typically used on partially meshed networks; each link is treated as a point-to-point link.

point-to-multipoint nonbroadcast mode — Operation of OSPF on nonbroadcast multiaccess networks where circuits do not support dynamic discovery of neighbors; each link is treated like a point-to-point link.

point-to-point mode — An extension to RFC 2328, developed by Cisco, which treats point-to-point subinterfaces in NBMA topologies as if they are point-to-point links.

Point-to-Point Protocol (PPP) — A communication protocol used over serial links.

point-to-point subinterfaces — Logical interfaces in their own subnet.

point-to-point topology — A network topology that supports only two routers on a segment, such as a dedicated serial connection.

poison reverse update — An update sent by a router running a distance vector routing protocol about an unreachable network with a metric larger than the largest acceptable hop count, in order to avoid routing loops.

policy routing — *See* policy-based routing.

policy-based routing — Routing based on source, Quality of Service, load sharing, or other packet characteristics; routers use route maps to match various criteria in the packets, and then route the packets as desired.

prefix — The leftmost bits in an IP address or network number, corresponding to the network bits (equivalent to a network number).

prefix list — A list of prefixes used to filter BGP updates received or sent.

prepending — When a router places its own AS number at the beginning of a route's AS_PATH attribute.

priority — Determines how likely a router is to be elected DR or BDR; higher priorities win the election, while priorities of zero indicate that a router isn't eligible to be DR or BDR.

process switching — The slowest switching method used in Cisco routers; when a packet arrives, the system processor is interrupted while the packet is copied into memory and the packet header is rewritten (and copied into the fast-switching cache).

protocol dependent module (PDM) — A module used by EIGRP to route a specific protocol, such as AppleTalk or IPX.

proxy ARP — When a router uses the Address Resolution Protocol for a host on an attached network to find the MAC address of a host (and hence where to send it).

Quality of Service (QOS) — Favoring different types of traffic over others, generally to ensure that certain kinds of traffic (often interactive traffic) arrive in a timely enough fashion to be useful.

query — *See* query packet.

query packet — A packet sent to request information about a route when a router doesn't have a feasible successor in its topology table for a particular destination, which requires acknowledgement from the receiving router.

query range — The possible paths that a query made in an EIGRP Autonomous System could travel.

query scoping — Efforts made to limit the query range in an EIGRP Autonomous System.

queue count — The number of packets in the queue waiting to be sent to a particular EIGRP neighbor.

queueing — A scheme that allows routers to reorder packets to ensure that certain types of traffic arrive in a timely manner, or aren't overwhelmed by other types of traffic.

redistribute — The process of importing or exporting routing information between one Autonomous System and another, or between two different routing protocols.

redistribution — The process of injecting routing information from one routing protocol or source of routing information into another.

Regional Internet Registries (RIRs) — The organizations (including ARIN, RIPE NCC, and APNIC) that provide IP registration services for the Internet.

reliable transmission — To ensure that a packet arrives, the receiver must send an acknowledgement packet to the sender, or the sender will retransmit the packet.

Reliable Transport Protocol (RTP) — The protocol used by EIGRP routers to communicate with each other, which sends routing updates using reliable transmission.

reply — *See* reply packet.

reply packet — A unicast packet sent in response to a query packet, requiring acknowledgement from the receiving router.

Réseaux IP Européens Network Coordination Centre (RIPE NCC) — The Regional Internet Registry for Europe, the Middle East, and parts of Africa.

reset — When a neighboring router fails to send an acknowledgement to a query packet, a router puts all of its routes through that neighbor into active mode in order to verify that they are still valid.

retransmission list — The list of packets sent by RTP that a neighboring router has yet to acknowledge; each packet is retransmitted if an acknowledgement isn't received up to 16 times or the hold time (whichever is longer).

retransmit timeout (RTO) — The length of time (in milliseconds) an EIGRP router waits before retransmitting a packet, determined by the size of the smooth round trip timer.

reuse limit — A value used to determine whether or not a suppressed route will be advertised when it comes up again; if the penalty is less than the reuse limit and the route is up, the route will be advertised again.

route dampening — A mechanism that promotes stability in BGP by suppressing unstable routes after excessive flapping.

route damping — *See* route dampening.

route filter — A method of filtering routing updates that uses an access list to select which routes to filter.

route flapping — When a route goes up and down repeatedly.

route map — A series of permit or deny statements used to match packets based on source address, protocol used, or other packet characteristics; if a statement is marked as permit and the packet matches the conditions for that particular statement, the route map does additional processing on the packet, as specified, after the match statements.

route reflector — A router that runs an IBGP session and passes routes onto its clients so that the clients do not need to be included in a full mesh with the other IBGP peers.

route reflector client — A router that receives routes from a route reflector.

route summarization — The combination of many routes that share their leftmost bits into one route, called a summary route.

route tag — A numeric value assigned to a route in a route map, which can be used in other route maps to match particular routes.

routed protocol — A protocol that uses Layer 3 addresses and can be carried over multiple networks.

router — A device that forwards packets to their destinations, or to the next hop towards their destinations based on Layer 3 addresses; a router also keeps a routing table, which it uses to make decisions about where to forward packets.

router ID — The 32-bit number representing a router on an OSPF network; usually this number is either the highest IP address of an active interface, or the highest IP address of a loopback interface.

router link entry LSA — A LSA (of type 1) generated by each router in an OSPF area, describing the state of its links and flooded throughout the area containing those links.

routing domain — Another term for autonomous system.

Routing Information Protocol (RIP) — An Internet standard distance vector routing protocol defined in RFC 1058.

routing loop — When two routers pass a packet back and forth without it ever reaching its destination; the next hop for that packet in each router's routing table is the other router.

routing protocol — A protocol used by routers to dynamically exchange information about routes, including which routes are best to each destination.

routing table — A table built by a router containing a list of networks, and the next hop to reach those networks.

scalable network — A network that remains stable and smooth while continually growing.

secondary address — An additional IP address added to an interface in order to allow an interface to be on more than one network at a time; Cisco routers support multiple secondary IP addresses.

seed metric — The initial metric for routes redistributed into another routing protocol.

segmentation — The process of breaking a network into smaller domains.

shortest path first (SPF) algorithm — *See* Djikstra algorithm.

smooth round trip timer (SRTT) — The interval (measured in milliseconds) between the time a router sends an EIGRP packet requiring acknowledgement, and the time the router receives the ACK packet from the other router.

soft inbound reset — An event that requires a BGP router to request all of the update messages from one or more peers without completely resetting the BGP connection.

soft outbound reset — An event that requires a BGP router to resend all of the update messages from one or more peers without completely resetting the BGP connection.

soft reset — An event that requires a BGP router to resend all its update messages, and request all of the update messages from one or more of its peers without completely resetting the BGP connection.

SPF delay timer — The timer that specifies how long a router will wait after receiving a LSU before undergoing the SPF calculation; the default is five seconds.

SPF holdtime timer — The amount of time between two consecutive SPF calculations; the default is 10 seconds.

split horizon — A router running a distance vector routing protocol refuses to send routing information back out of the same interface through which it learned it in the first place.

standard area — An area that can accept link updates and route summaries from both routers within the area, and from ABRs outside the area, as well as external routes from an ASBR.

standard IP access list — An access list that filters primarily based on source address; standard access lists may be identified using a name or a number between 1 and 99.

star topology — All remote sites are connected to a central site.

Start event — An event sent manually or automatically that tells a BGP router to attempt to establish a peer relationship with one of its neighbors.

Stop event — An event that tells a BGP router to reset its relationship with a peer.

stub area — An area that does not accept information about routes external to the Autonomous System; routers inside the stub area instead use a default route to reach these destinations.

Stuck-in-active (SIA) state — The state an EIGRP router enters when it sends out query packets and it does not receive a response before the active state timer expires (three minutes by default); an EIGRP router responds to this by resetting any neighbor that doesn't respond.

subinterface — A logical interface used to divide a physical interface into multiple parts, each of which can be associated with a different virtual circuit.

successor — A neighboring router with the lowest loop-free path to a particular destination.

summary link entry LSA — A LSA (of types 3 or 4) advertising inter-area routes, sent by ABRs, and usually flooded throughout the backbone area.

summary route — A route formed through route summarization.

supernet — Using a subnet mask or prefix shorter than the traditional class boundaries.

suppress — To prevent a route from being advertised for a period of time by BGP route dampening because of excessive flapping, even if the route goes back up.

suppress limit — The maximum value of the penalty set on a route by BGP's route dampening algorithm before the route is suppressed.

suppressed route — A route suppressed for excessive flapping by BGP route dampening.

Switched Multimegabit Data Service (SMDS) — A public packet-switched data communications service.

switched virtual circuit (SVC) — A virtual circuit established dynamically and torn down when no longer needed; used in NBMA topologies, such as frame relay.

synchronization — The process of not advertising routes learned through IBGP unless the routes are either local, or also advertised through an IGP.

syslog — A facility used to send log messages to a remote server; in Cisco routers, the syslog facility is used to send console messages to a server where they can be logged.

tagging routes — Identifying routes with the COMMUNITY attribute in order to allow filtering based on BGP communities.

third-party next hop — When a BGP router specifies the NEXT_HOP attribute of a route as another router on a multiaccess network in order to prevent packets from taking an extra hop.

third-party next hop — When a BGP router specifies the NEXT_HOP attribute of a route as another router on a multiaccess network in order to prevent packets from taking an extra hop.

Time to Live (TTL) — a timer that is increased by one after each hop on a network; a router discards packets if the TTL has expired.

topology database — *See* link-state database.

topology table — In EIGRP, the topology table contains all destinations advertised by neighboring routers.

totally stubby area — An area that does not accept routing information about routes external to the Autonomous System, or about routers outside its own area; to reach any destination outside the totally stubby area, routers use a default route.

transit area — The area through which a virtual link passes.

transit autonomous system — An autonomous system used to transmit traffic between two or more external autonomous systems; a service provider's autonomous system is typically a transit AS.

Trivial File Transfer Protocol (TFTP) — A file transfer protocol that you can use to transfer router configurations and access lists and Cisco IOS images; TFTP does not support authentication.

two-way state — A router receives a hello packet from a neighbor containing its own address; at this point, the two routers may form an adjacency with each other, depending on the network topology.

Type of Service (TOS) — An 8-bit field in an IP packet header that is used to determine the priority of a particular packet; it includes a 4-bit field, also known as the IP TOS field, and a 3-bit field, known as the IP Precedence, as well as a 1-bit Must Be Zero (MBZ) field that isn't used.

unfeasible routes — Routes that are no longer reachable by a BGP peer, and that it no longer advertises; a BGP router notifies its peers of these in update messages.

unnumbered interface — An interface without a specifically assigned IP address; these interfaces must reference another interface with an IP address (often a loopback interface).

update message — A message used by BGP routers to exchange information about either a single route, or one or more unfeasible routes.

update packet — An EIGRP packet containing updated information about routes.

update timer — The timer that controls the interval between routing updates.

uptime — The amount of time in seconds since a router first heard from a neighbor.

variable-length subnet mask (VLSM) — A subnet mask not on a class boundary.

variable-length subnet mask (VLSM) — A subnet mask with a variable prefix so that the same network may have many different subnet masks with prefixes of different lengths.

variance — A parameter used by EIGRP to configure load balancing over unequal paths; the variance is taken into account when choosing feasible successors.

virtual link — A logical link used to logically connect an area to the backbone area when it isn't physically connected; a virtual link must be between two ABRs over a common area.

weight attribute — A path attribute proprietary to Cisco, which is used on local routers to help a router choose a path; this attribute is not advertised to other BGP peers, internal or external.

Well-behaved route — A route that, according to BGP's route dampening algorithm, has proved to be stable over an extended period of time.

well-known discretionary attribute — A BGP attribute that must be recognized by all BGP implementations, but which a router does not need to include in its update messages.

well-known mandatory attribute — A BGP attribute that must both be recognized by all BGP implementations and included in all update messages.

withdrawn routes — *See* unfeasible routes.

Index